From Armstrong to Nuffield

From Armstrong to Nuffield

Studies in Twentieth-Century Science Education
in England and Wales

E. W. Jenkins

John Murray, Albemarle Street, London

To
I.J.
S.R.J.
C.E.J.

Printed in Great Britain by
Cox & Wyman Ltd, London, Fakenham and Reading

ISBN 0 7195 3585 9 (cased)
ISBN 0 7195 3586 7 (limp)

Foreword

In 1900, there can have been few, if any, concerned with science education who were not acquainted with at least the surname of Henry Edward Armstrong and who did not know, however imperfectly, something of the heuristic method of teaching of which he was such a zealous advocate and with which his name was, and still is, identified. In much the same way during the 1960s, a later generation of science educators associated a different name, that of the Nuffield Foundation, with another and more extensive programme of science curriculum reform which, in so far as it placed particular emphasis on the processes of scientific investigation, could claim a recognisable, if somewhat remote, ancestor in Armstrong's heurism. Each of the names 'Armstrong' and 'Nuffield' thus evokes an era in the history of school science education and they may be used, as in the title of this book, to define the period from approximately 1900 to 1962 with which the present work is concerned.

During the early years of the twentieth century, a number of legislative and administrative decisions were taken which were of seminal importance for school science education in England and Wales. Some of these decisions, the assumptions upon which they were based and the controversies associated with them, are discussed in Chapter 1. Chapter 2 describes the manner in which science was accommodated within public elementary, grant-aided secondary and public schools in the years up to 1918. It examines a number of factors which combined to provoke a reassessment of the contribution which natural science could make to a liberal education and thereby led to the search for a broad course which presented science as a humanising study, unspecialised and 'not determined by reference to prospective occupation or profession'. The most elaborate prescription for such a course was undoubtedly general science and the factors governing the implementation of this curriculum innovation within the schools and its eventual decline in popularity during the late 1950s are considered in Chapter 3.

Chapter 4 is concerned with biology, a subject which, despite its recognised importance for senior pupils intending to study medicine and its affinity with the long-established tradition of teaching botany and natural history, made slow progress towards a secure place in school curricula during the twentieth century. The chapter offers a number of reasons for the initial failure of schools to accommodate biology on a par with physics and chemistry, and examines the implications for biological education of that coalition of interests – economic, moral, social and political as well as educational – which encouraged the greater degree of acceptance of the subject by schools of all types towards the end of the inter-war period.

Chapter 5 describes the salient features of the scientific education of girls during the twentieth century. It identifies some of the ways in which such education has been influenced by views about the status and function of women within society and reviews the arguments which have been put forward from time to time to account for the alleged aversion of girls to the systematic study of physical science.

Chapter 6 is a study of science teaching manpower which assesses the significance of some of the factors which have governed the supply of, and demand for, school science teachers at various times since 1900. Chapter 7 reviews the provision and design of school science laboratories and, perhaps more clearly than any of the other chapters in this book, highlights the disparity in the resources made available to schools of different types in accordance with the different social functions they were intended to fulfil. The final chapter is an exploratory account of some of the ways in which science has been taught, and of the influence of School Certificate and G.C.E. examinations on the work of science teachers in selective schools.

This book is not offered as a history of twentieth-century school science education and, as its sub-title indicates, each of its eight chapters may, to some extent, be regarded as self-contained. It is hoped, however, that the reader will readily perceive sufficient continuity and coherence in the text to encourage him or her to read the work in its entirety.

In writing this book, I have attempted to do more than describe a number of the significant features of twentieth-century school science education in England and Wales. In particular, I have sought to explore, in a preliminary way, some of the complex factors which have shaped school science curricula since 1900 and to examine, in the historical context within which they arose, several fundamental problems relating to the educational function of science. The book may thus prove of particular use to those with a scholarly interest in investigations of this kind. However, my own inquiries have led me to believe that, despite the transformation of the social context of science education which has occurred during the twentieth century, many of the issues raised in this book show a remarkable similarity with those which are the concern of science educators at the present time. The book, therefore, may claim a degree of contemporary relevance which I hope will also commend it to practising science teachers and others responsible for providing a liberal scientific education in the last quarter of the twentieth century.

The Centre for Studies in Science Education   E. W. Jenkins
The University of Leeds

Notes and Acknowledgements

Unless otherwise indicated, the statistical data abstracted from official publications and quoted in this book refer to England and Wales.

All references to Reports of the Annual Meetings of the British Association for the Advancement of Science specify the year in which the meeting was held and not the subsequent year of publication. Thus, B.A.A.S., *Report*, 1907, refers to the *Report* of the 77th meeting of the B.A.A.S. held in 1907 (in Leicester).

It is a pleasure to record my thanks to the librarians and staff of the following institutions for their help and for permission to consult the sources listed:

Association for Science Education, Minute Books of the A.P.S.S.M.
Imperial College of Science and Technology, London, correspondence and papers of H. E. Armstrong.

Public Record Office, Ed. 14, London General Files; Ed. 24, Private Office Papers 1851–1935; Ed. 109, Reports of inspections by H.M.I. and Ed. 136, Private Office Papers, Series II, 1936–45.
University of Leeds, correspondence and papers of A. Smithells and exercise books in the Bicknell collection, University Museum of the History of Education.
University of Sussex, correspondence and papers of R. A. Gregory. I wish also to acknowledge the help of a number of colleagues and friends in the preparation of this book. Dr P. R. Sharp, Lecturer, University of Leeds, drew my attention to unpublished material relating to the early years of the West Riding Education Committee; Dr P. H. J. H. Gosden, Reader in Educational Administration and History, and Dr W. B. Stephens, Senior Lecturer, both of the University of Leeds, offered helpful comment on parts of Chapter 1; Mr Peter Collins and Miss Rowena Shepherd, former higher degree students in the School of Education, University of Leeds, were kind enough to discuss with me several of the points raised in Chapters 4 and 7 respectively. I owe a special debt to Professor D. Layton, Director of the Centre for Studies in Science Education, University of Leeds, for his advice, encouragement and scholarly comment extending over a number of years.

I am grateful to the following for permission to reproduce plates or to redraw diagrams from the sources quoted in the text references:

Plate 3 (Greater London Council Photographic Library); Plate 8 (Hertfordshire County Council); Figs. 5.2*a* and *b*, 6.1, 6.2, 6.3, 6.4 (Controller of Her Majesty's Stationery Office); Figs. 7.4, 7.5, 7.6 (John Murray).

Finally, I would like to thank the University of Leeds for granting me study leave during the 1975–6 session and for a generous grant in aid of publication of the present work.

E.W.J.

Contents

Plates

1
Science Education and Administrative Reform to 1918

Under the provisions of the 1902 Education Act, the councils of counties and of county boroughs became the local education authorities responsible for education in England and Wales. These councils were empowered by Part II of the Act to 'take such steps' as seemed to them desirable 'to supply or aid the supply of education other than elementary' and to promote the 'general coordination' of all forms of education.[1] Powers to administer elementary education were also granted to the so-called Part III authorities,[2] those non-county boroughs and urban districts with populations in excess of 10,000 and 20,000 respectively.[3] This distinction between Part II and Part III authorities, a major weakness of the Act,[4] reflected both the need to secure adequate Parliamentary support for the Education Bill and the separate roles that were generally ascribed to elementary and secondary education at the beginning of the twentieth century. As Morant[5] explained in the Report of the Board of Education for 1908–9,

> the idea that elementary and secondary schools (represented) not successive stages of education but alternative kinds of education for different social classes (was) deeply rooted and may be said to have dominated practice until recently.

Despite the social assumptions behind the 1902 Act, the controversial nature of its provision of rate aid for voluntary schools[6] and the evident weakness of having separate authorities for elementary and secondary education in some areas, the legislation did much to convert the long-endured administrative chaos of nineteenth-century education into something approaching a 'regulated system'.[7] In conjunction with subsequent legislation during the period 1902–18, the Balfour Education Act provided the framework within which education was administered for much of the present century.

Educational reform was an important part of the social programme of the reconstructed[8] Liberal party which formed the new administration in 1906. In that year, local education authorities were given the power to provide school meals and to subsidise them to a maximum of the product of a halfpenny rate. A year later, they were compelled to provide medical inspection for pupils in schools and were authorised to spend public money on play centres and vacation courses. A Probation of Offenders Act was passed in 1907 and, by 1910, rate aid could be given to finance a juvenile employment service. By the end of the First World War, local education authorities had the powers to act in almost all the major fields in which they act today, although they were not necessarily compelled to do so. Indeed, in the years immediately after 1902, local campaigns were often necessary to encourage individual authorities to take advantage of the powers available to them.[9] None the less, the period 1902 to 1918 is one in which the responsibility of the state for wide areas of social and educational welfare became firmly established and widely accepted.

The introduction of the so-called 'free place' system in 1907 made grants to secondary schools dependent on their keeping at least 25 per cent of the available places for public elementary school pupils who were required to pass an 'attainment test' as a condition of entry. Some secondary schools were initially reluctant to cooperate, preferring to forego the grant rather than submit to the new requirements. Others, facing the prospect of closure, saw the free place system as a 'means of deliverance' from their financial difficulties.[10] Although the introduction of free places was an attempt to 'secure that all secondary schools aided by the state' were accessible to all scholars who were 'qualified to profit' by the instruction they offered, it was well short of the secondary education for all demanded from some quarters, notably the T.U.C. As Tawney wrote[11] in 1922, the free place system

> though useful as making a break, if a small one, in the walls of educational exclu-
> siveness, was really the product of an age in which secondary education was regarded
> as an exceptional privilege, to be strained through a sieve and reserved, so far as the
> mass of the people were concerned, for children of exceptional capacity.

In 1905–6, there were 482 secondary schools recognised by the Board of Education for grant purposes, accommodating approximately 86,000 pupils.[12] By 1916–17, almost 200,000 pupils were attending grant-aided secondary schools and these offered a total of nearly 62,000 free places.[13] The formal education of most children remained confined to elementary schools and access to the privilege of a secondary education continued to be available, for the most part, only to those who could afford to pay the fees[14] and to meet the costs of remaining at school beyond the statutory leaving age.

In the two years immediately following the passage of the 1902 Act, grant-aided secondary schools were classified into two Divisions, A and B. The Division A schools provided a thorough course in science 'together with the subjects of a general education'. They were required to allot not less than thirteen hours each week to instruction in physics, mathematics, chemistry, drawing and practical geometry and not less than ten hours to other approved subjects which included English and at least one foreign language. At the discretion of the school, two of these ten hours could be used for manual instruction and another two for teaching mathematics or art.[15] In reality, therefore, the Division A secondary schools were Schools of Science, obtaining Parliamentary funds for science teaching, in the form of capitation and attendance grants, together with other grants dependent upon the results of the examinations taken by pupils who had followed the advanced courses. In 1902 there were 27,852 pupils following[16] organised day-courses of instruction in 214 Division A schools, an average of 130 pupils per school, in receipt of an overall *per capita* grant of £4.46.

Science occupied a much less prominent position in the curricula of secondary schools in Division B which were recognised for Parliamentary grant in respect of an approved scheme for a three- or four-year science course, based upon nine hours of instruction each week in science and mathematics. Of the 144 Division B schools in receipt of such grant in December 1902, eighty-three were in England and, of these, eight were county schools, four were run by voluntary authorities and the majority, sixty-nine, were endowed grammar schools. The preponderance[17] of the endowed schools reflects not only the small number of county secondary schools which had been established by 1902 but also the reluctance of some traditional grammar schools to adapt their curricula in order to meet the conditions specified for the award of grant under the Regulations governing Division A schools.

. **Table 1.1   The provision and finance of secondary education within the administrative area of the West Riding Education Committee, 1902–3**

No. of Division A schools	10
„ „ „ B schools	11
„ „ Science & Art day schools	13
Grant per pupil, Div. A schools	£3.50 to £9
„ „ „ , Div. B schools	£2 to £3.50
„ „ „ , per 20 hours advanced maths or science	7.5p. to 62.5p.
Maximum grant earned by a school*	£5.64 } per
Minimum „ „ „ „ „	£0.102 } pupil

* This was regarded as unsatisfactory since it was 'below the £8 which ought to be found by the Government to make up a revenue of £15 per scholar'.

There was a marked difference in the level of grant which could be earned by secondary schools in the two Divisions. The extent of the difference in the case of one large local education authority is illustrated by the data in Table 1.1, taken from a report[18] prepared for the West Riding County Council at the time of the enactment of the 1902 legislation. In the national context, 229 Division A schools in 1903–4 received a total of £137,568 in Parliamentary grant aid, compared with the £37,680 devoted to 253 Division B schools in the same period.[19] Table 1.2 indicates the geographical distribution of the schools in the two Divisions at this time.

In addition to the higher level of grant available to Division A schools, the Board of Education further encouraged the teaching of science by means of a relatively generous scholarships and bursary policy and by the grants which it was authorised to pay for scientific and practical subjects taught in 'Science Classes'. In 1902, 143,556 students attended such classes, held in 1,524 schools and other institutions in England and Wales, mostly in the evenings. The total grant paid 'on account of instruction in Science Classes' in 1902 amounted to £96,252, equivalent to 13s 5d per student under instruction.[20]

Table 1.2   Distribution of Division A and Division B Secondary Schools by County,* 1903–4 or 1904 (England only)

County/area	No. of Schools		County	No. of Schools	
	Div. A	Div. B		Div. A	Div. B
Bedfordshire	1	0	Middlesex	1	7
Berkshire	0	3	Norfolk	4	3
Buckinghamshire	0	2	Northants.	0	3
Cambridgeshire	2	4	Northumberland	2	5
Cheshire	7	9	Notts.	1	4
Cornwall	1	1	Oxfordshire	4	0
Cumberland	3	1	Rutland	0	1
Derbyshire	10	2	Shropshire	1	2
Devonshire	7	2	Somerset	10	2
Dorset	5	2	Staffordshire	8	6
Durham	14	2	Suffolk	1	5
Essex	7	6	Surrey	5	7
Gloucestershire	5	4	Sussex	2	4
Hampshire	9	4	Warwickshire	8	6
Hertfordshire	3	4	Westmoreland	2	1
Huntingdonshire	0	2	Wiltshire	6	5
Kent	8	4	Worcestershire	2	1
Lancashire	28	16	Yorks. E.R.	4	3
Leicestershire	6	1	„ N.R.	3	3
Lincolnshire	4	7	„ W.R.	22	21
London	22	17			

* The figures for the County Boroughs are incorporated within those of the Counties in which the Boroughs are located. Because the school year ended at different times in different parts of England, the figures relate to 31 July 1904 except for a few schools where the school year ended on 31 December 1904.

The grants available to Division A schools offered a financial lifeline to the more impecunious grammar schools, some of which altered their curricula so as to take advantage of them. In 1902–3, concern at this development, which has been described[21] as 'the indiscriminate conversion of impoverished small grammar schools into scientific and practical schools', was allied with a more general anxiety about the degree of early specialisation in science and the corresponding neglect of the other, non-scientific elements of a liberal, secondary education. The Bryce Commission had warned of such a 'lopsided' development of the secondary school curriculum in 1895. Noting that the Department of Science and Art was concerned with 'science, in a very liberal sense of the term, and art but not literature', the Commissioners explained[22] that this had produced two noteworthy effects.

> ... on the one hand, it ... made possible the creation of higher grade elementary schools as organised science schools and so ... added Secondary Education of a peculiar and limited character as a crown to our elementary system and on the other hand, it ... made a demand of time for science that the endowed grammar schools could not very well satisfy without unduly contracting their literary instruction.

In 1899 the *Journal of Education* referred[23] to the 'well-meant efforts ... made by well-meaning people' to produce 'scientific experts at the age of sixteen' and recorded 'the very large measure of support given by public speakers of weight to its contention that technical education was the 'narrowing *coping-stone*' to be built upon the foundation of a sound and general secondary education. For the Incorporated Association of Assistant Masters, those who preached 'the necessity of a sound literary groundwork' were as 'voices crying in the wilderness'.[24]

In 1903 the Headmasters' Conference claimed[25] that 'By their organisation, by their inspectorate and by their grants', the government had pushed the scientific and mathematical studies and 'neglected to furnish any means to advance literary subjects'. Michael Sadler, for whom the task of the secondary school was first and foremost 'to humanise' and only then to 'impart efficiency for life as it has to be lived',[26] commented[27] that it was as if the Board of Education had woken 'suddenly to the idea that science (was) neglected or badly taught' and had stepped in to try 'to force the growth of scientific feeling artificially by making the matter a question of increased grants'.

Evidence of an 'undue concentration' upon scientific instruction, at least in some schools, was provided by the Inspectorate. In 1902, Buckmaster, H.M. Chief Inspector of Schools and Classes in the Southern Division, warned[28] that while the science subjects were well taught, it was difficult for him 'to make the same statement with regard to English and other literary work'. The timetables were 'distinctly overloaded' with science in several cases, and 'insufficient attention' was given to languages, history and geography.

The most influential commentary, partly because it was the most decisive in its opinions, was the report produced[29] in 1902 by J. W. Headlam, H.M.I. As far as literary studies were concerned, he found 'the first elements of good work' to be absent. In many cases, the traditional principles underlying the grammar school curriculum appeared to have been replaced by 'scientific principles'. While large grants were available for teaching the science subjects, pupils were sometimes charged extra fees if they wished to study Greek. As a result, Greek had almost disappeared from the curriculum of these schools, the position of Latin was seriously threatened and, in almost every case, boys were 'completely and absolutely ignorant' of elementary facts in the 'history and life of the people whose language they were learning'. In addition, the lack of books and library facilities for teaching history, language and literature was in marked contrast to the apparatus and laboratories provided for the work in science.[30]

Headlam's report generated the impression that the literary and humanistic studies were not so much in danger of being dominated by the science subjects in the curriculum as of being superseded by them, a view shared by Bryce in his admission[31] that the 'lopsided' development of secondary education he had anticipated in 1895 had already taken place. For Headlam, a continuing indifference to the teaching of subjects other than the natural sciences would inevitably have 'a most harmful influence on the intellect and character of the nation'.[32]

Sir William Anson, the Parliamentary Secretary of the Board of Education, suitably alarmed by the contents of Headlam's report, urged that the problem of the lopsided development of the secondary school curriculum be solved either by altering the system for the payment of Parliamentary grant or by paying such grants for scientific and technical subjects only when the Board was satisfied that a reasonably balanced curriculum was being provided.[33] There were, however, problems in defining a secondary education in terms which would not only reflect this reasonable balance but also make clear how secondary education differed from elementary on grounds other than those of social class. In the 1904 Secondary School Regulations, Morant attempted to sidestep these difficulties by defining[34] a secondary *school*.

> The term 'Secondary School' means a Day or Boarding School which offers to each of its scholars, up to and beyond the age of sixteen, a general education, physical, mental and moral, given through a complete graded course of instruction, of wider scope and more advanced degree than that given in Elementary Schools.

The 1904 Regulations abolished the distinction between Division A and Division B schools and required that a secondary school course be both 'general' and 'graded', i.e. not confined to one branch of knowledge whether that be scientific, literary or linguistic, and so arranged as to avoid any repetition of work already covered. In addition, such a course had to be 'complete', i.e. planned so 'as to lead up to a definite standard of acquirement in the various branches of instruction'.[35]

Secondary schools in receipt of Parliamentary grant under the 1904 Regulations were required to provide an approved course of general instruction which extended over at least four years and which was based upon English Language and Literature; at least one language other than 'English; Geography, History, Mathematics, Science and Drawing'. Grant-aided schools were also advised to make 'due provision' for Manual Work and Physical Exercises and, in the case of girls, for Housewifery.[36] The minimum time to be allotted to individual subjects or groups of subjects was specified. At least seven and a half hours were to be devoted each week to the teaching of science and mathematics and eight hours to English, history, geography and one foreign language. The instruction in science was to be both 'theoretical and practical' and could not occupy less than three hours each week. If two foreign languages were offered, one of these had to be taken unless the Board could be satisfied that the omission of this subject was 'for the advantage of the School'. In the opinion of the Board, these minimum provisions allowed 'ample time' for other subjects to be added in order to produce a well-balanced curriculum which took some account of the needs of a particular school.[37]

The conception of a liberal, secondary education embodied in the 1904 Secondary School Regulations has been criticised on numerous occasions. By far the most important[38] and sustained criticism is that, in framing the Regulations, too much attention was given to the classical, literary, academic curriculum of the traditional grammar and public schools and not enough to the scientific, practical and quasi-vocational work which is said to have developed during the last quarter of the nineteenth century in the Higher Elementary and other schools, principally in response to grants available from the Department of Science and Art and, later, from the Technical Instruction Committees. Some critics have gone further and attributed the ideas underlying the Regulations to Morant, who, as Permanent Secretary of the Board, was responsible for drafting them. Thus Chuter Ede, in the debate on the 1944 Education Act, accused Morant of attempting to develop a system of grammar schools which would 'as nearly as possible reproduce the system he had known at Winchester'.[39] Among historians of education, Dent has expressed sympathy towards this view, adding that, 'thanks to Robert Morant', the idea 'that secondary education was 'inclusive of technical' was rejected.[40]

There is no doubt that Morant's conception of a liberal secondary education was firmly in the public school mould and that he was unsympathetic to the earlier work of the School Boards which he regarded as having supplied 'a sort of Pretence-Secondary School' and, thereby, 'headed off the natural local pressure in the big towns for the development of the true Secondary Schools'.[41] None the less, as Simon has pointed out,[42] Morant was not an individualist, 'rather he was and felt himself to be a part of the engine which motivated the machinery of state'. As such, his role in the formulation of the 1904 Secondary School Regulations was that of an able and ambitious civil servant who 'with supreme confidence and conscious rectitude' set out to implement a policy which was formulated at a time of mounting concern at the neglect of literary and humanistic studies, which commanded a wide measure of political and public support, and towards which he was almost certainly sympathetic.

The immediate response to the 1904 Regulations was, in general, favourable, particularly among the newly created education authorities responsible for the administration of secondary education at the local level. The abolition of the dual system of classification of secondary schools was particularly welcome.[43] Michael Sadler found[44] that the 1904 Regulations in no way interfered with 'any sound definition of secondary education'. For the *Journal of Education* in July 1904, the Regulations were[45] a portent of 'a revolution' which was, none the less, welcome since it had 'urged it for some time past'. Writing in the same journal two months later, T. L. Humberstone recorded[46] that the reviews of the new Regulations which had appeared in newspapers and educational journals had, for the most part, been 'expressions of approval of the broadmindedness' which the Board had shown and 'of congratulation to secondary schools that the "tyranny" which South Kensington (had) exercised' over them was to be mitigated, if not abolished.

The contemporary reaction of those concerned with scientific and technical education is of particular interest in the present context. The National Association for the Promotion of Technical and Secondary Education detected 'the ... broad spirit of educational statesmanship' in the Regulations which, it was felt, would 'contribute much towards building up an organised system of national education'.[47] An article in *Nature* determined[48] that secondary education, as outlined in the Regulations, would meet with the approval of every man of science, adding:

> We are promised exactly that for which men of science have frequently and con-
> sistently pleaded in these columns.

This extremely hospitable response is not, perhaps, that which might have been expected. Between 1902 and 1904, the majority of secondary schools in receipt of Parliamentary grant from the Board of Education belonged to Division A rather than to Division B. As such, these schools received a higher level of grant and offered a curriculum with a marked scientific bias. The purpose of the 1904 Regulations was to abolish this distinction and to introduce a uniform scale of grant applicable to 'all types of school' which came within the general definition of a secondary school given in the Prefatory Memorandum. In curriculum terms, the thirteen hours of instruction in scientific and allied subjects, com- pulsory in the Division A schools, was to be replaced by the stipulation that science teaching must occupy a minimum of three hours each week.

Moreover, the 1904 Regulations made it clear that Parliamentary grant for 'Science Classes' was to be discontinued. Institutions which provided such classes but which did not meet the requirements of the Board for recognition as secondary schools under the Regulations were to be given no more funds for such work after 1905, unless they could satisfy the Board that they had a reasonable prospect of developing into grant-earning secondary schools by the end of the 1905–6 school year.[49]

It would not have been difficult for those who wished to do so to present a case for the general development of secondary education along the lines of the Division A schools rather than as envisaged in the 1904 Regulations. Such a case could have rested principally on the grounds of the connection widely assumed to exist between scientific and technical education on the one hand and national economic prosperity on the other. There was ample evidence of a relative decline in the trading position of the United Kingdom and, more often than not, this was attributed to a lack of investment in scientific and technical education. The proportion of manufactured goods produced in Britain, which had stood at one-third of the entire world output in 1870, had fallen steadily as the country was overtaken in economic terms, first by the United States in 1880 and later by Germany.[50] During the final decade of the nineteenth century, exports of coal tar dyes, an industry which Britain had pioneered barely a generation earlier, fell from £530,000 to £366,500 while imports had risen by 15 per cent to £720,000. As the distinguished German chemist, von Baeyer, discerned[51] as early as 1878, 'the chief industrial nation and the most practical people in the world' had been 'beaten in the endeavour to turn to profitable account' the coal tar which it possessed.

In addition, attention could have been drawn both to the work of the Technical Instruction Committees, whereby the state had interfered[52] 'with a view to equipping its citizens with such knowledge as (would) fit them to meet foreign competition' and to the dominant position of science and technology in the newer institutions of higher education, many of which had recently acquired, or were shortly to acquire, the status of independent universities.

The nature of the response to the 1904 Regulations of those who might have been expected to criticise strongly the reduced amount of time specified for science teaching can be understood, at least in part, by a closer scrutiny of the Regulations themselves. The somewhat inelastic requirements of these Regulations were qualified by several important provisions. Two[53] of these were of particular significance for secondary school science education since they safeguarded, to some extent, the favourable position given to science subjects in the Secondary School Regulations issued in the previous two years.

In accordance with paragraph eleven of the 1904 Regulations, a secondary school recognised for the purposes of Parliamentary grant was permitted to offer a 'special course' of instruction in science 'of an advanced character', provided that the Board were satisfied that such a course was 'specially suitable' for the requirements of a given locality. Recognition of a special course for grant purposes was conditional upon a secondary school providing instruction in at least two distinct branches of science, each supported by 'adequate laboratory accommodation, equipment and appliances'. While it was not necessary that the same branches of science were studied in each year of the course, any selection of subjects was to be such as to secure 'continuous and progressive instruction in science suited to the special circumstances of the school'. Not less than thirteen hours were to be given to mathematics (including theoretical and practical geometry), science and drawing. At least five hours were to be allotted to science and, of these, not less than three were to be devoted to practical work covering both of the selected branches. Manual instruction or cookery, laundry work, dairy work, needlework or housewifery in the case of a girls' school, was also a compulsory component of the first two years of the special course.[54]

Finally, provision was made in paragraph thirteen of the Regulations for a school to submit, for the approval of the Board, a scheme of work which incorporated some differentiation of the curriculum after the first half of the four-year course had been completed. This provision permitted those secondary schools which obtained the Board's approval to offer a two-year course of advanced science to some of their pupils while retaining a more general curriculum for the remainder. Since special courses were confined to the science subjects, secondary schools were, in effect, invited to consider developing a science 'side' with the aid of additional Parliamentary grant. The Regulations did not, however, specify the level of grant to be paid 'on account of each scholar' attending a special course. This was left to the Board to determine in the case of each school, although it could not exceed the level of the attendance grants payable under the main body of the Regulations.[55]

With some justification, those who had objected to the advantage given to the science subjects by earlier Regulations claimed that this advantage was being perpetuated under the provisions relating to the special courses.[56]

The favoured position of science was further protected, at least temporarily, by the fact that the 1904 Regulations permitted[57] the existence for a further two years of those schools which had been recognised for grant purposes as Division A schools under the Regulations for 1903–4. A special grant was authorised to support the work of these schools where the cost of maintenance was said to be 'enhanced' by the 'more expensive nature' of their apparatus and 'general organisation'. The level of this grant was to be determined by the Board using a scale described as 'the practical equivalent of the scale previously applied to schools of this type'. Since this augmented grant could double the total amount of the ordinary grant, this was an important exception to the uniform scale of grant and one which the Board sought to justify 'on historical and practical grounds and as necessary for continuity of administration'.

The Board clearly recognised[58] that the policy of giving grants of exceptional amount to a particular type of school, even though these grants were 'necessary for the maintenance of the school at a due level of efficiency' was one which was both unpopular and represented a breach of the principle it was trying to establish in the Regulations. In addition, such a policy was seen as tempting school authorities to choose curricula which were not necessarily suited to the immediate circumstances of the school or which involved an unreasonable degree of specialisation in science. Two 'precautions' were therefore introduced in an attempt to ensure that schools in receipt of the exceptional grant offered curricula which provided the basis of a sound general education. The age at which pupils could begin the course which gave these schools their specific character was raised from twelve to thirteen and it became necessary to satisfy the Board that such a course was 'specially suitable for the circumstances of the locality'.

The change in regulation relating to age brought this provision into line with that which governed the four-year special courses in advanced science. However, as the *Journal of Education* pointed out, the reference to the 'circumstances of the locality' was 'educationally meaningless' since every locality had 'a certain proportion of boys' who, at the age of fifteen or sixteen, could 'benefit by seven hours a week of science instruction'.[59]

Not surprisingly, a detailed examination of the financial implications of the 1904 Regulations led the local administrative bodies to modify their earlier, favourable opinion and opposition to the Board's arrangements for grant was expressed by the secretaries to the Education Authorities and by the Education Committee of the County Councils Association.[60]

The response to the 1904 Regulations of those with an interest in the educational function of science was not, of course, determined simply by the amount of time to be given to science in the schools or by the level of the grant to be paid for teaching it. For many with such an interest, the most important feature of the Regulations must have been the guaranteed place offered to practical science in the curricula of the new secondary schools being developed by the Board in conjunction with the local authorities. This guarantee was of ideological as well as educational significance. Where the State had previously given financial support to the teaching of science, it had done so principally because of the importance of science in its practical applications in industry and trade. The Department of Science and Art was originally responsible to the Board of Trade, and the Technical Instruction Committees, although operating in very different ways in different parts of the country, were the realisation of an ideal which was primarily industrial and which aimed at 'making efficient the merchant and the workman'.[61] In contrast, the 1904 Regulations offered science a place in the curriculum alongside those subjects whose intrinsic educational value was not generally questioned. Whereas, for the Department of Science and Art, science was useful knowledge, the 1904 Regulations finally established science as a compulsory component of a sound, general education.

The Board, however, was less than fully committed to this ideological change since it wished it to be 'clearly understood' that the application of a uniform scale of grant to those schools which it categorised as literary, scientific or commercial, in no way implied a belief that such schools were of equal importance or had 'indiscriminate claims' to state aid.[62] Which type of school the Board thought to be most important is clear from the functions attributed to them in the Prefatory Memorandum to the Regulations. The scientific school was concerned to 'train the intellect towards understanding and applying the laws of the physical universe'. The literary school, on the other hand, paid 'special regard to the development of the higher powers of thought and expression and that discriminating appreciation of what is best in the thought and art of the world' which formed the 'basis of all human culture'. Fortunately, this somewhat bombastic assessment of the worth of the literary school, which not only revealed Morant's prejudice but also rendered scientific imagination and achievement eccentric to human culture, was at odds with the substance if not the spirit of the Regulations.

Ideology apart, there is some reason to believe that a broadening of the curricula of secondary schools along the lines prescribed by the 1904 Regulations would have been welcomed by many of those anxious to secure a proper place for science in a scheme of general education. In 1903 a statement on scientific education in schools, prepared by the Royal Society, drew attention[63] to the 'many students trained in the recent foundations for technical scientific instruction' who had remained 'ignorant of essential subjects of general education'. In the opinion of Sir William Huggins, President of the Society from 1900 to 1905, only by widening the general education common to all who eventually went on to university, could the 'gap between scientific students careless of literary form, and classical students ignorant of scientific method' be filled.[64] In addition, there was the earlier experience of the Technical Instruction Committees who had found that 'a good secondary education' was not only a necessary supplement to, but the very basis of, a sound technical education in all its higher branches.[65] As a result, many of these Committees had been forced, sometimes reluctantly, into the field of secondary education in order to make their more strictly technical work effective.[66]

The extensive involvement of the Technical Instruction Committees in secondary education towards the end of the nineteenth century is important in another respect. It permits the conjecture that the distinction between secondary education on the one hand and technical education on the other has perhaps been drawn too sharply[67] by some historians of education and notably by Dent. In support of this conjecture it may be noted that much of the money available to the Technical Instruction Committees was eventually used to provide grants and scholarships to grammar schools and to institutions of higher education and; in the case of one county, to establish four entirely new grammar schools.[68] In addition, by allowing a particularly liberal interpretation of the word 'technical', the Committee were able to give financial support to the teaching of such subjects as English[69] and modern languages.[70]

Given these circumstances and the provisions relating to Division A schools and to special courses, it is clear that the introduction of the 1904 Secondary School Regulations led to a less drastic revision of the curricula of at least some schools than has conventionally been assumed to be the case.

Before concluding this discussion of the 1904 Regulations, it is necessary to acknowledge that, at the time the Regulations were issued, the attention of many of those concerned with science and education were, in large measure, directed elsewhere, particularly towards the elementary and the public schools. Many of the controversies associated with the 1902 Education Act had centred not on the secondary schools, but on the elementary schools where the major innovations lay. Moreover, the abolition of the system whereby grants were paid for the teaching of specific subjects in favour of a 'connected and coherent' curriculum, the decline of object lessons and the rise of nature study meant that some reconsideration of the science to be taught in public elementary schools was necessary and the British Association, among others, gave attention to this problem between 1903 and 1908.[71] As far as the public schools were concerned the 'neglect of science' was an important element of the sustained and often bitter criticism to which these schools were subjected during the early years of the century. Some of the issues related to the reform of both elementary and public school education are considered further below.

In addition, many of the leading members of the community of professional scientists were engaged in a campaign to develop scientific and technical education not in the schools but in the universities and other institutions of higher education. Their apparent self-interest in seeking state aid for research in pure science was easily justified by reference to the national interest. As Sir William Huggins remarked[72] in an address on Science, Industry and Education delivered to the Royal Society in December 1902, the 'supreme value of research in pure science for the success and progress of the national industries of a country' could 'no longer be regarded as a question open to debate'. Much had, of course, already been achieved during the last two decades of the nineteenth century. Applied chemistry under Roscoe at Manchester was 'in no way inferior' to that in the Zurich Polytechnic[73] and similar comparisons could have been made with respect to metallurgy at Sheffield, textile technology at Leeds or shipping at Liverpool. Nevertheless, even more remained to be done, and Germany and, to a lesser extent, the United States were regarded as offering models of successful state intervention in scientific research. A visit to a Technische Hochschule by the Liberal politician, R. B. Haldane, in 1901 was an important factor in his subsequent 'conspiracy' to establish a 'London Charlottenburg' at South Kensington.[74]

The Board of Education, meanwhile, continued to influence secondary school curricula via its Regulations which were issued annually. There were several important revisions between 1904 and 1909. In 1905, the minimum weekly time specified for the teaching of mathematics and physical science was reduced from seven and a half hours, including not less than three for science, to seven of which only two were reserved for science.[75] Some flexibility in planning curricula was conceded to girls' secondary schools[76] and the special courses, confined to science under the 1904 Regulations, were extended to Language and Literature. This was an important development which, in the words of the Board,[77] placed 'the types of School commonly known as "classical" and "modern" ... on the same footing as those formerly known as "Schools of Science"'. The conditions governing the entry of pupils to these special courses in such subjects as English, Latin and French were similar, in all essentials, to those which operated in the case of the advanced courses in science. The former 'Schools of Science' were allowed to continue, subject to the rule that the Board be satisfied of the suitability of their curricula for the locality but, under the 1905 Regulations, the Board's sanction to courses which specialised 'on the side of Applied Science from the first' was henceforth confined to those schools in which such courses already existed.[78] Many secondary schools were thus permitted to retain a bias towards science in their curricula and to receive the correspondingly higher level of grant.

In 1907, the Board dispensed with the rules whereby a definite minimum time had to be given to individual subjects or groups of subjects in each year of a secondary school course, requiring instead that the curriculum and timetable provide for 'due continuity of instruction in each of the subjects taken' and that 'an adequate amount of time' be given to each subject.[79] The compulsory subjects of the curriculum remained 'English Language and Literature, at least one language other than English, Geography, History, Mathematics, Science and Drawing' but, for girls over fifteen years of age, an approved course in practical housewifery could be substituted for the work in science. The emphasis in the 1907 Regulations was thus placed on the curriculum of a secondary school as a whole[80] rather than on its 'indispensable minimum' components, a change of emphasis explained by the additional funds made available to the Board[81] and said to be justified by the 'growth of interest, of knowledge, and of experience'[82] of secondary education in the previous three years. Special courses could thus be assimilated to the more general work of the secondary school, although approval by the Board of the curriculum and timetable remained a condition of grant aid. The Board retained the right to require modifications of the scheme of work if a subject were taught which was 'not of educational value', if the time spent on particular subjects interfered with 'proper instruction in other subjects', or if the time given to any subject were deemed 'insufficient to allow of effective progress being made in it'.[83]

The Secondary School Regulations of 1909 introduced a further element of differentiation of the curricula of secondary schools for boys and those for girls. Girls' secondary schools were required to provide practical instruction in domestic subjects 'such as Needlework, Cookery, Laundry Work, Housekeeping and Household Hygiene' and the permission to substitute an approved course in a combination of these subjects 'partially or wholly' for the work in science normally undertaken by girls over fifteen years of age, was extended[84] to include mathematics 'other than Arithmetic'.

The Regulations issued between 1904 and 1909 provided the framework within which science was taught at grant-aided secondary schools up to the end of the First World War. As Morant made clear in successive Prefatory Memoranda, these Regulations applied to grant-aided schools which were very different in origin and outlook. They were schools which, for the most part, had grown up as 'isolated units, untended, unregarded, undirected by any common standard'.[85] In some, notably those which had once been 'Schools of Science' or Division A schools, the position of science and the facilities available for teaching it were, in general, satisfactory. Indeed, it would be fair to say that the problems of developing satisfactory schemes of work in such subjects as English and history within these schools have not received the attention they deserve.[86] In other grant-aided secondary schools, particularly those most closely allied with the public schools in outlook, science was tolerated rather than accepted or encouraged.

The varying degree of hospitality accorded to science by grant-aided secondary schools of different origin and tradition may be detected in the Report of the Thomson Committee, published in 1918. While able to accept[87] the assurance of the Assistant Masters' Association that science occupied a position in the grant earning secondary schools which was 'in no way inferior to that of any other subject', the Committee could still record that in a 'considerable number of schools', the time for science was 'as little as four three-quarter-hour periods a week, or even less'.[88] The Committee's conclusion, that the Board had accepted too low a minimum time for science, seems inescapable. However, it should be set against the fact that the number of awards in science made by the University of Cambridge to boys from 113 grant-earning secondary schools between 1906 and 1915 was larger than for any other subject for which awards were offered, an achievement attributed by the Thomson Committee to the stronger position of science and mathematics in sixth-form work compared with either classics or modern studies.[89]

Despite the low minimum of two hours for science teaching, prescribed initially in 1905, it seems likely that the various transitional arrangements between 1904 and 1906 together with the amendments embodied in subsequent Regulations, permitted a number of grant-aided secondary schools to retain a strong commitment to science in their curricula. As such, for these schools at least, the 1904 Secondary School Regulations were a less significant watershed than has often been claimed.

There is one other administrative reform of direct relevance to the work of the secondary schools which took place between 1900 and 1918 and to which brief reference must be made, namely the evolution of a coordinated system of secondary school examinations. At the beginning of the century, secondary schools were confronted with a large number of different examinations set by a variety of examining authorities.[90] There was considerable duplication of function and one examining authority often failed to recognise the examinations of another for qualifying purposes. Not surprisingly, schools sometimes succumbed to the temptation to enter their more able candidates for one examination after another.

The Consultative Committee of the Board of Education considered[91] ways of developing a coordinated system of examinations but no action followed the Committee's recommendations in 1904. Five years later, the Board again referred the examinations issue to the Consultative Committee whose report, published[92] in 1911, provided the basis of the system of secondary school examinations established at the end of the First World War.

The First School Examination, the School Certificate, required candidates to pass in five or more subjects including at least one from each of three main groups: English subjects, languages, mathematics and science. To pass the examination, a candidate was required to satisfy the examiners in each of the groups. Since mathematics and science formed a single group, a candidate could gain a School Certificate without presenting himself for examination in a science subject. The choice of subjects for inclusion in a group thus undermined to some extent the position established in the earlier Regulations issued by the Board of Education.

The Second School Examination, the Higher Certificate, was much more specialised in nature, candidates being required to choose subjects from only one of three groups: classics, modern studies, and mathematics and science. In 1917, the Secondary Schools Examination Council was established[93] to advise upon and to regulate the system of School Certificate examinations which, with a number of important modifications, was to serve the secondary schools until 1951.

In 1899, the last year in which the Committee of the Privy Council on Education was responsible for elementary education in England and Wales, the subjects for which grants could be given to elementary schools were divided into three categories: elementary, class and specific. The elementary subjects included the obligatory reading, writing and arithmetic together with needlework and drawing for older girls and boys as appropriate. Elementary science appeared in the list of approved class subjects and several alternative schemes of work were available. In each case, the instruction of the first three Standards was to be based on object lessons although the Committe of Council advised that the teaching in general should be 'mainly by experiment and illustration' rather than by 'definition and verbal description'.[94] To encourge such teaching, the Inspectorate was required to examine pupils in elementary science in a manner likely to elicit from them, 'as far as possible in their own language', the ideas they had formed of what they had seen. Specific subjects such as chemistry, physics, mechanics, botany, animal physiology and horticulture were taken by small numbers of the more senior pupils attending public elementary schools and it was possible for a school to submit its own scheme of work for approval in this category.

The Elementary School Code specified[95] the rate of grant to be paid for each of the various categories of subject and the relevant syllabuses were elaborated in a series of Schedules.[96] (See Figs. 1.1 and 1.2.)

Figure 1.1 Scheme of work in Elementary Science, a Class Subject under Article 101(e) of the Elementary Code, 1898

—	Standard I	Standard II	Standard III
Elementary Science (Scheme A) or	Thirty object lessons on the chief tribes of animals and their habits, on common plants and their growth, and on common inorganic substances and their properties.		
Elementary Science (Scheme B)	Thirty lessons on common objects, e.g.: A postage stamp; the post; money; a lead pencil; a railway train, Foods and clothing materials, as bread, milk, cotton, wool. Minerals; natural phenomena, as gold, coal, the day, the year.	Thirty lessons on common objects, such as animals, plants, and substances employed in ordinary life, e.g.: Horse, Leaves, Sparrow, Candles Roots, Soap, Stems, Cork, Buds, Paper.	Simple principles of classification of plants and animals. Substances used in the arts and manufactures. Phenomena of the earth and atmosphere.

Standard IV	Standard V	Standard VI	Standard VII
Simple mechanical laws in their application to common life and industries. Pressure of liquids and gases.	Simple chemical laws in their application to common life and industries.	Outlines of physiology in its bearing on health and work.	Familiar illustrations of applied science: *e.g.* the dwelling; fabrics and clothing; food; warming; lighting, etc.
A more advanced knowledge of special groups of common objects, such as:	(a) Animal or plant life; or	(a) Animal and plant life; or	(a) Distribution of plants and animals, and of the races of mankind; or
(a) Animals, or plants, with particular reference to agriculture; or	(b) The principles and processes involved in one of the chief industries of England; or	(b) The commonest elements and their compounds; or	(b) Properties of common gases; or
(b) Substances employed in arts and manufactures; or	(c) The physical and mechanical principles involved in the construction of some common instruments, and of some simple forms of industrial machinery.	(c) The mechanical powers.	(c) Sound, or light, or heat, or electricity, with applications.
(c) Some simple kinds of physical and mechanical appliances: *e.g.* the thermometer, barometer, lever, pulley, wheel and axle, spirit level.			

Figure 1.2   Scheme of work in Specific Science Subjects,* under Article 101(f) of the Elementary Code, 1898

	Mechanics	Animal Physiology	Botany	Principles of Agriculture	Chemistry
1st stage	Matter in three states; solids, liquids, and gases. The mechanical properties peculiar to each state. Matter is porous, compressible, elastic. Measurement as practised by the mechanic. Measures of length, time, velocity, and space.	The build of the human body. Names and positions of the internal organs. The properties of muscle.	Characters of the root, stem, leaves, and parts of the flower. Illustrated by specimen of common flowering plants.	The principles influencing the supply of plant food in the soil, and necessity for cultivation, and the circumstances making tillage more or less effective.	Elementary and compound matter, illustrations of combination and decomposition in such bodies as hydrochloric acid, water, oxide of mercury, and rust of iron.
2nd stage	Matter in motion. The weight of a body, its inertia and momentum. Measures of force and work.	The mechanism of the principal movements of the limbs and of the body as a whole. The organs and functions of alimentation, circulation, and respiration. The use and abuse of foods and drinks.	Structure of wood, bark, and pith. Cells and vessels. Food of plants and manner in which a plant grows. Functions of the root, leaves, and different parts of the flower.	The principles regulating the more or less perfect supply of plant food; manures as supplemental sources of plant food.	Preparation and properties of the common gases, such as oxygen, hydrogen, nitrogen and chlorine. The chemical character and constituents of pure air, and pure water and the nature of the impurities sometimes found in both. Effects of plants and animals on air.
3rd stage	The simple mechanical powers, viz., (1) The lever; (2) the wheel and axle; (3) pulleys; (4) the inclined plane; (5) the wedge; (6) the screw. Liquid pressure; the hydrostatic press; liquids under the action of gravity. The parallelogram of velocities. The parallelogram of forces. Examples commonly met with illustrating the mechanical powers N.B.—*Instructions in this subject should be purely descriptive and experimental.*	The general arrangements of the nervous system. The properties of nerve. Reflex action. Sensation. The organs and functions of touch, taste, smell, hearing, and sight. N.B.—*Instruction in this subject should be illustrated by diagrams or models only.*	The comparison of a fern and a thorn with a flowering plant. The formation of different kinds of fruits. The structure of a bean and of a grain of wheat or barley. The phenomena of germination.	The principles regulating the growth of crops, and the variations in their yield and quality.	The properties of carbon and its chief inorganic compounds. Differences between metallic bodies. Combination by weight and volume. The use of symbols and chemical formulæ.

* The three stages of 'such of these subjects as admit of it' could be taken in any order.

Physics			
Sound, Light, and Heat	Magnetism and Electricity	Elementary Physics and Chemistry	Domestic Economy (Girls)
The three modes in which heat may be conveyed from place to place. Effects of heat on solids, liquids, and gases. Expansion by heat. The thermometer. Latent heat. Elementary notions of specific heat. Heat produced by mechanical, chemical, and vital action.	Attraction, repulsion and polarity, as illustrated by the magnet. Terrestrial magnetism, and the mariner's compass.	Properties of common stuffs: relative density of solids and liquids: flotation of solids. The barometer and thermometer; their use; graphic representation of daily readings. Solution. water as a solvent: solubility of metals, etc., in acids: crystallisation of salt, soda, alum.	Food: its composition and nutritive value. Clothing and washing.
Sources and propagation of light. Intensity, shadows, shadow photometer. Reflection, mirrors. Refraction, lenses. Elementary explanation of the microscope, camera obscura, and magic lantern. Dispersion, prisms. The rainbow. Reflecting and refracting telescopes.	Attraction of light bodies by rubbed sealing wax and glass. Experimental proof that there are two forms of electricity. Attraction and repulsion. Gold-leaf electroscope. Construction of electrophorus, electrical machine, and Leyden jar. Explanation of atmospheric electricity.	Evaporation and distillation: heat absorbed in fusion of ice and in conversion of water into steam: density of ice; change in density of water on heating: moisture in air: wet and dry bulb thermometer. Study of iron rusting and of combustion of candle, gas, oil, phosphorus: effect on metals of heating in air: discovery of active constituent of air.	Food: its functions. The dwelling: warming, cleaning and ventilation.
Propagation of sound. Elementary notions of vibrations and waves. Reflection of sound echoes. Musical notes, simple instruments. Simple explanation of beats and nodes.	Voltaic or chemical electricity. The voltaic battery and notions of a current. Chemical effect of a current. Electrolysis. Magnetic effect of a current. Galvanometer. Induced currents. Electro-magnets. The electric telegraph.	Chalk and lime: the burning of chalk or limestone: action of muriatic acid on chalk or limestone: carbonic acid: reformation of chalk. Discovery of carbonic acid in air: its formation by combustion of carbonaceous materials and in respiration. Study of action of muriatic and vitriolic acids on zinc; combustion of the gas obtained and discovery of the composition of water. Presence of air and solids dissolved in water: sea-water; hardness of water.	Food: its preparation and culinary treatment. Rules for health; the management of a sick room.

In 1898 elementary science was taught as a class subject in 2,143 'departments', compared with 17,049 for geography, 5,780 for history and 13,456 for
English.[97] Even so, as Table 1.3 indicates, there had been a considerable
growth in the teaching of elementary science in the public elementary schools
during the last decade of the nineteenth century. Table 1.4 records a similar
growth in the numbers of day scholars presented for examination in specific

**Table 1.3 No. of departments in day
elementary schools in which elementary science
was taught as a class subject, 1890–1900**

Year	No. of departments in which Elementary Science was taught
1890	32
1891	173
1892	788
1893	1,073
1894	1,215
1895	1,396
1896	2,237
1897	2,617
1898	2,143
1899	(21,301)*
1900	(19,998)

* It is not possible to compare these figures with those
for earlier years. The marked increase is explained by
alterations to the Elementary Code in 1895, 1896 and
1898. For details see Board of Education, *Report for the
year 1900–1*, vol. 2, p. 468.

**Table 1.4   Numbers of Scholars presented in specific subjects
under the Elementary Code, 1890–1900**

Year	Animal Physiology	Botany	Chemistry	Sound, Light and Heat	Magnetism and Electricity
	No. of Scholars presented in				
1890	15,842	1,830	2,007	1,183	2,293
1891	15,050	2,115	1,847	1,085	2,554
1892	13,622	1,845	1,935	1,163	2,338
1893	14,060	1,968	2,387	1,168	2,181
1894	15,271	2,052	3,043	1,175	3,040
1895	17,003	2,483	3,850	914	3,198
1896	18,284	2,996	4,822	937	3,168
1897	19,989	3,377	5,545	1,040	3,431
1898	22,877	4,031	6,978	1,155	3,905
1899	41,244	8,833	14,737	1,943	7,697
1900	36,810	8,905	13,557	1,730	7,026

science subjects during the same period,[98] and shows that the rate of increase in the numbers of pupils qualifying for grants in respect of these subjects was particularly marked after 1897.

In 1900 the elaborate system whereby different grants had been paid for different parts of the curriculum was replaced by a block grant calculated at the rate of twenty-two shillings per pupil 'in average attendance',[99] although special grants were made available to support the teaching of a number of domestic and related subjects. The tripartite classification of the subjects of the elementary school curriculum was also abolished and a two-fold division introduced. The first group of subjects consisted of those taught 'as a rule' in all public elementary schools, although not necessarily to every class in a given school. Science was represented in this group only by a reference to 'lessons, including object lessons, on ... common things', and the Board provided some examples of the work it envisaged under this heading in a set of 'Revised Instructions' issued in 1902. Science was much more strongly represented in the second group of subjects, one or more of which was to be taken when 'in the opinion of the Inspector' circumstances made this desirable. The subjects in this second category were those formerly referred to as 'specific subjects' under earlier Regulations but no additional grant was, of course, payable for teaching them. Unfortunately, a change in the manner in which the statistics are presented[100] prevents even an indirect comparison of the position of individual science subjects in the public elementary schools shortly before and after 1900.

In 1903, the Board issued[101] a provisional code of Regulations for public elementary schools to cover a period which was essentially transitional in character since a number of schools were still managed by School Boards or by voluntary agencies while the responsibility for others had already passed to the new local education authorities.

In the following year, the distinction between subjects which were common to all public elementary schools and those which could be taught in appropriate circumstances was finally abolished. Instead, the 1904 Regulations attempted 'to exhibit, without undue elaboration, the course of instruction as a connected and coherent whole'.[102] While allowing for local variation, public elementary schools were expected to provide[103] a 'graduated course of instruction, suitable to the age and capacity of the scholar', in English Language, arithmetic, geography, history, drawing, singing, physical exercises, plain needlework for girls and 'knowledge of the common phenomena of the external world'. In the Regulations[104] of 1905, this last element of the curriculum was replaced by Observation Lessons and Nature Study' which, ideally, were taught with special reference to the surroundings of the pupils and to the natural features, industries and plant life of the locality, with the view of forming the habit of intelligent and accurate observation'. Further advice was offered in the Board's *Suggestions to teachers and others concerned in the work of Public Elementary Schools*, also published[105] in 1905.

In the opinion of the Board, the 1904 Regulations introduced no 'important changes of substance' into the Elementary School Code and the Prefatory Memorandum advised against any far-reaching and sudden change in the instruction given in the schools.[106] Morant's introductory statement of the true purpose of the public elementary school, widely regarded by his contemporaries as 'excellent'[107] and described by his biographer[108] as 'ennobling', was, in reality, an assertion that elementary education under the 1904 Code was to be 'training in followership, rather than leadership'[109] and, as such, eminently suited to the majority of the population, particularly the working classes, whose education was to be confined to an elementary school throughout the next forty years.[110]

As far as science is concerned, the ending of the payment of grants for the teaching of specific subjects inevitably diminished the status of science within the elementary school curriculum. In addition, with the abolition of specific subjects and their prescribed syllabuses, the responsibility for devising adequate schemes of work in 'Observation Lessons and Nature Study' passed, in large measure, to the teachers in the elementary schools. There is little doubt that despite the Board's 'Suggestions' and the advice and practical help offered by a variety of individuals and organisations,[111] it was a responsibility which the majority of public elementary school teachers were ill-prepared to discharge. Despite the improvements in training facilities initiated in 1904, the lack of an adequate number of trained elementary school teachers with a sound knowledge of science, particularly of physical science, was a major obstacle to a more generous development of elementary school science teaching after 1900. Since this problem is considered further in Chapter 6, it will be sufficient, at this point, to note that, in the opinion[112] of the Thomson Committee in 1918, a 'considerable number' of the students passing out of the training colleges were incapable of maintaining, let alone raising, the low level of science found in most public elementary schools.

Although there were a number of important changes in the Elementary School Regulations after 1905, these, for the most part, were concerned with adjustments to the grant or with provisions designed to raise the level of qualification of elementary school teachers. Higher Elementary and Central Schools are discussed, in the context of their curricula, in Chapter 2.

References

[1] For accounts of the background to the legislation see Simon, B., *Education and the Labour Movement, 1870–1918*, 1965, chapter VI; Eaglesham, E., *From School Board to Local Authority*, 1956 and Cruikshank, M., *Church and State in English Education*, 1963.

[2] Part III of the Act was concerned with elementary education.

[3] The figures were based on the 1901 Census.

[4] The distinction was not removed until 1944.

[5] Board of Education, *Report for the Year 1908–9*, HMSO, pp. 31–2. Morant was Permanent Secretary of the Board from 1903 to 1911 and responsible for drafting the Education Bill. For an account of his life see Allen, B. M., *Sir Robert Morant*, 1943.

[6] Labour and Nonconformist opposition to this provision was intense and the problem of financing voluntary schools was a major issue in the General Election of 1906. This

returned a Liberal Government with an overwhelming majority, pledged to 'undo the damage' caused by the religious clauses of the 1902 Act.

[7] Magnus, P., *Educational Aims and Efforts, 1880–1910, p. 217.*

[8] The 'new liberalism' embraced such concepts as 'social equality' and the 'democratic' welfare state. Thompson, H. J., *The New Liberalism in Great Britain: The Liberal Mind and Party Politics in a Time of Crisis and Reconstruction (1890–1914)*, Ph.D. thesis, Harvard University, 1954.

[9] For a sympathetic indication of the 'strenuous agitation' necessary to force an authority to operate in the areas where it had the power to do so, see Simon, B., op. cit., p. 283.

[10] Curtis, S. J., *Education in Britain since 1900*, 1952, p. 62.

[11] Tawney, R. H., *Secondary Education for All,* 1922, pp. 83–4.

[12] Board of Education, *Report for the Year 1905–6*, HMSO, p. 47.

[13] Lawson, J., Silver, H., *A Social History of Education in England*, 1973, p. 382. Apart from prestige, there was an important distinction between free places and scholarships. The former were 'free of tuition and entrance fees' and most carried extra allowances for books or travel. However, the important maintenance allowances were, more often than not, confined to scholarship holders, although there were considerable regional variations.

[14] In 1913–14, when the Board supplied grant-aid to over 1,000 secondary schools, only six charged no fees. Tawney, op. cit., pp. 81–2, 84, reports that of the remainder, 242 charged up to 5 guineas per year, 623 between 5 and 10 guineas, 107 between 10 and 15 guineas and 47 over this latter sum.

[15] Board of Education, *Regulations for Secondary Day Schools*, HMSO, 1902, p. 8 and *Report for the Year 1909–10*, HMSO, p. 73.

[16] Board of Education, *Report for the Year 1902–3*, Cd. 1763, HMSO, p. 55. In 1900, the corresponding numbers of schools and students were 183 and 24,639 respectively. It should be noted that only a small proportion of the grant was paid 'on the results of Examination'. Of the total grant of £124,300 10s 9d paid in 1902, £120,619 10s 9d was for Capitation and Attendance.

[17] By 1906, when 600 secondary schools were aided by the Board of Education, 335 of these were endowed schools and 157 were provided by L.E.A.s. Of the remainder, seventy-four were 'allied to the endowed schools in outlook'. Board of Education, *Summary of Figures relating to State aided Secondary Schools under Regulations for the School Year, 1906–7*, Cmd. 3538, HMSO, 1907.

[18] West Riding County Council, Education Committee, *Report on Secondary Schools (Existing Conditions)*, Wakefield, February 1904, p. 22.

[19] Board of Education, *Statistics of Public Education in England and Wales*, 1903–4–5, Cd. 2782, HMSO, p. 172. The data in Table 1.2 are taken from ibid, pp. 173–86 which lists individual schools.

[20] The 'Special Aid to Students and Schools of Science' in 1902 included seven Exhibitions, twenty-two National Scholarships and six Free Studentships to the Royal College of Science, London; twenty-seven Local Exhibitions to universities and colleges; 629 Science Scholarships to enable pupils under the age of sixteen to pursue more advanced instruction and a total of thirty-four Whitworth Scholarships and Exhibitions. Board of Education, *Report for the Year 1902–3*, HMSO, pp. 56–67. In addition there were grants to teachers to enable them to attend inservice courses.

[21] Kazamias, A. M., *Politics, Society and Secondary Education in England*, Philadelphia U.P., 1966, p. 133.

[22] Royal Commission on Secondary Education, *Report*, vol. 1. Cd. 7862, HMSO, 1895, p. 98.

[23] *Journal of Education*, November 1899, p. 684.

[24] Quoted in Banks, O., 'Morant and the Secondary School Regulations', *B. J. Ed. Studies*, III, November 1954, p. 35.

[25] *Journal of Education*, January 1903, pp. 25–6. The comment was made by W. H. D. Rouse, Headmaster of the Perse Grammar School, Cambridge, who argued that the elementary and technical 'parts of education' were 'very strongly organised' at the Board but that the secondary branch was, for the most part, in the hands of those with 'no practical experience of what the schools wanted'.

[26] Sadler, M. E., *Report on Secondary and Technical Education in Huddersfield*, 1904, pp. 26–7.

[27] *Journal of Education*, April 1903, p. 289.

[28] Board of Education, *General Reports of Higher Education with Appendices for the Year, 1902*, HMSO, 1903, p. 11.

[29] Headlam, J. W., Report on the Teaching of Literary subjects in some Secondary Schools for Boys, in Board of Education, *General Reports of Higher Education with Appendices for the Year, 1902*.

[30] Ibid, pp. 62–5.

[31] Hansard, vol. 125, 1903, cols. 230–3.

[32] Headlam, J. W., op. cit., p. 66.

[33] Hansard, vol. 125, 1903, col. 181.

[34] Board of Education, *Regulations for Secondary Schools*, Cd. 2128, HMSO, 1904, p. 17.

[35] Ibid, pp. 7–8.

[36] Ibid, para 4, p. 18.

[37] Ibid, p. 9.

[38] For some other criticisms, e.g. that the Regulations were based on a faulty faculty psychology, see Board of Education, *Report of the Consultative Committee on Secondary Education with Special Reference to Grammar Schools and Technical High Schools* (Spens Report), HMSO, 1938, pp. 68–72.

[39] Hansard, 8 February 1944, col. 1697.

[40] Dent, H. C., *Secondary Education for All*, 1949, p. 33. For other similar opinions which place less emphasis on the personal contribution of Morant, see Curtis, S. J., *History of Education in Great Britain*, 1945 and Barnard, H. C., *A Short History of English Education from 1760 to 1944*, 1947.

[41] Eaglesham, E., op. cit., p. 190. Eaglesham quotes from a memorandum prepared by Morant.

[42] Simon, B., op. cit., p. 239. Simon also quotes from an unpublished letter, written by Morant shortly after he had been knighted in 1907, in which he reveals his attitude to the role of the civil servant.

[43] See, for example, Local Inquiries Respecting Secondary Schools in English Counties, Lancashire, *The Record of Technical and Secondary Education*, XIII, 1904, pp. 448–9. The West Riding in 1902 claimed that in order to obtain the higher level of grant, a secondary school was required to 'sacrifice educational aims' and to 'necessarily forego ... instruction in certain general subjects'. West Riding County Council, op. cit., p. 22. In 1906, the 1904 Regulations were said to have encouraged a more liberal and elastic scheme of instruction. W.R.C.C., *Second Annual Report*, 1906, p. 19. For another reaction see Balfour, G., *Education in Staffordshire, 1903–13*.

[44] Sadler, M. E., *Report on Secondary and Technical Education in Huddersfield*, 1904, p. 27.

[45] *Journal of Education*, July 1904, p. 459.

[46] Ibid, September 1904, p. 605.

[47] *The Record* ..., XIII, no. 55, 1904, p. 279.

[48] *Nature*, 11 August 1904, p. 346.

[49] Board of Education, *Regulations for Secondary Schools*, 1904, p. 25, para 39 and Prefatory Memorandum, para. xviii.

[50] For details, see Deane, P., Cole, W. A., *British Economic Growth 1688–1959, 1967*. For some discussion of the influence of economic arguments on education, see Wardle, D., *The Rise of the Schooled Society*, 1974, p. 58.

[51] B.A.A.S., *Report*, 1901, p. 259. For the coal tar dye statistics, see p. 257. Much was made at this meeting of the failure of British industry to seize its opportunities.

[52] Macan, H., The New Official Return Respecting Secondary Schools in England, *The Record* ..., VII, 1898, p. 302.

[53] Possibly three since, in girls' secondary schools in which the total number of hours of instruction was less than twenty-two, the time given to science and mathematics could be reduced to one-third of that total, provided that not less than three hours were given to science. In addition, the Regulations allowed the language requirements to be waived in any secondary school if, in the opinion of the Board, the English course provided 'adequate linguistic and literary training' and the staff were 'specially qualified' to give the necessary instruction. Board of Education, *Regulations for Secondary Schools*, 1904, paras 5 and 6.

[54] It was merely 'desirable' for the ordinary course in the sense that 'due provision' was to be made, ibid., para 4.

[55] Ibid., chapter III, para 35.

[56] Humberstone, T. L., 'Notes on the New Regulations for Secondary Schools', *Journal of Education*, September 1904, p. 607. Humberstone regarded the 'vicious Regulations for Division A schools' as perpetuated 'under the specious title of "Special Courses".'

[57] Board of Education, *Regulations for Secondary Schools*, 1904, para x and para 37.

[58] Ibid., para xi.

[59] *Journal of Education*, September 1904, pp. 593–4.

[60] Ibid., p. 593. The Secretaries to the Education Authorities passed a 'strong resolution' against the Regulations and the Education Committee of the County Councils Association 'followed suit in a general protest'.

[61] Macan, H., op. cit., p. 302.

[62] Board of Education, *Regulations for Secondary Schools*, 1904, para ix.

[63] Statement regarding Scientific Education in Schools, drawn up by a Committee of the Royal Society, October 1903, reproduced in Huggins, Sir W., *The Royal Society or, Science in the State and in the Schools*, 1906, p. 121.

[64] Science in Education, ibid., p. 116. Huggins was in no doubt that 'notwithstanding the immense intrinsic value of its teaching', science was 'but one of the studies ... necessary for a wide and liberal education' and he was generous, perhaps overmuch so, in his estimation of the contribution to be made by the study of literature and languages. Ibid., pp. 113, 114.

[65] Macan, H., op. cit., p. 302.

[66] For an account of the work of the Technical Instruction Committees, see Gosden, P. H. J. H., 'Technical Instruction Committees' in History of Education Society, *Studies in the Government and control of education since 1860*, 1970, p. 27 et seq.

[67] For the Bryce Commission in 1895, secondary and technical education were 'inseparable'.

[68] For details of scholarships, grants etc. in 1894 and in 1899 see Gosden, P. H. J. H., op. cit., p. 36. For the four new schools, see ibid., pp. 36–7.

[69] The 'lament' of the Headmasters' Conference in 1903 that 'Shakespeare' had been introduced into a Durham School as 'commercial English' may be taken not as evidence of the threat to the humanities but as an indication that literary subjects were being taught in institutions financed by funds made available for scientific and technical education. For report of Conference, see *Journal of Education*, January 1903, pp. 24–8.

[70] The Surrey Technical Instruction Committee, for example, provided the services of a modern languages master at Richmond County School in 1896. Backhurst, A., *The Record* ..., x, 1901, pp. 363–8.

[71] See B.A.A.S., *Report*, 1903 and 1908.

[72] Huggins, Sir W., op. cit., p. 21. As a result of this address, a letter was sent to the universities, together with the statement about scientific education to which reference has already been made, urging them 'respectfully' to take such steps as were in their power to 'ensure that a knowledge of science is recognised in schools and elsewhere as an essential part of general education'. The letter, dated 21 January 1904, is reproduced in ibid., pp. 120–2.

[73] Ashby, E., Anderson, M., *Portrait of Haldane at Work on Education*, 1974, p. 42. See also Wardle, D., op. cit., pp. 55–6.

[74] Ashby, E., Anderson, M., op. cit., chapter 4 *passim*.

[75] Board of Education, *Regulations for Secondary Schools, 1905*, Cd. 2492, HMSO, para V (c) and para 5.

[76] Ibid., para vi and para 5.

[77] Ibid., para ix.

[78] Ibid., para viii.

[79] Board of Education, *Regulations for Secondary Schools 1907*, Cd. 3592, HMSO, para 7 of the Prefatory Memorandum and para 4 of chapter 1.

[80] It is necessary to point out that, between 1902 and 1918, the Board was much exercised with the problem of 'early leaving'. The average length of secondary school life was less than three years for both boys and girls until after the First World War when the Board introduced some measures to try to deal with the problem. See Board of Education, *Report for the Year 1912–13*, Cd. 7341, HMSO, pp. 105–10 and *Report for the Year 1920–21*, Cd. 1718, HMSO, p. 25.

[81] The expenditure on grants to secondary schools in the years ending 1905, 1906, 1907 and 1908 was £254,237, £239,640, £254,210 and £342,584 respectively. The latter figure excludes grants for day-classes which had been abolished. *Statistics of Public Education in England and Wales*, 1906–7–8, Cd. 4286 and 1905–6–7, Cd. 3886 and 1903–4–5, Cd. 2782, HMSO.

[82] Board of Education, *Regulations for Secondary Schools, 1907*, para 7. According to the Board, the strict rules of the 1904 Regulations were 'contemplated from the first as being only a temporary expedient'.

[83] Ibid., chapter 1 para 4. In February 1907, a 'Welsh Department' was set up at the Board. From 1908 onwards the Annual Reports of the Board were rearranged to accommodate this change and separate, but similar, Secondary School Regulations were issued.

[84] Board of Education, *Regulations for Secondary Schools, 1909*, Cd. 4691, chapter II, para 9. This decision provoked strong, but ultimately ineffective opposition, notably from the G.P.D.S.T. See Dyhouse, C., 'Social Darwinistic ideas and the Development of Women's Education in England, 1830–1920, *History of Education* vol. 5, no. 1, 1976, pp. 41–58.

[85] Board of Education, *Report for the Year 1905–6*, HMSO, p.49.

[86] Some insight into these problems is given in ibid., pp. 50–2.

[87] *Natural Science in Education*, HMSO, 1918, para 10.

[88] Ibid., para 11. In this paragraph, the Thomson Committee also drew attention to the problem of 'early leaving', pointing out that the position of science, 'or indeed of any other subject', would never 'be satisfactory' until the schools could depend 'on the great mass of their pupils entering at an age which should certainly not be later than twelve, and remaining at least to the stage marked by the First School Examination'.

[89] The figures for Scholarships and Exhibitions were respectively eighty-eight and forty-five (science); thirty-four and twelve (classics); eighty-two and twenty-six (mathematics); nine and one (science *and* mathematics); thirty-six and twelve (other subjects). Of ninety-five advanced courses in secondary schools, recognised by the Board of Education in 1917, sixty-three were in science and mathematics, thirteen in classics and nineteen in modern studies. Ibid., para 10 (footnotes).

[90] For example, the Oxford and Cambridge Locals, London Matriculation, Victoria Preliminary, Law Preliminary, Medical Preliminary, Responsions and Previous Examinations; those set by the College of Preceptors, by 'South Kensington', the Army or Navy and by the Civil Service together with a number of 'scholarship' examinations.

[91] See Board of Education, *Report for the Year 1904–5*, Cd. 2783, HMSO, p. 69. The report of the Consultative Committee was published separately. The British Association was also active in the field of school examinations. See B.A.A.S., *Report*, 1904, pp. 845–8 and pp. 360–77.

[92] Board of Education, *Report of the Consultative Committee on Examinations in Secondary Schools*, Cd. 6004, HMSO, 1911.

[93] The S.S.E.C. was replaced by the Schools Council in 1964. For details of the establishment of the S.S.E.C. see *P.R.O.*, *Ed* 24/1243–1245. A detailed investigation of its work and influence remains to be undertaken.

[94] The Committee of Council on Education (England and Wales), *Report 1898–9*, Cd. 9401, HMSO, 1899, p. 540 and pp. 582–3. Providing a subject was not 'taken up as a specific subject', it could be taught as one of the alternative courses known collectively as elementary science, e.g. mechanics, horticulture, magnetism and electricity, chemistry.

[95] For example; one shilling or six pence for specific subjects and one or two shillings for class subjects, ibid., pp. 558–9.

[96] The Figures are taken from ibid., Schedule II, pp. 574–5 and Schedule IV, pp. 594–5.

[97] Ibid., Table 53, p. 116.

[98] Data from ibid., Table 52, pp. 114–15 and Board of Education, *Report for the Year 1900–1*, vol. 2, Cd. 757, HMSO, pp. 468–9.

[99] This rate applied to 'older' scholars, that for infants being seventeen shillings per pupil. However, in 1909, the Board introduced a rate which depended simply upon the age of a pupil on a given day in a year, thus relieving Local Authorities and Managers of the temptation to classify the pupils 'not on educational grounds alone, but with regard to financial considerations also'. The Board, of course, retained the right to reduce or withhold grant on grounds of inefficiency. Board of Education, *Report for the Year 1908–9*, Cd. 5130, HMSO, p. 11.

[100] Board of Education, *Revised Instructions Applicable to the Code of 1902*, Cd. 1120, HMSO. The difference is essentially between numbers of 'departments' on the one hand and of pupils on the other. In 1898–9, 2,876 'departments' prepared pupils for examination in specific subjects. Of those pupils who were presented, 'nearly 70 per cent' were examined in algebra, mechanics, animal physiology and domestic economy. Recognising that some candidates entered for the maximum of two specific subjects and that some departments taught more than one specific subject, an approximate figure of 500

may be conjectured for the number of public elementary schools which taught specific science subjects, other than those mentioned, in 1898. This, tentatively, may be compared with 574 departments in which science was taught in 1902. Committee of Council on Education, *Report 1898–9*, Cd. 9401, p. xxi and Board of Education, *Report for the Year 1910–11*. Cd. 6116, p. 20.

[101] Board of Education, *Provisional Code of Regulations for Public Elementary Schools and Training Colleges with Schedules, 1903*, Cd. 1509, HMSO.

[102] Board of Education, *Code of Regulations for Public Elementary Schools with Schedules, 1904*, Cd. 2074, HMSO, p. iv.

[103] Ibid., chapter 1, p. 1.

[104] Board of Education, *Code of Regulations for Public Elementary Schools with Schedules, 1905*, Cmd. 2579, HMSO, chapter 1, p. 2.

[105] The function of the 'Suggestions' was 'to spread as widely as possible a knowledge of the best that was being thought and done in the whole sphere of elementary education throughout the country'. Board of Education, *Report for the Year 1910–11*, Cd. 6116, HMSO, p. 21. The 1902 'Revised Instructions' were, of course, withdrawn.

[106] Board of Education, 1904, op. cit., Prefatory Memorandum.

[107] For example, *The Record* ... vol. XIII, no. 55, 1904, p. 278.

[108] Allen, B. M., op. cit., p. 212.

[109] Eaglesham, E., *Foundations of Twentieth Century Education*, p. 52.

[110] It is easier to sympathise with the view that the 1904 Regulations prescribed a near standstill in elementary education, rather than presaged the dawn of a new era. Ibid. and Birchenhough, C., *History of Elementary Education*, p. 322.

[111] There was no shortage of advice and help from local authorities, the Nature Study Union, Museums, the Royal Society for the Protection of Birds. See Board of Education, *Report for the Year 1910–11*, p. 29.

[112] *Natural Science in Education*, HMSO, 1918, para 89. The Committee also found it necessary to deprecate the continuing employment of peripatetic teachers of science.

2
Practice and Rationale to 1918

As has been noted, the position which science should occupy in school curricula was the subject of considerable controversy in the years between the passage of the Balfour Act and the end of the First World War. The debate took place in a society which was characterised, at least initially, by all the optimism associated with the new century and much influenced by those developments in science and technology which were suggesting 'if not a material, at any rate a mechanistic universe'.[1] The response of those who saw themselves as especially concerned with the more spiritual aspects of life was generally predictable, occasionally extreme[2] and it inevitably encouraged competing claims about the contribution which science could make to a liberal education and the role it should fulfil in contemporary society. As the scope of science and technology widened and alternative ideas about the nature and function of education became more widely diffused, the aims, content and methods of science teaching were subjected to mounting scrutiny.

The extent of the concern is indicated by the number of investigations into school science teaching carried out between 1900 and 1918. The British Association for the Advancement of Science discussed school science at several of its annual meetings,[3] and committees it had established to examine the position of science in the schools reported in 1908 and in 1917. The Association of Public School Science Masters reviewed public school science teaching in 1907 and, four years later, the Board of Education gave particular attention to science teaching in the maintained secondary schools in its Annual Report.[4] Elementary school science was similarly investigated, by the British Association[5] in 1907 and by the Board[6/7] in 1911 and 1914. Finally, during the First World War, the Government appointed a committee, under the Chairmanship of Sir J. J. Thomson, the President of the Royal Society, to 'inquire into the position occupied by Natural Science in the Educational System of Great Britain, especially in Secondary Schools and Universities' and to advise what measures were 'needed to promote its study'.[8]

The reports of the investigations carried out at different times between 1900 and 1918 are important sources of information about the content and methods of science teaching in elementary, secondary and public schools. The Committee which reported to the British Association in 1908 examined the work of twenty-two public and twenty-five boys' secondary schools and discovered 'general agreement among the curricula'.[9] It proved possible to identify the general patterns of subjects taught in two types of secondary schools, A and B, classified on the basis of the age at which pupils normally left; fifteen to sixteen in the Group A schools, compared with eighteen or nineteen in the schools of

Group B. Tables 2.1 and 2.2 summarise[10] the findings of the Committee as published in its report.

Table 2.1   Usual Science Subjects in Boys' Schools where the leaving age is sixteen: 1908

Subjects	Average Age						
	10	11	12	13	14	15	16
Nature Study	———	———	———	–	–	–	–
Elementary Physical Measurements	–	–	═══	═══	═══	–	–
Elementary Heat	–	–	–		═══	═══	
Mechanics	–	–	–	———	———	———	
Heat and Light	–	–	–		———	———	———
Electricity	–	–	–	–	–	–	═══
Elementary Chemistry	–	–	–	–	═══	–	–
Systematic Chemistry	–	–	–	–	–	═══	═══

For Key: See Table 2.2

Table 2.2   Usual Science Subjects in Boys' Schools where the leaving age is eighteen: 1908

Subjects	12	13	14	15	16	17	18
Nature Study	═══	═══	═══	–	–	–	–
Elementary Physical Measurements	–	–	═══	═══	–	–	–
Elementary Heat	–	–		═══	═══		–
Mechanics	–	–	–	═══	═══	═══	
Heat and Light	–	–	–	–	–	═══	═══
Electricity	–	–	–	–	–	———	———
Elementary Chemistry	–	–	–	═══	═══	–	–
Systematic Chemistry	–	–	–	–	–	═══	═══
Biology	–	–	–	–	———	———	———
Sound	–	–	–	–	———	———	———

Subject taught by a few schools: ————————
Subject taught by a majority of schools: ════════
Subject taught by nearly all schools: ════════

As the Tables indicate, most boys were introduced to secondary school science through a course of nature study, a 'conveniently elastic term', which covered work 'of the most various kinds'.[11] Such a course rarely led to the subsequent, systematic study of one or more of the biological sciences which were virtually excluded from the curricula of secondary and public schools for boys at this time. There were, of course, exceptions, the most important being the provision of sixth-form courses in botany and zoology for small numbers of intending medical students.[12] In girls' secondary schools, on the other hand, where an introductory course of nature study was also common, botany was the dominant science and few pupils studied physics[13] beyond a 'very elementary' level. (See Tables 2.3 and 2.4.) Much of this botany teaching appears to have been inadequate. In the opinion of the Board of Education, the subject was still too often 'regarded somewhat in the light of an accomplishment, making no very serious demands on the pupils' intelligence and requiring little more by way of equipment than a classroom and a bunch of flowers'.[14]

Table 2.3   No. of Grant-aided Girls' Secondary Schools (leaving age sixteen) teaching science subjects at a given age: 1917

	36 Typical Schools							
AGE	8–10+	11+	12+	13+	14+	15+	16+	17+
Nature Study	25	18	6	3	–	1	–	
General Elementary Physics	–	11	26	18	9	4	2	
Elementary Chemistry	–	1	9	16	17	9	4	
Systematic Chemistry	–	–	–	1	7	9	9	
Mechanics	–	–	–	–	1	1	1	
Heat	–	–	–	3	3	2	–	
Light	–	–	–	–	–	2	2	
Botany	–	6	9	11	21	30	28	
Hygiene	–	1	3	4	3	2	2	
Domestic Science	–	–	4	6	8	8	3	

Table 2.4   No. of Grant-aided Girls' Secondary Schools (leaving age eighteen) teaching science subjects at a given age: 1917

	103 Typical Schools								
AGE	8–10+	11+	12+	13+	14+	15+	16+	17+	18+
Nature Study	90	70	21	7	1	–	–	–	–
General Elementary Physics	3	31	78	78	31	11	8	5	–
Elementary Chemistry	2	8	27	50	54	30	11	4	–
Systematic Chemistry	–	–	1	3	16	28	35	47	4
Mechanics	–	–	–	3	1	1	6	16	2
Heat	–	–	1	8	10	11	7	16	3
Light	–	–	–	3	6	3	7	13	3
Botany	3	17	31	33	57	83	87	80	2
Biology	–	–	1	2	–	2	3	11	–
Hygiene	1	3	8	6	10	10	7	7	–
Domestic Science	3	9	10	19	24	23	16	13	–
Physiology	–	–	–	–	–	1	2	2	–
Physiography	–	–	1	–	–	–	–	–	–
Zoology	–	–	–	1	–	–	1	3	1
Mag. and Electricity	–	–	–	–	1	1	–	–	–
Sound	–	–	–	–	–	–	1	2	–
Geology	–	–	–	–	–	–	–	2	–

A course in elementary physical measurements also seems to have been practically universal in boys' secondary and public schools at this time. Examining authorities offered syllabuses in the 'subject' and its teaching was encouraged by a number of professional organisations, including the Headmasters' Association.[15] The A.P.S.S.M. noted that science courses in over half of the forty-six schools which responded to its questionnaire in 1907 began with mensuration and that, in all cases, measurement was the beginning of a more systematic study of science:

> Measurements of length, area, volume, mass and densities (are) the foundation on which practically all rest their superstructure.[16]

Additional insight into the teaching of physical measurements in the schools may be gained from the textbooks in use at the time. *Practical Lessons in Physical Measurement*, written by Alfred Earl, the Senior Science Master at Tonbridge School, was first published in 1894 and ran to several editions in subsequent years. Intended as an introduction to the 'serious study of science', the author provided a lengthy justification of the emphasis placed in the book on accurate observation and measurement.[17] His rationale included the following assertion:

> The real beginning of exact knowledge, or science, lies in measuring and a faithful observer is always occupied in measurement.

The book, 350 pages long, contains much that would form part of a conventional course in the properties of matter, but the emphasis, as the above quotation suggests, was always on the accuracy and reliability of the measurements rather than on any physical significance which might be attributed to them.

The same emphasis is evident in the first book of Arthur Mason's *Systematic Course of Practical Science for Secondary and Other Schools*, first published in 1904, and entitled *Introductory Physical Measurements*. Described by a reviewer in *Nature* as 'quite one of the best books of its kind', a more cautious and perceptive tone was evident in the comment to be found in the journal, *Secondary Education*:

> If science is measurement, this book will help beginners to be accurate, observant and neat in measurements.[18]

The following question, taken from D. Rintoul's *Introduction to Practical Physics*, illustrates clearly the manner in which pupils were often expected to display those skills acquired from a course of elementary physical measurements:

> A circular cardboard disc whose diameter is 10.2 cm is found to weigh 7.5 g. What will be the area of a circular piece of the same cardboard weighing 10.0 g?

The answer to this problem was to be 'worked out to four significant figures'.[19]

Elementary heat was also a subject widely taught in secondary and public schools where it was considered to be a necessary preliminary to, or an accompaniment of, a course in elementary chemistry. *A Student's Heat*, published in 1916 and intended for the higher forms of secondary schools, begins with a chapter entitled 'The Measurement of Temperature'. The book contains[20] numerous examination questions which, in addition to confirming the importance attached to physical measurements, indicates the work likely to have been included in a course of elementary heat.

> In virtue of what properties would you select a liquid for use in a thermometer and what would determine the dimensions you would give to the instrument?
>
> *(Oxford and Cambridge Higher Local)*

> A Scotch shepherd, if his plaid is partly wet through and he is out at night, turns his plaid with the wet side in. Explain why this proceeding is a safeguard against chills and describe any one experiment to illustrate your answer.
>
> *(Army Entrance)*

It is clear that courses such as elementary heat or physical measurements were derived from those prescribed by the Department of Science and Art for the science classes and schools to which it had given grant support in the nineteenth century.[21] As such, systematic instruction in physics, where this existed, was provided by sequencing the individual courses, usually in the order: mechanics, heat, light and electricity. According to the Thomson Committee[22] this was apt to lead to 'the neglect of very important parts of the subject', e.g. the conservation of energy, surface tension and diffusion through membranes, simply because they were related to more than one branch of physics or lay outside the conventional divisions.

Systematic courses in chemistry, on the other hand, were well established in the higher forms of secondary, public and later, of central schools.[23] Newth's *Textbook of Inorganic Chemistry*[24] and Shenstone's *Elements of Inorganic Chemistry*[25] were two popular texts in use at the time, particularly in the public schools.[26] The chemistry taught at this level was largely inorganic, with an emphasis on systematic qualitative analysis. Physical chemistry was represented by topics such as the equilibrium law, the ionic hypothesis and associated phenomena, elementary thermochemistry and the colligative properties of solutions. Lower down the school, elementary chemistry had much in common with that which was to be taught for another fifty years; equivalent weights, acids and bases, metals and non-metals, methods of preparing salts and the properties of individual elements and their compounds.[27]

Most of the secondary and public school teachers involved in the British Association survey in 1908 appear to have been satisfied with their existing curricula since they required 'few changes to realise their ideals'. These changes included the incorporation of mensuration and elementary physical measurements within mathematics rather than science teaching and the introduction of nature study if such a course were not already available to pupils.[28]

The state of science teaching in the public schools at this time is of particular significance, since these schools were not affected directly by the legislative and administrative reforms discussed in Chapter 1 and, as the more socially prestigious institutions providing a secondary education, set an example which many grammar schools sought to emulate. In addition, the position accorded to science in the curricula of the public schools was an important element in the vehement and widespread criticism to which these schools were subjected in the early years of the twentieth century.

The public schools were attacked from many quarters and for a variety of reasons.[29] G. B. Shaw and H. G. Wells, both radical critics who sought the abolition of the public schools rather than their reform, were unrelenting in their hostility. Shaw's target was the 'flogging, punishing, coercing and retaliating' which, in his view, characterised English public schools.[30] Wells, characteristically, focused his attack[31] on the public school teachers who made the schools 'places of refuge' and the boys unfit for life or for any real leadership. Less radical opposition came from those involved directly with public school education but even this, in Mack's estimation, amounted to something of a 'revolt from within'. Thus, Norwood and Hope in 1909 could describe[32] public school boys as 'ignorant of life, contemptuous of all outside the pale of their own caste, uninterested in work, neither deserving nor revering knowledge'.

As far as science was concerned, the principal issue was the dominating influence of the classics upon all aspects of public school life. Public school science masters were often paid less than their classically educated colleagues who also enjoyed more favourable career prospects.[33] Of 224 Higher Certificates awarded by the Oxford and Cambridge Board to Eton, Winchester, Rugby, Cheltenham, Clifton and Marlborough in 1902, only twenty-nine were in science subjects.[34] Few pupils from public schools were entered for the Preliminary, Intermediate or Matriculation examinations in science conducted by the University of London. As a correspondent to *Nature* pointed out[35] in 1902, these examinations, generally held in high esteem, 'scarcely (touched) the education of the country as represented by the great public schools of England'. Not surprisingly, the Royal Society concluded[36] that the public schools had failed to devise for themselves any 'adequate way of assimilating into their system of education, the principles and methods of science'.

To some extent, they were discouraged from doing so by the pattern of awards available from Oxford and Cambridge, the two universities with which the public schools were most intimately connected. Table 2.5 records the distribution of scholarships and exhibitions made, over the period 1906 to 1915, by the University of Oxford where a definite number of scholarships was awarded annually for natural science and this number was announced in advance of the examinations.[37] At Cambridge, where there was no prior allotment of scholarships to individual subjects and the number of scholarships in a given subject was determined by the relative performance of the candidates overall, 228 scholarships and 109 exhibitions were awarded for science, or science and mathematics jointly, during the same period out of respective totals of 895 and 375. To gain the maximum number of awards, therefore, the public schools encouraged their most intellectually able pupils to specialise in classics or, to some extent, mathematics, rather than in natural science.[38] It was this specialisation and the value judgements put forward to support it which led Wells to refer to 'the blackmail of the Greek language specialists'[39] and to describe the classical prize scholar as an image of 'ignorance classically adorned'.

Table 2.5   Subjects of Scholarships and Exhibitions Awarded by Oxford Colleges, 1906–15

| | Number of | |
Subjects	Scholarships	Exhibitions
Science	115	59
Classics	650	358
History	122	137
Mathematics	141	61
TOTAL:	1,028	615
Science as % of Total	11.2	9.6

In these circumstances, the optimistic tone of the report on public school science teaching prepared by the A.P.S.S.M. in 1907 and published[40] two years later by the Office of Special Inquiries and Reports of the Board of Education, is somewhat surprising. It was claimed that 'about 90 per cent' of those passing through the public schools in 1907–8 were compelled to take a 'longer or shorter course of science'[41] and that 9,013 or approximately 61 per cent, of the 14,714 pupils attending the forty-six schools surveyed by the A.P.S.S.M. were receiving 'more or less' training and instruction in science as part of their regular school course. Laboratories and classrooms specially designed and equipped for science teaching were 'the rule' and in nearly every instance where the accommodation was inadequate, new buildings were being, or were 'about to be' erected. Not one of the questionnaires returned to the Association contained 'any grumble or even hint' that supplies for science teaching were inadequate or that the subject was 'starved of funds'.[42] Figure 2.1 illustrates the scheme of work in one boys' public school in 1908–9.

However, the report is open to criticism on the grounds that it neither seriously challenged the division of public schools into separate 'sides' nor fully explored the consequences of such divisions for the teaching of science. In twenty-six of the schools investigated, complete division was the norm and this was often accompanied by further subdivision into an army class and into mathematics, engineering and science sides. Ten schools were described as chiefly 'classical' and the remainder were said to have 'no definite line of cleavage'. The forty-six schools in the sample were, therefore, widely different in character and mode of organisation.[43]

The proportion of pupils studying science at any one time was highest in

Figure 2.1   Scheme of Work in a Boys' Public School in 1908–9

Forms I and II

Nature Study

Botany: Roots, stems, leaves, fruits, etc. with reference to a few typical plants.
Elementary plant physiology.
Animals, etc.: Rabbit, Dog, Cat, etc.
Birds.
Butterflies, Moths, etc.

Objects in Common Life

Air. Barometer.
Water. Clouds, Rain, Snow, etc.
Some lighting problems, e.g. flame, Bunsen Burner, electric light.
Electric Bell, etc., etc.
Elementary Astronomy.

Form IIIB

Elementary Science

Measurement of length, area and volume.
Simple Effects of Heat: Thermometer.
Weighing: The Balance: Densities.
Solution, etc.
Simple chemical operations and construction of apparatus.
Examination of Air and Water.

Form IIIA

Physics

Mechanics: Graphs: Springs and Spring Balances.
Levers, Moments: The Balance, Steelyard.
Forces: Parallelogram and Triangle.
Parallel Forces.
Centre of Gravity.
Mechanical principles, etc.

Heat: Heat and Temperature.
Fixed Points of Thermometer: Scales.
Measurement of Heat: Calorimetry.
Expansion of Solids, Liquids, Gases.
Change of State.
Hygrometry.

Form IV

Also doing Heat *this year*.
Syllabus like IIIA, rather more fully;
also:

Light: Shadows.
Reflection and Refraction of Light at Plane and Curved Surfaces.
Formation of Images.
Simple Optical Instruments.
The Spectrum.

Form V

Chemistry

The study of air and water, carbon, salt, without the introduction of theory, symbols or equations.
The gas laws – leading to Avogadro's Hypothesis.
The laws of chemical combination – leading up to the Theory.
The further study of non-metals and metals – in the light of the Theory, especially the 'equation'.
Volumetric Analysis.

SP. V and SP VI

Work up to Scholarship Standard (Chemistry and Physics) – subjects varying from term to term.

those public schools which were not divided into sides. Significantly, none of these ten 'single-barrelled' schools, with the exception of Winchester, could be regarded as a public school of the first rank.[44] Where a school possessed a 'definite line of cleavage', science was either not taught at all to boys on the classical side or, more commonly, allocated insufficient time to allow the subject to have much importance in the eyes of the pupils.[45] It was a situation which Edmond Holmes, a former H.M.I. writing in 1911, summed up as follows:[46]

> Science is, I believe, seriously taught to those who wish to take it seriously; but, if taught at all, it is certainly not taught seriously to the rank and file of the boys, who belong to the 'Classical side'.

The same point was made by the Thomson Committee which concluded that in the public schools 'as a whole' there had been 'no general recognition of the principle that science should form an essential part of secondary education'.[47]

The reluctance of some public schools to accommodate science fully within their curricula was, in part, a consequence of the fact that these schools provided a socially prestigious, classical education for which a sufficient number of parents were prepared to pay the fees. When the parents did not want scientific instruction to be provided on an equal footing with the classics, a public school was under little pressure to change its curriculum.[48] Many public schools, with a status which never approached that of Eton or Marlborough, did adapt their curricula in order to survive and, by 1918, the majority offered adequate opportunities for the study of science to those boys whose parents desired it.[49] Those schools which failed to adapt to changing circumstances found it difficult to recruit pupils, or even closed down.[50] This operation of relatively free market forces ensured that a number of public schools retained a classically dominated curriculum at least until 1918 and, in some cases, well beyond that date. Paradoxically, the First World War, to which scientific knowledge had made such an obvious contribution, may have delayed further the reform of the small number of classically orientated public schools of the first rank. The advent of war scotched the demand for reform which, in 1914, seemed likely to exceed 'in extent and thoroughness the two engineered by Arnold and the public school commissioners'[51] and the contribution of former public school boys to the war itself made subsequent criticisms of these schools much more difficult.

In 1917, the British Association published the report of a committee chaired by Sir Richard Gregory and appointed to inquire into the position of science in secondary and public schools. Hampered by the circumstances of the war and aware that the Committee under Sir J. J. Thomson was conducting its own investigation, the Gregory Committee was content to identify any significant changes which had taken place in the teaching of school science since the committee had last reported to the Association at its Dublin meeting nine years earlier.[52] It recorded 'a tendency to begin electricity' before the final year in those boys' secondary schools where significant numbers of pupils remained to the age of sixteen. Otherwise, the subjects were found to be 'in much the same position'[53] as they had occupied in 1908. In the public schools, Gregory's committee concluded[54] that less importance was being attached to a course of elementary physical measurements, that there was a growing tendency to leave the teaching of mechanics to mathematics staff and that biology was receiving more attention than it had been given in 1908.

These changes in no way mitigated the persistent criticism that the schemes of work followed in many schools made too little reference to the everyday experiences of pupils and largely excluded the commonplace applications of scientific knowledge. In 1906, the British Association was advised[55] that school science teaching was usually detached 'from the concerns ... of common life'. In 1911, the Board of Education, complaining of the 'curious, if not inexplicable limitations' of some school science courses, noted 'a tendency to refrain from all mention of scientific matters of common interest'. The motor and the dynamo were not discussed in courses on electricity and magnetism and, despite the widespread teaching of heat, it was said that a boy who left school with any knowledge of how a locomotive worked usually did so as a 'result of his own unaided researches'. The Board concluded[56] that the science syllabuses 'may and sometimes do err in the direction of being inhuman'. It was a conclusion shortly to be substantiated by the experiences of the First World War.[57]

By 1918, when the Thomson Committee presented its report, there was little new in its findings that the interpretation given to science in many secondary schools was severely restricted, that the number of girls studying physics beyond an introductory level was 'quite insignificant'[58] and that too few pupils of either sex were offered adequate opportunities to study biology. The narrowness of the customary secondary school science course was 'agreed on almost all hands'.[59]

In the early years of this century, a pupil's first contact with scientific knowledge in the elementary schools was often via a series of object lessons. There was an abundance of books offering advice to elementary school teachers on how to organise and conduct their work along these lines and that written[60] by Louisa Walker, Headmistress of a Hampstead Board School, is typical of them. Her book, likened by an H.M.I. to a 'good bag of tools' from which a pupil teacher 'could always pick out a lesson' suitable to his or her needs, catalogued a large number of objects from 'apple' to 'zinc', each of which formed the basis of a standardised lesson. Every lesson was divided into three sections, qualities named and described, uses and sources and was prefaced by a clear statement of aims coupled with a list of the apparatus required. In some instances, the facts were woven 'together in rhyme' in order to help the pupils retain the necessary information. The following extract from the object lesson on cork illustrates the recommended procedure:

> Shew a large piece of cork. Ask what it is (a piece of cork). Where do we find bark? (On trees.) On what part of trees? (On the stem.) Teacher to shew the stem of a tree on which the bark still remains. Tell the children the bark before them is from the cork oak and is called 'cork bark'. Repeat together 'Cork is the bark of a small oak tree.' Write on blackboard, etc.

The versified mnemonic began thus:

Teacher:

This cork which I hold is part of a tree
Which part? and where found, on mountain or sea?
From whence and for what? How, why and wherefore
Was this beautiful substance first brought to our shore?

Children:

Cork is the *bark* of a little oak tree,
Which grows on the shores of a very blue sea.[61]

The contribution of the Board of Education to the teaching of object lessons was published as an Appendix to its 1901 Regulations for Elementary Schools. The lessons were divided into seven categories, covering plant life, animal life, the sky, object lessons for town schools and for country schools, the science of common things and measuring, weighing and testing. Elementary school teachers were invited to select topics other than those listed in the Appendix but such selection was subject to approval by the Inspectorate. The following extracts indicate the kind of work encouraged by the Board at this time:[62]

Sunrise, noon and sunset. (Note the object over which the sun is seen to rise from month to month. Note sun's position at noon and its varying height above the horizon.)

Mole – shape, snout, teeth, paws, claws, eyes, ears, fur, food.

Volcanic rocks, lava, brimstone, pumice stone, basalt or whinstone. (According to the nature of the district.)

Measurements of length – first by eye, then with rule.

As far as the Board was concerned, object lessons were to be distinguished from instruction in natural science, the former constituting elementary science only in so far as they helped pupils 'to observe some of the facts of nature upon which Natural Science is founded'.[63] However, the distinction was not always evident in the reports on object lessons prepared by members of the Inspectorate.[64] In addition, many of the topics suggested by the Board could be taught adequately only by those elementary school teachers with a sound knowledge and understanding of scientific principles.

The quality of the work done in object lessons varied widely.[65] Very good object lessons were given in the best elementary schools, but many were clearly inadequate and often seriously so. Too many teachers ignored the interests of their pupils. There were few successful attempts to provide a coherent pattern of work, the objects selected for study often being chosen simply on the grounds of convenience. The result, as the Board admitted[66] in 1910, was that a sequence such as 'the camel', 'an orange' and a 'pair of scissors' was by no means uncommon. For H. E. Armstrong the conventional object lesson in 1902 provided a model of 'what should be avoided'[67] and the British Association was left in no doubt that, by 1908, the object lesson had often deteriorated to become little more than 'a laborious elucidation of the obvious'.[68]

However, even by the beginning of the century, schemes of work based upon object lessons were giving way to more systematic courses based upon nature study, although the significance of the change was not always realised immediately.[69] The development of nature study in the elementary schools, strongly encouraged by the Board of Education in its Regulations and 'Suggestions' is described in Chapter 4.

The variety which existed in elementary school science teaching in the early years of the century was, to some extent, in accord with the Board's view that such teaching should reflect local conditions.[70] H. M. I. Ward, reporting[71] on the North-Western Division in 1913, found it difficult to describe a typical elementary school science course. In the good country school, it was 'closely associated with practical gardening and, at its best in a town school, involved some simple knowledge of animals, birds and flowers, with older boys following a simple course of experimental physics'. What seems beyond doubt is that many nature study exercises were no better than the object lessons they had replaced. As with the contemporary nature study movement in the United States, the subject was hampered by a lack of definition, obstructed by an expanse of material, deflected by sentimentality of the worst kind, and, with the younger pupils, even pressed into service as a kind of auxiliary Scripture.[72]

The Thomson Committee, while acknowledging that in some elementary schools, especially those in which significant numbers of boys remained until the age of fourteen, a 'master with exceptional character and qualifications' could provide science teaching of great value, concluded[73] that work of this 'comparatively advanced nature' was confined to some 300 or 400 of the total of about 24,000 elementary departments for children other than infants in England and Wales in 1918. It is possible that some of this advanced work was described in a Memorandum[74] on the teaching of science to boys in certain elementary schools in London, prepared by the Board of Education in 1914. At Ensham Council Boys' School, Wandsworth, where there was a good laboratory, experimental science was taught to Standards VI and VII for four and a half hours each week. At Denmark Hill Council Senior Mixed School, the facilities included metal and wood lathes and other craft machinery, as well as a suitably equipped science laboratory.[75] Practical work in physics 'with an emphasis on measurement' was often the basis of the work provided for older boys, the girls being encouraged to study such topics as soap, soda, baking powder, bleaching and dyeing.[76] As in the better elementary schools in other parts of the country, some pupils were encouraged to undertake what would now be known as projects, involving the manufacture of simple electrical equipment.[77]

However, it is likely that much of the comparatively 'advanced' work referred to by the Thomson Committee was undertaken in the Higher Elementary Schools, legalised in 1900, and in the Central Schools, established in significant numbers in large cities and towns after 1911, to continue the general education of public elementary school pupils while, at the same time, giving them 'a definite bias towards some kind of industrial or commercial work'.[78] As such, the curricula of many of these schools had a marked scientific or technical and vocational character.[79]

The Higher Elementary Schools were an unpopular development with the Board of Education since they represented a blurring of the distinction between elementary and secondary education.[80] They operated under a special section, Chapter VI, of the Elementary Code and were obliged to submit details of their curricula and timetables, together with such other information as may have been required, for the approval of the Board.[81] The number of Higher Elementary Schools was never large. There were[82] twenty-nine in 1902, accommodating a total of 7,459 pupils. In 1910, thirty-eight such schools in England provided an education for 7,125 pupils of whom 5,446 were between thirteen and fifteen years of age.[83] When the first series of full inspections of Higher Elementary Schools was completed between 1909 and 1911, the Inspectors concluded that only a minority had succeeded in fulfilling 'the double purpose of developing the education given in ordinary public elementary schools and of providing special instruction bearing on the future occupation of the scholars'.[84]

Central Schools operated under the normal Elementary Code and, by July 1912, six such schools had been established in Manchester and thirty-one in London.[85] Other towns followed the example of these two Authorities and the Board received a report on the London 'experiment' in 1914. The Inspectors concluded that the standard of work in the ordinary elementary subjects was 'considerably higher'[86] than that reached normally in the upper classes of a public elementary school and noted that, in sixteen of the forty-two central schools then existing in London, ten to twelve hours per week were given to practical studies in science and handicraft in each year of the course. In the case of boys, the practical teaching involved mensuration, drawing, clay-modelling, woodwork and metalwork. Girls studied elementary science (principally nature study), together with domestic economy, drawing or other approved subjects. The staffing of the Central Schools was said to be on a 'liberal scale' with a 'fair proportion' of the teachers holding degrees in arts and science and able to display 'considerable professional skill'. The problems of bringing the instruction into 'close and definite relation' with the future employment of the pupils attending these Central Schools, however, were regarded as far from solved, partly because most of the teachers had been trained along conventional academic lines.[87]

No account of school science teaching during this period can ignore the influence of H. E. Armstrong and the heurism now generally associated with his name, although he was not the first to employ or to refer to a heuristical method.[88] Armstrong initiated his campaign to establish science teaching along heuristic lines in a lecture delivered to an International Conference on Education held at South Kensington in 1884. As a Fellow of the Royal Society, Secretary of the Chemical Society and, in the following year, President of the Chemistry Section of the British Association, Armstrong had a wide range of professional contacts and was able to exert considerable influence. He used the Association as a platform for his developing ideas, presenting the Newcastle Meeting in 1889 with his suggestions for a course of elementary instruction in physical science and adding a selection of 'illustrative exercises' in the following year. From 1890 onwards, Armstrong engaged in most of the activities now associated with curriculum development, addressing meetings, writing articles for the educational press, conducting in-service courses for teachers and serving on numerous committees. He was largely responsible for a science-teaching syllabus produced by a committee of the Incorporated Association of Headmasters, published in 1896 and approved[89] by the Oxford and Cambridge Boards as an examination subject. In 1898, the Board of Education published[90] his account of the 'Heuristic Method of Teaching or the Art of Making Children Discover Things for Themselves' in a volume of its *Special Reports on Educational Subjects*. He was a member of a committee appointed by the British Association in 1903 to advise upon the 'course of experimental, observational and practical studies most suitable for elementary schools'.[91] The final report of this committee, presented to the Association five years later, included two detailed schemes of work in elementary experimental science, one for boys, the other for girls.[92] The syllabuses were the work of a subcommittee which, in addition to Armstrong, consisted of W. M. Heller, Professor Arthur Smithells and Dr C. W. Kimmins. The appointment of Heller to the membership of the subcommittee is of particular significance since he was a former student of the Central Institution in London, where Armstrong had been a teacher, and he had considerable experience of teaching science along heuristic lines. Together with Armstrong and the headmaster, C. M. Stuart, Heller had introduced the heuristic system into St Dunstan's College at Catford near where Armstrong lived[93] and, from 1894 to 1897, he had been a peripatetic teacher of science, employed by the London School Board. In 1900, Heller was appointed senior organiser and Inspector of science instruction for the Irish Board of National Education and was able to introduce 'General Elementary Science' as a compulsory part of the curricula of Irish Schools.[94]

The influence of Armstrong and Heller is evident in most of the syllabuses prepared by the British Association Committee.

> Weight of volumes of water (30, 40, 50 cc, etc.) measured from burette and pipette, leading to the fact that one cubic centimetre of water weighs one gram. Repeat these experiments with hot and lukewarm water.
>
> Weigh volumes of milk, spirit, brine, mercury ... to calculate the weight of 1 cc of each.[95]

The contribution of Arthur Smithells, known to have an interest in the science of common things and in the teaching of domestic science,[96] is also readily detected:

> Textile fabrics (especially woollens) have power of absorbing water vapour from the air. Weigh roll of dry flannel and again weigh after exposure to air for a couple of days. Make daily weighings of a bag of seaweed, also observations of thermometer, barometer, and the kind of day.
>
> Burn some finely divided animal and vegetable material, e.g. lean and fat meat, cheese, bread, potato and notice carefully all changes that occur.[97]

By the early years of the century, therefore, there was considerable evidence that Armstrong's campaign to introduce the heuristic method into the schools was meeting with success. Many schools had been equipped with laboratories for practical science[98] and it had been shown that large classes and the requirements of external examinations were not incompatible with heuristic methods of teaching.[99] A small nucleus of teachers had been trained to use heuristic methods[100] and some advertisements for teaching appointments even specified that a knowledge of the 'Armstrong Method' was desirable or essential. By 1907, the heuristic method 'with modifications' was 'very general'[101] in the public schools although it is clear that this was only one of the many 'methods' used at this time. At Berkhamsted, lectures were used to teach senior pupils on the science side. At Harrow, an early course on mensuration was followed by lectures which, in the case of chemistry were 'somewhat heuristic' and, to a certain extent, followed 'Armstrong's method of dealing very completely with some one substance'. At Clifton, in 1907, laboratory work was generally 'carried on independently of lecture work', a situation which prevailed at Gresham's School until the work was reorganised so that 'if a boy is doing heat theoretically, he will also be doing it practically'.[102] This degree of independence of theoretical and practical science studies is difficult to reconcile with a heuristic approach and is somewhat surprising when regarded from a more modern viewpoint.

By 1908, laboratory classes were almost universal in maintained secondary schools and Armstrong's heuristic method was 'widely used',[103] particularly when teaching chemistry to younger pupils. In many instances, pupils were introduced to the matter to be investigated by means of a general class discussion or by writing answers to questions set before the experimental work 'in order to focus the ideas of the class upon its purpose'.[104] Pupils were required to present written accounts of their work, notes made by the pupils being the widely accepted practice. The Board of Education was critical[105] of some of these accounts. 'While accurate as mere description', they often failed to state the assumptions which had been made or to elaborate the relationship between the observations and the conclusions drawn from them.

In the elementary schools, Armstrong could have pointed not only to the solid achievements in London during the last decade of the nineteenth century but also to the policy being pursued by the new Board of Education. By 1908, workshop exercises, nature study and domestic science were regarded as essential parts of the curricula of elementary schools, although this was by no means due entirely to Armstrong's influence and it is doubtful whether he would have regarded these developments as unqualified progress. Others, however, were willing to do so. Philip Magnus detected the 'true spirit of educational reform' in the prefatory memoranda to some of the Regulations of the Board of Education which he saw as reflecting an official move in the direction urged by the British Association in a succession of reports on elementary school science teaching.[106]

Yet, even as early as 1900, heurism was under attack and there were unmistakable signs that, in the hands of inexperienced or inadequate teachers, the heuristic method was being misapplied. In 1909, the Board warned[107] of a 'slavish adherence' to heurism, an Inspector commenting[108] that it was 'rare' to find boys who could apply the methods learnt in a given situation to the solution of a new problem, 'even of a related kind'. Teachers were divided about the effectiveness of the heuristic method, so much so that the Gregory Committee in 1908 found it impossible to summarise its opinions.[109] For some, the method had failed completely. Others, after some years of heuristic teaching, were 'more than ever convinced' of its value.

In 1918, the Thomson Committee severely criticised the heuristic method of teaching which it held responsible for the narrowness of school science education. In a passage that does less than justice to Armstrong's views, the Committee warned that a pupil could not 'expect to rediscover in his school hours all that he may fairly be expected to know', adding that to insist that he should do so was to waste his time and his opportunities.[110] Armstrong was hurt and angry at this travesty of his intentions, although it was by no means without precedent. Ramsay, in 1891, had claimed[111] that 'the conclusions to be drawn' were those which it had taken men of genius '150 years to deduce' and, as such, it was not to be expected 'that an average schoolboy should make out such deductions for himself'.

Armstrong dismissed the Thomson Report as worthless and unlikely to influence educational opinion.[112] He was wrong on both counts. By 1925, he was forced to admit that he had lived long enough to be 'out of fashion' and 'to see the attempt to develop the experimental method in schools a practical failure'.[113]

Armstrong himself must take some responsibility for the manner in which his case was misrepresented. His insistence that

> the beginner not only may but must be put absolutely in the position of an original discoverer

easily led others to assume that he expected a pupil to discover everything for himself. This Armstrong regarded as 'the greatest nonsense' since

> no one asks that [he] should, or believes that [he] can, only that [he] shall learn at first-hand how discoveries are made.[114]

Unlike some reformers, Armstrong did not provide his would-be followers with a comprehensive and coherent statement of his educational beliefs. *The Teaching of Scientific Method and Other Papers on Education*, first published in 1903, was a haphazard compilation of some of his speeches and articles which lacked many of the qualities he advocated so strongly. Smithells, reviewing the book for *Nature*, noted[115] 'a want of system and co-ordination' and expressed his regret that Armstrong had not 'mixed the twenty-three outpourings and ... subjected the mixed liquid to a process of fractional distillation'. In the Preface to the 1903 edition, Armstrong admitted[116] that he was 'open to the charge' of somewhat unduly repeating his argument but the damage was done and the impact of the work significantly reduced by its lack of structure and coherence.[117]

Armstrong encountered other difficulties when trying to persuade others to his point of view. He was too nervous to be an outstanding lecturer[118] and was at his most stimulating in an informal context. His disciple and biographer, J. Vargas Eyre, disposes 'to some extent'[119] of the belief that he was difficult to get along with but there is little doubt that many with whom he had contact shared this belief. It was claimed[120] that opposition had 'made him dogmatic' and Smithells went so far as to say[121] that it was 'not the matter of Armstrong's proposals' which had created opposition, but the manner in which they had been presented. He described Armstrong as 'vigorous almost to violence, red-hot, scathing, scornful, uncompromising and incessant'. Certainly Armstrong was no respector of persons or institutions and, as his obituarist shrewdly recalled[122] he felt it his duty 'to point out clearly ... the errors of governments, departments, universities and individuals and to indicate the true path they ought to take'.

Brock has attributed[123] Armstrong's rude 'bedside' manner to a deliberately aggressive policy designed to disturb the complacency of his audience. If this attribution is correct, it is not difficult to sympathise with Armstrong's messianic approach to reform which sometimes made him enemies when he needed friends. Moreover, it is important to acknowledge Fowles's claim[124] that Armstrong's 'fiery zeal' was responsible for persuading many teachers to give the heuristic method an extended trial.

Armstrong's uncompromising manner also helps to explain why he sometimes appeared blind to the fact that not everyone who took issue with his ideas was totally opposed to them. In a book published in 1909, F. Hodson, a former science master at Bedales School, found it possible to defend the heuristic position while being fully 'alive to its dangers'.[125] He prescribed the use of heurism at an introductory stage, followed by 'speedier methods of accumulating information', a prescription consistent with the practice found in many schools. Although Hodson acknowledged the worst excesses of the heuristic fanatics, he was full and generous in his estimation of Armstrong's many and vigorous contributions to creating new practice; 'spreading conviction in favour of training alertness, self-reliance, rather than of communicating information alone'. It is doubtful whether Armstrong would have thought this sufficient testimony.

Armstrong himself attributed the decline of the heuristic movement to the teachers and there is no doubt that they were 'the method's weakest point'.[126] By 1900 he had witnessed his exercises in physical measurements being worked in too mechanical a manner, 'much as were the conventional examples in mathematical textbooks'.[127] In 1909, the schemes of work suggested by the British Association were found[128] to have led to 'considerable repetition' and, occasionally, to teaching which was 'grotesquely unsuited to the ages and abilities' of the pupils in some elementary schools in London. Armstrong was particularly critical of the knowledgeable but 'impractical' science graduate[129] and of the 'anti-heuristic' instruction provided by the teacher training colleges wherein the 'Beckmessers' reigned supreme.[130] His remedy, characteristically, was the wholesale reform of teaching within the universities which 'directly or indirectly' governed everything.[131]

However, there were a number of other factors which contributed to the decline of heurism. These were the undermining of faculty psychology, principally by Herbartian ideas, an increasing scepticism of the validity of the transfer of training accepted by Armstrong and a growing awareness of the inadequacy of the concept of science implicit[132] in heurism and, hence, of the limitations of the teaching of 'scientific method' as an educational objective. Each of these factors will now be considered in some detail.

The analysis of the human intellect in terms of distinct faculties was not, of course, new[133] even in the nineteenth century when one of its most influential manifestations was the pseudo-science of phrenology.[134] Although phrenology was discredited by Armstrong's day, the belief that the mind consisted of faculties such as 'reasoning', 'imagination', 'memory' or 'will' and that these could be developed by appropriate training and experience, provided a convenient means of justifying individual elements of a curriculum. The analogy usually drawn was between training the mind by education and training the muscles by suitable physical exercises, an 'unused faculty' eventually becoming 'unusable' unless exercised.[135] The analogy was easily extended. Just as physical fitness enabled the execution of physical tasks other than those used to develop the physically fit condition, so, it was held, could the trained faculties be applied to the solution of other problems, i.e. training could be transferred.

Throughout the nineteenth century, a faculty psychology was used widely to legitimise the aims, methods and content of school curricula, although its influence was probably greater on secondary than on elementary education.[136] This is not to imply that such curricula were determined logically by the ideas of a faculty psychology or that practising teachers were necessarily much concerned with faculty psychology as the dominant theory of learning. Indeed, as Selleck has observed,[137] it is likely that 'educationists placed no great emphasis on learning theory at all' in deciding their curriculum or methods. It does mean, however, that Armstrong, like many of his contemporary 'new' educationists, was obliged to argue his case in terms of a faculty psychology which was widely accepted and generally understood. Heuristic methods 'trained the faculties of thoughtfulness and power of seeing; accuracy of thought, of word and of deed'.[138] As a practical educationist, arguing for the teaching of experimental science, Armstrong claimed that these faculties could be developed only if pupils were made to reason for themselves. He therefore carefully distinguished scientific fact from scientific method, a distinction with antecedents in a Report[139] prepared by the British Association in 1867 and in the writings of the secular educationist, George Combe.[140]

The psychological support of heurism was undermined by the growing influence of the ideas of Froebel, Pestalozzi and Herbart, all of whom had been dead for many years before their writings had a major impact on English educational practice. Although the late nineteenth-century 'naturalist' disciples of Pestalozzi and Froebel were far from unanimous in their views,[141] they all shared the belief that the prime aim of education was to develop the latent powers of each pupil 'in accordance with nature's laws'. The naturalists thus placed their emphasis on freedom rather than on method, and on self-development rather than on faculty training, thereby helping to generate a 'new spirit', the essentials of which were[142] 'reverence for the pupil's individuality and a belief that individuality grows best in an atmosphere of freedom'. Such ideas, while not themselves destructive of faculty psychology, clearly threatened to infuse it with such a generous spirit as to alter its significance for the curriculum.

One of the principal difficulties associated with the naturalist view of education was the imprecise nature of the role it prescribed for the teacher.[143] His essential task was 'simply to interfere as little as possible' with the 'natural development' of the pupil. In this respect, he was at a disadvantage when compared with those of his colleagues who subscribed to the ideas of the Herbartian school. The Herbartian teacher was given not only a positive, directing role in pupil development, but also a well-defined plan for organising instruction, based upon the five formal steps of preparation, presentation, association, generalisation and application.[144] For the naturalist, the child developed; for the Herbartian, he was to be made by the teacher. The practical advantage of Herbartianism is obvious and teachers were quick to recognise it. H. M. I. Potter, writing[145] much later of this period, records that the five steps were the 'fashionable' lesson pattern. Selleck comments[146] that, in the ten years after 1897, Herbartianism supported a minor publishing industry and the *Journal of Education* observed[147] in 1911 that 'all students of education were stepping to the tune of the five steps' not long after they had been introduced.

The Herbartians differed from the members of the naturalist school in one other important respect. The concept of mental faculties was specifically rejected.[148] Sir John Adams disposed[149] of faculty psychology in true Herbartian style in an influential book published in 1897 and, ten years later, it was claimed[150] that the doctrine had ceased to have the respect of serious students of the mind. The attack was so vigorous that some contemporary writers saw[151] Herbartian ideas as directed *primarily* at the overthrow of faculty psychology. Intentionally or otherwise, this was undoubtedly the effect.

The success of Herbartian ideas cannot be explained simply in terms of the enthusiasm of its advocates or of their appeal to the practical or professional instincts of teachers. For the Herbartians, education was essentially moral education,[152] a message readily perceived by many who saw society as 'undermined and enfeebled'[153] and 'no longer assured of certain certainties'.[154] Herbartianism, in effect, offered to counteract the consequences of apparently crumbling moral and religious beliefs.

This concern for moral education led the Herbartians to press for major changes in the curriculum, particularly in that of the elementary school.[155] Herbart himself had argued[156] for a balanced curriculum but many of his followers in early twentieth-century England chose to emphasise history and literature since these were seen to hold the greatest potential for moral education.[157] Heurism was attacked directly by Hayward, a leading exponent of Herbart's ideas. He claimed in 1904 that the great need was not that a pupil's mind should be exercised but that it should be 'fed with a rich repast of historical and biographical ideas'.[158] This was too much for Armstrong who had ignored the earlier Herbartian onslaught on faculty psychology. Like Magnus,[159] he saw the Herbartians as responsible for a 'new crusade', favouring literary studies at the expense of workshop or laboratory instruction and he was to spend the remainder of his long life thundering against 'the revival of the literary cult', reserving the 'more vitriolic portions of his extensive vocabulary for psychologists'.[160]

The rapid and widespread acceptance of Herbartian ideas and the collapse of faculty psychology were of more immediate significance for heurism than the evidence emerging from the work of the experimental psychologists on the transfer of training. The conclusion that such transfer as occurred was always specific rather than general, began to accumulate after the publication[161] of the work of Thorndike and Woodworth in 1901. Although the validity of some of the experimental findings was questioned, there was ample ammunition for the critics of heurism. The cautious statements of some of the experimental psychologists were roughly treated for the sake of the cause, particularly, as might be expected, by the Herbartians.

> Accuracy does not transfer; neatness does not transfer; observation does not transfer.[162]

Nor, it might have been added, does scientific method.

The decline of faculty psychology as a learning theory and the hardening of opinion against the transfer of training paved the way for teaching methods based upon a different perception of learning. It also encouraged the introduction of long-overdue subject matter into school science curricula. In particular, it was no longer possible to defend the exclusion of biology on the grounds that it provided a less satisfactory 'mental training' than the physical sciences, allegedly because the subject lent itself less well to precise measurement or was 'inferior from the experimental point of view'.[163]

When the public school science masters met in conference in 1912, they spent much of their time discussing the order in which various scientific topics should be presented, e.g. static before current electricity or 'physical measurements' before chemistry. As the more perceptive members of the A.P.S.S.M. realised, such discussion belonged to an order which was passing. The new problems were those of matching the subject matter and the order of its presentation with the maturing intelligence and developing interests of the pupils. Armstrong, predictably, maintained his opposition, accepting 'neither the experiments of the psychologists nor their inferences'[164] and remained as convinced as ever of the importance of training pupils in the scientific method.

By his own admission, Armstrong's interest in the practice of scientific method was originally literary. At school, he was much influenced by Trench's *Study of Words*[165] and he referred to this work in his statement on heurism published by the Board of Education in 1898. According to Armstrong, Trench's book made him 'critical and anxious to get behind meanings'. Another seminal experience was his involvement in 1880 in a patent dispute about a process for the production of salicylic acid. The display of judicial method, 'the stringent examination and cross-examination of every particular' came to him 'as the acme of scientific thought'.[166]

For Armstrong, scientific method was the methodical, logical use of systematised knowledge. This interpretation is confirmed by his choice of 'text-books': Herbert Spencer's *Essays on Education* and Charles Kingsley's *Scientific Lectures and Essays* were to be followed by a liberal course of detective literature, 'beginning perhaps with Edgar Allan Poe's *The Murders in the Rue Morgue*'.[167]

There is much in common between Armstrong's view of science and that expounded[168] by T. H. Huxley in 1854:

Science is nothing but trained and organised common sense, differing from the latter only as a veteran may differ from a raw recruit.

For Huxley, the 'vast results obtained by Science' were won by 'no mental processes other than those which are practised by every one of us, in the humblest and meanest affairs of life'. Huxley admitted no distinction between the sciences 'on the grounds of method' and, like Armstrong, used a detective analogy to emphasise his point. Huxley's view of scientific method was derived from J. S. Mill's *System of Logic*, as he readily acknowledged, and Armstrong, in turn, acknowledged[169] his own debt to Huxley:

If ever (a) man sought to mould himself upon another ... it is I.

Typically, Armstrong added that much as he owed to the inspiration and support of the Spencer-Huxley 'school', it was mainly 'after the event' and he was particularly critical of Huxley for failing to develop the scientific method in education.

If, as Westaway claimed[170] in 1912, science was 'the most perfect embodiment of the Truth and of the means of getting at the Truth', it was inevitable that attempts would be made to apply the scientific method to diverse areas of human endeavour. The most systematic and comprehensive attempt to emerge in the nineteenth century was Comte's positivism which sought to establish a science of society based upon a body of certain, positive knowledge. Huxley clashed with the small group of well-organised, vociferous English positivists, principally because he sensed that positivism as a social and political creed was becoming too closely identified with science itself. Although he stripped[171] positivism of its scientific respectability, Huxley acknowledged that positivism had awakened in him the idea that the organisation of society upon a new and purely scientific basis was not only practicable but 'an ideal worth fighting for'. Armstrong would have subscribed to such an ideal, which clearly rests upon a particular view of the nature of science and of scientific method. W. K. Clifford's *The Common Sense of the Exact Sciences*, first published in 1885, is the classic statement of that view. More influential, because it was more widely read and amalgamated Comtian and Spencerian ideas, was Karl Pearson's *The Grammar of Science* which appeared in 1892. Two quotations[172] will illustrate the claims made for science and scientific method:

The classification of facts, the recognition of their sequence is the function of science, and the habit of forming a judgement upon these facts, unbiased by personal feeling, is characteristic of the scientific frame of mind. The scientific method ... is not peculiar to one class of phenomena and to one class of workers ... We must carefully guard ourselves against supposing that the scientific frame of mind is a peculiarity of the professional scientist.

... the material of science is co-extensive with the whole life, physical and mental, of the Universe.

Others were ready to share Pearson's views and, where possible, to act accordingly. Leslie Stephen, the political economist, argued for a scientific theory 'which defined the limits within which institutions might be modified by any proposed change'. The sociologist Benjamin Kidd included[173] 'politics, history, ethics, economics and religion' within his 'science of life'. Lord Acton initiated the Cambridge Modern History series to 'meet the scientific demand for completeness and certainty' and J. B. Bury, Acton's successor in the Regius Chair at Cambridge, used his inaugural lecture in 1903 to assert that history was a science 'no more and no less'.[174] The British Science Guild, established in 1905 as a result of Lockyer's initiative, sought 'to apply the methods of science to all fields of human endeavour and thus to further the progress and increase the welfare of the Empire'.[175] The Educational Science section which Armstrong forced upon the British Association in 1900 was an attempt to align education with the physical sciences. The assumption was that if educational science could not aspire to the 'finality' of the results obtained by the established sciences, it could, at least, emulate their methods.

The equation of science with organised common sense and of scientific method with little more than rational, scholarly thought was not without practical consequences for science itself. In 1916, Frederick Soddy referred to the one million pounds provided by Carnegie for 'improving and extending the opportunities for scientific study and research in the Universities of Scotland'. He noted[176] that, at Aberdeen, 'a bare one quarter' had gone to science. The remainder of the bequest had been used to establish one professorship in history and five lectureships in French, political economy, German, education and constitutional law and history. For Soddy, 'calling science what is not science' needed to be 'watched and checkmated'.

Although Soddy did not indicate the criteria whereby science could be distinguished from non-science, there were several developments at the turn of the century, both in science and philosophy, which made it impossible to sustain the view that science was merely organised common sense. The fundamental obscurity of the apparently simple foundations of Newtonian mechanics was exposed by Mach and Hertz. Einstein's Theory of Relativity raised the important question of how science could claim to progress by accumulating knowledge if major advances required the destruction of previously held theories. The conception of science implicit in heurism could not account for developments such as thermodynamics or quantum theory, any more than it could accommodate Newton's assertion that a body is at rest only because there are forces acting upon it or Galileo's 'rape of the senses' in advocating a heliocentric universe. As the concepts and imagery of science were seen to be removed further and further from 'common sense', it became increasingly difficult to argue convincingly that pupils must be put in the position of an original discoverer[177] and to maintain that science owed its achievements to a method which was merely 'a game' whose rules could be learnt and applied.

Armstrong claimed[178] that he had elaborated these rules in *The Teaching of Scientific Method*. The game was 'without end'. 'Trumps' were rarely turned up and 'low cards prevailed'. The essential items of apparatus for learning how to play the game were 'centimetre-foot rules, drawing boards, T- and set-squares and balances', the latter being the 'primary weapons' of heuristic instruction and, as such, to be treated with the 'utmost care and reverence'.[179] For Armstrong, all true science rested on exact measurement, all exact coordinated knowledge could be called science and no subject was mastered until it was reduced to scientific terms.[180]

By the early twentieth century, this view of science and of scientific method was philosophically unacceptable. Moreover, it contained an inherent educational paradox. In arguing simultaneously that the scientific method was not confined to natural science and that the chief function of science teachers was to teach scientific method, Armstrong was close to denying science any educational advantage over other subjects in the curriculum and to surrendering the claim of science teachers to a special existence.

This paradox was discussed in 1917 in the Report of a Committee appointed by the British Association to inquire into the position of science in secondary schools. The Committee found the paradox to rest upon the false assumption that the method of science could be regarded as separable from the matter:

> The scientific method is an abstraction which does not exist apart from its concrete embodiments.[181]

The term 'concrete embodiments' is an unfortunate one and the Committee's conclusion takes the paradox no nearer to resolution unless scientific method is given a more generous interpretation than that implicit in Armstrong's 'game'. Science can clearly claim no monopoly of the skills associated with activities such as observing, testing hypotheses, thinking logically or verifying provisional ideas. Similarly, attitudes such as curiosity, willingness to suspend judgement or intellectual honesty cannot be regarded as associated uniquely with the practice of science. None the less, the Committee's conclusion, that it was possible to use scientific method only when dealing with scientific matters, was essentially correct.

Armstrong remained unrepentant, asserting in 1924 that the method of science was 'far more widely applicable' than was generally supposed.[182] Armstrong's failure, perhaps to appreciate, but ultimately to respond to shifts in the philosophy of science and to recognise their implications for heurism may be partially explained by the fact that he was an organic chemist, trained and nurtured in the nineteenth-century German tradition. As such, he was eccentric to the great achievements of the school of mathematical physicists and chemists who, in creating thermodynamics, relativity and quantum theory, contributed to the most profound and fruitful change in the conception of reality since Newton. It is astonishing but significant that Armstrong in 1902 could only lament 'a dearth of imaginative power ... in science' and a 'prevailing tendency ... to imitate rather than to originate and individualise'.[183]

Armstrong's attitude is well illustrated by his reactions to the emergent physical chemists, many of whom applied mathematical considerations to what he regarded as chemical phenomena. In a lengthy correspondence with Whetham in *Nature* in 1906, Armstrong objected to the application of 'thermodynamic reasoning' – 'a favourite device of the mathematical mind' – to osmotic phenomena. Whetham was obliged to remind[184] Armstrong of that most basic of points, the independence of thermodynamic reasoning of the view held about the fundamental nature of the osmotic process. To some extent, Armstrong was reflecting a difference in the points of view of the classical, synthetic organic chemist and the new school of physical chemists, a difference he expressed[185] in the following terms:

> ... the chemist ... though able perhaps to imagine a frictionless piston, yet desires, in the first place, to get nearer to a knowledge of what happens to the real tangible piston of practice.

Moreover, in so far as he was objecting to a possible blurring of the distinction between an observation and a hypothesis, Armstrong could probably have counted upon a degree of support. Berry, for example, was later to complain[186] that an *analogy* drawn by van't Hoff between the behaviour of gases and of solutions was practically 'dogma' for students.

Unfortunately, it seems likely that Armstrong had a more fundamental aversion to physical chemists who, in his view, 'put facts aside and fitted curves to suit their assumptions'. His objection was to the use of mathematical models *per se* in chemistry. He refused to recognise the usefulness of such models in guiding and provoking experimental studies and, in his usual blunt manner, proclaimed the need to 'cast out, root and branch', the physical element in chemistry.[187]

Despite the virtual eclipse of the heuristic method of teaching science, many of Armstrong's ideas were to continue to influence school science education. An emphasis on practical experimental teaching and a belief in the importance of learning by doing became established features, and science curriculum reform, a generation after his death in 1937, was to incorporate Armstrong's view that science could best contribute to liberal education by initiating pupils into its greatest professional mystery, its method.[188]

Resolution of the paradox posed by Armstrong's conception of scientific method ultimately lies in a recognition that the logical and imaginative operations of science are conducted with what Ravetz has called[189] 'intellectually constructed things and events' and not with the objects of common-sense experience. Although these intellectual constructs are designed to relate as closely as is possible to the inaccessible reality of the external world, they are not, as Armstrong's scientific method seemed to imply, identical with it. It follows that some aspects of scientific method cannot readily be taught and that an appreciation of the methodology of science requires that students be introduced to these intellectually constructed 'things and events'. Hence, as heurism lost its philosophical support, the stage was set for a reassessment of the contribution of natural science to liberal education and for a renewed emphasis on the acquisition of scientific knowledge as an educational objective.

The drift from process to content was strongly encouraged by the experience of the First World War which highlighted a widespread ignorance of common scientific facts among both officers and men. In 1916, Napier Shaw, a former director of the meteorological department, complained of the difficulty of teaching army officers the rudiments of weather forecasting when they had 'no more knowledge about the air than a clodhopper's experience'.[190] Smithells, who served as chemical adviser in charge of the anti-gas training in the Home Command, encountered a similar problem. He later claimed that a 'vast number and probably the majority of ... casualties' during gas attacks had been sustained as a result of 'ignorance of the elements of natural science on the part of officers and men'[191] and that heroism had become 'a substitute for intelligence'.

A lack of knowledge of scientific matters of importance to the prosecution of the war was not confined to serving members of the armed forces. A Government Minister, replying to criticisms of a decision to allow the export of lard from which glycerine and hence much-needed nitroglycerine could be manufactured, sought to exonerate his colleagues by claiming that the relevant process had been discovered only recently.[192] Since the hydrolysis of fats to produce an alcohol such as glycerol had been known for centuries, this incident became something of a *cause célèbre* among the scientific community.

The war also revealed the dependence of British manufacturing industry on the scientific and technological expertise of other countries, even in a sector such as the production of dyestuffs which Britain had pioneered little more than a generation earlier. When the war began, the country thus found itself without adequate or even any sources of materials as diverse as optical glass, needed to produce such items as binoculars and range-finders, and acetone, used as a solvent for guncotton. According to Ray Lankester, acetone was made eventually 'by the aid of a Russian chemist of Manchester'.[193]

On 2 February 1916 a memorandum appeared in *The Times* claiming that people were being 'destroyed from lack of knowledge' of science 'on the part of ... legislators and administrative officials'. The memorandum, entitled 'The Neglect of Science' was initiated by M. D. Hill of Eton, signed by many Fellows of the Royal Society and ultimately supported by many other leading members of the scientific community and by most of the professional scientific and technological institutions.[194] Publication of the memorandum provoked lively correspondence in the national press and the principal issues were debated at a conference convened at the Linnæan Society on 3 May 1916. A Neglect of Science Committee was formally established and 13,000 copies of the report of the conference proceedings were sent[195] to Members of both Houses of Parliament, Fellows of the Royal Society, governors of public schools, members of the Courts of City Companies, principals of all universities in the Empire, the Ministers of Education in the colonies and even to the 'Mayors of English and Scotch Municipalities'.

A deputation of five members of the committee, under the Chairmanship of Lord Rayleigh, met Lord Crewe, Lord President of the Council, on 7 June 1916. According to Crewe[196] the members of the deputation undoubtedly represented those 'best qualified to judge the needs of the case' and the accounts of the meeting offered independently by each side show that the meeting was characterised by a marked unanimity of view rather than by any clash of opinion. The Neglect of Science Committee regarded the subsequent appointment of the Thomson Committee in August 1916 as a direct consequence of its efforts but this is not supported by the evidence. The Government had already accepted that national interests were suffering from the 'neglect of science' and the Thomson Committee, although formally a Committee appointed by the Prime Minister, worked in, and was serviced by, officials of the Board of Education.[197] Not surprisingly, many of its recommendations were an endorsement of the policy pursued by the Board of Education for several years before the outbreak of the war.

The agitation of the Neglect of Science Committee provoked a prompt and vigorous reaction from humanist and classical scholars and those anxious to defend their educational interests. Ramsay MacDonald told[198] the House of Commons that the Neglect of Science Committee were 'practically telling us to clear the humanities out of our schools'. *Blackwood's Magazine* referred[199] to the 'ferocious attack' on the humanities as evidence of the 'unbalanced men of science who wish to kill off all learning other than their own'. Those who had hitherto praised German scientific and technological achievements had their own evidence used against them. Replying to an eloquent and reasoned speech by Haldane, Lord Cromer told[200] the House of Lords that the German emphasis on science had led not only to great national prosperity but also to moral collapse, responsible for the war in which the Allies were then engaged.

A more direct challenge came from Sir Richard Livingstone in his *Defence of a Classical Education*. He claimed that the fundamental weakness of science as a vehicle of liberal education was that:

> ...it tells us hardly anything about man. The man who is our friend, enemy, kinsman, partner, colleague, with whom we live and (have our) business, who governs or is governed by us, (never comes) within our view.[201]

H. G. Wells, never reluctant to take up the cause of science education, claimed[202] that Livingstone's case rested on two misconceptions; namely that an attempt was being made to abolish classics from general education and that a scientific education could be equated with the acquisition of facts. Livingstone's claim that he had been misrepresented left Wells unrepentant.[203]

Controversy was also engaged at a more formal level. At a meeting held in October 1916 the Historical, Classical, English, Geographical and Modern Language Associations, in conjunction with the British Academy, elected a Council of Humanistic Studies to protect their educational interests. A joint meeting of the Council with the Neglect of Science Committee, held two months later, proposed three Resolutions, two of which were concerned with the amounts of time to be devoted to various subjects in the secondary school curriculum. After due consultation, the Classical Association rejected the time proposed for classics as 'manifestly too little'. The English Association suggested that the allocation of time to specific subjects was more properly the task of individual headteachers and the Geographical Association found itself with an unexpected battle on its hands since, in framing the Resolution, geography had been amalgamated with natural science.[204]

The haggling, reminiscent of a dispute 'whether a tailor should make coats or trousers',[205] continued at a further meeting in January 1917, until little difference remained, at least outwardly, in the positions of those claiming to represent the sciences and the humanities respectively. The bartering over the time to be allowed for science in school curricula and the quibbling about the wording of formal Resolutions did nothing to resolve the issue raised by Livingstone, namely, how science could justify its claim to being a humanising study. The case could not be argued solely in terms of the acquisition of scientific knowledge and it was no longer possible to proclaim the near universal applicability of scientific method. Overtly utilitarian arguments were also suspect, despite the role of science in the war and the revelations, by the British Science Guild and others, of the continuing scientific inadequacy of much of British industry. Moreover, there was some concern within the scientific community that if utilitarian arguments were pressed too strongly, the value of science would be measured simply by its practical utility. Andrade warned of[206] the danger of a preoccupation with applied science and a correspondent to *Nature*, although arguing a somewhat different case, reflected accurately the concern that too much emphasis might be placed on the usefulness of science in justifying its inclusion within the curriculum.

> We hear much of the place of science in education, but it seems sometimes as if its advocates would say: 'When I mention science, I mean experimental science and not only experimental science, but industrial science and not only industrial science, but paying science.'[207]

In these circumstances, the most immediately distinctive achievement of the Thomson Committee when it reported in 1918 was its forceful reassertion of the humanising influence of the proper study of science.[208]

> How necessary Science is in War ... we have learnt at a great price. How it contributes to the prosperity of industries and trade, all are ready to admit. How valuable it may be in training the judgement, in stirring the imagination and in cultivating a spirit of reverence, few have yet accepted in full faith.

There is, in this assertion, a clear debt to Sanderson of Oundle, and to those who shared his vision.

> The Romance of Science opens out ideals, the wondrous experiments stir up faith and belief.

> Men and women may learn to appreciate the art (of science) as they appreciate music and painting, though they have no skills as musicians or painters.[209]

Nature study is not designed to produce naturalists any more than music is taught to make musicians . . .

Natural history should . . . give the child a sense of his oneness with all forms of life.[210]

Smithells, noting in 1918, that science had 'edified and instructed far less than was reasonably to be expected' from a movement that had been carried on for so long and with such vigour, attributed this failure to the fact that science had not been taught as a humanity: it had not been brought to bear 'upon the environment and avocations of human life'.[211]

The most influential of those who pressed that science should be studied in more effective relation with life and things as they are in the everyday world rather than 'as it is dealt with by "professionals" in seminaries'[212] was Richard Gregory. His book, *Discovery or the Spirit and Service of Science*, published in 1916, is described by his biographer as an 'eloquent and effective plea for the abandonment of the view that scientific and humanistic studies were mutually antipathetic' and 'a synthesis of the arguments (Gregory) had been steadily advancing in *Nature, The School World, Cornhill, Fortnightly, Sunday at Home*, and other magazines'.[213] Science was to be taught because it provided 'an intellectual outlook, a standard of truth and a gospel of light'[214] and illustrated the nobility of scientific aims and the spiritual aspects of scientific endeavour. Here indeed were high sentiments and a new morality for science, 'that compensation which takes the place of worldly riches and enables unselfish work to be done from which others make commercial gain'.[215]

It is hardly surprising that Gregory warmly welcomed the recommendations which the Thomson Committee made. He pressed his case at the British Association in 1919 and 1921, pleading for science as part of a general education, 'unspecialised . . . and without reference to prospective occupation or profession'.[216] There was, of course, opposition; from Armstrong, despite his membership of the B.A.A.S. Committee of which Gregory was Chairman, and from those, like H. H. Turner, who challenged[217] the possibility of a 'science for everybody'. However, the forces which had initiated the science-for-all movement were too strong to be resisted and there remained only the formidable problem of translating lofty ideals into practical proposals.

A start had been made by the British Association Committee under Gregory which had included in its report schemes of work for several different types of school. Each scheme, prepared by a different author, contained subject matter drawn from several of the conventional sciences. Each attempted to present science in its relationship to the lives and environment of the pupils. The scope of some of the schemes was wide. *Science for All in a Public School*[218] moved from cosmology to the gramophone and is of particular significance for the general science movement considered in the next chapter.

One feature of the British Association Report deserves mention. Addressing itself to the question whether there were any general principles to guide a teacher in ordering a curriculum to meet the needs of his pupils, the Committee sought criteria to 'discriminate between things suitable and things unsuitable for pupils at different stages of progress'.[219] The Committee detected three conspicuous motives among those which had prompted men of science to try to understand their world.

> First is delight in the intrinsic beauty and charm of natural phenomena. . . . Next, the motive that springs from the perception that man can exploit the forces of nature only if he is prepared to understand them. . . . Lastly, there is the motive that prompts men to seek 'fundamental principles' in nature.

These motives of 'wonder, utility and systematisation' were present in all scientific activity to different degrees and at different times.[220] The Committee convinced itself that they were also present in the minds of the pupils. There were few children, if any, who did not 'feel the charm of natural phenomena'. The utility motive was 'notoriously conspicuous' and, in boys, 'may reach the force and volume of a passion'. The systematising motive gained dominance only with the 'full advent of adolescence'.[221]

The assertion that the interest of children in science exhibited a rhythm corresponding to the rhythm of its history was due principally to T. P. Nunn[222] who had first elaborated this view in 1905. Nunn's ideas had obvious implications both for the sequencing of topics within a school science course and for the strategy by which they should be taught. Elementary physical measurements were to be replaced by studies more likely to appeal to the wonder motive, e.g. nature study, astronomy. Archimedes' Principle was to be taught not as a 'property of fluids' or as a method of determining specific gravity but as the principle which explained why ships were able to float. Moreover, it was to be taught when pupils' minds were most receptive to the utility motive.

It is inappropriate to consider either the genesis or the validity of Nunn's ideas[223] in this book. However, it is important to recognise that they constituted a new 'learning theory' which was consistent with, and supportive of, the view that science should be taught as an essential humanity. In addition, they reflected a greater feeling for the personal and historical dimensions of scientific activity than that implied by either Huxley's science as 'organised common sense' or by Armstrong's scientific method. The inclusion of historical and biographical studies within a science course could be justified not only because they provided an opportunity to humanise the subject and to introduce 'more of the spirit and less of the . . . dry bones',[224] but also because such studies could be matched to the appropriate stages of pupil motivation.

Finally, Nunn's conception of the historical development of science constituted yet another challenge to heurism which had worked the systematising motive 'beyond its natural strength'.[225] It was inevitable that Armstrong would be hostile to the science-for-all movement with its necessarily reduced emphasis on laboratory exercises.

> The 'damned boy' needs drilling. We forget this and ever twaddle of playing on his interests,[226]

he wrote in 1924. None the less, it was to be Gregory's and not Armstrong's hour. Science was to provide a liberal education by 'the study of nature, the sight and history of men and the setting forth of noble objects of action'.[227]

References

[1] Ensor, R. C. K., *England, 1870–1914*, 1936, p. 552. Ensor likens the mood of early twentieth-century society, compared with that of the last decade of the previous century, to one of 'sunrise succeeding sunset', ibid., p. 527.

[2] See, for example, Holmes, E., *What is, and What Might Be*, 1911, in which the former H.M.I. condemns the 'externalism' of the West. The reaction to the widening influence of science and technology is discernible in other aspects of early twentieth-century society, notably the 'back to the land' movement, the 'back to the wild' movement (Boy Scouts, Boys' Brigade) and even in a 'back to childhood'. *Peter Pan* was produced in 1904.

[3] For example, at the Leicester Meeting in 1907.

[4] Board of Education, *Report, 1909–10*, Cd. 5616, HMSO, pp. 73–82. For an account of the founding and work of the A.P.S.S.M., see Mikhail, N. H., *A Historical Review of the Development of the Main Associations Concerned with the Promotion of Science Teaching in Secondary Schools in England ...*, London M.A. Thesis, 1961.

[5] B.A.A.S., *Report*, 1908, p. 495.

[6] Board of Education, *Report*, 1910–11, HMSO, p. 28.

[7] Board of Education, *Memorandum on the Teaching of Science to Boys in Certain Public Elementary Schools in London*, P.R.O., Ed. 14/96.

[8] *Natural Science in Education*, HMSO, 1918. The Committee was also required to give due regard 'to the requirements of a liberal education, to the advancement of Pure Science and to the interests of the trade, industries and professions which particularly depend upon Applied Science' and to take into account the Report of the Consultative Committee of the Board of Education on the provision of Scholarships and Bursaries.

[9] B.A.A.S., *Report*, 1908, p. 528. The report was nominally the work of a Committee chaired by Sir Oliver Lodge, but the inquiry was undertaken by a much smaller Committee under the Chairmanship of Sir Richard Gregory. The other members of this subcommittee were G. F. Daniell, W. D. Eggar, C. M. Stuart and O. H. Latter. Eggar and Latter were two of the founders of the A.P.S.S.M.

[10] Ibid., pp. 528–9.

[11] Board of Education, *Report for the Year 1909–10*, Cd. 5616, HMSO, p. 75.

[12] At least one of the public schools investigated by the A.P.S.S.M. in 1907 offered a thorough course in biology to lower forms on the classical side occupying two and a half hours each week. Board of Education, *Educational Pamphlet No. 17*, HMSO, 1909.

[13] B.A.A.S., *Report*, 1917, p. 131. Tables 2.3 and 2.4 are taken from this source but almost certainly represent the general position in 1908.

[14] Board of Education, *Report for the Year 1909–10*, HMSO, p. 82.

[15] B.A.A.S., *Report*, 1908, p. 529.

[16] Board of Education, *Educational Pamphlet No. 17*, HMSO, 1909, p. 19.

[17] Earl, A., *Practical Lessons in Physical Measurement*, 1894, p. 6.

[18] The significance of this comment and that of the author of the review in *Nature* are enhanced by their selection, presumably by the publishers, for inclusion in the frontispiece of the second volume in the series, *Experimental Heat*.

[19] Rintoul, D., *Introduction to Practical Physics*, p. 10. Rintoul was an assistant master at Clifton College. His book, like many others of its kind, can be regarded as derived from the pioneering work of another Clifton science teacher, A. M. Worthington. The latter's *Physical Laboratory Practice: A First Course* was described in 1909 as 'the parent of a

large family of laboratory guides which have seen the light during the last ten or fifteen years', Board of Education, *Educational Pamphlet No. 17*, 1909, p. 6.

[20] Hart, I. B., *A Student's Heat*, 1916, p. 25 and p. 127. The author was Senior Science Master at Leamington Municipal Secondary School and a 'lecturer in physics' at the municipal technical school in the same town.

[21] Referring to the *ad hoc* grant system of the Department of Science and Art, the Thomson Committee commented in 1918 that 'though these conditions no longer hold, their effect to some extent persists'. *Natural Science in Education*, HMSO, 1918, para. 9.

[22] Ibid., para. 50.

[23] See p. 41.

[24] Newth, G. S., *A Textbook of Inorganic Chemistry*, Longmans Green. The ninth edition, 'revised and enlarged' was issued in 1902 and Newth is described as 'Demonstrator in the Royal College of Science, London' and 'Assistant-Examiner in Chemistry, Board of Education, South Kensington'.

[25] Shenstone, W. A., *The Elements of Inorganic Chemistry for Use in Schools and Colleges*, Edward Arnold. First published in 1900, a second and revised edition was issued in the following year. Shenstone, a Fellow of the Royal Society, taught Chemistry at Clifton College.

[26] Board of Education, *Educational Pamphlet No. 17*, HMSO, 1909, p. 24.

[27] See, for example, Wilson, F. R. L., Hedley, G. W., *A School Chemistry*, O.U.P., 1912, published in two parts but also available as a single volume. Wilson was an assistant master at Charterhouse and Hedley was 'Head Science Master' on the Military and Civil Side of Cheltenham College.

[28] B.A.A.S., *Report*, 1908, p. 531.

[29] For a detailed account, see Mack, E. C., *Public Schools and British Opinion since 1860*, Columbia U.P., 1941, Chapters VIII and IX.

[30] In 1923, Shaw wanted 'Eton, Harrow, Winchester ... and their cheaper and more pernicious imitators' to be 'razed to the ground and their foundations razed with salt'. Shaw, G. B., *Sham Education*, 1931, p. 359, quoted in Mack, E. C., op. cit., p. 266.

[31] For a summary of Wells's views, see Mack, E. C., op. cit., p. 275 ff. For an account of his ideas on science education, see Stephenson, C., *The Educational Ideas of H. G. Wells with Particular Reference to the Contribution of Science*, Leeds, M.Ed. Thesis, 1974.

[32] Hope, A. H., Norwood, C., *The Higher Education of Boys in England*, 1909, quoted in Mack, E. C., op. cit., p. 282. The 'Caste' problem was thoroughly aired by Galsworthy in an article written on 27 May 1912. See Marrot, H. V., *The Life and Letters of John Galsworthy*, New York, 1906, pp. 703–5.

[33] Baker, H. B., *The Teaching of Science as it Exists Today*, Report to the A.G.M. of the A.P.S.S.M., *Minute Books*, A.S.E., Hatfield, p. 28.

[34] *Nature*, 11 September 1902, p. 459. The individual figures are Eton (45, 0); Winchester (48, 4); Rugby (58, 6); Cheltenham (32, 7); Clifton (23, 8) and Marlborough (18, 4). These figures are quoted in a letter which the author advised was 'not written in a spirit of hostility to classical and literary society'.

[35] Letter from Irving, A., *Nature*, 31 July 1902, p. 320. A similar picture emerges from the report prepared by the A.P.S.S.M. in 1907. See Board of Education, *Educational Pamphlet No. 17*, 1909, p. 25 for details.

[36] Royal Society, *Statement Regarding Scientific Education in Schools, Drawn up by a Committee of the Royal Society*, reproduced in Huggins, Sir W., *The Royal Society ...*, 1906, p. 121.

[37] Data for both universities from *Natural Science in Education*, HMSO, 1918, para. 18.

[38] M. D. Hill, one of the founders of the A.P.S.S.M. recognised this point from the beginning. *Journal of Education*, 1903, p. 331.

[39] Wells, H. G., 'A Modern Education', in Lankester, Sir R. (ed.), *Natural Science and the Classical System in Education*, 1918, pp. 202, 205. See also Mack, E. C., op. cit., p. 269. Wells wanted a curriculum which included law, history and those political subjects which would give information about contemporary developments 'such as Communism and tariff problems'.

[40] Board of Education, *Report on Science Teaching in Public Schools Represented on the Association of Public School Science Masters, Educational Pamphlet No. 17*, HMSO, 1909. The Board naturally disclaimed responsibility for opinions expressed in the Report. For O. H. Latter of Charterhouse, who edited the Report for the A.P.S.S.M., the improvements which had taken place in public school science teaching amounted since 1883, to 'a revolution'. Ibid., p. 7.

[41] Ibid., p. 10.

[42] Ibid., p. 17. The Table is taken from Appendix II.

[43] Ibid., p. 12. A somewhat different emphasis to that of the text of the Report is found in a footnote inserted by the Director of the Office of Special Inquiries and Reports. 'The smallest percentage of boys learning science ... is 21.8, the largest 100. If the forty-six Schools are arranged in the order of the percentage of boys returned as learning science, they fall into two fairly well-defined groups, viz. (i) a group of twenty-five schools in which less than 63 per cent of the boys are learning science, and (ii) a group of twenty schools in which more than 73 per cent are learning science. ... On the whole there is in the first group a majority of schools who are most closely identified with the classical tradition, while the second group contains a preponderance of those schools which are not divided into 'classical' and 'modern' sides.

[44] They were Aldenham, Battersea G.S., Perse School, Dean Close School, Exeter School, Giggleswick, Gresham's School, Plymouth College, Winchester and Wyggeston School.

[45] The A.P.S.S.M. recognised this point (ibid., p. 23), but it is difficult to make much sense of the figures since they generally excluded time allowed for 'prep' and some were quoted in 'periods' of 45 to 105 minutes' duration and others in 'hours per week'.

[46] Holmes, E., *What is and What Might Be*, 1909, p. 260 (footnote). For Holmes, the study of science in a public school was 'as a rule, a pure farce'.

[47] *Natural Science in Education*, HMSO, 1918, para. 13. For the effect of organising a school into 'sides' on the amount of science taught, see para. 14.

[48] This 'social determination' of public school curricula is most clearly evident in a Memorandum entitled 'The Influence of Science on Classical Studies' prepared for Morant in 1911 by 'the very best man we have on the subject'; *P.R.O., Ed.*24/287. '50 years ago, men occupied in commerce and industry were trained in Private Academies or local Grammar Schools. Now, nearly all who could afford it go to large Boarding Schools and these ... prepare boys, not only as was formerly the case for professional work and public life, but for commerce and industry.... The great development of modern subjects is an inevitable result of social changes.' By modern studies, the author of the Memorandum means not only science but also modern languages.

[49] *Natural Science in Education*, HMSO, 1918, para. 13.

[50] Ogilvie, V., *The English Public School*, 1957. Ogilvie (p. 196) relates how Bath College, founded in 1867 had to close down in 1909. The 'basic defect' was a social one, the School Council refusing to allow the sons of tradespeople into the school. This, allied with 'an education that was too strictly classical' caused the collapse of the school.

[51] Mack, E. C., op. cit., p. 305. How much remained to be done is clear from Sir Alec

Douglas-Home's account of his science teaching at Eton in 1917. John Christie, the science teacher, used to appear 'late in a dressing gown', distribute a book on 'Levers' and then 'ring the bell for his butler', who entertained 'the young gentlemen' with coffee and biscuits while Christie had a bath. When Christie was ready, he delivered a short dissertation on leverage and never questioned the pupils. This made Sir Alec and his fellow pupils 'suspect that it was ground which was too dangerous for the teacher'. Douglas-Home, Sir, A., *The Way the Wind Blows*, 1976, p. 60.

[52] Because of the war, the British Association did not hold an Annual Meeting in 1917.

[53] B.A.A.S., *Report*, 1917, p. 129. The Committee was required to 'consider and report upon the method and substance of science teaching in secondary schools, with particular reference to the essential place of science in general education'. It contained three members of the 1908 Committee (Gregory, Armstrong and Daniell) with T. P. Nunn, C. A. Buckmaster, F. W. Sanderson, A. Vassall and A. M. Worthington as 'newcomers'. Unlike the earlier Committee, it included girls' secondary schools in its investigation. It differed from the Thomson Committee in that a number of its members were practising schoolteachers.

[54] Ibid., pp. 130–1.

[55] B.A.A.S., *Report*, 1906, pp. 782–3.

[56] Board of Education, *Report for the Year 1909–10*, Cd. 5616, HMSO, 1911, pp. 76–7. The Board's conclusion should be assessed in the light of a claim such as the following, made in the Report: 'Every child is interested in soap bubbles but the majority ... are not introduced to ... the phenomena connected with surface tension.'

[57] See p. 53.

[58] *Natural Science in Education*, HMSO, 1918, para. 27.

[59] Ibid., para. 40.

[60] Walker, L., *Cusack's Object Lessons*, 1895. 'Professor' Cusack's series of educational books was very wide-ranging indeed. His 'copy' books for teaching handwriting were adopted by the London School Board and said to be very widely used.

[61] Ibid., Part II, pp. 169, 172.

[62] Board of Education, *Report for the Year 1900–1*, vol. III, Cd. 758, HMSO, pp. 270–80.

[63] Ibid., p. 268.

[64] See, for example, H.M.I. Currey's Report on Class Subjects and Object Lessons in Elementary Schools in the Eastern Division in 1898 in which there is a reference to 'Elementary Science (Object Lessons)'. *Report of the Committee of Council on Education*, 1898–9, Cd. 9401, HMSO, p. 177.

[65] For a vivid but depressing account of an object lesson see ibid., 1877–8, pp. 438–9.

[66] Board of Education, *Report for the Year 1910–11*, Cd. 6116, HMSO, p. 28.

[67] Armstrong, H. E , 'Training in Scientific Method as a Central Motive in Elementary Schools', in van Praagh, G. (ed.), *H. E. Armstrong and Science Education*, 1973, p. 104.

[68] B.A.A.S., *Report*, 1908, p. 503.

[69] McDonald, R. M., *The History of the Teaching of the Biological Sciences in English Grammar Schools, 1850–1952*, M.Ed. Thesis, Durham, 1953, p. 152.

[70] Birchenhough, C., op. cit., p. 309.

[71] Board of Education, *Report for the Year 1913–14*. Mr Ward's Report on Elementary Education in the North-West Division, Cd. 7934, HMSO, pp. 223–24.

[72] Allen, D. E., *The Naturalist in Britain; A Social History*, Allen Lane, 1976, p. 204. Allen refers to *Insect Lives as Told by Themselves*, published by the Religious Tract Society in 1898, to illustrate his point.

[73] *Natural Science in Education,* HMSO, 1918, para. 87.

[74] Board of Education, *Memorandum on the Teaching of Science to Boys in Certain Public Elementary Schools in London*, 14:5:1914, *P.R.O.*, Ed. 14/96.

[75] Ibid., p. 26 and p. 1. In contrast, Wordsworth Road Council Boys' School, Stoke Newington, had to make do with trestles in front of the desks in a classroom.

[76] Ibid., p. 16.

[77] Turner, D. M., *History of Science Teaching in England*, 1927, p. 150.

[78] Board of Education, *Report for the Year 1911–12*, Cd. 6707, HMSO, p. 42.

[79] For example, the 1902 Regulations required that not less than thirteen hours per week be devoted to teaching mathematics, physics, chemistry and drawing in a Higher Elementary School.

[80] They were investigated by the Board's Consultative Committee which reported in 1906, recommending that L.E.A.'s should be 'discouraged from trying ... to raise the schools into the secondary rank'. *Report of the Consultative Committee upon Higher Elementary Schools*, HMSO, 1906.

[81] After 1919, Higher Elementary Schools were no longer treated differently in the matter of Regulations or grants from ordinary public elementary schools. For sample Regulations governing Higher Elementary Schools, see Board of Education, *Code of Regulations for Public Elementary Schools (Exclusive of Wales and Monmouthshire)*, Cd. 3594, HMSO, 1907, Chap. VI, paras. 37–42A.

[82] Board of Education, *Report for the Year 1902–3*, Cd. 1763, HMSO, p. 46.

[83] Board of Education, *Report for the Year 1911–12*, p. 47.

[84] Ibid., p. 41.

[85] Ibid., pp. 42–3.

[86] Board of Education, *Report for the Year 1913–14*, Cd. 7934, HMSO, p. 61.

[87] Ibid., pp. 60–2.

[88] For an account of some antecedents, see Brock, W. H. (ed.), *H. E. Armstrong and the Teaching of Science, 1880–1930*, 1973, pp. 19–21.

[89] Ibid., p. 30. Brock points out that Armstrong had doubts whether the Examination Boards 'really understood the point of heurism'.

[90] Reprinted from Board of Education, *Special Reports on Educational Subjects*, vol. ii, HMSO, 1898, in van Praagh, G., op. cit., pp. 60–79.

[91] B.A.A.S., *Report*, 1903, p. 433. He was also Secretary of the earlier Committee which recommended the establishment of the 1903 Committee.

[92] B.A.A.S., *Report*, 1908, pp. 495–526. The schemes of work are given as Appendices A and B. Appendix C was a 'contracted scheme of work for small schools' and Appendix D a list of apparatus for an elementary school not provided with a special room. The prices are of some interest. Burettes 50 cc – 2s 2d; Pipettes 50 cc – 7d; Clock glasses (4-in. diameter) – 1¼d.

[93] Armstrong lived at Lewisham. His eldest son, Edward Frankland, 'passed through' St Dunstan's. Brock, W. H., op. cit., pp. 31–2.

[94] B.A.A.S. *Report*, 1908, p. 500. Kimmins was a former Headmaster of the Shoreditch Technical Day School who became Chief Inspector of Schools and Technical Adviser to the L.C.C. He was sympathetic to Armstrong's heuristic method.

[95] Ibid., p. 510.

[96] For an account of Smithells's contribution to science education, see Flintham, A. J., *The Contribution of Arthur Smithells, F.R.S. (1860–1939) to the Development of Science Education in England*, M.Ed. Thesis, Leeds, 1974, *passim*.

[97] B.A.A.S., *Report*, 1908, p. 515 and p. 516.

[98] See Chapter 7 and B.A.A.S., *Report*, 1903, p. 875.

[99] This was one result of the work of Armstrong, Heller and Stuart at St Dunstan's.

[100] In 1896, Armstrong held Saturday morning sessions for nearly 200 London Teachers. The course was repeated over the next three years. Eyre, J. V., *Henry Edward Armstrong*, 1958, p. 135.

[101] Board of Education, *Educational Pamphlet No. 17*, 1909, p. 20. The ensuing comments on public school science teaching are taken from this source.

[102] Ibid., p. 22.

[103] B.A.A.S., *Report*, 1908, pp. 531–2.

[104] B.A.A.S., *Report*, 1908, p. 531.

[105] Board of Education, *Report for the Year 1909–10*, HMSO, p. 79.

[106] B.A.A.S., *Report*, 1908, p. 495. Magnus was Chairman of the Committee. For an account of Magnus' life and work, see Foden, F., *Philip Magnus, Victorian Educational Pioneer*, 1970.

[107] Board of Education, *Report for the Year 1909–10*, HMSO, p. 79.

[108] B.A.A.S., *Report*, 1908, p. 532.

[109] Ibid., p. 533.

[110] *Natural Science in Education*, HMSO, 1918, para. 42.

[111] *Educational Times*, 44, 1891, p. 228. There were, however, other dimensions to Ramsay's assessment of Armstrong's ideas. Armstrong was more than reluctant to believe that Ramsay and Rayleigh had discovered argon in the atmosphere and used his Presidency of the Chemical Society to challenge their work in a manner which gave considerable offence. Since the discovery was based on attaching significance to small differences in density, it is interesting that Armstrong did not seize the opportunity to drive home the obvious message. That he did not do so subsequently may be explained by his sour personal relationships with Ramsay.

[112] Brock, W. H., op. cit., p. 48 and *Nature*, vol. 104, 1919, pp. 521–2.

[113] Armstrong, H. E., *Sanderson of Oundle*, in Brock, W. H., op. cit., p. 137.

[114] Eyre, J. V., op. cit. This biography is subtitled 'The Doyen of British Chemists and Pioneer of Technical Education' and dedicated to Armstrong 'my beloved Mentor and Friend' and to his youngest daughter. The 'refutation' is also found in Browne, C. E., *Henry Edward Armstrong*, 1954, and quoted in van Praagh, G., op. cit., p. 5, who adds (p. 9) that the heuristic method is 'still mis-stated and then criticised'. It is clearly still a touchy point for those infected with the '*virus heuristicum Armstrongii*'. In his 'authoritative' statement published by the Board of Education, Armstrong wrote, 'young scholars cannot be expected to find out everything themselves'. Van Praagh, G., op. cit., p. 69.

[115] *Nature*, vol. 69, 1903, p. 289.

[116] Armstrong, H. E., *The Teaching of Scientific Method and Other Papers on Education*, 1903. A second edition was published in 1910 and reprinted in 1925 with a new Preface in which Armstrong reviewed the developments which had taken place a quarter of a century after 'the winter of our discontent'.

[117] Brock, W. H., op. cit., p. 51.

[118] Ibid., p. 53.

[119] Eyre, J. V., op. cit., p. 61.

[120] *Journal of Education*, 1903, p. 666. It was added 'that like many reformers', Armstrong weakened his case by exaggeration.

[121] *Nature*, 28 January 1904, p. 290. In this connection, some earlier acrimonious correspondence between Smithells and Armstrong is of interest. See *Nature*, 1893, pp. 150, 172, 198.

[122] *J. Soc.Chem.Ind.*, 56, 1937, p. 669.

[123] Brock, W. H., op. cit., p. 52.

[124] Fowles, G., *Lecture Experiments in Chemistry*, 1948, 3rd edn., p. 505.

[125] Hodson, F., *Broad Lines in Science Teaching*, 1909, p. 83. Some of Hodson's own 'projects' are remarkable by any standards. Pupils at his school had arranged wireless signalling over half a mile, separated cerium, lanthanum and didymium in cerite and studied the absorption spectrum of the last named 'element', etc. See ibid., p. 91.

[126] Brock, W. H., op. cit., p. 51. The Thomson Committee noted in 1918 that much of the science taught in the training colleges ought to have been done in the secondary schools or in a pupil-teacher centre. (*Natural Science in Education*, 1918, para. 89.)

[127] Armstrong, H. E., *Juvenile Research* (an address to a Conference of Science Teachers), *London Technical Education Gazette*, March 1900, reproduced in van Praagh, G., op. cit., p. 80.

[128] *Report on the Teaching of Science in London Elementary Schools*, 1909, *P.R.O.*, Ed.14/95, dated 21/1/08 and signed E. D. F. Bloom.

[129] For Smithells's views, B.A.A.S., *Report*, 1906, pp. 782–3.

[130] Armstrong, H. E., Address to Section L of the B.A.A.S., 1902, reproduced in van Praagh, G., op. cit., p. 120. See also 'The Heuristic Method' in ibid., p. 70. Beckmesser is a character in Wagner's *Die Meistersinger* and Armstrong is suggesting that the training college staff were pedants capable only of following fixed rules.

[131] Armstrong, H. E., 'An Appeal to Headmasters', reproduced in van Praagh, G., op. cit., p. 98.

[132] A reviewer in *Nature*, 23 September 1909, p. 361, noted 'the growing importance attached to the philosophy of science'. George Sarton can be regarded as having played a major role in institutionalising the history and philosophy of science as an academic study and *Isis* was founded in 1912. In the United Kingdom, Whitehead and Singer persuaded the University of London to introduce a degree course in the history and philosophy of science in 1924.

[133] It can be traced back perhaps to Aristotle. Selleck, R. J. W., op. cit., attributes the 'modern' form to Christian Wolff whose *Rational Psychology* appeared in 1734. See also Murphy, G., *Historical Introduction to Modern Psychology*, New York, 1950.

[134] One of the most important phrenologists who influenced education was George Combe (1788–1859). See Chapter 4.

[135] This was the warning of Fitch in 1900. Fitch, J., *Educational Aims and Methods*, 1900, pp. 102–3.

[136] Selleck, R. J. W., op. cit., p. 75.

[137] Ibid., p. 49. The failure of English elementary school teachers to pay due regard to theory and principles was commented upon by many educationists. See, for example, Hayward, F. H., *The Reform of Biblical and Moral Education ...*, 1902, p. 29.

[138] Armstrong, H. E., *The Teaching of Scientific Method and Other Papers on Education*, 1925, p. 196.

[139] B.A.A.S., Report of the Committee appointed ... to consider the best means for promoting Scientific Education in Schools, *Report*, 1867, p. xli.

[140] Combe's distinction was between *positive* instruction and *instrumental* instruction. For an account of Combe's educational ideas see Jolly, W., *Education: its Principles and Practice as Developed by George Combe*, 1879. For a Biography, see Gibbon, C., *The Life of George Combe*, 2 vols., 1878.

[141] They included Margaret McMillan, Maria Montessori, John Dewey and Homer Lane and, as may be imagined, embraced a wide range of opinion. See Selleck, R. J. W., op. cit., p. 212.

[142] *Report of the Conference of New Ideals in Education*, August 1915, quoted in Selleck,

R. J. W., op. cit. The influence of the naturalists is discernible in the Board of Education *Suggestions* issued in 1925, e.g. 'The leading principle which determines the methods of education suitable to early childhood is the recognition of the spontaneous activities of the children.' (*Suggestions*, p. 22.)

[143] It is here that the differences between the individual members of the naturalist school showed most clearly. For Margaret McMillan 'free expression' followed drill, in the nursery school. Montessori denied that the teacher was a passive force but for Mac-Munn, the teacher was the servant not the master of the child. Rusk, writing as late as 1928, claimed that 'the outstanding problem in educational method ... (was) the extent to which, if at all, the teacher should intervene in the educative process'. Rusk, R. R., *The Philosophical Bases of Education*, 1928, pp. 18–19.

[144] The five steps, derived by dividing the first of Herbart's original four steps into two, were known by a variety of names. Perhaps inevitably, ends and means became confused and many lessons based on the Herbartian steps were absurdly rigid and contrived. M. Fennell, *Notes of Lessons on the Herbartian Method*, 1902, offered eighty lessons, each complete in itself and lasting thirty to forty-five minutes and illustrates the point particularly well.

[145] Potter, F. F., *Educational Journey*, 1949, p. 26.

[146] Selleck, R. J. W., op. cit., p. 243.

[147] *Journal of Education*, vol. XXXIII, January 1911, p. 39.

[148] Faculties were 'merely logical designations for the preliminary classification of phenomena'. Herbart, J. F., *A Textbook in Psychology*, 1897, pp. 186–7.

[149] Adams, J., *The Herbartian Psychology Applied to Education*, 1897, pp. 107–34.

[150] Adamson, J. W., *The Practice of Instruction*, 1907, p. 87.

[151] Laurie, A. P. (ed.), *The Teachers Encyclopaedia*, vol. 7, 1911–12, p. 189.

[152] 'Instruction will form the circle of thought and education the character. The last is nothing without the first.' Herbart, J. F., *The Science of Education*, 1904, p. 93.

[153] Seeley, J. R., *Ethics and Religion*, Society of Ethical Propagandists, 1900, p. 12.

[154] Selleck, R. J. W., op. cit., p. 301.

[155] They met with considerable success. The 1906 Elementary School Regulations provided that 'moral instruction should form an important part of every Elementary School curriculum'.

[156] Herbart had distinguished content which supplements 'experience' (natural science) from that which augmented 'social intercourse' (historical-humanities) and had insisted that each be given due place in a balanced curriculum. Felkin, H. M. and E., *An Introduction to Herbart's Science and Practice of Education*, 1901, pp. 121–2.

[157] Catherine I. Dodd, in her *Introduction to The Herbartian Principles of Teaching*, 1906, pp. 35–6, claimed that history was pre-eminent among the school studies. 'History ... is placed first in the scheme of instruction because it is ... of primary importance in moulding the character and in stimulating interest.' This attitude was reinforced by nationalist/imperialist writers who claimed that 'well-taught' history provided the basis of patriotism.

[158] Hayward, F. H., *The Secret of Herbart*, 1904, p. 76.

[159] Magnus, P., *Educational Aims and Efforts, 1890–1910*, 1910, p. 176.

[160] Brock, W. H., op. cit., p. 39.

[161] Thorndike, E. L., Woodworth, R. S., 'The Influence of Improvement in one mental function upon the efficiency of other functions', *Psychol. Rev.*, 8, 1901, pp. 247–61, 384–95 and 553–64.

[162] Hayward, F. H., *Day and Evening Schools*, 1910, pp. 211–12. See also Nuth, M. E., Hayward, F. H., *Child Study*, vol. IV, 2, 1911, p. 65.

[163] Board of Education, *Educational Pamphlet No. 17*, 1909, p. 19.

[164] See *Nature*, 18 January 1912, p. 394.

[165] Armstrong, H. E., *Our Need to Honour Huxley's Will*, 1933, reproduced in Brock, W. H., op. cit., p. 61. R. C. Trench was, from 1863, Archbishop of Dublin and he founded the scheme for the Oxford English Dictionary in 1867. *On the Study of Words* was published in 1851. Armstrong claimed that Trench's book made him unable to appreciate Huxley's 'didactic teaching, perfect though this was'.

[166] Armstrong, H. E., *Journal of the Central Institution Old Students' Association*, 35, 1938, quoted in Brock, W. H., op. cit., p. 11.

[167] Armstrong, H. E., How Science must be Studied to be Useful, *The Technical World*, 1896, in van Praagh, G., op. cit., pp. 43–4. Other 'choices' were Ruskin's *Sesame and Lilies* and Carlyle, 'studied in moderation'. The only technical work was Black's tract on *Magnesia Alba*.

[168] Huxley, T. H., 'On the Educational Value of the Natural History Sciences', *Science and Education*, 1905 edn., p. 45.

[169] Armstrong, H. E., *Our Need to Honour Huxley's Will*, 1933, in Brock, W. H., op. cit., p. 55.

[170] Westaway, F. W., *Scientific Method: its Philosophy and its Practice*, 1912, p. 50.

[171] He denounced it with the telling phrase, 'Catholicism minus Christianity' in a lay sermon in Edinburgh in 1868. See Eisen, S., 'Huxley and the Positivists', *Victorian Studies*, vol. VII, no. 4, June 1964, p. 341.

[172] Pearson, K., *The Grammar of Science*, 1892, pp. 6–7, 15. The irony of science as organised common sense was that such common sense needed several lengthy books to explain it.

[173] Kidd, B., *Social Evolution*, 1894, p. 26.

[174] For an account of 'scientific history' and an interpretation of Bury's claim, see Marwick, A., *The Nature of History*, 1970, Chapter 4, *passim* and p. 52.

[175] British Science Guild, *Report of the Inaugural Meeting*, 1905. Further insights into the conception of scientific method discussed in these paragraphs are gained from the items under the heading 'Musings in Unscientific Method' which appeared in the Guild's *Journal* after 1915.

[176] Soddy, F., *Nature*, vol. 98, 16 September 1916, p. 91.

[177] Armstrong, H. E., *The Heuristic Method ... etc.* Board of Education, *Special Reports on Educational Subjects*, vol. ii, 1898, reproduced in van Praagh, G., op. cit., p. 68.

[178] Armstrong, H. E., *Sanderson of Oundle, The Fundamental Problems of School Policy and the Cult of the Turned-up Trouser Hem*, reproduced in Brock, W. H., op. cit., p. 144.

[179] Armstrong, H. E., *The Heuristic Method ... etc.*, reproduced in van Praagh, G., op. cit., pp. 78–9. Armstrong was scathing in his comments about the cheaper balances devised, for example, by A. M. Worthington of Clifton and H. M. I. Rooper. Armstrong recommended a balance costing about £3 in 1891 compared with those improvised by Worthington and Rooper for 4s and 2d respectively. None the less, Worthington was one of the first to show that it was possible to select experiments and to employ simple inexpensive apparatus capable of yielding quantitative results of accuracy sufficient to allow sound deductions to be drawn. Board of Education, *Educational Pamphlet No. 17*, 1909, p. 6.

[180] Armstrong, H. E., *Sanderson of Oundle*, in Brock, W. H., op. cit., p. 140.

[181] B.A.A.S., *Report*, 1917, p. 134.

[182] Armstrong, H. E., *Sanderson of Oundle*, in Brock, W. H., op. cit., p. 145.

[183] Armstrong, H. E., Address to Section L, B.A.A.S., 1902, reproduced in van Praagh, G., op. cit., p. 110.

[184] *Nature*, vol. 74, 31 May 1906, pp. 102–3 and 30 August 1906, p. 443.

[185] Ibid., vol. 74, 24 May 1906, p. 79.

[186] Berry, A. J., *J.Soc.Chem.Ind.*, 55, 20 November 1936, pp. 944–5.

[187] Armstrong, H. E., *J.Soc.Chem.Ind.*, 55, 13 November 1936, pp. 916–17. According to Armstrong, physical chemists 'never' used their eyes and were 'most lamentably lacking in chemical culture'.

[188] The Nuffield Science Teaching Project stressed the teaching of science 'as an inquiry' and encouraged pupils 'to think about scientific things in the way that practising scientists do', van Praagh, G., op. cit., p. 13 and Nuffield Foundation Science Teaching Project, *Progress Report*, 1964, p. 5. Armstrong's heurism also had important ideological features. Scientific knowledge was seen as neutral, objective and value free so that science could claim a special, even unique place among human activities. Scientific method was presented as the sword of truth with which to smite superstition and dogma. Ravetz regards the acceptance of this ideology by historians of science as 'a tragedy'. See his article in Teich, M., Young, R., *Changing Perspectives in the History of Science*, 1973, pp. 204–22.

[189] Ravetz, J. R., *Scientific Knowledge and its Social Problems*, 1971, p. 110.

[190] Shaw, N., *The Lack of Science in Modern Education*, 1916, p. 8.

[191] Smithells, A., *The Ways of Chemistry*. Supplement to *The Listener*, 26 February 1930, p. ii. It was necessary to point out that 'the potency of different gases bore no proportion to the unpleasantness or violence of their smells' and that 'liquids evaporate more in sunlight than in the dull of night'. The matter is discussed in some detail in Flintham, A. J., op. cit., p. 157. The Navy and the Medical Corps deserve to be exempted from most of the criticism levelled at the Army.

[192] League for the Promotion of Science in Education, *Report 1916–19*, 1919, p. 21 and 'The Neglect of Science', *The Times*, 2 February 1916, p. 10.

[193] League for the Promotion of Science in Education, op. cit., p. 21. Report of speech by Sir Ray Lankester. The continuing export of cotton from which nitro-cellulose could be made was another controversial issue. See also British Science Guild, *Ninth Annual Report*, 1915, for further examples.

[194] These included not only the institutions concerned with chemistry and the biological sciences, but also those with professional responsibilities in the fields of medicine, engineering, horticulture, architecture, metallurgy and geography.

[195] League for the Promotion of Science in Education, op. cit., p. 61.

[196] *P.R.O., Ed.* 24/1174, 7 June 1916.

[197] For detailed accounts of the establishment of the Thomson Committee, see Jenkins, E. W., 'The Thomson Committee and the Board of Education, 1916–22', *B.J.Ed.St.*, vol. XXI, no. 1, February 1973, pp. 76–87 and 'The Board of Education and the Reconstruction Committee', *J.Ed.Admin. and History*, vol. V, no. i, 1973. For further comment on the work of the Committee, see Feheney, J. M., *The Thomson Report (1918): A Critical Evaluation*, M.Ed. Thesis, King's College, London 1976.

[198] 5 Hansard 84, 18 July 1916, col. 906.

[199] See *Nature*, 6 April 1916, p. 120. The editorial is in the March 1916 issue of *Blackwood's Magazine*, pp. 407–18.

[200] Quoted in *Nature*, 20 July 1916, p. 418.

[201] Livingstone, R. W., *A Defence of Classical Education*, 1916, pp. 30–1.

[202] *Nature*, 1 March 1917, p. 1. Wells reviewed the book for *Nature*.

[203] Ibid., 10 May 1917, p. 205.

[204] For details of the Resolutions, see Armytage, W. H., *Sir Richard Gregory*, 1957, pp. 71–4.

[205] *Nature*, 11 May 1916, pp. 240–1. It is a quotation from J. S. Mill.

[206] *Nature*, vol. 97, 29 June 1916, pp. 361–2.

[207] Ibid., vol. 98, September 1916, p. 69. In contrast, note Schuster's view that a 'fatal distinction' was emerging between 'men of theory' and 'men of practice'. B.A.A.S., *Report*, 1915, pp. 3–23, and *Nature*, vol. 96, 9 September 1915, p. 37.

[208] *Natural Science in Education*, HMSO, 1918, para. 4.

[209] Sanderson, F. W., *Science in a Public School*, B.A.A.S. *Report*, 1917, pp. 155, 157. See also Wells, H. G., *Sanderson of Oundle*, 1923, p. 257. According to Armstrong, Sanderson was 'nothing short of inconsequent in his ravings – they were nothing less – on science'. See Armstrong, H. E., *Sanderson of Oundle*, 1924, reproduced in Brock, W. H., op. cit., p. 139.

[210] Thomas, E., 'The Scope of Nature Study', in Hodson, F., op. cit., pp. 21–2. Thomas (1878–1917) was a poet and essayist who was killed at Arras.

[211] Flintham, A. J., op. cit., pp. 159 and 160, quoted from Smithells, A., School and University Science, *S.S.R.*, vol. 5, 1924, p. 131 and *Nature*, vol. 98, 1917, p. 400. The account in *Nature* is of an address by Smithells to the A.P.S.S.M.

[212] The phrase is Smithells. See *S.S.R.*, vol. 5, 1924, p. 131.

[213] Armytage, W. H., op. cit., pp. 68–9. Much of Gregory's influence was due to his leading articles in *Nature*. Armytage describes these as situation reports from the battlefront 'where science was struggling to obtain full recognition in both state and school'. However, see *Nature*, vol. 224, 1 November 1969, p. 463.

[214] Gregory, R. A., *Discovery or the Spirit and Service of Science*, 1916, p. vi.

[215] Ibid., p. 17.

[216] From Gregory's address to the Conference of Delegates of Corresponding Societies at the Edinburgh Meeting of the B.A.A.S. in 1921 and quoted in Armytage, W. H., op. cit., p. 81. For a review of the Thomson Report, see *Nature*, 6 June 1918, pp. 265–6.

[217] Flintham, A. J., op. cit., discusses some of the private correspondence between Turner and Smithells on this issue. Turner was Professor of Astronomy at Oxford and President of the A.P.S.S.M. in 1916. For Smithells' views, see *The School Guardian*, 18 November 1916, pp. 3–4, and 16 December 1916, pp. 27–8.

[218] B.A.A.S. *Report*, 1917, pp. 149–54. This scheme of work was prepared by Archer Vassall of Harrow. Another scheme, of practical food studies, was prepared by Armstrong. His introduction showed that he had not yielded one inch on the question of transfer of training or, for that matter, in his attitude to women. 'If girls were made scientific thinkers in relation to home matters ... they would stand on an intellectual plane far higher than they now occupy.' The tone of Armstrong's contribution differs noticeably from that of the others.

[219] B.A.A.S., *Report*, 1917, p. 135.

[220] Ibid., pp. 135–6.

[221] Ibid., p. 136.

[222] T. P. Nunn, 1870–1944. After fourteen years teaching in secondary schools, Nunn became Vice-Principal of the London Day Training College in 1905. From 1922 to 1936, he was Director of the London Institute of Education. His most famous work, *Education: Its Data and First Principles*, was first published in 1920. He wrote extensively about the teaching of mathematics and science and was a philosopher of some distinction. Between 1917 and 1924 he held, at various times, the Presidency of the Mathematical Association, of Section L of the British Association and of the Education Section of the British Psychological Society.

[223] Nunn's ideas were accepted by the Spens Committee in its discussion of the principles of the curriculum. Although the Science Masters Association was critical of the Spens

Report, it did not challenge Nunn's views. Board of Education, *Report of the Consultative Committee on Secondary Education*, HMSO, 1938, p. 163. See also Nunn, T. P., op. cit., p. 271, and Whitehead, A. N., The Rhythm of Education, 1922.

[224] B.A.A.S., *Report*, 1917, p. 140.

[225] Ibid., p. 137.

[226] Armstrong, H. E., *Sanderson of Oundle*, 1924, in Brock, W. H., op. cit., p. 145. Armstrong appears to have regarded 'science-for-all' as written in deliberate opposition to heurism. This was denied, much later, by Bryant. *S.S.R.*, vol. 32, no. 117, 1951 pp. 143–4.

[227] The phrase is Ruskin's and was quoted by Michael Sadler in his introduction to Hodson, F., op. cit., 1909, p. xl.

3
The General Science Movement

'What do we hope to accomplish by teaching more science?' For Sir William Tilden, writing in the first issue of *The School Science Review* in 1919, the answer was 'furnishing the mind and giving some knowledge of the world in which we live ... without obtruding the notions of discipline and training in method'.[1] Tilden's reply suggests that he would have sympathised both with Smithells's attempts to bring science 'into the homes of the people'[2] and with Gregory's assertion that school science must be 'science for all and not for embryonic engineers, chemists ... or biologists'.[3] The views of these three men, expressed within a few years of the ending of the First World War, reflected a wider measure of agreement that school science courses should be broadened and humanised and this was seen as 'the common aim'[4] by the science masters at their annual meeting in 1920.

However, there was much 'less confidence, less sureness of touch' and 'a good deal of disagreement' among the science masters about how their common aim might be realised. For some, school science could be infused with breadth and humanity by the introduction of ancillary courses in the methods and philosophy of science, based principally upon the ideas of Whitehead and Russell.[5] For others, notably E. J. Holmyard, science could be humanised by adopting the historical method of teaching. The absence of a significant number of teachers with an adequate training in the history and philosophy of science was a major obstacle to the widespread adoption of either of these solutions. In addition, the historical method too easily degenerated into the teaching of a mere smattering of historical facts, a procedure which was justly condemned.[6]

The most detailed prescription for a broad science course in which 'the humanising method' was 'the vital point' was undoubtedly general science. Although elements of this curriculum innovation may be detected in Huxley's physiography and in developments in other countries,[7] particularly the United States, the more immediate origins of general science lay in two pamphlets published by the A.P.S.S.M. in 1916: *The Aims of Science Teaching in General Education* and *Science for All*. These pamphlets, produced as part of the 'Neglect of Science' campaign, were the work of an A.P.S.S.M. subcommittee, consisting of W. D. Eggar, F. M. Oldham and A. Vassall. Vassall, a former pupil of Oswald Latter at Charterhouse, was also responsible for the scheme of work included in the Report of Gregory's British Association Committee in 1917 and entitled *Science for All in a Public School*.[8]

The qualification attached to 'all' is significant. Only after 1919, when the A.P.S.S.M. opened its ranks to graduate science masters in secondary schools and became the Science Masters' Association, did the phrase 'science for all' acquire a somewhat broader meaning.[9] Even after this date, severe constraints on membership continued to apply. Eligibility for membership of the S.M.A. was confined to male graduates in secondary schools until 1946 when it was extended to secondary school science masters in general and to male student science teachers in training. Only in 1965, following amalgamation with the Association of (Women) Science Teachers in 1961, can the descendant of the A.P.S.S.M. claim to have produced a policy statement on science education which was formally concerned with the teaching of science to *all* pupils.[10] The Association of Women Science Teachers was formed in 1912 by some members of the Association of Assistant Mistresses but, according to Mikhail,[11] it had little in common with the A.P.S.S.M. until 1919.

The second volume of *The School Science Review*, the journal of the newly formed S.M.A., contained a reprint of the original 'science for all' proposals which had been approved, without dissent, at the annual meeting of the A.P.S.S.M. in 1917. Science for all in a boys' public school thus became science for all in boys' secondary schools. The proposals, summarised in Figure 3.1, did not constitute a 'strict syllabus' but it was suggested that adequate treatment of the work required 'not less than five hours in school and one hour's preparation per week for six terms'.[12] Practical work throughout the course was regarded as essential, 'as much as possible being done by the boys', although it was recognised that some topics were more appropriately taught by other methods, e.g. by 'illustrated lectures'. The scheme of work was intended for the 'middle forms' of secondary schools. General Science was thus to be a sequel to introductory courses and a prelude to post-certificate specialisation.

> Practical measurements (in mathematical classes), nature study and 'object' courses such as the experimental investigation of chalk or of a candle, provide suitable employment in the lower forms.[13]

General Science was given a more precise formulation by the Oxford and Cambridge Examination Board in 1921 when the new subject was added to those already included in the list of Group III subjects for the School Certificate Examination.[14] The fact that the Oxford and Cambridge Joint Board was the first of the Examination Boards to recognise General Science in this way reflects the close connection between the Joint Board and the public schools, the science staff of which still dominated the policies and attitudes[15] of the S.M.A. Even so, it appears that considerable opposition had to be overcome before General Science was granted the status of a Group III subject, even by the Oxford and Cambridge Board.[16]

The S.M.A. expressed approval of the Board's General Science syllabus, on the grounds that it would 'enable papers to be set which would go far to meet [the Association's] wishes'.[17] Candidates were required to sit two papers, each of two hours' duration, which included questions on physics, chemistry, biology, astronomy, geology and meteorology. Questions of a 'biographical nature' could also be set. In 1925, the Oxford and Cambridge Board examined 500 candidates in General Science, drawn from twenty of the 120 schools which normally entered boys for the Board's Certificate examinations.[18]

Figure 3.1   Summary* of 'Science for all' – S.M.A., 1920

The universe. Solar System. Earth. Igneous and Sedimentary rocks.
Volcanoes. Glaciers. Fossils. Coal.

Atmosphere. Life of a plant. Fermentation. Pasteur. Animal Kingdom.
Balance of Nature. Darwin. Simple agriculture. Simple physiology and hygiene.

Natural resources of the Empire.

Mass. Weight. Density. Falling bodies (Galileo and Aristotle). Force and
work. Liquid and gaseous pressure. Diffusion. Capillarity and surface tension.
Applications of the above.

Study of atmosphere. Combustion. Respiration. Water. Limestone, sandstone,
clay. Conservation of mass. Laws of combination introducing chemical theory.
Flame. Hydrocarbons. Coal-gas. Nitrogen, sulphur, chlorine and their simple
compounds. Acids, bases and salts. Properties and extraction of metals. Alloys.
Iron and steel. Petroleum. Coal-tar products. Oils, fats, soap, glycerine. Sugar.

Sources, effects and transference of heat. Thermometers. Investigation of heat
quantity. Heat and temperature; thermometric scales. Calorimetry. Change of
state; vapour pressure. Heat values of fuels. Heat and work. Horse-power.
Mechanical equivalent. Engines.

Rectilinear propagation of light. Photometry. Reflection and refraction. Mirrors
and lenses. The eye. Telescopes and microscopes. Dispersion.

Wave motion. The ear. Pitch, loudness, quality. The gramophone.

Magnets. Lines of force. Terrestrial magnetism. Cells. Electromagnets.
Telegraphs. Conductors and insulators. Electroscope. Potential. E.M.F. Effects
of current. Resistance. Ohm's Law. Current induction. Microphone and
telephone. Dynamo and motor. Electrical energy. Lamps. Heat and work.
Units.

It was several years before the other Examination Boards followed the
example of the Oxford and Cambridge Joint Board and the growth of General
Science as an examination subject was slow. For the S.M.A., the majority of the
Examination Boards simply failed to respond to the demands of the school
science teaching profession.[19]

> A progressive examining body takes the opinion of those immediately concerned
> with science teaching and ventures to introduce a paper. . . . The stationary examining
> body undertakes to set a paper 'if and when there is a sufficient number of candidates
> wishing to take it'.

However, such a view begs the question of how the demands of the science
teachers were to be identified and articulated. It is doubtful whether the
public school-orientated S.M.A. could have claimed legitimately to represent
the views of secondary school science teachers in general and the public school
origins of 'science for all' were only too evident.[20] The examining bodies could

* Each of the sections was illustrated by a number of examples, but 'the details' were 'not
prescribed nor even recommended'.

also have pointed out that opinion about the merits of General Science was divided, not least among the membership of the S.M.A. itself and that, far from there being a widespread demand by the schools for the introduction of General Science, the post-war changes in secondary school science curricula seemed to be in the direction of increased, rather than of reduced, specialisation. Of thirty-nine boys' secondary schools investigated by the Board of Education just before 1925, only two had submitted any candidates for the examination in General Science set by the Oxford and Cambridge Joint Board.[21] More significantly, the investigation showed that the first two years of work in the grammar schools was still largely confined to nature study, although there were a few schools in which elementary physical science was taught to eleven- to twelve-year-old pupils. In only three of the thirty-nine schools had any attempt been made to broaden the curriculum for twelve- to sixteen-year-old pupils by introducing any science subject other than chemistry or physics, and, in general, physics was taught up to the level of the School Certificate only 'in patches'.[22]

> Some kindergarten Mechanics illustrated by toy models and rather trivial experiments is very commonly taken at the age of 13. Heat is taught in all schools, but light is occasionally neglected. Sound is not, as a rule, taken seriously. Some schools take practically only heat, light and sound at the Certificate stage and relegate Electricity and Magnetism to post-Certificate work.

Such specialisation was encouraged by the requirements of the University of London Matriculation Examination in which a paper in heat, light and sound was an alternative to examination in electricity and magnetism and a separate syllabus and examination were offered in mechanics. In addition, the rubric of the composite papers permitted candidates to avoid answering questions on one of the branches of physics which the examinations were designed to test. It was thus possible for candidates to satisfy the examiners in, for example, magnetism and electricity, without displaying any knowledge of one of these two aspects of the discipline.[23] The influence of the London Matriculation Examination on secondary school science teaching between the wars was considerable, not only because the Examination was prestigious in its own right, but also because the University of London refused to recognise the Matriculation Certificates issued by other Matriculating Authorities.[24]

The fragmentary nature of secondary school science courses was confirmed by a committee which reported to the British Association at its annual meeting in Glasgow in 1928.

> There are syllabuses of mechanics and hydrostatics, light and heat, electricity and magnetism, chemistry, botany, natural history and many other separate divisions of science.[25]

The Committee, chaired yet again by Richard Gregory, reaffirmed the need to 'widen the scope of science teaching' and to 'bring it into closer contact with living things as well as with the many natural phenomena of our changeful earth and man's relationship to them'.[26] However, the Committee was severely critical of the General Science Examinations set by the Oxford and Cambridge

Board. The interpretation of the General Science syllabus by the examiners 'often showed a misconception of what (the) science of everyday life should signify', many of the questions were judged to be 'more appropriate to physics or chemistry papers' and it was felt that too much emphasis had been placed on the recall of facts rather than of principles.[27] The censure was extended to the Joint Board's syllabus in General Science which was regarded as too comprehensive to allow anything other than a superficial treatment. It is not surprising, therefore, that the schemes of work produced in 1917 were appended to the 1928 Report on the grounds that they still contained 'so much of value and so clearly indicated the spirit' which, by implication, had failed to animate secondary school science teaching.[28]

Table 3.1

a   Number and distribution of State Scholarships in Science subjects, 1926 and 1927

	1926	1927
Physics	11	7
Chemistry	19	9
Biology	5	7
Engineering	4	3
Other Science	8	8
Total Science	47	34
Total Scholarships Taken up	225	172

b   Subjects followed by graduate trainee teachers, 1926

	Maths	Chemistry	Physics	General Science	Botany
Bristol	3	4	2	–	–
Manchester	5	13	8	3	1
London Day T.C.	10	12	8	–	8
Sheffield	2	5	3	–	–
Cardiff	–	4	3	–	2
North Wales	3	7	4	–	–
Swansea	–	–	–	–	2
Reading	1	2	1	–	3
Cambridge (women)	5	–	–	5	–

Some of the obstacles to broadening school science curricula were only too obvious to Gregory's Committee. In 1926, of 100 teachers offering to teach science, thirty-eight offered chemistry, twenty-three physics, twelve botany, fifteen science (unspecified) and only twelve 'natural science'.[29] The entrenched position of physics and chemistry is confirmed by the pattern of results in the State Scholarship examinations and by the subjects followed[30] by trainee graduate science teachers. (See Table 3.1.) Secondary school headmasters, in general, preferred to appoint science teachers with specialist Honours degrees and, because of the surplus of qualified applicants, particularly chemists,[31] they were usually able to do so. Of sixteen advertisements for teachers of science subjects which appeared in *The Times Educational Supplement* between 22 October and 12 November 1927, eight specified science graduates with 'Honours' or 'high' Honours.[32] Many of the applicants for these posts would have been Honours graduates of the University of London[33] and, as such, would have studied one science subject in depth and another to a subsidiary level in reading for their degrees. The reluctance of such teachers to teach subjects which had not formed part of their degree courses is not difficult to understand.[34]

Specialisation was also encouraged by the grants paid by the Board of Education for approved courses of advanced study. While these grants had undoubtedly raised the general standard of sixth-form work in science, they had also, unintentionally, led to an increased degree of specialisation earlier in the secondary school. In the physical sciences, the School Certificate courses came to be regarded less as a contribution to a general secondary education and more as the foundation of advanced and more specialised studies.

Viewed in the broader context, the inter-war years as a whole were not an auspicious period in which to promote science curriculum change. A grudging growth in the number of grant-aided secondary schools from 1,081 in 1919 to 1,354 in 1930 was followed by a decade of virtual stagnation.[35] The extent to which the 'bright hopes'[36] engendered by the Fisher Act were dashed by a succession of economic crises is only too clear from the data[37] in Table 3.2. School science teaching could not hope to be immune from the persistent cry for, and practice of, economy. New apparatus and equipment were difficult to obtain and cuts in the school building programmes meant that, in many secondary schools, laboratory accommodation was severely limited and classes became seriously overcrowded. In the elementary schools, adequate, purpose-built laboratory accommodation was the exception rather than the rule and this often remained the case when these schools were reorganised in accordance with the recommendations of the Hadow Committee in its Report, published in 1926.

By 1930, six of the eight Boards conducting School Certificate examinations offered a syllabus and examination in General Science. In addition, all the Examination Boards allowed schools to submit for approval their own syllabuses as alternatives to those published in the Regulations. Little advantage was taken of this provision. Of 379 schools examined by the London Board in 1931, only five offered their own syllabuses in science subjects.[38] The exclusion of General Science syllabuses from the Regulations of the Durham Board and of the Northern Universities' Joint Board was probably more significant than appears, at first glance, to be the case. In 1930, the N.U.J.M.B. was the largest Examination Board conducting School Certificate Examinations, examining 28 per cent (17,664) of all the candidates presented for examination in that year. In contrast, the Durham Board examined 1.9 per cent (1,178) of the entry, drawn from only forty-two schools.[39]

Table 3.2 Pupils and Educational Expenditure, 1920–38

Years	Secondary Schools		Elementary Schools	Approved Capital Expenditure Elementary and Secondary Education £	Education Expenditure as % of national expenditure (d)
	No. on list (a)	No. of pupils (b)	No. of pupils on register (average) (c)		
1920–21	1205	336,836	5,933,458	2,274,521	4.52
1921–22	1249	354,956	5,878,792	1,546,608	6.06
1922–23	1264	354,165	5,759,363	1,093,816	10.84
1923–24	1270	349,141	5,670,052	1,762,016	6.00
1924–25	1284	352,605	5,597,816	4,166,363	6.10
1925–26	1301	360,503	5,631,560	5,493,144	5.80
1926–27	1319	371,493	5,635,412	5,295,678	6.25
1927–28	1329	377,540	5,611,063	5,773,367	6.35
1928–29	1341	386,993	5,574,254	6,153,848	6.04
1929–30	1354	394,105	5,546,002	7,801,651	6.03
1930–31	1367	411,309	5,538,772	11,614,238	6.25
1931–32	1379	432,061	5,576,419	7,221,275	6.51
1932–33	1378	441,883	5,635,216	3,817,225	6.00
1933–34	1381	448,421	5,649,354	3,254,630	6.56
1934–35	1380	456,783	5,468,960	6,604,003	6.62
1935–36	1389	463,906	5,321,065	8,556,655	6.63
1936–37	1393	466,245	5,185,298	10,073,280	6.48
1937–38	1398	470,003	5,087,485	12,955,205	–

NOTES

(a) To 1928 the data refer to a year ending 31 July. From this year onwards they refer to 31 March.

(b) These and the figures in column (a) refer to England and Wales.

(c) Data refer to a year ending 31 March. Average attendance was of course lower than the average number on the register.

(d) The data refer to the U.K., to year ending 31 March and to *all* education expenditure as a percentage of national expenditure.

Table 3.3   Schools Taking Various Subjects in Certificate Examinations and Periods per week for that Subject and Hours Practical Per Week (Average): 1932

	O. & C.	Oxf.	Camb.	Lond.	N.U.J.B.	C.W.B.	Brist.	Dur.
No. of Schools	82	125	111	114	142	56	6	14
% Schools Taking Physics	68.3	73.0	62.0	91.0	91.0	77.0	83.0	78.0
Total Periods	4.1	4.1	4.3	4.4	3.2	5.1	4.2	3.5
Practical Hours	1.7	1.7	1.7	1.8	1.6	1.9	1.9	1.6
% Schools Taking Chemistry	67.1	75.0	92.0	91.0	94.0	93.0	100.0	72.0
Total Periods	4.1	4.2	4.5	4.3	3.9	4.9	4.3	3.7
Practical Hours	1.6	1.8	1.8	1.9	1.6	2.0	1.9	1.8
% Schools Taking P. & C.	58.5	5.0	4.5	7.0	20.0	1.8	–	29.0
Total Periods	4.9	5.0	4.0	6.0	5.0	–	–	5.5
Practical Hours	2.5	1.6	1.7	2.7	2.1	–	–	3.0
% Schools Taking Gen. Science	28.1	21.0	1.8	7.0	–	3.6	–	7.0*
Total Periods	4.4	4.1	6.0	6.1	–	4.0	–	4.0
Practical Hours	1.8	1.8	3.0	2.3	–	2.0	–	2.5
% Schools Taking Biology	3.7	2.4	1.8	3.5	4.2	1.8	–	7.0
Total Periods	3.9	4	3.5	4.8	3.6	4.0	–	2.0
Practical Hours	1.4	4	1.7	2.7	1.4	1.8	–	1.5
% Schools Taking Agric.	–	2.4	2.7	–	0.8	–	16*	–
Total Periods	–	5.0	4.0	–	4.0	–	2.0	–
Practical Hours	–	2.4	2.0	–	1.0	–	1.0	–

* Figures for a single school.

None the less, the wider availability of General Science as an examination subject after 1930 was of considerable importance since secondary schools tended to retain established relationships with individual Examination Boards rather than change from one Board to another. The relative popularity of General Science as an examination subject in 1931 may be inferred from the data[40] in Table 3.3. The greater popularity of the subject in the public and other schools entering candidates for the examinations of the Oxford and Cambridge Joint Board is only to be expected.

Table 3.4 (a)   Percentage of Secondary Schools Teaching Given Science Subjects, 1932 (B.A.A.S.)

	Boys'	Girls'	Mixed
Number of Schools	98	198	62
Schools Taking Chemistry	97	83	92
Schools Taking Physics	97	72	87
Schools Taking General Science	56	69	50
Schools Taking Biology	25	41	32
Schools Taking Botany	22	84	52
Schools Taking Zoology	16	27	21

Table 3.4 (b)   Subjects Taught Not Necessarily for Examination. Percentage of Secondary Schools Teaching Given Subjects, 1932 (S.M.A.), by Examination Board

	O. & C.	Oxf.	Camb.	Lond.	N.U.J.B.	C.W.B.	Brist.	Dur.
Number of Schools	82	125	111	114	142	56	6	14
Chemistry	100	95	98	98	99	98	100	100
Physics	100	97	92	96	99	93	100	90
Biology	22	9	9	17	10	13	1 sch.	1 sch.
General Science	37	24	5	14	6	7	1 sch.	3 sch.
Bio. or Gen. Sci.	49	30	13	25	16	20	2 sch.	4 sch.
Agric. or Rural Sci.	4	5	7	–	1	11	1 sch.	–

It is not possible to establish with equal precision the extent to which General Science was taught to non-examination classes in public and secondary schools at this time. Tables 3.4 and 3.5 summarise the relevant results of an S.M.A. investigation, reported in 1932, and of an inquiry conducted by a B.A.A.S. Committee[41] which reported to the Association in 1933. Both sets of data confirm that General Science was making an inroad into the grammar school curriculum but that physics and chemistry continued to dominate the science work in boys' schools. A more varied pattern, involving botany, prevailed in the secondary schools for girls. The discrepancy in the reported extent to which General Science was taught can, in part, be explained by differences in the samples upon which the two sets of results were based. The S.M.A. investigation involved 'about 700' schools, all of which were boys' secondary or public schools. The B.A.A.S. Committee received 358 replies to its questionnaire and these were heavily weighted in favour of girls' schools (98 boys', 198 girls' and 62 co-educational schools). Both the S.M.A. and the B.A.A.S. studies involved 'non-aided secondary schools', i.e. independent schools, but the extent to which such schools were represented in the final samples was not revealed.

Table 3.5   Percentage of Secondary School Pupils Studying Various Science Subjects, 1931

	Boys'	Girls'	Mixed
Number of Schools	98	198	62
Average % Pupils Taking Chemistry	50	26	51
Average % Pupils Taking Physics	55	21	50
Average % Pupils Taking General Science	37	40	42
Average % Pupils Taking Biology	21	26	28
Average % Pupils Taking Botany	4	31	24
Average % Pupils Taking Zoology	4	4	3

Particular interest attaches to the data relating to the N.U.J.M.B. Six per cent of the schools which habitually entered their pupils for the examinations of this Board taught science to their pupils as General Science, even though the N.U.J.M.B. offered no syllabuses in General Science at this time. This suggests that a number of schools offered courses in General Science to a level below that of the School Certificate, a suggestion confirmed by the finding of the B.A.A.S. Committee that only thirty-five of 137 girls' schools 'taking General Science', 'took the subject in School Certificate'.[42] In the view of the British Association Committee, General Science was 'usually taken as an introduction for pupils of ages eleven to thirteen'. This is in marked contrast to the original intention of the S.M.A. that General Science should be taught in the 'middle forms of secondary schools'.[43]

General Science in the schools differed from the S.M.A. prescription in one other important respect. In many schools, General Science was 'taken to mean chemistry and physics only'.[44] In the words of the panel of investigators appointed by the Secondary School Examinations Council to inquire into the School Certificate examinations held in 1931, the practice was 'to confine science work too narrowly'.[45]

This practice was undoubtedly encouraged by the structure of the School Certificate system of examinations and it is significant that the section of the S.S.E.C. Report dealing with science was the longest of the subject reports. The recommendations of the investigating panel were to have a seminal influence on the science curriculum of secondary schools. Impressed by the number and diversity of 'science' syllabuses offered by the Examination Boards, the panel recommended that a 'genuine' physics syllabus should be developed and that no candidate be allowed to obtain a School Certificate pass in science without presenting himself for examination in both the physical and biological sciences. It was proposed to implement this latter recommendation by restricting the number of science papers available within the scheme of examination to four: physics, chemistry, biology and Elementary Science.[46] Candidates who wished to obtain a pass in science at School Certificate level were to be required to present themselves for examination in Elementary Science unless they chose to be examined in each of the three other subjects when exemption from the otherwise compulsory paper in Elementary Science could be granted.

The title of the compulsory paper was carefully chosen to distinguish the associated scheme of work from that known as 'General Science'. The S.S.E.C. investigators were critical of the various attempts that had been made to define a syllabus of General Science and to devise an appropriate examination. The detailed nature of this criticism was not revealed in the published Report but it seems clear that the dissatisfaction stemmed from the difficulty of producing a scheme of work which was sufficiently broad without being superficial. It also seems likely that the panel of investigators sought to overcome this difficulty by devising a syllabus which was both wide and *elementary*. The notes on the suggested paper in Elementary Science confirm that the scheme of work would 'not be enough' for those schools which attempted to 'give a liberal education in which Science has a prominent part', nor 'might it suit candidates preparing to take Science as a main subject in the Sixth Form'.[47] Despite the similarities between Elementary Science and General Science, e.g.

> ... children should understand ... the general methods by which knowledge has been won and the way in which it is applied (or even misapplied?) in social affairs,[48]

it is evident that the S.S.E.C. proposals constituted a much less ambitious innovation than that of the S.M.A. The examination paper in Elementary Science was to consist of 'easy and straightforward' questions and the time proposed for teaching the subject was four, forty-five minute periods per week, an allowance considerably less than that recommended by either the Thomson Committee in 1918 or by the S.M.A. in 1920.

The publication by the S.M.A. in 1932 of a pamphlet entitled *General Science* virtually coincided with the release of the S.S.E.C. Report and its recommendations relating to Elementary Science. This appears to have caused some confusion among members of the Association, despite the fact that the S.M.A. pamphlet was a reissue of the 1917 publication which had been printed before the recommendations of the Examinations Council were made public.[49]

It is doubtful whether the proposal for a paper in Elementary Science, which would have been 'obligatory for virtually all candidates desiring a (School Certificate) pass in Science', was a realistic one in 1932. Most secondary schools taught little or no biology and the implementation of the S.S.E.C. proposals could have led some schools to abandon science in favour of some other Group III subject, for example, arithmetic or elementary mathematics, since it was not necessary for pupils to pass in a science subject in order to gain a School Certificate.[50] None the less, the S.S.E.C. proposals rekindled the debate about the kind of science course which was appropriate for secondary school pupils up to the level of the School Certificate examination. A memorandum on the curriculum issued by the London County Council in 1933 came down firmly in favour of General Science:[51]

> Science teaching should help pupils ... to see life steadily and see it whole. We wish them to obtain a broad view of nature, to study man ... from the points of view of both the biological and the physical sciences.

W. Mayhowe Heller told Section L of the British Association in 1932 that 'our subject must be General Science'.

> We cannot work in the corners of knowledge ... we must be free to trample down half a dozen fences in one and the same lesson.[52]

An article in *Nature* attributed excessive specialisation in science to the false belief that it was impossible to obtain science scholarships to the universities unless the detailed study of physics and chemistry began before the School Certificate examination and commented that it was 'educationally criminal' for fourteen-year-old pupils to begin to 'learn more and more about less and less'.[53]

Several books were published at this time in an attempt to illustrate how physics, chemistry and biology could be presented as a 'living body of knowledge ... interwoven into everything around us'.[54] Newbury's book, while dealing with the teaching of chemistry, indicated how the individual science subjects could be grouped around a central theme in such a way that stress was 'laid upon the inter-relationship of the sciences'.[55] It also incorporated several suggested schemes of work, including a three-year course devised by Andrade and Huxley. Appropriate school texts also became available, sometimes with such confusing titles as *A Short Course of General Science: Vol. 1, Physics*, and *Elementary General Science: Chemistry*.[56]

In 1933, following the publication of the S.S.E.C. Report, the S.M.A. accepted that the position of General Science was in need of review and a subcommittee was set up to 'consider the aims, content and method of Science regarded as suitable for Elementary Science as suggested by the Investigators Panel'.[57] The interim report of this subcommittee in October 1933, provided the initiative for the following Resolution, adopted by the science masters at their annual meeting in 1934:

> A paper in Elementary Science should be obligatory for all pupils taking the general schools examination.[58]

The S.M.A. expressed this view at a conference, held in April 1934, with four of the Examination Boards; Oxford, Cambridge, London and the Northern Universities. Since it was clear that, without authority from the Board of Education, it would not be possible for an individual Examination Board to make a paper in Elementary Science a compulsory part of the School Certificate examination, the conference resolved to invite the Examining Bodies 'to consider the desirability of including "Elementary Science" on the lines of the Science Masters' suggestions as a subject in the School

Certificate examinations for which they were responsible'. It was agreed that 'General Science' should be used as a title in preference to 'Elementary Science' and that the title should be used only for a subject which included biology as well as the physical sciences.[59] One direct consequence of this conference was that the N.U.J.M.B. introduced a General Science syllabus into its scheme of examination in the following year.

The way was also clear for the S.M.A. to undertake a major review of its own proposals for General Science and yet another subcommittee was constituted to 'consider the problems presented to teachers in Secondary Schools by the introduction of General Science'. The subcommittee was also asked to make specific suggestions about 'the aims to be kept in view', the basic principles of the subject, the material to be included, the method(s) of its treatment and the timetable requirements at different stages of secondary education.[60] The subcommittee was chaired by C. L. Bryant, an assistant master at Harrow, and convened by J. A. Lauwerys, lecturer in the methods of science at the University of London Institute of Education. It was Lauwerys who wrote most of the report of the subcommittee and who provided some psychological support for the teaching of General Science rather than the single sciences by claiming that General Science was more likely to illustrate the 'common elements of matter or method between disciplines' which could foster a limited degree of transfer of training.[61]

The Teaching of General Science, Part I, appeared in 1936 as an interim report. The subcommittee noted that 'the numerous reasons urged to justify the inclusion of any subject in the curriculum'[62] could be classified under three headings: utilitarian, disciplinarian and cultural. Whilst the usefulness of scientific knowledge was beyond question, the inclusion of general science in the secondary school curriculum could not be justified simply, or even primarily, on the grounds that the subject helped 'pupils in their everyday life'. Such grounds implied an unacceptable vocational bias in the school science course and, like the disciplinary aim, placed an excessive degree of confidence in the possibility of transferring skills acquired in one context to another.

Since claims based upon utilitarian considerations or on the transfer of training were rejected, it became necessary to justify the teaching of General Science on cultural grounds. The subcommittee had no doubt that 'of all the claims made for the inclusion of science in a school curriculum', this was the strongest.[63] To fulfil its cultural function, a school science course must be broadly conceived, 'touching ordinary life at many points', placing an emphasis on scientific principles of broad generality and finding its starting point and inspiration in the human environment.[64] General Science was thus defined[65] as:

A course of scientific study and investigation which has its roots in the common experience of children and does not exclude any of the fundamental special sciences. It seeks to elucidate the general principles observable in nature, without emphasising the traditional division into specialised subjects until such time as this is warranted by the increasing complexity of the field of investigation, by the developing unity of the separate parts of that field, and by the intellectual progress of the pupils.

Having clarified the nature of the contribution that General Science might make to a liberal secondary school education, Bryant's subcommittee turned its attention to the problem of selecting the content of a General Science course. Since it failed to detect any principles governing the selection of the contents of existing syllabuses in science, the subcommittee felt compelled 'to fix clearly the rational basis'[66] of its own proposed curriculum and the following criteria were adopted.

First, the subject matter had to be such as to 'call forth activity on the part of the pupils'. The appeal was clearly to pupils' interests and attitudes.

... every item ... should help the boy toward an intelligent understanding of his immediate environment, his own body being the central figure in it.[67]

The importance of pupils' attitudes to their eventual achievement in science was also clearly recognised by the subcommittee.

... the importance of the *sentiments* which grow up around any subject cannot be over-estimated. It is essential for future success that a child's first introduction to Science should not lead to boredom, to a feeling of failure or insufficiency, or to an impression that it is a formalised study not directly applicable to things that interest them.[68]

Secondly, content was to be selected so as to help pupils perceive relationships by 'systematising their knowledge'.

... every item ... should lead to the understanding of fundamental scientific principles.[69]

The final consideration related as much to teaching methods as to content and showed a concern for the future well-being of the scientific disciplines.

... our syllabus (must provide) a field suited to the cultivation of those habits, interests and sentiments which are fundamental to science.

To 'give effect to these criteria', the subcommittee established two working groups, each with three members. The first group 'tried to find out things a boy wanted to know, the questions a boy wants to be answered'. In the light of the answers received, it produced a list of topics, A, suitable for teaching and 'necessary to explain the most important contacts between the pupil and his environment'. The second group, operating independently, selected a few very important scientific ideas and worked outwards from these to a second list, B, which exemplified them.[70]

The subcommittee found that there was a considerable amount of material common to both the 'A and B lists, and this was used as the 'backbone' of the General Science syllabus. The syllabus was completed by the addition of such content as was necessary for an adequate understanding of this core material. It is unfortunate that the interim report does not reveal in detail how the subcommittee eventually established its syllabus, i.e. how the 'contacts of the "A" men and the fundamental principles of the "B" men' related to particular items in the General Science course. The reason given for the omission of this detail is not entirely convincing:[71]

... no practical method has been found of indicating (the relationship) within a reasonable space and with clearness.

An appreciation of the significance of each item of the General Science syllabus was made more difficult by the decision of the subcommittee to maintain the customary classification into the three main branches of science when presenting their scheme of work. The syllabus was printed in three vertical columns, headed Physics, Biology and Chemistry respectively, and in horizontal rows which encompassed work from the three sciences thought to be suitable for pupils within a given age-range.

The subcommittee's decision to retain the conventional modes of classifying the natural sciences stems from the attitude of its members towards the 'topic' method of teaching said to be commonly used by those who taught General Science.[72] This method involved the selection of a topic, e.g. air, water, radiation, which would then be studied from several points of view. 'Air' might thus lead to considerations of pressure, respiration, burning and the solubility of the atmospheric gases in water. Advocates of the topic method claimed that it allowed the teacher to ignore the conventional barriers between physics, chemistry and biology and thus to reveal the fundamental unity of science. However, the subcommittee found this unity 'very elusive'[73] and claimed that it 'must exist mainly as an ideal aim in the mind of the teacher'. As such, it did not need to appear explicitly in the syllabus.

Such a claim asks much of the methods used to teach General Science and here the advice of the S.M.A. subcommittee was more positive. The 'purely didactic' method, whereby a teacher began his lesson by stating a principle or law and followed this by 'practical verification, numerical examples and ... everyday application' was dismissed, on the grounds that it was opposed to the empirical and inductive spirit of science, lacked any element of active inquiry and was 'singularly ineffective' in making a pupil 'love his work'. The subcommittee favoured the so-called 'problem method' which, in its view, tended to reverse the order of the more didactic presentation. The lesson began with a consideration of either 'some ordinary phenomenon or some practical application'.

> Discussion leads to the clear statement of a problem which can be answered by careful experiment, and suggestions are obtained from the class as to how the apparatus is to be arranged to obtain an answer. Finally, results are gathered together and, from them, a law or general statement emerges.[74]

The antecedents of this procedure clearly include Dawes's 'science of common things',[75] the views of the Thomson Committee with its emphasis on ordinary phenomena and the practical applications of scientific knowledge, and Armstrong's heurism which required that pupils be placed, as far as possible, in the position of an original discoverer.

The interim report of the subcommittee was approved by the General Committee of the S.M.A. and, shortly afterwards, in January 1937, discussed at the annual meeting of the Association in Manchester. Not one of the 400 members present raised a voice 'against General Science as an ideal' and many 'expressed their agreement with the guiding principles' set down in the Preamble to the Scheme of Work.[76] However, there was considerable criticism of the syllabus itself and of the time suggested for teaching it. Some of the science masters found the syllabus overlong.[77] Others were concerned to increase the amount of time suggested for the teaching of individual topics or disciplines. Chemistry teachers, in particular, felt that the subcommittee's recommendations showed scant courtesy to their subject, especially its quantitative aspects.[78] The Institute of Chemistry sent a letter to the S.M.A. pleading for more chemistry to be included in the General Science syllabus,[79] although the proportion of the total time devoted to chemistry was in fact in excess of that suggested by the Panel of Investigators into the School Certificate examination of 1931. The response of the subcommittee was essentially that chemistry was a less effective medium than physics for inculcating the quantitative basis of science and lent itself less readily to experiments which led to useful generalisations.

> What generalisations has Chemistry to compare with (Boyle's Law, Archimedes' Principle, Ohm's Law) as suitable educational material? ... The Conservation of Mass ... the law of Gay-Lussac, perhaps? ... What is to be done with them when they are established? They do not lend themselves to direct everyday applications.[80]

Much of the criticism of the S.M.A. proposals was directed at the suggested time allowance of four periods per week for four years, totalling 480 periods. The subcommittee claimed that the scheme of work they had devised could be taught in 453 periods of which 197 were allotted to physics, 159 to biology and ninety-seven to chemistry.[81] Critics were quick to point out that the Thomson Committee had recommended an allowance for science of four periods per week in the first year, rising to six periods per week for each of the three succeeding years of a secondary school course up to the age of fifteen or sixteen. In addition, some schools already devoted as much as eight periods per week to the teaching of science subjects. Such criticisms involved a failure to appreciate that the subcommittee, recognising that there were many schools in which the science teaching was confined to four periods per week, had decided to 'try to help these schools first of all'.[82] The General Science syllabus appended to the interim report thus represented the 'barest minimum of Science' with which all boys who passed through secondary schools 'should be acquainted'.[83] When the second part of The Teaching of General Science was published in 1938, an extended syllabus provided for an additional 360 periods and the proportion of time to be devoted to chemical ideas was increased, principally to accommodate aspects of elementary quantitative and organic chemistry.[84]

The Teaching of General Science, prepared as it was by a subcommittee of the Science Masters' Association, was inevitably drawn up with the interests of boys particularly in mind. The Association of Women Teachers, whilst adopting a generally favourable attitude to the first part of the report of the subcommittee, commented that the syllabus was too long and that parts of it needed modification to cater for the 'normal interests of the average girl'.[85] The S.M.A. subcommittee seems to have ignored these comments in producing the second part of its report and it is perhaps surprising that the interests of girls' secondary schools were not represented by the co-option of an A.W.S.T. member to the subcommittee. However, since the General Science syllabus was founded on the coincidence of fundamental scientific principles and the dominant interests of boys, it is unlikely that minor modifications of, or adjustments to, the scheme of work would have accommodated satisfactorily 'the normal interests of the average girl'.

Despite detailed criticism of the proposals of the S.M.A. subcommittee, the view that all secondary school pupils should follow a broad course in natural science was endorsed by both the Spens Committee in 1938 and the Norwood Committee five years later. The Spens Committee[86] received written evidence from the S.M.A. and one of the witnesses before it, C. J. R. Whitmore, H.M.I., a staff Inspector for science, had attended all the meetings of the subcommittee in an advisory capacity.[87] The relevant section of the Spens Report, intended as 'a contribution to the solution'[88] of the problem of providing an adequate, broad course in science for secondary school pupils up to the age of sixteen, included specific reference to the publications of the S.M.A. The report presented the case for General Science in virtually the same terms as the S.M.A., even to the extent of adopting Nunn's ideas on the wonder, application and systematising 'motives'. Not surprisingly, the Association found itself 'in close agreement with the Spens Committee about the aims of school science teaching'.[89]

However, the agreement did not extend to the more practical matter of the timetable which, as has been noted, was a sensitive issue amongst the members of the S.M.A. The Association was particularly hostile to the suggestion that a course intended to 'arouse a general interest in science and its applications in everyday life' might be taught in less time than a course based upon a more formal treatment of the disciplines.[90] The Spens Committee, anticipating criticism on this matter, resorted to quoting the Thomson Committee in defence of its recommendation and claimed that the suggested time would be adequate if 'better use' were made of the time allotted to science in the schools. 'Better use' in this context meant increasing the proportion of time devoted to teacher demonstration at the expense of pupil-based laboratory work, a change of emphasis supported by a reference to Nunn's psychology.[91]

> By a greater use of good demonstration ... science teachers will more commonly stimulate wonder and imagination.

The recommended reduction in the time 'hitherto given to mathematics and science' was a consequence of the acceptance by the Spens Committee of the opinion that English and related subjects should form the 'unifying principle'[92] of the secondary school curriculum. The S.M.A., attacking this 'literary bias' found it 'difficult to conceive of weaker arguments than those advanced by the Spens Committee for protecting literary subjects at the expense of science'.[93]

Despite its outwardly favourable attitude to General Science, the Spens Committee seriously underestimated the potential of the subject as a vehicle of liberal education. It also largely ignored the contribution which General Science could make to the development of those reading and writing skills to which the Committee itself attached such great importance.[94] If, as the Spens Committee claimed, many pupils passed through the grammar schools 'without acquiring the capacity to express themselves in English', the explanation, as Bryant was quick to point out,[95] might have been that such pupils had 'been expected too often to write sensibly about matters of which they had little knowledge and in which they took even less interest'.

The Spens Committee also anticipated the criticism that a course of General Science might prejudice the future careers of the minority of pupils who would later specialise in some branch of science. However, its assertion that a general course in science up to the age of sixteen was both necessary and desirable, that 'children should be given a bird's eye view of a wider field'[96] before settling down to the formal study of physics, chemistry or biology, did little to meet this criticism or to reassure those science teachers who sensed that General Science might disadvantage their future sixth-form specialists.

The problem of accommodating these specialists in a more general scheme of work was considered by a Committee of the Secondary School Examinations Council, under the chairmanship of Cyril Norwood, which reported[97] in 1943. The Norwood Committee expressed support for a General Science course and subscribed to the aims elaborated by the Spens Committee.

> We have studied with considerable care the case for General Science and the case against it. . . . In our view, it holds out great promise and is much to be encouraged.[98]

The S.S.E.C. Committee suggested that, in some schools, the General Science course up to the age of sixteen could be divided into two stages, the first to be undertaken by all pupils. The subsequent stage would then consist of two different schemes of work in General Science, one for pupils not intending to treat science as a main subject and the other, 'though still General Science', placing sufficient emphasis on one or more of the constituent sciences to provide an adequate basis for sixth-form specialisation in science. In other schools, 'depending upon the sympathies and qualifications of the staff and upon the laboratory accommodation available', a single course in General Science for all up to the level of the School Certificate might be more appropriate. The case for General Science put forward by the Norwood Committee was thus heavily qualified in respect of its suitability as a preparation for more advanced study.

> . . . the foundation can be sound enough for a structure of good sixth-form work to be erected upon it, if, in the last stage of General Science in the Main School, the specialist teacher . . . is given opportunity to assert his special point of view.[99]

Despite differences of opinion about the nature and scope of General Science[100] and doubts about its adequacy as a prelude to sixth-form courses in science, the need to broaden school science curricula became more widely accepted by schools towards the end of the 1930s. Between 1922 and 1930, the percentage of all candidates offering General Science as a subject in the School

Certificate examinations rose by only 0.1 to 2.7. It reached 6 per cent by 1936, 11.4 per cent by the following year and increased to 23 per cent by 1942. The numbers of candidates entering for various science subjects in the three years 1936, 1939 and 1942 confirm that it was this period which saw General Science gain a position as an examination subject close to that of the three principal sciences. (See Table 3.6.) The increase from 4,847 to 17,817 in the entry for General Science during the period 1936–42 was accompanied by a decline from 29,975 to 23,067 in the entry for chemistry and the near extinction of botany as an examination subject in the School Certificate. During the same six-year period, the total numbers of candidates taking School Certificate examinations differed by less than 1 per cent[101] but the number of schools entering candidates in General Science rose from 240 in 1936 to 680 in 1942. These latter figures represented 8 per cent and 34 per cent respectively of the total number of schools entering candidates in each of these years,[102] a total which had actually fallen from 1,910 in 1936 to 1,520 in 1942.

Table 3.6   School Certificate Entries by Subject: 1936, 1939 and 1942

Year	Physics	Chemistry	Physics with Chemistry	Biology	Botany	General Science
1936	21,676	29,975	5,128	14,003	10,307	4,847
1939	21,493	29,475	7,737	18,071	6,240	12,497
1942	23,686	23,067	7,115	19,004	3,383	17,817

By 1943, it seems likely that 'about 40 per cent' of the secondary schools in England and Wales presented candidates for examination in General Science at School Certificate level.[103] Of 225 schools submitting 'effective replies' to a questionnaire distributed in 1943 on behalf of the S.M.A., there were 108 in which General Science was the only science subject offered in the School Certificate or in which all candidates offered the subject. This latter condition tended to prevail in the smaller schools of 150–200 pupils, presumably because larger secondary schools were able to offer a number of science options. In those schools in which General Science was the only science presented by candidates for examination, the course varied from five years (sixty-two schools) to three years or less (fourteen schools) in length. Where General Science was one of a number of science subjects taught in a school, it tended to be taught to the 'weaker' candidates and/or to non-science specialists, usually as a course of three or four years' duration up to the School Certificate year.

The S.M.A. questionnaire revealed considerable variety in the manner in which the teaching of General Science was organised within the secondary schools. There were 'as many instances of two or more masters teaching different portions of the same subject in the same Form as of one master only teaching a given Form'. Where a division of labour existed, it appears to have been between the biological and the physical sciences. However, the replies to the questionnaire were collected during the Second World War and the extent to which the findings may be extrapolated to more normal conditions is difficult to assess. The circumstances of the war were probably of particular significance for the availability and deployment of science teaching staff. Some schools were seriously affected by a shortage of qualified science teachers for part or all of the war and this, in itself, may have contributed to the growth of General Science in the schools after 1939.

Since the membership of the S.M.A. at this time was drawn predominantly from grammar and public schools, the Association did not concern itself directly with the teaching of science in other types of schools which provided an education for the majority of pupils of secondary school age. Few of these schools entered pupils for School Certificate examinations so that it is not possible to use examination statistics to estimate the growth of General Science teaching within them. A detailed investigation[104] carried out by the Board of Education in 1930, involving 584 senior schools, showed that of 144,854 pupils, almost all (144,812) were following science courses. The sample included selective and non-selective central schools and ordinary senior schools, together with a few 'Higher Tops' in County Durham, i.e. parts of elementary schools in which the pupils had passed Standard VII and remained at school for more advanced work. Perhaps the most significant finding of the Board's inquiry was that many of the schools had not been in existence long enough to develop complete courses so that the number of pupils studying science within them decreased rapidly with successive years.

Most of the schools allowed two or three forty to forty-five minute periods per week for science, but the range was wide, from one to eight periods per week. In general, senior schools tended to allow rather more time for teaching science than the selective central schools.

The investigation also revealed that the science teaching in senior schools had several features in common with the corresponding work to be found in the grammar and public schools. The physical sciences dominated the science curricula, 264 of the 584 schools returning the Board's questionnaire giving no attention at all to the teaching of biology. In six schools, chemistry was the only science taught and, in another thirty-six, science was represented exclusively by physics. In coeducational schools, the curriculum showed the familiar, marked differentiation between the sexes, botany being taught to the girls and the physical sciences to the boys.[105] As in the grammar schools, the science staff was highly specialised, few of the men graduates being competent to teach anything other than physics or chemistry. Of 599 male science graduates teaching in the sample of schools in 1930, 547 were regarded as qualified to teach physics, 510 to teach chemistry, but only thirty to teach botany. A more balanced position prevailed among the women graduates teaching science. Of the 198 involved in the investigation, 129 were competent to teach chemistry, 111 to teach physics and 117 to teach botany.[106]

The 1932 *Memorandum on the Teaching of Science in Senior Schools* was an attempt by the Board of Education to encourage a new approach[107] to the teaching of science in this sector of post-primary education. Such an approach was inevitably constrained by the limited length of senior school life, less than three years for most pupils, and by the social functions ascribed officially to the senior schools. It was suggested that the curriculum might be designed to encourage the health of the individual, to provide a knowledge of man's dependence on science and to foster an appreciation of the wonders of nature.

The many ideas for a detailed syllabus offered in the Memorandum clearly owe much to those influences which are also evident in the general science syllabuses of the S.M.A. Scientific principles were to be taught, as far as possible, in relation to their application in the everyday experience of the pupils. Thus, the study of heat would enable pupils to appreciate that heat was a form of energy, necessary for human health and having numerous applications in the household and in locomotion. Similarly, light was to be presented in connection with the eye and with telescopes: 'pins and parallax' were 'out of place'. Electricity was to be taught with reference to its thermal, chemical and magnetic effects, i.e. insulators, fuses, conductors, the dynamo, motor and wireless. Like the S.M.A. subcommittee, the Board was of the opinion that chemistry could make only a limited contribution to the general scientific education of pupils between the ages of eleven and fifteen because the chemistry of the materials of everyday life was too complex. A substantial chemical component in the senior school science curriculum was thus justified only if local industry had 'important chemical interests'.[108]

The pressures to broaden the science curricula of senior schools and to focus the teaching upon the interests and experiences of the pupils are also evident in a Memorandum produced by the London County Council in 1933 and in a Report published by the London Teachers' Association three years later.

> The course should be a broad study of nature.[109]
> No attempt should be made to pigeonhole the various branches of science: ... the general science should be based on the process of living and its centre should be the child.[110]

It is a reasonable inference that, despite these pressures for reform, only slow progress was made during the 1930s in broadening the science teaching within senior schools and in relating scientific knowledge to the immediate environment of the pupils. In addition, given that many such pupils left school as soon as they were permitted legally to do so, some senior schools can have had little time to develop full general science courses before they were reorganised as secondary modern schools, in most cases as a result of the 1944 Education Act.

In 1944, the S.M.A. appointed a new subcommittee to review *The Teaching of General Science* in the light of the experience gained in the schools. The subcommittee decided that 'the time was not ripe for the discussion of changes'[111] and, in view of the circumstances then prevailing, there is little doubt of the wisdom of this decision. Three-quarters of a million children had been evacuated at the beginning of the war and, by 1944, over half the schools in towns and cities had been damaged or destroyed by enemy action. The need to reorganise the educational system was widely accepted, the broad, legislative guidelines for reform being laid down in the 1944 Education Act. This Act raised the Presidency of the Board of Education to Ministerial status, abolished the distinction between Part II and Part III local education authorities and established the tripartite system of 'secondary education for all'. It promised [112] a higher school leaving age of fifteen and revived the scheme for county colleges and compulsory part-time education up to the age of eighteen. In addition to this legislation, the future of the public schools had been reviewed by the Fleming Committee[113] and major changes in the training of teachers had been recommended in the Report of the McNair Committee.[114]

The S.M.A. subcommittee was therefore reconstituted in 1947 when some of the salient features of the post-war educational system had become more firmly established. It reported in 1950, affirming that the reports issued in 1936 and 1938 were 'sound in principle' and required no serious amendment of their 'philosophical background'.[115] The imminent introduction of a subject-based First School Examination, the General Certificate of Education, to replace the system of School Certificates was an important factor governing the sub-committee's deliberations since it was hoped that the scheme of work in General Science could form the basis of an Ordinary level syllabus in the subject. An attempt was made to correct the 'unfortunate impression' that earlier reports had encouraged the use of demonstration experiments at the expense of individual laboratory work conducted by the pupils themselves,[116] by including a chapter dealing with practical work and by incorporating a schedule of suggested experiments and demonstrations. The 'chemistry section' of the report was redesigned to meet the criticism that this subject had been neglected and 'a more equitable distribution' of time between the principal sciences was established. However, attention was largely confined to the teaching of General Science in the grammar and public schools, secondary modern science teaching being the subject of separate and later publications.[117]

With the advantage of hindsight, it is possible to discern that the popularity of General Science as an examination subject began to decline even before the S.M.A. Report was published in 1950. Bull showed[118] in 1949 that the emerging and dominant post-war pattern in the grammar schools was one in which General Science provided an introduction, of one to three years' duration, to the study of the separate science subjects. (See Table 3.7.) This pattern, similar in some respects to that urged by the Norwood Committee, came to be reflected in the number of pupils entered for General Science in the G.C.E. examinations. Table 3.8 provides an analysis of selected entries for G.C.E. Ordinary level examinations in the summer of 1951 and Table 3.9 indicates the relative popularity of General Science as an O-level subject after this date.[119] It is clear that the position established by General Science relative to the single science subjects during the war years was not maintained. The proportional decline in the number of O-level entries in General Science gave way to a fall in the actual numbers of entries during the 1960s and, by the middle of the following decade, the majority of G.C.E. Boards had withdrawn their O-level syllabuses in this subject.[120]

To understand the steady and eventually rapid decline in General Science it is necessary to refer both to the criticisms levelled at the innovation itself and to those social and educational factors which exerted a powerful influence on the curriculum of the secondary school after the end of the Second World War. It is not, of course, suggested that these variables governing curriculum reform have operated independently of each other.

Table 3.7   The Accommodation of General Science in the Curricula of Grammar Schools, 1949

	Number and Percentage of Schools	
1 General Science as an Introduction (1–3 years) to the study of separate subjects	121	(33.7)
2 General Science as an Introduction for all pupils and also figuring as an alternative to separate subjects to complete the course	87	(24.2)
3 General Science (one subject) taken by all pupils for 4 years and by most for five years	31	(8.6)
4 General Science (2 subjects) taken by most pupils, some taking it as one subject	20	(5.6)
5 'Physics-with-Chemistry' figuring among a variety of alternatives	36	(10.0)
6 Science Courses arranged in completely separate subjects, e.g. Physics, Chemistry, Biology	40	(11.1)
7 Courses in transition	22	(6.1)
8 Unclassified	2	(0.5)
Total	359	(100.0)

The most frequent and persistent criticism of General Science was that it consisted of a miscellany of odds and ends[121] lacking any coherence and founded upon inadequate integrating principles. Critics were quick to point out that the 'unity' of General Science was far from evident in syllabuses or examination papers. Many syllabuses, including that devised by the S.M.A., presented the contents of a General Science course under the conventional headings of physics, chemistry and biology. The 1950 *Report on the Teaching of General Science* contained the revealing comment that the work on electrolysis and cells had been 'removed to the chemistry section'.[122] Examinations in General Science often involved papers in which physics, chemistry and biology questions appeared in separate sections and, in some instances, a separate paper was set in each of these three principal branches.[123]

Similar conventions were observed by the authors of General Science text-books, despite the use of 'some ingenious chapter headings',[124] and titles such as *General Science: Physics* or *General Science: Chemistry* were relatively common. For some advocates of General Science, a tripartite division of General Science textbooks constituted no argument against General Science itself. J. A. Lauwerys, a member of the 1936 S.M.A. subcommittee and an

Table 3.8 Entries for Ordinary Level G.C.E., Summer 1951, by Sex and Subject

Subject	BOYS			GIRLS			TOTAL		
	Entries	Number Passed	% Passed	Entries	Number Passed	% Passed	Entries	Total Passes	% Passes
English Language	57,603	32,682	56.7	51,291	34,432	67.1	108,894	67,114	61.6
Physics	18,819	10,619	56.4	2,729	1,531	56.1	21,548	12,150	56.4
Chemistry	16,005	9,329	58.3	4,672	2,486	53.2	20,677	11,815	57.1
Biology	6,935	3,882	56.0	22,079	12,551	56.8	29,014	16,433	56.6
General Science	12,538	6,657	53.1	9,134	5,037	55.1	21,672	11,694	54.0
History	33,890	17,925	52.9	32,360	19,939	61.6	66,250	37,864	57.2

Table 3.9   O-Level Entries in General Science, Physics, Chemistry and Biology, 1951–62

	Number of Entries (Boys and Girls)					General Science As	
Year	General Science (a)	Chemistry (b)	Physics (c)	Biology (d)	All Subjects (e)	(a/e)%	(a/b+c+d)%
1951	21,672	20,677	21,548	29,014	738,717	2.93	30.4
1952	22,378	25,255	25,888	34,252	829,710	2.69	26.2
1953	25,688	30,915	31,875	39,717	979,769	2.62	25.0
1954	25,325	32,079	33,701	42,681	984,243	2.57	23.3
1955	25,207	34,954	37,157	46,952	1,043,864	2.41	21.2
1956	25,747	36,390	39,455	50,138	1,068,813	2.40	20.4
1957	24,299	40,357	43,632	54,890	1,128,421	2.15	17.4
1958	24,929	46,158	50,973	62,588	1,274,768	1.95	15.6
1959	25,643	53,803	60,029	73,001	1,449,995	1.76	13.7
1960	26,431	59,643	68,080	83,989	1,603,894	1.64	12.5
1961	27,647*	62,221	71,157	89,214	1,872,194	1.47*	12.4*
1962	27,891*	67,371	79,691	99,531	2,100,256	1.32*	11.3*

* The General Science entries for these years refer to summer and winter examinations, i.e. Summer 1961 and Winter 1961–2 and Summer 1962 and Winter 1962–3. All other entries refer to Summer examinations only. The General Science entries for the earlier years also include a very small number of entries in the History and Philosophy of Science.

influential figure in science education at this time, claimed that, in so far as the function of a textbook was to 'expound a well-ordered scheme', it did not amount to a replacement of the teacher but was merely a tool for him to use. As such, it was 'convenient' if a textbook adopted the 'traditional divisions of the field'. Lauwerys's argument seems to underestimate the influence exerted by textbooks in lesson planning and organisation and it is not surprising that, in many schools, General Science appeared on the timetable as largely separate courses of physics, chemistry and biology.

The S.M.A. was challenged frequently to identify the principles which would enable a scheme of work in General Science to be distinguished from the sum of separate courses in physics, chemistry and biology. It became increasingly obvious that this was a challenge which the Association was unable to meet. 'Though they occasionally tell us what General Science is not, nowhere do [they] tell us what it is', complained[125] H. S. Shelton of the 1932 General Science pamphlet. In Shelton's view, the authors of this pamphlet had 'acquired an idea' which they did 'not fully understand' and which they 'could not properly apply'.[126] Shelton was an active figure in the debate about General Science which took place among educationists during the 1930s, expressing his ideas in a variety of articles[127] in *The School Science Review*, *The Schoolmaster* and *The Contemporary Review*. He was also a member of the S.M.A. sub-committee which produced the 1936 Report, but he 'ceased to attend' after two meetings.[128] In 1939, he wrote a book, *The Theory and Practice of General Science*, in which he criticised the syllabuses devised by the S.M.A. and offered an alternative 'rational scheme' of work based, not upon 'the technology of the specialist sciences' but upon 'what ought to be familiar to the ordinary educated man'.[129]

Shelton's claim that the S.M.A. had failed to provide a clear and practical definition of a general course, based upon scientific principles of wide applicability,[130] is supported by the evidence given by the Association to the Norwood Committee.

> It would be true to say that a school is teaching General Science even if its pupils study Physics, Chemistry and Biology separately with separate teachers; do some Geology as part of their Geography course, and take separate subjects in S.C., not the subject General Science.[131]

It is difficult to reconcile this statement, given in reply to a question asked by the Norwood Committee, with many of the earlier pronouncements of the Association about General Science. There was, as Shelton observed,[132] a 'very small relation' between the theoretical exposition and the actual schemes of work. Moreover, in so far as the statement equated general science with a mere broadening of the science curriculum, the case for teaching the new subject was to be undermined by the introduction and growth of biology courses in secondary schools.[133]

The defence offered by the S.M.A. to the charge that General Science lacked coherence and led to the acquisition of 'cigarette-card knowledge' was not convincing. The subcommittee which prepared the 1936 and 1938 Reports admitted that it required 'imagination to see much unity between the particular phenomena which a biologist, a physicist, a chemist and a geologist would abstract for study' from a given landscape and acknowledged that 'there would not be much similarity' in the methods or principles they would use in their work.[134] Failing to detect a fundamental unity in the methods and principles of the natural sciences, yet 'feeling' that some unity 'must exist',[135] the S.M.A. subcommittee concluded that this was probably only 'an ideal in the mind of the man of science'[136] and that, as such, the 'essence of general science' lay 'not in the syllabus, but in the interpretation of it'.[137] Conclusions of this kind, which were of little help to practising teachers, did nothing to place the debate about General Science on a more secure footing and strengthened the belief that General Science was no more than a device for broadening the school science curriculum.

In seeking to undermine this belief, the S.M.A. subcommittee touched upon a fundamental issue, with a significance extending beyond the general science movement itself. According to the subcommittee, whatever desire existed to 'break through the boundaries between the three main divisions of science' was due, not to any reaction against a 'perfectly reasonable classification of phenomena', but rather to opposition to the 'excessive formalism' of school science teaching. 'Formalism', as used in this context, refers to the content and methods of teaching the professionally orientated grammar school science courses, intended to introduce pupils to the concepts and logical structures of the established scientific disciplines of physics and chemistry.

The aims of such courses, although expressed in different terms at different times, were concerned essentially with training the mind, the acquisition of scientific skills, attitudes and techniques, or, to use a much more modern phrase, with 'getting pupils to think ... in the way practising scientists do'.[138]

General Science, in reaction to this formalism, embodied a different and more radical conception of the contribution that science could make to general education in the secondary school. It involved a rejection of the assumption that an initiation into the professional world of precise and abstract scientific ideas could provide an adequate basis of 'science for all', even within the selective grammar school. Starting with the experiences and interests of the pupils rather than with the needs or attributes of the scientific disciplines, General Science reasserted the usefulness of scientific knowledge and sought to relate such knowledge to its applications in the everyday lives of the pupils. In this way, pupils were to be helped to understand both the scientific conception of the world in which they lived and some of the ways in which science and technology were able to transform the intellectual and material condition of mankind. General Science was thus a challenge to the 'professionalism'[139] of school science and an attempt to emphasise what the Council for Curriculum Reform referred to as 'recognition' knowledge, i.e. knowledge which could contribute to satisfying a pupil's need to feel 'at home in the universe' and to his capacity for 'intelligent criticism of social policy'.[140]

As Bradley was quick to realise, the teaching of General Science involved sacrificing 'the continuity of classical physics and of classical chemistry'.[141] Science teachers, highly trained in one branch of science and identifying themselves professionally with the individual scientific disciplines, were unlikely to make such sacrifices readily or easily. Arthur Smithells had recognised the severity and dimensions of this problem as early as 1924. In a discussion of school and university science, he commented[142] that the greatest difficulty facing a new entrant to school science teaching was that of divesting himself of ' ... the University or professional outlook in science'. The S.M.A. subcommittee returned to this theme in 1938, warning that the professional mind could not attain maturity 'in a meagre environment of specialised abstractions, starved of the realisation of other values and points of view'.[143]

The 'A' and 'B' lists drawn up during the construction of the General Science syllabus thus constituted a bold attempt to marry the alternative views of the role that science should fulfil in a liberal secondary education. However, the two sets of educational objectives associated with these different conceptions of school science teaching were, in some elements, incompatible. The Institute of Chemistry assessed the worth of General Science by estimating its contribution to the future well-being of the profession of chemistry rather than by reference to the personal development of the pupils in the secondary schools. As the S.M.A. soon discovered, it was not possible to reconcile the demands made by the Institute with a broad course of general science, every item of which helped a pupil 'toward an intelligent understanding of his immediate environment'.[144] The difficulty was highlighted by Marchant's investigation in 1943. He reported[145] that while many teachers accepted that General Science was more satisfactory 'culturally and educationally' than courses based on the individual sciences, the latter continued to be taught because of the widely held assumption that General Science was an inadequate basis for more specialised work in science at sixth-form level.[146] Thus, while the 'educational faith' of the science teacher may have inclined 'towards General Science', 'he dare not act accordingly'.[147] The more radical aspects of General Science were thus in conflict with the pre-professional function ascribed to grammar school courses in the science subjects, a function which was strongly supported by the structure and format of public examinations.[148]

As might be expected, this conflict was somewhat less in evidence in other types of school which also offered a post-primary education but which were intended to fulfil a different social function from the grammar schools. In so far as an understanding of the everyday applications of scientific knowledge was seen as more compatible with the future occupations prescribed for pupils attending elementary or senior schools than a rigorous introduction to the vocabulary, grammar and syntax of the scientific disciplines, these schools provided a more hospitable environment than the prestigious secondary schools for the growth of alternative courses in science. Such growth was encouraged by a variety of official publications. The Hadow Committee recommended[149] that science syllabuses in senior schools should vary according to the type of school and the facilities available. Schools located in industrial areas were urged to give particular attention to elementary physics and mechanics and to provide their pupils with opportunities to use the machinery found in local industries. Schools in rural areas were advised to introduce a corresponding agricultural bias into the curricula provided for pupils between the ages of eleven and fifteen. An emphasis on making senior school pupils aware of the practical applications of science in their everyday lives was advocated by the Board of Education in its *Handbook of Suggestions for Teachers*[150] but, as the Board admitted, successful science teaching in senior schools often required that teachers abandon the 'academic tradition' in which they had been nurtured.[151] That they did not do so is one of the reasons why General Science made little progress in senior schools before these were reorganised as secondary modern schools after 1944.

For science education, as for much else, the Second World War was a watershed. In the years between the two World Wars, the percentage of Higher School Certificate candidates offering physics and chemistry had declined, despite a substantial increase in numbers, and the demand for qualified scientists and technologists had almost stagnated.[152] (See Tables 3.10 and 3.11.) Of the seventy-one new Chairs created during the period, only twenty-two were in science and technology. In 1944, the Government established a Committee, under the chairmanship of Lord Eustace Percy, to consider the needs of higher technological education and the response that could be made by the universities and technical colleges. Together with the Report of the Barlow Committee[153] on scientific manpower, the Percy Report[154] established the framework of an unprecedented expansion in scientific, technical and technological education. Although some of the Committee's recommendations

Table 3.10   Higher School Certificate Entries, By Subject: 1920 and 1938

	1920		1938	
	Number of Entries	% of Total	Number of Entries	% of Total
Latin & Greek	1,196	17	3,470	9
French	996	15	4,752	13
German	90	1.5	899	2
English	573	8	4,734	13
History	472	7	3,880	10
Geography	100	1.5	1,795	15
Economics	–	–	179	–
Mathematics	1,289	19	5,501	15
Biology (and Zoology)	26	–	1,480	4
Chemistry	1,016	15	3,934	11
Physics	1,006	15	4,040	11

Table 3.11   Science and Technology Students in English Universities and University Colleges: 1922–3 and 1938–9

	1922–3		1938–9	
	No.	%	No.	%
Science	5,970	19.3	6,061	16.2
Technology	3,882	12.5	4,217	11.3
Science & Technology	9,852	31.8	10,278	27.5

were implemented only after much delay,[155] post-war British society was committed to economic planning and to the production of scientists and technologists in greatly increased numbers. The important White Paper[156] on Technical Education in 1956 led to the establishment of the Colleges of Advanced Technology and greatly encouraged the expansion of courses in local, area and regional colleges. In 1938, the estimated output of professional scientists and technologists from all sources was about 5,000. By 1960, it had risen to about 17,000.[157] In the three years after 1955, the numbers qualifying as professional technologists in the United Kingdom increased by one-quarter,[158] the country acquired a Minister for Science and the Advisory Council on Scientific Policy publicised the need to attract able boys and girls into careers in science and technology. Girls became classified as part of the 'pool of untapped scientific ability' and manpower predictions were made in units of QSP, qualified scientific personnel.[159]

Within the schools, there was a massive expansion in the numbers of sixth-form pupils, sustained by the so-called 'trend' to stay on at school beyond the statutory leaving age and by the 'bulge' in the birth-rate. Between 1955 and 1965, the numbers of pupils in the sixth form doubled,[160] a growth which reflected the greater degree of national prosperity and the close association of educational achievement with future occupation and status. The shortage of an adequate number of well-qualified science teachers was a chronic problem but the twenty years following the end of the Second World War were, as a whole, remarkably hospitable for science in the schools, colleges and universities. The 'swing' to science subjects in the sixth form during the 1950s was astonishing. By 1960, over 60 per cent of sixth-form boys were specialising wholly in science and/or mathematics.[161] One non-scientist, reviewing the post-war grammar schools in 1960, concluded that the arts subjects were forced to recruit 'the weak students or the careful plodders' and the occasional 'gifted eccentric' flying in the face of fashion.[162]

These developments inevitably reinforced the pre-professional function of grammar school science courses and, in such a climate, General Science could not hope to flourish. Developments in the modern schools were handicapped by a crippling shortage of qualified science teachers,[163] an inadequate provision of laboratory accommodation and equipment, the suspicion of employers[164] about the value of General Science and, in some instances, by the under-standable pressure to seek parity of esteem with the grammar schools. Schools were urged to allow the three major sciences to gain 'their just places' in the curriculum, each taught from the outset by specialists. Connell and James, writing[165] in 1958, expressed the mood accurately.

> An improvement in ... school science teaching is a requirement for the continued existence of this country as a leading scientific and industrial nation. As a first step in this direction general science ... should be abandoned.

After reprinting the *Report on the Teaching of General Science* in 1960, the S.M.A. made no further attempt to argue the case for General Science.[166] The interests of the Association moved to the production of specialised G.C.E. courses, designed to attract even more boys and girls into science- and technology-based careers.[167] Even as it did so, the schools were embarking on changes which threatened to render such courses obsolescent. The introduction of the Certificate of Secondary Education, the advent of comprehensive re-organisation and the eventual raising of the school leaving age, coupled with a growing disillusionment with some aspects of science and technology,[168] paved the way for a renewed debate about the contribution that science could make to the general education of all pupils up to the age of sixteen. As before, the problem was to be the degree of compatibility between the aims and objectives of the new curricula and those of the science teachers in the schools. There is, however, one significant difference. General Science was an attempt to sup-plant the specialised grammar school science courses, determined primarily by the needs of future science specialists. Many of the more modern curriculum 'packages' of the sixties and seventies, derived from such specialised courses, must seek accommodation within non-selective comprehensive schools, estab-lished to provide, among much else, a general education in science for all. As Greenwood has remarked,[169] many of these recent attempts at curriculum reform may represent the end, rather than the beginning, of an era in school science education.

References

[1] *S.S.R.*, vol. 1, no. 1, 1919, p. 12.

[2] Ibid., p. 29.

[3] B.A.A.S., *Report*, 1922, p. 207.

[4] Tancock, E. O., The Annual Meeting: A General Impression, *S.S.R.*, vol. 1, no. 2, 1919, p. 100.

[5] *S.S.R.*, vol. 1, no. 4, 1920, p. 133.

[6] The 'average method' of teaching the history of science was also subjected to criticism in later years. See, for example, the account of Lancelot Hogben's 'onslaught' at the British Association Meeting in Blackpool in 1936 and reported in *Journal of Education*, October 1936, pp. 657–8.

[7] The first volume of *The School Science Review* carried a review of an American text, *The Elements of General Science*. According to the reviewer, the value of the 'enlarged and revised edition' lay in its suggestions of 'ground to be covered'. *S.S.R.*, vol. 1, no. 1, 1919, p. 31.

[8] B.A.A.S., *Report*, 1917, pp. 149–54.

[9] The Association grew rapidly after 1919, both in terms of numbers of members and the schools they represented. The following data are taken from Mikhail, N. H., op. cit.

Year	1920	1921	1922	1923	1928	1938
No. of members	494	600	729	805	1,408	2,548
No. of Schools	258	325	376	429	672	886

According to C. L. Bryant, Secretary of the A.P.S.S.M. from 1915 to 1918, the extension of membership beyond the public schools was 'hotly disputed', but the 'progressives got their way'. *S.S.R.*, vol. XXVI, no. 100, 1945, p. 256.

[10] For a comment on this issue see a letter from H. P. Ramage, *Education in Science*, no. 64, September 1975, p. 33.

[11] Mikhail, N. H., op. cit., p. 51. The S.M.A. and A.(W.)S.T. were the principal organisations professionally concerned with school science teaching at this time. The Association of Science Teachers, founded in 1912, gave evidence to the Thomson Committee and there was a suggestion from Fairbrother, a science master at Leeds Grammar School, that it should amalgamate with the A.P.S.S.M. and the Yorkshire Natural Science Association to form a National Science Association, concerned with science education and analogous to the Chemical Society. The S.M.A. Committee rejected the idea. The A.S.T. became the A.W.S.T. in 1922. *S.S.R.*, vol. 2, no. 6, December 1920, p. 228.

[12] Science for All, *S.S.R.*, vol. 2, no. 6, 1920, pp. 203 and 204. This was a reprint 'without material alteration' of the A.P.S.S.M. *Science for All* pamphlet prepared for the Thomson Committee in 1917.

[13] Ibid., p. 203.

[14] *S.S.R.*, vol. 1, no. 4, 1920, p. 150. The syllabus is also reproduced in this issue (pp. 150–1). The Army Council considered 'Science for All' in 1920 and a general science paper was set in the Sandhurst Scholarship Examination after 1925.

[15] For some years after 1919, the *S.S.R.*, made reference to 'prep' rather than to 'homework'. More significantly, the Officers of the S.M.A. continued to be drawn from schools which could hardly claim to be representative of secondary schools in general. The editorial panel of the *S.S.R.* in 1926 was drawn from Harrow, Clifton College,

Charterhouse, St Olave's School and Balliol College. The public school dominance of S.M.A. affairs continued until well after the end of the Second World War.

[16] *S.S.R.*, vol. 1, no. 2, 1919, p. 55.

[17] *S.S.R.*, vol. 1, no. 4, 1920, p. 150.

[18] *S.S.R.*, vol. 7, no. 26, 1925, pp. 71 and 220-1.

[19] Conditions for Effective Science Teaching, *S.S.R.*, vol. VII, no. 26, 1925, p. 70.

[20] It should also be noted that the Oxford and Cambridge Joint Board differed from other local Examination Boards in its origins and methods of operation. See Montgomery, R. J., *Examinations*, 1965, p. 63.

[21] Board of Education, *Report of an Inquiry into the Conditions Affecting the Teaching of Science in Secondary Schools for Boys in England*, HMSO, 1925. See also *S.S.R.*, vol. VII, no. 26, December 1925, p. 70.

[22] Ibid., p. 68.

[23] Ibid., pp. 68-9.

[24] For an account of the rigidity of the London Matriculation requirements see Montgomery, R. J., op. cit., p. 135, et seq. 'London Matric' was in great demand between the Wars and when 'grievances were aired in national conferences' about matriculation, 'Matric tended to be London Matriculation and no other'. Petch, J. A., *Fifty Years of Examining*, 1953, ch. 10.

[25] B.A.A.S., *Report*, 1928, p. 443.

[26] Ibid., p. 444.

[27] Ibid., p. 469.

[28] The B.A.A.S. Report was given a cool reception by the S.M.A. which expressed concern over the reappearance of the 1917 Schemes of Work and described the report as 'overwritten'. *S.S.R.*, vol. XI, no. 43, 1920, p. 236.

[29] B.A.A.S., *Report*, 1928, p. 454.

[30] Ibid., p. 455.

[31] The D.S.I.R. warned in 1925 that the number of students who had graduated recently in chemistry was so large that many of them could not 'hope to obtain satisfactory employment, including teaching employment, in the near future'. *S.S.R.*, vol. VII, no. 26, 1925, p. 70. The S.M.A. was quick to claim, somewhat unconvincingly, that, since chemistry (and physics) were no longer the route to a lucrative career, the argument in favour of 'confining the attention of schoolboys to the physical sciences' was much weakened. Ibid., p. 69.

[32] B.A.A.S., *Report*, 1928, p. 456.

[33] Of the 1,311 degrees obtained in pure science in England in 1924-5, 477 were awarded by the University of London. The corresponding figures for 1930-1 are 1,968 and 562; for 1937-8, 2,157 and 676. *Returns from Universities and University Colleges*.

[34] Board of Education, *Report of an Inquiry ...*, 1925, p. 8.

[35] The 1930 figure of 1,354 had risen to 1,398 by 1938.

[36] The phrase is Fisher's, used in a speech in Birmingham in February 1922. He expressed the view that in a few years, 'the clouds' would 'pass away'. *Education*, 3 March 1922, p. 142.

[37] Taken from Board of Education, *Annual Reports and Statistics. Education in 1938; Statistical Abstract 1937*, Cmd. 5353, p. 61 and ibid., 1938, Cmd. 6232, p. 64 and *Memoranda on the Board's Estimates, 1925-6, 1930, 1938* and *1939*. The quoted capital cost excludes charges (e.g. loan charges) other than that approved by the Board for the financial year in question.

[38] *The School Certificate Examinations*, HMSO, 1931, p. 43.

[39] Ibid., p. 19.

[40] Science in Secondary Boys' Schools – Statistics, *S.S.R.*, vol. XIII, no. 52, 1932, p. 386.

[41] The B.A.A.S. Committee was chaired by Dr Lilian Clarke. The S.M.A. data are taken from ibid., p. 387 and the B.A.A.S. data from the *Report* of the 1933 Meeting, p. 319.

[42] B.A.A.S., *Report*, 1933, p. 319.

[43] Science for All: Outline of the Course, *S.S.R.*, vol. II, no. 6, 1920, p. 203.

[44] B.A.A.S., *Report*, 1933, p. 319.

[45] *The School Certificate Examination*, HMSO, 1932, p. 123. There were earlier investigations of a similar nature in 1918 and 1924 but the reports were not published, although the 'subject reports' of the 1918 investigation were issued as three pamphlets in 1920. See *Journal of Education*, February 1920, p. 94.

[46] The Investigators (twenty-three in all, chaired by Cyril Norwood and including Headteachers, H.M.I.s, two assistant teachers, a senior science master and the senior science master at Rugby) were also critical of some of the questions which had been set in the School Certificate papers in science; ibid., pp. 124–30.

[47] Ibid., p. 159.

[48] Ibid., p. 158.

[49] *S.S.R.*, vol. XIV, no. 56, 1933, p. 466. The 1932 publication was a 'second reprint' of the 1917 document.

[50] The number and titles of the subjects in Group III varied from one Board to another. To qualify for a School Certificate of the N.U.J.M.B. in 1918, a candidate had to reach a satisfactory standard in each of five subjects, including at least one from each of Groups I and II and one at least from Group III which included Mathematics, *either* Mechanics *or* Physics, Chemistry, Geography, *either* Natural History *or* Botany, Domestic Science. Petch, J. A., *Fifty Years of Examining*, 1953, p. 82.

[51] L.C.C., *Memorandum on Curricula – Science*, 1933, p. 2.

[52] B.A.A.S., *Report*, 1932, p. 216. W. Mayhowe Heller was President of Section L in 1932.

[53] *Nature*, 7 October 1933, p. 531.

[54] Andrade, E. N. da C., Huxley, J. S., *An Introduction to Science*, 1933.

[55] Newbury, N. F., *The Teaching of Chemistry*, 1934, p. 25. A second edition appeared in 1958.

[56] Published in 1933 by John Murray in two volumes and by Blackie in three volumes respectively.

[57] *S.S.R.*, vol. XIV, no. 56, 1933, p. 466.

[58] *S.S.R.*, vol. XL, no. 140, 1958, p. 119.

[59] *S.S.R.*, vol. XVI, no. 61, 1934, p. 125.

[60] S.M.A., *The Teaching of General Science, Part I*, 1936, p. 3.

[61] Lauwerys, J. A., The Teaching of Physical Science, *S.S.R.*, vol. XVII, no. 66, 1935, p. 164. The arguments presented in this article parallel those in the Interim Report on Teaching General Science. For a note on Lauwerys, see n. 124 below.

[62] S.M.A., *The Teaching of General Science, Part I,* 1936, p. 10.

[63] Ibid., pp. 14–15.

[64] Ibid., pp. 11 and 13.

[65] Ibid., p. 30.

[66] Ibid., p. 17. It is interesting that the S.M.A. subcommittee failed to perceive that at least one syllabus, Armstrong's scheme as presented to the B.A.A.S. in 1889, was carefully constructed on explicitly stated principles. This syllabus was intended for a wider age and ability range than the syllabus incorporated in *The Teaching of General Science*.

[67] Ibid., p. 18.

[68] Ibid., p. 13.

[69] Ibid., p. 18.

[70] Ibid., pp. 19–20.

[71] Ibid., p. 20.

[72] Ibid., p. 22. Faraday's 'Chemical History of a Candle' was quoted as an outstanding example of the topic method of teaching.

[73] Ibid., p. 23.

[74] Ibid., p. 27.

[75] Layton, D., *Science for the People*, 1973, especially Chapter 5.

[76] S.M.A., *The Teaching of General Science, Part II*, 1938, p. 3.

[77] See, e.g., *S.S.R.*, vol. XIX, no. 73, 1937, p. 136, where C. L. Bryant discusses the question of length in reply to comment by the A.W.S.T.

[78] *S.S.R.*, vol. XIX, no. 74, 1937, p. 299 and ibid., vol. XVIII, no. 72, 1937, p. 473 and 594.

[79] *S.S.R.*, vol. XVIII, no. 72, 1937, p. 595.

[80] *The Teaching of General Science, Part II,* 1938, p. 19.

[81] Ibid., Part I, 1936, p. 35.

[82] Ibid., Part II, 1938, p. 11.

[83] Ibid., Part I, 1936, p. 21.

[84] Ibid., Part II, 1938, pp. 20 and 22.

[85] *S.S.R.*, vol. XIX, no. 73, 1937, pp. 134–5.

[86] *Report of the Consultative Committee on Secondary Education With Special Reference to Grammar and Technical High Schools,* HMSO, 1938; hereafter referred to as *Spens Report*.

[87] *The Teaching of General Science, Part II*, 1938, p. vii.

[88] *Spens Report*, p. 244.

[89] Bryant, C. L., 'Science and the Spens Report', *S.S.R.*, vol. XXI, no. 82, 1939, p. 783.

[90] *Spens Report*, p. 165.

[91] Ibid., p. 250.

[92] Ibid., p. 173.

[93] *S.S.R.*, vol. XXI, no. 82, 1939, p. 787. There was more to the Spens Report than a mere 'literary bias'. Citizenship, fostered by English and related subjects, especially history, was a very important issue although the Committee rejected the teaching of 'citizenship' itself as a subject in the timetable. See Chapter 4, p. 134.

[94] *Spens Report*, p. 174.

[95] *S.S.R.*, vol. XXI, no. 82, 1939, p. 787.

[96] *Spens Report*, p. 250.

[97] Report of the Committee of the S.S.E.C. appointed in 1941, *Curriculum and Examinations in Secondary Schools*, HMSO, 1943.

[98] Ibid., p. 109.

[99] Ibid., p. 110.

[100] For example, should elements of geology, astronomy, meteorology be included in a General Science Course? The S.M.A. subcommittee and the Spens Committee differed on this point. The Norwood Committee found itself attracted by the old-fashioned title 'physiography' and by much that this implied.

[101] 78,856 in 1936 and 79,085 in 1942. Between 1936 and 1942, the physics and biology entries increased by 3 per cent and 6 per cent respectively. Figures from Board of Education, *Annual Reports*.

[102] *S.S.R.*, vol. XXV, no. 96, 1944, p. 255.

[103] Ibid., p. 241. Forty per cent of boys' schools and 38 per cent of coeducational schools.

The data in this and the ensuing paragraph are taken from the investigation conducted by Marchant and reported in this issue of the *S.S.R.*

[104] Board of Education, *Memorandum on the Teaching of Science in Senior Schools*, Educational Pamphlet, no. 89, HMSO, 1932. In addition to the questionnaire data, the Memorandum was based upon the visit of H.M.I.s to a smaller sample of eighty schools. It should be noted that a substantial minority (134 out of 308) of central schools entered at least some of their pupils for School Certificate examinations. Ibid., p. 8.

[105] Ibid., p. 7–8.

[106] Ibid., p. 10.

[107] Ibid., p. 15.

[108] Ibid., pp. 17–20.

[109] L.C.C., *Senior Schools: Memoranda on the Curriculum*, no. 1, *Science*, 1933, p. 5.

[110] London Teachers' Association, *The Teaching of Science in Senior Schools*, Pamphlet no. 9, 1936, p. 17.

[111] S.M.A., *Report on The Teaching of General Science*, 1950, pp. 6–7.

[112] The raising of the school leaving age was postponed until 1947 and the proposal to establish county colleges has not been implemented.

[113] *The Public Schools and the General Educational System*, HMSO, 1944.

[114] *Teachers and Youth Leaders*, HMSO, 1944.

[115] S.M.A., *Report on the Teaching of General Science*, 1950, p. 1.

[116] Ibid., pp. 3–4.

[117] S.M.A., *Secondary Modern Science Teaching*, Part I, 1953, Part II, 1957.

[118] Bull, M., *An Investigation into the Teaching of Science in Secondary Grammar Schools*, 1949. Bull's analysis was based on replies to questionnaires sent to all the grammar schools in five northern counties and to 'arbitrarily selected' schools elsewhere in England and Wales. The Tables are taken from Bull's report.

[119] Data from *Education in 1951, etc.,* Annual Reports and Statistics of the Ministry of Education.

[120] A number of other 'combined science' syllabuses remained available to the schools, e.g. 'physics with chemistry' and some 'new' schemes were also devised such as 'physical science'.

[121] Pingriff, G. N., Science for All – Some Criticisms. *S.S.R.*, vol. II, no. 8, 1921, pp. 323–6.

[122] S.M.A., *Report on the Teaching of General Science*, 1950, p. 17.

[123] Connell, L., James, W. S., General Science Today, *S.S.R.*, vol. XXXIX, no. 138, 1958, p. 280.

[124] Lauwerys, J. A., General Science, *S.S.R.*, vol. XVIII, no. 72, June 1937, p. 471. At this time, Lauwerys was lecturer and tutor in the methods of science at the University of London Institute of Education. He was an advocate of biology teaching in the secondary schools and was actively involved with the Committee (later Council) for Curriculum Reform in the early years of the Second World War. He eventually became Professor of Comparative Education in the University of London. He has acknowledged the influence of T. P. Nunn, the Director of the London Institute, on the development of his educational and philosophical ideas. See Lauwerys, J. A., *Education and Biology*, 1934, p. ix.

[125] Shelton, H. S., Essay-review of General Science, *S.S.R.*, vol. XIV, no. 56, 1933, p. 459.

[126] Shelton, H. S., *The Theory and Practice of General Science*, 1939, p. 29.

[127] For a list of some of these articles, see ibid., Preface, pp. v and vi.

[128] S.M.A., *The Teaching of General Science*, 1936, p. 2.

[129] Shelton, H. S., op. cit., 1939, p. 118.

[130] E.g. ibid., p. 35. 'The central idea of general science is that you are teaching *science*, not specialised subjects.' Shelton was also critical of the publicity given to the S.M.A. scheme, by a conference held at the Institute of Education, opened by the President of the Royal Society in the presence of other 'prominent men of science'. In Shelton's view, whatever the merits of the S.M.A. subcommittee in devising curricula, they understood 'thoroughly well the arts of propaganda'. Ibid., p. 33.

[131] *S.S.R.*, vol. XXIV, no. 92, 1942, p. 97. The Norwood Committee issued a questionnaire and the replies of the S.M.A. and of the A.W.S.T. are given separately.

[132] Shelton, H. S., op. cit., 1939, p. 33. Shelton was referring to the 1936 Report, written by Lauwerys whose 'literary effort' disguised this 'small relation'. The S.M.A. statement also embodies a different conception of general science from that eventually recommended by the Norwood Committee, i.e., 'an elementary course ... (in which) the traditional divisions' ... did not arise. Board of Education, *Report of the S.S.E.C.*, HMSO, 1941, p. 108.

[133] Lauwerys, among others, maintained that general science was not an attempt simply 'to widen the content of school science courses' but rather 'an attempt to alter the spirit' in which they were tackled. *S.S.R.*, vol. XVIII, no. 72, 1937, p. 467. Lauwerys was also able to press for the teaching of general science via the Council for Curriculum Reform of which he became Chairman in January 1943. Council for Curriculum Reform, *The Content of Education*, 1945, Chapter IX.

[134] S.M.A., *The Teaching of General Science*, Part I, 1936, p. 23.

[135] S.M.A., *The Teaching of General Science*, Part I, 1936, p. 23.

[136] Ibid., p. 24.

[137] Shelton, H. S., op. cit., 1939, p. 32, describes this as a 'cryptic remark, worthy of Captain Bunsby'.

[138] Nuffield Foundation Science Teaching Project, *Progress Report*, October 1964, p. 5.

[139] The S.M.A. subcommittee discussed the effect of 'professionalism in knowledge' upon school science in its 1938 Report. The term is, of course, Whitehead's. See S.M.A., *The Teaching of General Science,* Part II, 1938, pp. 7–9, and Whitehead, A. N., *Science and the Modern World*, 1925, pp. 244–5.

[140] Council for Curriculum Reform, *The Content of Education*, 1945, p. 141. The Council contrasted 'recognition' knowledge with 'active' or 'utilisable' knowledge of science. The amount of this latter knowledge required was 'really quite small'.

[141] Bradley, J., General Science, *S.S.R.*, vol. XVIII, no. 70, 1936, p. 182.

[142] Smithells, A., School and University Science, *S.S.R.*, vol. V, no. 19, 1924, p. 133.

[143] S.M.A., *The Teaching of General Science,* Part II, 1938, p. 8.

[144] S.M.A., *The Teaching of General Science,* Part I, 1936, p. 18. The subcommittee, however, did not seem to realise the basis of the 'dilemma' posed by the Council of the Institute and denied that it was necessary to choose between 'teaching useful facts' and 'educating in generalisations'. Ibid, Part II, 1938, p. 18.

[145] Marchant, D. H. J., An Inquiry into the Present Position of Science in Secondary Schools (August 1943), *S.S.R.*, vol. XXV, no. 96, 1944, p. 245.

[146] There was no real evidence to support this assumption and Christopher eventually showed it to be groundless. Christopher, R., *The Effectiveness of General Science as a Preparation for Sixth-Form Studies* ... M.Ed. Thesis, Manchester, 1953. None the less, schools acted on this assumption, some requiring general science pupils to spend three rather than the usual two years preparing for H.S.C. examinations in science. Marchant (ibid.) reported that 113 out of 152 schools regarded general science as a less satisfactory pre-sixth-form course for science specialists than any two of the three principal sciences.

[147] S.M.A., *The Teaching of General Science*, Part II, 1938, p. 7.

[148] 'If matriculation provided the bricks with which this structure of conservatism and narrowness was built, the University scholarship was the keystone which locked it immovably.' Ibid., p. 5.

[149] *The Education of the Adolescent*, HMSO, 1926, p. 222 et seq.

[150] Board of Education, *Handbook of Suggestions for Teachers ...* , HMSO, 1927, p. 218. See also the 1937 edition.

[151] Board of Education, Educational Pamphlet, no. 89, 1932, HMSO, p. 64.

[152] The data in the Tables are taken from Edwards, A. D., *The Changing Sixth Form in the Twentieth Century*, 1970, pp. 37–8; U.G.C., *Annual Returns from Universities and University Colleges in Receipt of Treasury Grant* and U.G.C., *University Development from 1935 to 1947*.

[153] Lord President of the Council, *Scientific Manpower*, HMSO, 1946. The membership of the Committee included P. M. S. Blackett, G. Crowther, S. Zuckerman and C. P. Snow.

[154] Ministry of Education, *Higher Technological Education*, HMSO, 1945.

[155] For example, the recommended Diploma in Technology was not introduced for another decade.

[156] *Technical Education*, HMSO, 1956.

[157] Advisory Council on Scientific Policy, *Annual Report*, 1960–1, HMSO, 1962, and Committee on Manpower Statistics, *Report*.

[158] Argles, M., *South Kensington to Robbins*, 1964, p. 121.

[159] It was also the period of the 'two cultures', a term introduced by C. P. Snow in the Rede Lectures of 1959; *The Two Cultures and the Scientific Revolution*.

[160] Edwards, A. D., op. cit., Ch. 4, contains a detailed account of 'The Explosion in Sixth-Form Numbers'.

[161] Ibid., p. 71.

[162] Stevens, F., *The Living Tradition*, 1960, pp. 79–80.

[163] Secondary modern schools were much more seriously affected than the grammar schools by the shortage of qualified science teachers; see Chapter 6.

[164] A similar uncertainty has been evident in some employers' reactions to 'physics-with-chemistry'. In addition, a general science qualification has sometimes failed to allow exemption from some course requirements where such exemption would have been granted for physics or chemistry. See General Science on Trial – Pooling of Ignorance, *T.E.S.*, 28 September 1956, p. 1171 and Marchant, D. H. J., op. cit., p. 250.

[165] Connell, L., James, W. S., op. cit., p. 285.

[166] A draft policy statement, issued in 1957 for discussion amongst members of the Association, suggested that the introductory phase (eleven to thirteen years) of a secondary school science course be taught on a topic basis by one teacher. For a comment on this, see *S.S.R.*, vol. XXXIX, no. 138, 1958, p. 323.

[167] The S.M.A. produced three suggested syllabuses for physics, chemistry and biology in the early 1960s, but these were for use in *grammar* schools.

[168] The Biological Sciences and Medicine escaped this disillusionment, as did the various social sciences.

[169] Greenwood, N., *Ed. in Chem.*, vol. 9, no. 1, January 1972, p. 36.

4
The Biological Sciences

During the latter half of the nineteenth century, the biological sciences were represented in the schools by botany and, to a lesser extent, by zoology, biology, the agricultural and horticultural sciences and by animal physiology. The latter was included in the list of subjects approved by the Department of Science and Art as early as 1861, principally as a result of the pioneering efforts of George Combe, the phrenologist.[1] His pamphlet, *On Teaching Physiology and its Applications in Common Schools*, published in 1857, shows that Combe was concerned to teach pupils the 'structure, functions and relations' of the 'various organs of the human body on which health and life depend', together with the 'causes of good and bad health and the means that should be used in ... daily habits to secure the one and avoid the other'.[2] The 'various organs' excluded those concerned with reproduction and, as a further precaution against alienating public opinion, Combe was careful to refer always to animal rather than to human physiology. In common with other contemporary Utilitarians, Combe believed that the widespread introduction of 'animal' physiology into the curricula of the public elementary schools would help to improve the health of the industrial classes and hence to secure their greater happiness and usefulness to society. Although he was a keen supporter of the movement to develop a national system of secular schools, Combe 'did not hesitate' to teach classes in such schools that it was 'their duty towards God to preserve the health of the bodies which God had given them'.[3] By obviating the more predictable objections to the teaching of physiology and by admitting the religious element into his lessons, Combe was able to overcome the opposition expected from the churches and his schemes of work exerted a considerable influence on the work done for the Department of Science and Art examinations throughout the remainder of the century.

Although botany had long been taught as an ancillary subject to medicine,[4] its more general educational importance and popularity in schools in the latter half of the nineteenth century owed much to the Rev. J. S. Henslow, Regius Professor of Botany at Cambridge from 1827 to 1861. Like most contemporary botanists, Henslow's professional interest was systematic botany: the classification of plants in orders based upon their structures. In 1837, Henslow assumed responsibility for the parish of Hitcham in Suffolk and here, from 1853 onwards, he taught botany to the village children attending the National school. Each Monday afternoon, pupils conducted floral dissections and completed formidable floral schedules, in order to identify the specimens which Henslow provided. The work was completed by an 'instructional lecture' based upon preserved plant material from the school herbarium, in which Henslow reviewed the 'geographical distribution, structural peculiarities and historical, scriptural and economic connections'[5] of the species under consideration. For Henslow, the educational claims of systematic botany rested on the fact that it provided an excellent means of developing the powers of observation and logical thought and of 'improving the intellectual and moral status of the pupils'.[6] Many of the witnesses before the Clarendon Commission in 1864 expressed support for this view. Richard Owen, F.R.S., spoke of the power of botany to 'bring out the faculties of classification, order and method',[7] and W. B. Carpenter, another Fellow of the Royal Society, referred to the value of the subject in 'training the mind in the observation of complex phenomena'.[8]

Although Henslow's ideas were developed within the context of elementary education in a rural community, he was of the opinion that practical botany was suitable for the education of all classes of society and it was in the public and 'first-grade' schools that his ideas gained wider acceptance after his death in 1861. The rise in the fortunes of systematic botany in these schools was due largely to the efforts of Wilson, Temple[9] and Tyndall and of Huxley, who, more than any other single person, championed the biological sciences as instruments of education. Also of importance was Daniel Oliver, Keeper of the Herbarium and Library at Kew and Professor of Botany at University College, London. It was Oliver who edited and prefaced the manuscript of a book which Henslow had left unfinished at his death. By the time of the Devonshire Commission, *Lessons in Elementary Botany* was 'widely used' in the public and first-grade schools and, by 1900, it had sold 67,000 copies.[10]

In the hands of less than inspiring teachers, important elements of Henslow's methods were subsequently misapplied or ignored. As early as 1868, Wilson recorded[11] that boys were sometimes told to get a botany text and learn the details of the classification of plants directly from it. This practice eventually became so widespread that, by 1900, the teaching of systematic botany had largely degenerated to become a particular form of booklearning.[12] In many girls' schools, the status of botany was reduced to that of a mere accomplishment.[13] Not surprisingly, the Examiners appointed by the Department of Science and Art and by the Cambridge Local Examinations Board were persistent in their criticism of the tendency of the schools to neglect practical botanical studies.[14]

Between Henslow's death and the end of the century, there were several important developments within the science of botany itself. In particular, the development of anatomical, morphological and physiological studies of plants meant that botany could no longer be equated with systematic, taxonomic exercises. There was something of a struggle between the systematic and physiological botanists which the latter won, leaving the old school to complain that the new generation of botanists did not know their plants.[15] It was Huxley who attempted to break the stranglehold of systematic botany on school curricula by pioneering the introduction of plant anatomy, morphology and physiology into botany syllabuses. He devised the 'type' system of study and extended the scheme of work to include non-flowering as well as flowering plants.

The direction of change is recorded in J. D. Hooker's *Botany Science Primer*, published in 1876, and intended for students following the syllabuses of the Department of Science and Art. Hooker, who was Henslow's son-in-law, commented[16] that 'Botany is now also an experimental science' and included in the primer simple demonstrations intended to illustrate such phenomena as respiration, transpiration, germination and heliotropism. However, apart from some work at senior level, Huxley's ideas were not widely adopted by the public and first-grade schools, even by the end of the century.

The position of zoology in the schools during the latter half of the nineteenth century shows a number of parallels with that of botany. The subject was included in the examination schedule of the Department of Science and Art in 1861 and the syllabus, intended to foster the development of orderly and systematic habits of thought, was firmly based on taxonomic considerations, an emphasis characteristic of other zoology syllabuses of the period.[17] As with botany, it was Huxley who pressed for the inclusion of physiological and morphological features within zoology syllabuses and who sought to provide new content and direction for the teaching of the subject. He condemned the exclusive attention given to taxonomy, argued persuasively for the practical study of selected types and stressed the importance of demonstration and of dissection conducted by the pupils themselves. Under Huxley's influence, the syllabuses and examinations of the Department of Science and Art encouraged the new approach to zoology teaching and other Examining Authorities eventually followed the example of South Kensington, e.g. the University of London in 1877 for its First B.Sc. and Preliminary examinations, and, in the same year, the Oxford and Cambridge Schools Examination Board for its Higher Certificate.

It was in the senior classes of the public and first-grade schools that Huxley's ideas on zoology teaching were received most favourably. At the Leys School, a prize was awarded for physiology in 1884 and, by 1891, a small class carried out dissections, the cutting and staining of sections and microscopy exercises as part of the preparation for the London Intermediate B.Sc. Examination. It was a class of some distinction, including Barcroft, Bainbridge and Henry Dale among its members.[18] Charterhouse began to teach zoology in 1890, although boys taught 'out of school' had obtained scholarships in physiology to the universities in the 1870s. In other schools, where Huxley's influence was somewhat attenuated, the zoology teaching was often confined to the study of the few selected types required by the examination syllabuses. Pupils thus gained little or no insight into the variety and distribution of species within the animal kingdom. Moreover, practical methods of studying even the 'type' animal were all too often ignored. The Examiners of the Cambridge Local Examinations Board noted[19] in 1884, that, while candidates in general were 'able to write pages of classification of the animal kingdom from third-rate textbooks', hardly a single candidate had 'any knowledge even of the external characteristics of a frog or a leech'. In 1901, the Examiners returned to the same theme:

It does not appear to have been realised that without careful observation and dissection of well chosen 'types', a satisfactory study of zoology is impossible.[20]

Zoology was a much less popular examination subject with the schools than either botany or physiology (see Tables 4.1 and 4.2), and it was not included in the list of 'specific subjects' which formed part of the Code governing the curricula of public elementary schools[21] after 1870. Because of the small

Table 4.1   Numbers of Candidates Entering for Examinations in Biological Sciences under the Regulations of the Department of Science and Art, 1863–98

Year	Animal Physiology	Botany	Zoology	General Biology	Principles of Agriculture	Hygiene
1863	343	210	41	–	–	–
1873	6,834	1,194	181	–	–	–
1883	6,191	2,043	–	210	5,171	–
1893	8,015	3,309	92	183	6,046	6,048
1898	5,486*	2,911	69	258	975	7,557

* Called 'Human Physiology'

Table 4.2   Numbers Entering Examinations in the Biological Sciences held by the Cambridge University Local Examinations Board, 1879–1900 (Midsummer Figures Only)

Year	Botany				Zoology				Physiol. & Hygiene				Biology	
	Junior		Senior		Junior		Senior		Junior		Senior		Senior	
	B	G	B	G	B	G	B	G	B	G	B	G	B	G
1878	45	237	9	179	75	147	14	79	–	–	–	–	–	–
1880	76	277	13	189	118	157	32	108	–	–	–	–	–	–
1884	60	364	11	219	108	102	11	61	–	–	–	–	9	195
1890	25	569	2	305	26	62	3	39	–	–	–	–	–	–
1895	26	612	15	242	35	25	8	19	42	289	7	97	–	–
1900	24	725	2	282	22	3	1	6	95	737	22	205	–	–

demand for zoology teaching in the schools, the celebrated Elementary Science Series of class-books published by Macmillan did not include a volume on zoology although there were several affined texts, notably Huxley's *Lessons in Elementary Physiology*. The book corresponding to Hooker's botany primer was Andrew Wilson's *Zoology*, published in 1877 as one of Chambers' *Elementary Science Manuals* and intended for students preparing for the 'elementary stage of the zoology section of the Science and Art Examinations'.[22] The already slender popularity of zoology as an examination subject declined after about 1880, perhaps because of the association of zoology with the more controversial issues arising from Darwin's *Origin of Species* (1859) and his *Descent of Man*, published in 1871. The decline may also have been indicative of a mounting antagonism to the ideas of Huxley who had become well-known, even notorious, as an agnostic, evolutionist and ardent supporter of vivisection.[23] Huxley's principal achievement was, however, to endure; the study of animal life was recognised as a 'natural and respectable pursuit of the young and worthy of encouragement, not derision'.[24]

In the mid-nineteenth century, the work of Schleiden, Schwann, Schultze and von Mohl led to a realisation of the cellular, protoplasmic nature of life common to plants and animals. In response to this development and to his own continuing dissatisfaction with the teaching of botany and zoology in the schools, Huxley encouraged the schools to introduce the new subject of biology into their curricula. In 1874, biology, 'in which the former subjects of Zoology, Vegetable Anatomy and Physiology were absorbed',[25] was added to the list of subjects approved for grant-earning purposes under the Regulations of the Department of Science and Art. Despite the summer courses arranged for teachers and the publication[26] of *A Course of Practical Instruction in Elementary Biology* in 1875, the new subject was not an immediate success. The Cambridge Local Examinations Board added biology to its schedule for the Senior Certificate in 1884 but abandoned the examination following the poor performance by the candidates.[27] The University of London introduced biology papers into the First B.Sc. and Preliminary Examinations in 1880, but botanical and zoological topics were examined separately. In 1900, the title of the examination paper was changed from 'General Biology' to 'Zoology and Botany' and, in the following year, separate and alternative papers were set. The Oxford and Cambridge Joint Board included Elementary Biology as an optional subject in the schedule for its Higher Certificate in 1885, but there were only four candidates. Eton College, where Huxley was a governor, introduced a biology course in 1881, but it 'did not remain in favour very long'.[28] None the less, as with botany and zoology, it was the public and first-grade schools which were most receptive to Huxley's 'life science'. Elsewhere, biology was either not taught or was presented in a manner unlikely to realise Huxley's intention 'to get into the young mind some notion of what life is'.[29]

Some biological science was included within the syllabuses of subjects such as agriculture and horticulture. 'Principles of Agriculture' became a grant-earning subject under the Regulations of the Department of Science and Art in 1875, and the scheme of work included aspects of plant nutrition and structure, plant and animal breeding and animal physiology. Agriculture was also introduced into the Public Elementary School Code in 1882, becoming an alternative 'class' subject in 1890. Horticulture gained a similar status in 1894, with a scheme of work which included reference to structural, physiological and economic botany.

During the last decade or so of the nineteenth century, there were a number of attempts to stimulate the teaching of agricultural science. In 1889, the year following the County Councils Act, a Board of Agriculture was established with the responsibility of administering Government grants[30] for agricultural education. Almost all of this money was used to create grant-aided centres in association with universities and colleges. However, some of these institutions of higher education recognised the importance of stimulating agricultural studies in schools and organised a number of classes and vacation courses for school teachers.[31] These activities continued well into the twentieth century. In 1907–8, for example, staff of the University of Leeds delivered over 600 lectures, mostly extra-mural, on aspects of farming, gardening, farriery, dairying and poultry keeping and were involved in the supervision of demonstration plots and gardens attached to both day and evening schools. In addition, they provided Saturday classes for teachers.[32] In-service activities of this kind were particularly useful during the 1890s when Technical Instruction Committees were able to use 'Whisky Money' to encourage the teaching of agricultural subjects.

In 1899, an Agricultural Education Committee was established to secure 'systematic and efficient instruction ... in agricultural subjects' and to diffuse 'among the agricultural classes, a more thorough appreciation of the advantages of instruction bearing ... upon their industry'.[33] These narrowly economic considerations, prompted by a second ruinous collapse of the British agricultural industry,[34] were buttressed by reference to other and more educationally attuned arguments, such as 'an appreciation of nature', mental training or even moral improvement. An interest in nature, it was claimed, 'would not only make a better worker of the agriculturist'; it would 'strengthen him morally against, at any rate the lower, attractions of town life',[35] a reference to the contemporary concern about the continuing drift of population from the land into the urban areas.[36]

The new Board of Education responded to this complex of sentiments in 1900 with a Circular, urging that education in the village school be made 'more consonant with the environment of the scholars' than was 'usually the case',[37] and, in 1901–2, with specimen courses of nature study, gardening and rural economy.[38] In 1905, the Board's Regulations made nature study a compulsory part of the curriculum of the public elementary school and, in the following years, 'Suggestions' were offered for schemes of work in the new subject.

The teaching of nature study was also encouraged by the School Nature Study Union, an organisation founded in 1903 on the strength of the enthusiasm aroused by a fortnight-long Nature Study Exhibition held a few months earlier in Regent's Park. The Union used its journal, School Nature Study, to emphasise the importance and educational value of studying plants and animals in their natural surroundings and to provide ideas for the teaching of a subject regarded by the British Association as 'particularly suited' to elementary schools.[39]

Plates 1–4 illustrate some of the activities associated with nature study in the schools in the early years of the present century. Unfortunately, much of the work done under the guise of nature study seems to have been highly contrived

Plate 1   One of the exhibits at the Nature Study Exhibition held in Regent's Park, London, 1902

Plate 2   Pupils working in a school garden, 1906

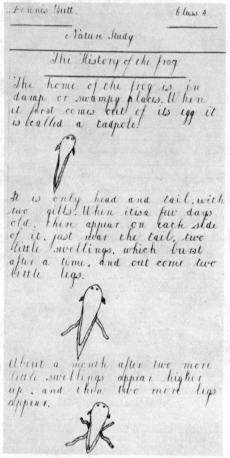

Plate 3 Part of a folio of work presented in 1907

and often invested with an excess of 'soggy idealism'.[40] Rather than undertake a systematic, long-term, scientific study of the fauna, flora or ecology of a particular locality, pupils watched and tended twigs, seeds and tadpoles in the classroom or had these pointed out to them on specially arranged rambles. Classes were usually too large to allow any genuine experimental work and, as with the earlier object lessons, teachers often attempted to cover too many topics, some of which were unseasonal or otherwise unsuitable for discussion.[41] In addition, nature study was often more a means of religious or moral instruction rather than an introduction to the scientific study of the natural world. Even school gardening easily degenerated into the 'mere employment of cheap child labour'.

Nevertheless, encouraged by the Board of Education, the British Association and the School Nature Study Union, fostered by the new 'naturalist' mood in education,[42] nourished by the nature notes and magazines of a popular

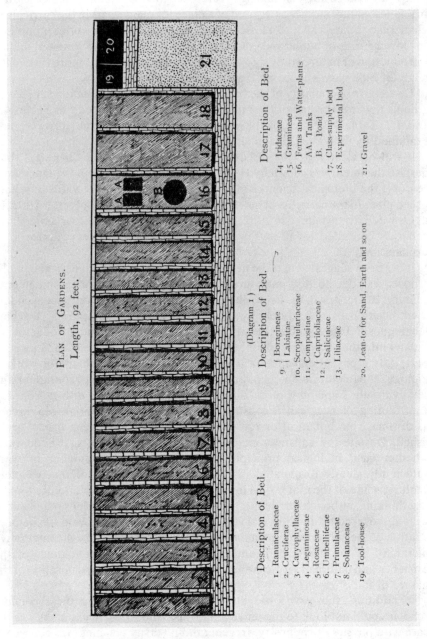

PLAN OF GARDENS.
Length, 92 feet.

(Diagram 1)

Description of Bed.

1. Ranunculaceae
2. Cruciferae
3. Caryophyllaceae
4. Leguminosae
5. Rosaceae
6. Umbelliferae
7. Primulaceae
8. Solanaceae

19. Tool-house

Description of Bed.

9. { Boragineae
   { Labiatae
10. Scrophulariaceae
11. Compositae
12. { Caprifoliaceae
    { Salicineae
13. Liliaceae

20. Lean-to for Sand, Earth and so on

Description of Bed.

14. Iridaceae
15. Gramineae
16. Ferns and Water-plants
    AA. Tanks
    B. Pond
17. Class-supply bed
18. Experimental bed

21. Gravel

Plate 4 Plan of an educational garden which won a silver medal at a Home
Counties Nature Study Exhibition, 1903

press[43] and increasingly sustained by reference to T. P. Nunn's 'wonder' motive in science, nature study was assured of a place for many years in the curricula of elementary schools and, to a lesser extent, in the schemes of work for pupils in the lower forms of public and grammar schools. Only rarely, however, did the introduction of nature study into a secondary school lead to a more systematic study of biological science by the more senior classes.

The relative popularity of the biological sciences as examination subjects in schools towards the end of the nineteenth century is indicated[44] in Tables 4.1 and 4.2. Table 4.3[45] records the years in which biological subjects were first examined by individual Examination Boards.

It will be clear from the discussion of general science in Chapter 3 that, despite the initiatives shown by Henslow, Huxley and others in the nineteenth century, the biological sciences made only slow progress[46] towards an established place in the curricula of most public and secondary schools after 1900. If, as Oswald Latter claimed in 1907, the right of biology 'to rank as a subject' was generally conceded and its merits recognised, this slow progress calls for some explanation.

It has been suggested that the neglect of biology by the secondary and public schools was due to the 'immaturity' of biological science in the nineteenth century. Being 'first in the field', physics and chemistry were able to consolidate their position in the schools by the development of appropriate teaching techniques.[47] This argument clearly cannot be applied[48] to the introduction of botany into the secondary school curriculum and, in the case of biology is, at best, only a partial explanation. However, a satisfactory scheme of work in biology, capable of involving pupils in both observation and experiment and self-evidently something more than an amalgam of topics drawn from the contributing sciences, can be constructed only after the appropriate biological – as distinct from botanical or zoological – principles have been firmly established. Despite the advances made in the nineteenth century, it is doubtful whether such biological principles existed in sufficient number or were sufficiently clearly formulated in 1900. At the beginning of the twentieth century, some of the major developments which were to revolutionise biological thinking, although imminent, had not yet occurred. Mendel's publications were discovered by de Vries in 1900. Almost contemporary were the demonstration of the existence of hormones (1903), 'the revelation of the integrative hierarchy of the nervous system' (c. 1902), and the 'first inklings of the existence and nature of viruses which necessarily led to a reconsideration of the nature of life'.[49]

In addition, those who sought to introduce biology into the secondary schools could not look to the universities for a 'model curriculum', as was the case with physics or chemistry. In general, university teaching was concerned with such specialisms as botany, zoology, forestry, biochemistry, genetics and physiology. The trend was towards increased specialisation and fragmentation of these life sciences rather than towards their consolidation and integration. After an uneasy accommodation during most of the last quarter of the nineteenth century, separate zoology and botany sections were created within

Table 4.3 Examination Boards Examining Biological Subjects by 1925 and Dates of Introduction of the Relevant Examinations (those in brackets were obsolete by 1925)

P = May also be offered in Preliminary or Matriculation
G = Group Subject
M = Exempts from First M.B. (in certain cases)
* = Date of introduction not available
S = Subsidiary Subject
I = Exempts from Inter Science (in certain cases)

Board	Lower Certificate						School Certificate				Higher Certificate					
	Botany	Natural History	Hygiene	Zoology	Botany	General or Elementary Science	Botany	Zoology or Natural History	Biology or Natural History	General or Elementary Sci.	Hygiene	Agric.	Botany	Zoology	Biology	General or Elementary Sci.
Oxford and Cambridge Joint	1910					1923	1915			1921			1875 GSM	1918 GM	1885 GSM	1918 GS
Oxford Local	1888	(1858)				1914	1884		(1858)	1917	1908	1916	1918 GS	GS	1924 GS	GS
Cambridge Local	1858		1895	(1858–1906)	1907		1858	1858	(1883–4)		1895	1902	1918 GS	1918 G	1923 G	GS
London	1905						1905 P	1905 P	1925		1906		1906 GSI	1906 GSI	1919 GS	GS
Northern							1918 P1905	1918 P1905					1918 GSMI	1918 GSMI	1924 GM	
Bristol							1917 P						1920 GI	1920 GI	1920 GM	
Durham							1917	1917	1924				1918 GI	1918 GI	1924 GM	GS
Central Welsh	* P						* P	*	*		*	*	GI	GI	GM	S

the British Association in 1895. When L. C. Miall retired from the chair of biology at Leeds in 1906, separate zoology and botany departments were created,[50] and this was followed by more specialised developments, e.g. of experimental plant physiology from 1911 and of a marine biological laboratory in conjunction with the University of Sheffield from 1912.

It was also by no means clear on what grounds the case for including biology in the curricula of secondary schools should rest. Henslow's arguments for botany and Huxley's claims for biology presumed a faculty psychology which, as noted in Chapter 2, was collapsing under an onslaught from the Herbartians. Moreover, if, as Huxley claimed,[51] no clear distinction could be admitted between the physical and biological sciences on the grounds of method and the primary aim of the science teacher was to teach scientific method, biology virtually ceased to have any educational advantage over physics or chemistry. In some respects, biology was often regarded as a less satisfactory vehicle for a scientific education than the physical sciences, even by those who advocated its introduction into the schools. As Oswald Latter admitted in 1907, biology lacked 'the advantage of physics and chemistry in providing a training in experiment, in precision and in exact reasoning'.[52] As such, it could not hope to be accommodated easily within a curriculum which still gave considerable emphasis to precise and exact measurement, 'the basis of all true science'.[53] While the introduction of experimental physiology into school biology courses helped to overcome this disadvantage, such a development seemed to indicate that pupils should study physics and chemistry *before* undertaking a systematic course in biology. Huxley had recognised this point as early as 1854, claiming that the systematic teaching of biology could not 'be attempted with success' until the student had 'attained to a certain knowledge of physics and chemistry'.[54] His view seems to have been borne out by subsequent experience. In 1900, the Chief Inspector of Schools for the Southern and Eastern Divisions of England reported that several girls' schools which had attempted to 'frame' their science courses on a scheme of work involving botany, physiology and biology had encountered difficulties because of the failure to base such work on a 'sound foundation of physics and chemistry in the first two years'.[55]

Like zoology, biology suffered from the view that dissection was an unsuitable task for the majority of pupils and particularly so for girls.[56] This objection almost certainly exaggerated the importance of dissection in the teaching of school biology but it was of particular significance at a time when the anti-vivisectionist cause was strong and the general question of the use of animals for the purposes of teaching or experiment was a matter of vigorous and often acrimonious public debate.[57] In so far as secondary school biology was identified with pre-medical education and the medical schools were regarded as sympathetic to vivisection, opposition to the more general teaching of biology in the secondary schools was likely to be strong.

The objection to dissection was sometimes pressed as part of a more general claim that anatomy and physiology were 'nasty' even 'indecent' subjects, unfit for the education of boys and girls at school. In these instances, the real point at issue, as Latter commented in 1907, could often be stated much more simply:

It is the processes of reproduction to which objection is made.[58]

The force of this objection is indicated by the fact that some objectors appeared to be willing to withdraw their opposition to the teaching of zoology or biology at school if these parts of the subject were omitted.

The close association of secondary school biology with medical education at the beginning of this century is significant in another respect. It indicates the restricted career opportunities available to those with biological qualifications and the consequent lack of incentive to extend the teaching of secondary school biology beyond that provided for intending medical students. The establishment of a number of National Institutes, such as that for Dairy Research at Reading in 1912, created a small number of specialised opportunities in the field of agriculture but, in the early twentieth century, those industries which were eventually to employ significant numbers of bacteriologists, biochemists, mycologists, plant or animal pathologists, virologists, microbiologists, parasitologists or nutritionists, together with their supporting technical staff, barely existed. As an example, the British pharmaceutical industry underwent a major expansion, based upon scientific research, only after the discovery of the first sulpha drug in 1935 and the subsequent isolation and clinical use of penicillin.[59]

The later growth of professional employment in the field of biology, compared with chemistry or physics, is illustrated by the dates at which the relevant professional institutions as distinct from learned societies, were founded. Whereas the academic interests of botanists had been institutionalised in the Linnaean (1788) and Botanical (1836) Societies before the corresponding societies were established for chemistry (1841) and physics (1874), the Institute of Biology was not set up until 1950, almost three-quarters of a century after the foundation of the Institute of Chemistry in 1877.

By the time the Thomson Committee reported in 1918, biology in boys' secondary schools was represented almost exclusively by nature study, taught to the lower forms, and by botany and zoology taught to the few senior pupils intending to study medicine. Only in a 'very few boys' schools' was there any 'systematic attempt to give a knowledge of the main facts of the life of plants and animals'.[60] In the secondary schools for girls, botany was the dominant and occasionally, the only, science taught, although it was becoming 'more and more common' to treat the plant as a living organism rather than as a herbarium specimen to be classified. The 'physiology of the plant and its relation to its surroundings' had become more important than 'the identification of wild flowers'.[61] In the public elementary schools, the teaching of biological science was usually confined to nature study. While some of this work was 'quite admirable', much of it was worthless. It was too commonly neither 'nature' nor 'study',[62] defects which the Thomson Committee attributed to the low standard of 'acquirement in Elementary Science of those trained for Elementary school work'.[63]

Although the Thomson Committee stressed that 'some knowledge of the main facts of the life of plants and animals should form a regular part of the teaching in every secondary school,'[64] its Report fell short of recommending the introduction of a systematic course in biology into the curricula for all pupils up to the age of sixteen in these schools:

> The science work ... should ... include besides Physics and Chemistry, some study of plant and animal life.[65]

'Some study' was defined as the 'main anatomical features of the higher plants', their elementary physiology, 'especially their relations to the soil and to the atmosphere', and a general knowledge of animal metabolism. It was claimed that this work did not require a specialist teacher of biology and that it could be accommodated within the curricula of boys' secondary schools by 'devoting to it part of the science time in the summer term'.[66] As far as girls' secondary schools were concerned, the Thomson Committee attached less importance to developing the teaching of biology than to expanding the opportunities for work in physics and chemistry.

> It is most desirable that girls should have an opportunity of discovering whether they have a taste for physics or chemistry and of developing such a taste where it exists.[67]

In discussing the teaching of science in elementary schools, the Committee was content to refer to the Board of Education *Suggestions For Teaching Elementary Science Including Nature Study* as an illustration of the kind of work it wished to encourage.[68]

It is clear that the Thomson Committee never seriously challenged the alleged educational superiority of the physical over the biological sciences. Whilst the teaching of some biological topics was encouraged, physics and chemistry were to 'continue to be the fundamental subjects'[69] of the secondary school curriculum. The subordinate position ascribed to school biology is illustrated by the Committee's reference to the difficulty of finding 'a competent biologist' who could teach 'even the most elementary physics with the requisite accuracy and definiteness'.[70]

The introduction of the system of School Certificate examinations at the end of the First World War provided another opportunity, this time for the Secondary School Examinations Council and the Examination Boards, to encourage the development of biology as a school subject. However, the initial proposal was to include the biological sciences in the list of Group IV subjects, in which a pass was not required for the award of a School Certificate.[71] This proposal was strongly resisted by the Association of Science Teachers and the subjects were eventually included in Group III, together with physics, chemistry and mathematics. Even so, in 1918, only four of the eight Examination Boards provided School Certificate syllabuses in natural history, zoology or biology whereas physics, chemistry and botany were examined by all. (See Table 4.3.)

Botany was further favoured by the panel of Investigators appointed by the Secondary School Examinations Council to review the new system of School Certificate examinations. The panel deemed natural history and zoology unsuitable subjects for a pass with credit in science[72] and claimed that the 'principles of biological science' could be illustrated better by botany than by biology or by zoology which was thought to have the additional disadvantage of not lending itself readily to an experimental treatment at school level.[73] In formulating these opinions, the S.S.E.C. must have been influenced by the problems of devising a satisfactory biology examination,[74] problems which stemmed, in part, from the continuing difficulty of constructing syllabuses in biology at School Certificate level. These syllabuses were prepared by botanists and zoologists rather than by biologists and the different interests were reflected both in the examination papers and in the textbooks which students used in preparing for them. Some examination papers were divided into two, occasionally three, distinct sections: animal biology, plant biology and general biology. Many biology textbooks were recognisably the work of two authors and might equally well have been published in two parts, the one a textbook of zoology, the other of botany.[75]

These circumstances, which hardly encouraged initiative in the teaching and examining of biology, were complicated by the attempt to introduce general science into the curricula of secondary schools. The views of those who argued that biology should 'merge imperceptibly' with the other sciences and 'be combined ... as general science'[76] were not easily reconciled with the development of a distinct biology course which, taught by suitably qualified teachers, could take an equal place alongside physics and chemistry in the secondary school curriculum.

Despite the conferences and meetings organised by the British Association and the Science Masters' Association, the vacation courses sponsored by the Board of Education and some local education authorities,[77] biology remained 'disgracefully neglected'[78] by the schools throughout the 1920s. In only three out of twenty-five boys' secondary schools investigated by H.M. Inspectorate in 1925 was there any attempt to broaden the curriculum for pupils between the ages of twelve and sixteen by including a science subject other than physics or chemistry within the curriculum. Further, only nine of the 210 teachers in the sample of schools taught any biology other than that which formed part of the nature study sometimes provided for the younger boys.[79] The more general position of biology in the schools in 1925 was described in the following terms by John Brown, an 'Inspector of Schools under the London County Council':

> ... in many boys' schools, the science teaching is confined entirely to certain sections of physics and chemistry. This is true also of central schools and of ordinary elementary schools after the nature study course has been completed.[80]

In 1927, when the 'inadequate provision for biological teaching' in 'every level and type of school' was brought to the attention of the Imperial Agricultural Research Conference in London, the Board of Education estimated that about one in ten grant-aided secondary schools for boys included biology in their curricula. The position of biology in the independent schools was said to have 'improved considerably' in the preceding five years.[81]

By 1929, when over 81 per cent of the secondary schools in England and Wales were preparing some of their pupils for Higher School Certificate examinations, biology was taught as a subject in only 16 per cent of them.[82] Not

Table 4.4   Numbers and Percentages of Candidates Offering Biology at the level of the First School Examination, 1922–50

Year	Number	Percentage
1922	Nil	–
1924	32	0.06
1926	86	0.2
1929	648	1.1
1930	1,021	1.6
1931	3,075	4.6
1932	4,551	6.6
1933	6,171	9.0
1934	7,383	11.1
1935	9,968	14.2
1936	13,467	17.5
1937	15,119	19.6
1938	15,852	20.6
1947	30,287	–
1948	32,961	–
1949	34,093	–
1950	31,070	–

Table 4.5   Numbers and Percentages of Candidates offering Biological Subjects at the Level of the Second School Examination, 1925–50

Year	Botany Number	Botany Percentage	Zoology Number	Zoology Percentage	Biology Number	Biology Percentage
1925	394	5.0	140	1.8	56	0.7
1926	411	5.0	177	2.2	66	0.8
1927	420	5.1	173	2.1	89	1.1
1928	455	5.2	175	2.0	95	1.1
1929	502	5.5	206	2.3	89	1.0
1930	543	5.7	260	2.7	116	1.2
1931	690	6.3	346	3.1	182	1.7
1932	823	6.7	414	3.4	245	2.0
1933	897	6.9	479	3.7	297	2.3
1934	831	6.7	454	3.7	315	2.5
1935	768	6.8	497	4.4	408	3.6
1936	655	5.8	451	4.0	543	4.8
1937	714	6.0	537	4.5	627	5.2
1938	757	5.7	679	5.1	801	6.1
1947	2,123	–	2,186	–	2,844	–
1948	2,261	–	2,359	–	3,275	–
1949	2,712	–	2,770	–	3,381	–
1950	2,948	–	3,047	–	3,706	–

surprisingly, botanists who could also teach chemistry, physics or mathematics were, in general, more likely to make a successful application for a teaching post than those whose second subject was zoology.[83]

The slow growth of biology in the secondary schools in the decade or so after 1918 is indicated by the examination statistics[84] in Tables 4.4 and 4.5. Although the number of candidates offering biology in the School Certificate examination rose from thirty-two (0.06 per cent of the total entry) in 1924 to 1,021 in 1930, this latter figure still represented less than 2 per cent of the total Certificate entry.

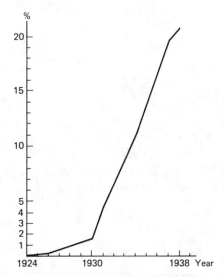

Figure 4.1 The percentage of candidates offering Biology as a subject in the First School Examination, 1924–38

It is clear from the data in Tables 4.4 and 4.5 and from Figures 4.1 to 4.4 that it was the decade after 1930 which, more than any other, saw biology gain an established place in the secondary school curriculum.[85] Boys' schools which had taught little or no biology before 1930 began to introduce it as an examination subject after this date and, in the secondary schools for girls, biology gradually replaced botany in the curriculum.[86] The decline of botany, which is particularly evident after 1933, was also encouraged by the introduction of courses of general science into secondary school curricula.[87] Zoology, in contrast, so strengthened its position in the secondary schools that, by the end of the Second World War, botany, zoology and biology enjoyed a similar degree of popularity as examination subjects. Tables 4.6 and 4.7, summarising data collected from a sample of 132 schools, provide some insight into the ways in which the biological sciences were accommodated within the secondary schools in the mid-1930s.[88]

The rapid development of biology as a school subject after 1930 may be regarded as a response to a succession of official and other reports which had

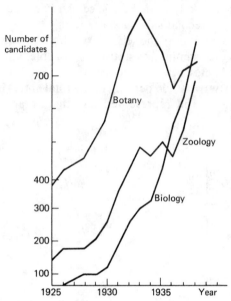

Figure 4.2 Numbers of Candidates in Botany, Zoology and Biology, Second School Examination, 1925–38

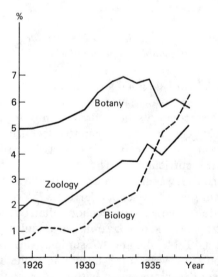

Figure 4.3 Percentage of Candidates offering Biological Subjects in the Second School Examination, 1925–38

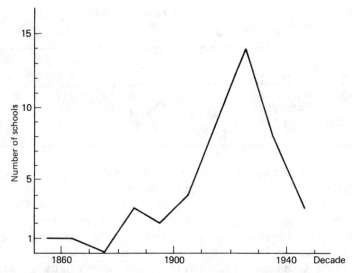

Figure 4.4 Numbers of Schools (as calculated from a questionnaire, S.S.R. XXXV, p. 74) which took up Biology in different decades

stressed the value of a biological education, promoted discussion of the contents of school biology syllabuses and encouraged a debate about teaching methods. The 1926 'Hadow' report[89] on the *Education of the Adolescent* affirmed the claims of biology to a place in the curricula of elementary, modern and central schools. The subsequent report[90] of the Consultative Committee on *Primary Schools* (1931) urged that nature study form an integral part of the curriculum for younger pupils and included illustrations of how schemes of work could be based upon a school garden or upon other practical exercises involving living things.

Table 4.6   Biological Sciences in Secondary Schools in 1934

	Boys	Girls	Mixed	Totals
Schools Teaching Botany	21	39	33	93
Schools Teaching Zoology	20	14	19	53
Biology in Lower School only	13	15	13	41
Biology in Upper School only	18	32	30	80
Some Biology Compulsory	11	19	24	54
Nature Study in Preparatory Forms only	32	5	9	46
Some Biology added recently	5	5	7	17

One report of seminal importance for the secondary schools was that produced by a committee of the British Association, appointed 'to consider and report upon the position of Animal Biology in the School Curriculum and matters relating thereto'.[91] Despite its terms of reference, the committee

Table 4.7   Teaching of Botany and Zoology in Secondary Schools in
1934

Botany and Zoology Taught	Boys	Type of School Girls	Mixed	Totals
Throughout the School	9	10	11	30
In Upper Forms Only	9	18	19	46
In Lower Forms Only	4	4	1	9
Total				85

concerned itself with biology rather than with animal biology and its extremely thorough report, presented to the Annual Meeting of the Association in 1928, included a comparison of the position of the subject in schools in England and Wales with that found elsewhere, notably in Japan, the United States, and several countries of Western Europe.[92] The report also highlighted the failure of three Examination Boards to provide syllabuses in School Certificate biology and of the University of London to include biology in its important and influential Matriculation schedule.[93]

The committee recommended that biology be a 'fundamental subject' in the curricula of all secondary schools and suggested timetables which would allow the subject to be studied on an equal basis with physics and chemistry up to School Certificate standard. Although 'deprecating uniformity' and 'preferring to see different syllabuses elaborated in different localities in accordance with local conditions',[94] the Committee presented a number of possible schemes of work in secondary school biology. These ranged from a complete, five-year course leading to the School Certificate, to suggestions for a two-year introductory course to be followed by all twelve to thirteen-year-old pupils. The schemes of work were supported by reference to suitable practical studies, books, apparatus and sources of specimens. The production of these realistic and practical biology syllabuses which 'avoided the complete separation of plants and animals into two unrelated 'kingdoms' for independent study, was an important contribution to the evolution of biology as a school subject.

By 1931, all eight Examination Boards examined biology at School Certificate level, although there was considerable variety both in the form of the examination and in the contents of the syllabus. These differences in syllabus content were an inevitable consequence of the immaturity of biology as a school subject,[95] of the different traditions of the individual Examination Boards and of the diversity of opinion which existed among science teachers about what should be included in a secondary school biology course. This diversity of opinion was clearly evident at the Annual Meeting of the S.M.A. in January 1930, when the members discussed the teaching of School Certificate biology. Some teachers considered field work to be one of the most valuable forms of practical work in biology and a number of Examination Boards, 'especially of Oxford and Cambridge' were said to be 'very anxious' to include such work in their syllabuses.[96] However, teachers working in urban schools insisted that appropriate field work of an adequate standard was impossible. The science masters were also unable to reach agreement on the 'types' of animal to be included in a biology syllabus. Amoeba, Hydra and the Frog were regarded by some teachers as 'well-chosen' while others mentioned the 'earthworm and insects'.[97] A proposal that a School Certificate biology syllabus should include 'an elementary knowledge of, at least, the evidences of evolution and the principles of heredity' seems to have caused particular difficulty. After discussion, the Resolution was amended to exclude all reference to heredity and eventually adopted by only twenty-nine votes to nineteen, at a meeting of about 'eighty to one hundred members' at which 'the views of a surprisingly large number' were heard.

In excluding heredity from School Certificate biology courses, it is possible that the majority of the science masters were seeking to dissociate themselves and their Association from the more contentious, even sensational, issues associated with the application of genetic ideas to human society. The worst excesses of Fascist Germany lay in the future and the need to control the genetic quality of a population was accepted by a number of eminent scientists and widely discussed in Britain and elsewhere for most of the inter-war period. The forum for much of the debate was the Eugenics Society which was active in its support[98] of the movement to extend contraceptive facilities within the population and which, in its own right, campaigned vigorously for the introduction of 'Eugenics Instruction' into the schools.[99] The teaching of eugenics in schools was discussed[100] within Section L of the British Association at its annual meeting in 1931, the year in which Julian Huxley's concern at the tendency of 'the stupid to inherit the earth' led him to suggest that the continuance of unemployment pay be made conditional upon a man having no more children and that any infringement of such a condition might be met by a short period of segregation in a labour camp.[101] Huxley was by no means alone[102] in his attitude towards 'racial decay' and opposition to his views and to those of the orthodox eugenists was fierce. Hogben, in particular, attacked the social Darwinistic assumptions implicit in the eugenic approach to the solution of social problems.[103]

By means of its meetings and journal, the S.M.A. did much to encourage an informed discussion of secondary school biology teaching. The publication within *The School Science Review* of articles intended to draw the attention of teachers to significant developments in the biological sciences[104] was particularly important at a time when most secondary school science masters had little or no formal biological education. The Association also took the initiative of establishing a subcommittee to design a biology syllabus which would 'command a wide measure of agreement'.[105] This was eventually published in 1935 and presented in four sections: general biology, animals, plants and ecology.

Although the activities of organisations such as the British Association and the Science Masters' Association were an essential component of biology curriculum development, the wider degree of acceptance of the subject by the schools after 1930 also owed much to the growing awareness of the economic and social benefits of a biological education. The provision of sixth-form courses in botany and zoology had long been justified by reference to the medical profession, but, until the 1920s, the employment prospects of professionally qualified biologists were sufficiently bleak to exert little or no positive influence on secondary school curricula generally. After the end of the First World War, there was a sudden increase in the demand for qualified biologists to meet the needs of new and expanding research organisations at home and in the various countries of the British Empire. The rapid development of agriculture in the colonies stimulated a corresponding expansion in the scientific work carried out under the authority of the Colonial Office and was of particular significance. Table 4.8 compares the numbers of Colonial Office appointments in biological science in two five-year periods separated by the First World War.[106] The highly specialised nature of some of these appointments is evident.

Table 4.8   Numbers of Colonial Office Appointments in Biological Science compared over two, five-year periods

	Total, 1909–14	Total, 1919–24
Agriculture	30	97
Economic and Systematic Botanists	5	11
Mycologists	6	15
Entomologists	10	12
Agricultural Chemists	6	11
Total	57	146

At home, an effort was made to increase the scientific support given to the agricultural, public health, forestry and veterinary departments of the administration, but the demand for suitably qualified graduates could not be met by the universities in which botany was still the dominant biological science.[107] The schools and universities were held responsible for the disparity between supply and demand and Headmasters and Vice-Chancellors were urged to publicise the career opportunities available to those with appropriate biological qualifications. The problem was discussed in the correspondence columns of *The Times* and, in 1929, the Ministry of Agriculture and Fisheries issued two leaflets[108] setting out the range of posts available to qualified biologists throughout the Empire. One of these leaflets was addressed to pupils and their parents, the other to teachers in the schools. Concern over the inadequate supply of biologists was also reflected in articles and correspondence in the educational press[109] and in the more specialised journals such as *The School Science Review*.

On 14 March 1930, the Government's Economic Advisory Council, chaired by the Prime Minister, set up a committee under Viscount Chelmsford to:

consider the obstacles which stand in the way of the education and supply of biologists for work in this country and overseas and to submit recommendations for the removal of such obstacles.[110]

The Chelmsford Report was published in 1933. Although the Committee found it impossible to quantify the 'substantial and growing demand'[111] for biologists, it confirmed that the supply fell short of the demand, adding that, in those specialist areas where the supply was sufficient in quantity, it was 'deficient in quality'.[112] The Committee also criticised the lack of accurate knowledge on the part of the public of the various biological posts available and of the mechanism for making such knowledge widely available.

The Chelmsford Committee was clearly very impressed by a shortage of qualified biologists at a time when 'every other profession calling for a certain high standard of educational attainment' appeared to be faced with 'a congested list of applicants clamouring to be admitted'.[113] Unfortunately, much of the evidence which led the Chelmsford Committee to its conclusions was undermined by the economic events of 1931. The world depression produced not an increased demand for biologists but a contraction, and the published Report was prefaced by a note from the Prime Minister which, by its understatement of the case, emphasised the harsh economic realities.

> The Secretary of State for the Colonies has asked that it should be made plain that since information ... was furnished to the Committee, the position has altered as a result of the existing economic stringency.[114]

The dramatic suddenness with which the conclusions of the Chelmsford Committee were invalidated had clear implications for those who used manpower arguments in an attempt to influence the curricula of schools and universities. Tizard discussed some of these implications at length in his Presidential address to Section L of the British Association in 1934, warning that 'public statements about the shortage of specialists in any branch of science and technology ... may be out of date before a normal period of advanced training is finished'.[115] Tizard was severely critical of the Chelmsford Report and, in particular, of its assumption that the lack of an adequate supply of biologists could be attributed to the neglect of biology in the schools. He argued for a *laissez-faire* economic determination of school biology teaching, advising that as soon as there was 'an assurance of reasonable careers in biology', suitable candidates would be forthcoming.[116]

Despite Tizard's criticism and the changed economic circumstances which prevailed at its publication in 1933, the Chelmsford Report was a significant document in the history of school biology teaching. The fact that the Committee had been set up at all was an official recognition of the importance of biological knowledge to national welfare and there is a suggestion that the economic measures introduced by the Government had an initially less severe effect on the recruitment of biologists by the Colonial Office than on other classes of appointment.[117] As an exercise in manpower planning, it was severely limited and, because of the small numbers of highly specialised biologists involved,[118] more than normally vulnerable to the winds of economic change. None the less, schools and universities had been reminded that there were important careers, other than medicine, available to qualified biologists and, as Tizard admitted in 1934, it needed 'no inspired prophet to foresee a great development some day of the biological sciences'.[119]

The Chelmsford Committee was excluded by its terms of reference from arguing a broad case for the teaching of biology in the schools. However, a number of the Committee's recommendations and conclusions related to issues which were of direct importance to the development of biology as a school subject, e.g. its encouragement of biology at the expense of botany and/or zoology and its condemnation of the excessive concentration on chemistry and physics by the schools and by the scholarship system.[120] The Committee's recommendation that 'none should leave school without some knowledge' of biology,[121] while far from new, was particularly timely and lent support to those who were pressing for the inclusion of biology in school curricula on grounds which were social rather than narrowly economic. These included individuals such as T. P. Nunn:

> It is far from fanciful to connect the low status of biological studies in our education ... with the decadence of rural life and activity,[122]

and Winifred Cullis, Professor of Physiology at the London School of Medicine for Women:

> Think what it would mean ... if we could give the children in the schools a working knowledge of the principles of good feeding,[123]

together with organisations as diverse as the Church of England Moral Welfare Council, the Marriage Guidance Council, the Central Authority for Health Education, the Eugenics Society,[124] the British Social Hygiene Council and the Board of Education.

Although established at different times and for different purposes, each of these organisations had a legitimate interest in the biological education of children at school. The Board of Education also had a statutory concern for the health of pupils in so far as this affected their educational attainment. In practice, this led to the official encouragement of health education and, in particular, of instruction in hygiene in the public elementary schools.

> ... the neglect of hygiene costs a nation dear, in money and life. It is the inhibitions and restrictions of ignorance in a right way of living which has imposed upon Great Britain much of its annual burden of disease ... its vast company of those who exist and toil, far below normal health, capacity and contentment.[125]

Although this was a particularly inflated claim for hygiene at a time when many people suffered from a lack of food as much as from a lack of knowledge, it is suggestive of the importance which the Board of Education attached to health education in the inter-war period. Two methods of teaching 'the principles and practice of good living' were recommended, each appropriate to a particular age or degree of experience. Young pupils of ten to eleven years of age could be taught by 'habit-training'. More mature adolescents were to be taught by methods which were based on an understanding of the scientific principles of hygiene.

The 'Suggestions' from the Board of Education were part of a more comprehensive government programme to raise the general level of the health of the population. The Central Authority for Health Education, founded in 1927, was established to help local education authorities with health propaganda,[126] using mass commercial advertising, exhibitions, films, rallies and 'health weeks'. The propaganda extended to the cinema where even newsreels were sometimes used to encourage the drinking of milk as part of the fight against tuberculosis. It seems likely that these methods, based upon the publicising of facts and appropriate accompanying exhortations, were of limited effectiveness in bringing about major changes in attitudes, habits or beliefs.

Sex hygiene was one aspect of health education which received particular attention during and immediately after the two World Wars when the need to curb the spread of venereal infection became urgent. There were, however, a number of difficulties associated with the various campaigns to raise the level of awareness of the facts about venereal diseases and the modes of their transmission. The first was the clear association of such diseases with sexual licence and hence with moral censure.[127] The second was an unwillingness to discuss the issues in public. The Chief Medical Officer of the Ministry of Health, Sir Wilson Jameson, created something of a sensation in 1942 by speaking frankly on the radio about venereal diseases. In addition, there was the more fundamental problem of ignorance of sexual anatomy and physiology.

Clearly, the teaching of biology in schools could help to overcome these difficulties, at least in the longer term. Information about venereal infection could be 'given naturally' in schools as part of a wider study of communicable diseases. Similarly, sexual reproduction could be taught as a general biological phenomenon and not singled out as a matter for special consideration. Pupils could acquire a sound knowledge of their own bodies and of those of the opposite sex and the sex act could cease to be a mystery, too often associated with the naughty, dirty or furtive.

Despite a growing recognition of the need to educate young people in sexual matters, the association of sex education with biological knowledge was not entirely to the advantage of biology, particularly in the elementary and senior schools. In 1932, F. Mander, the General Secretary of the National Union of Teachers, expressed the opinion that 'the prospects of biological teaching' were being 'tremendously prejudiced because of an association in the public mind with sex'.[128] He was referring to the suspicion entertained by some parents that biological education, particularly in the public elementary schools, could be identified with 'teaching sex hygiene in class'.[129] Another, related problem, was that many parents and teachers, recognising that views on sex varied 'between the scientific and the sacramental' felt that sex education was a sphere which teachers 'should vacate as much as possible'. In these circumstances, the following Resolution, adopted by the N.U.T. in July 1932, was of particular significance:

In view of the contribution which biology makes to a proper understanding of human life and the laws of health, the Executive commend to teachers in general the suggestion that the nature study commonly undertaken in the primary school should lead to further biological studies at the post-primary or secondary stage.[130]

Sex education was also the concern of organisations such as the Church of England Moral Welfare Council[131] and the Marriage Guidance Council[132] whose principal interests were in ethical and marital issues rather than in the dissemination of biological knowledge. While emphasising the moral basis of sound sex education and the importance of adequate personal relationships, these organisations, like a number of others, came to realise that 'adequate biological knowledge before puberty' was essential to the achievement of their primary objectives. As a result, they supported others campaigning for sex education and, more generally, for an extension of biological teaching in the schools.

The fact that the activities of the various organisations concerned with marriage guidance, sex education, eugenics or the teaching of hygiene were initially much less successful than they might have been because of the general level of biological ignorance of the population, was appreciated most fully by the British Social Hygiene Council. The Council was formed in 1925 from the National Council for Combating Venereal Disease[133] which, since its foundation in 1914, had pioneered sex education courses in the schools and marriage guidance classes in youth clubs and similar organisations. The work of the British Social Hygiene Council, involving 'close contact with the adult and adolescent in industry,.in agriculture and in family life' produced a conviction that its programme of health education was unlikely to influence widely 'either outlook or behaviour' until it could be based on an understanding by the population in general of the function and behaviour of living organisms. In the absence of an adequate background knowledge of biology, the population was 'a prey to every form of quackery'.[134]

Concluding that the relative ineffectiveness of its work in health education could be traced to the 'lack of balance' in the educational system, the Council devoted considerable effort to securing adequate opportunities for biological education in the schools. It arranged deputations to Government departments, conducted inquiries into particular aspects of biology teaching and organised several national and international conferences. One conference, held in London and concerned specifically with biological education, was of particular significance, both because of its timing and the wide range of interests represented at its discussions. The 1932 Conference on *The Place of Biology in Education* brought together a group of distinguished and influential men and women which included statesmen, scientists, educationists, inspectors, academics, local education authority administrators and teachers from elementary, secondary and public schools. Those addressing the conference included[135] Viscount Chelmsford, Michael Sadler, Selby-Bigge, Richard Gregory, Walter Morley Fletcher (the first secretary of the Medical Research Council), Frederick Mander of the N.U.T. and R. H. Cowley, Senior Medical Officer at the Board of Education. Detailed schemes of work were suggested by J. A.

Thomson (General Biology), by Winifred Cullis (Functional Biology, Physiology) and by Julian Huxley (General Science).

The conference was given generous publicity by the popular, educational and scientific press. Its proceedings were subsequently edited by J. G. Crowther, then the science correspondent of the *Manchester Guardian*, and published in 1933 as a handbook, entitled *Biology in Education*.[136] In his introduction, Crowther acknowledged the debt which the conference owed to Sir J. A. Thomson,[137] Professor of Natural History at the University of Aberdeen. Thomson had long campaigned for the teaching of biology in schools and colleges and, through his writings, had done much to extend biological knowledge to the public at large. He had participated in in-service courses for training college lecturers and, with Patrick Geddes, had written a lengthy and important book which emphasised the contribution of biological science to the 'relief of man's estate'.[138] Not only had biological knowledge helped man to explore nature, 'to get more fish out of the sea, to make two blades of grass grow where none had grown before', but it had strengthened 'his hands against his enemies'. Diseases 'like those caused by hookworm and bilharzia, the malaria organism and the diphtheria microbe' were 'shrinking every year'.[139] In addition, knowledge of the role of hormones and vitamins and of the mechanism of inheritance was enabling man to understand more of the functioning of his own body.

The views which Thomson expressed in his book were closely matched by many of the speakers at the national conference on biology in education and, in his introduction to the published proceedings, Crowther was able to present a strong case for the teaching of biology in schools. The claim of the subject to an established place in school curricula rested, first and foremost, on the general, cultural value of a biological education. Man could not 'understand what he is and how he came to be as he is, without appreciating himself as a biological entity'.[140] The utilitarian and subsidiary arguments in favour of biology teaching were based not only on the more obvious applications of biological knowledge,

> the improvement of agriculture ... the growing of plants ... the preparation of the land ... the control of insects and animals pestiferous to man ... the science of nutrition and healthy living,[141]

but also on the value of such knowledge in the determination of social policy. How were people to 'decide on suitable legislation for the treatment of the mentally disordered? How were the 'backward races' to be treated?'[142] In addition, it was suggested that the efficient and harmonious functioning of living organisms might provide a much-needed model for the integration of society and for the conduct of human affairs in the home or factory.

The 1932 Conference was only part of a wider and continuing programme of activities undertaken by the British Social Hygiene Council to promote 'the teaching of the biological sciences in all kinds of educational institution, to secure adequate recognition for biology as a general and as a specialist subject for examining bodies and to give guidance in the production of textbooks and teaching material for use at home and overseas'.[143] Guided by its Education Advisory Board, composed of representatives of the Board of Education, the universities, the Examination Boards and the major educational organisations, together with individuals prominent in biology and education, the Council published its views on examining biology at School Certificate level[144] and on the place of human biology within school science courses.[145] It collaborated with local education authorities[146] in the development of biology teaching in the schools and established a central exhibition of biology teaching equipment and materials.[147] In 1933, the Council began the publication of *Biology*, its official journal for 'schools and teachers'. Although the primary concern of the British Social Hygiene Council was health education, the editorial policy of its journal, as determined by an Education Advisory Board, was to 'foster the development of biological teaching'. The journal sought to expound 'no particular doctrine of biological teaching', and, 'to uphold no cut-and-dried method of presentation'.[148] As a forum offered 'impartially to all', *Biology* encouraged the discussion of many issues of contemporary significance in biological education, e.g. the position of biology within a scheme of general science, the supply of suitably qualified biology teachers. In addition, the journal provided a means of reporting biological research and of illustrating the application of biological knowledge to human affairs. The first issue of *Biology* included practical contributions on visual aids and laboratory work in elementary biology teaching, together with articles on ecology and malaria, the latter based on material 'supplied by the Ross Institute'. Subsequent issues 'leaned heavily towards the service of biology teachers, largely in the grammar and public schools', but the journal also developed an international outlook and included contributions which discussed aspects of biological education in Russia, Malaysia, West Africa, India and the United States.[149]

Notwithstanding this liberal editorial policy, many of the articles published in the Council's journal emphasised the social and economic value of biological knowledge, e.g. 'The Biological Significance of Milk' (1936), 'Education and Child Health' (1938), 'Health Research at Peckham' (1938). In 1943, after the health education function of the British Social Hygiene Council had been effectively assumed by the Central Council of Health Education established under the Ministry of Health in the previous year, the title of the journal was changed to *Biology and Human Affairs*. In 1950, the British Social Hygiene Council became the British Social Biology Council, a title which reflected more accurately the Council's concern with 'the application of biological knowledge to the solution of social problems and the promotion of human welfare'.[150]

A somewhat different interpretation of the social value of a biological education from that implicit in the activities of the British Social Hygiene Council was adopted by those who based their case for including biology within school curricula on the contribution which the subject could make to education for 'citizenship'.[151] The citizenship movement of the 1930s, another factor encouraging the introduction of biology into the schools, had several antecedents. The Board of Education, responding to the influence of the Herbartians and to pressure from the Moral Instruction League, had included a section on character training in the Elementary School Regulations for 1906, requiring that moral instruction 'shall form an important part of every Elementary School Curriculum'.[152] The emphasis placed by the progressive educationists on self-discipline and genuine school government, institutionalised in schools such as Abbotsholme and Bedales, contributed another element to an evolving tradition of education for citizenship. The founding of the League of Nations and the hopes of a new post-war era in the conduct of affairs by nations added an international dimension to this tradition, manifest by the formation of the New Education League[153] in Calais in 1921 and by the 'progressive' schools associated with A. S. Neill, the Russells and Kurt Hahn. Finally, there was the important ingredient of 'civics', a school subject the importance of which seemed to be reinforced by the extension of the franchise after 1917, by the need to forestall or mitigate the industrial unrest threatening to undermine the basis of post-war British society[154] and by the revolutionary political events which had taken place in other countries. In 1919, Section L of the British Association established a Committee on training in citizenship under the chairmanship of Bishop Welldon.[155] Before it was discharged in 1923, Welldon's Committee produced three reports, the first of which contained a somewhat unimaginative syllabus for civics, divided into twenty-one sections with titles such as 'Origins of the State', 'Temperance', 'Leisure' and 'Recreation'.

Although official belief in the value of civics in education was sustained throughout the 1920s by a series of books and pamphlets, the subject made little headway in the schools. In the elementary schools, civics was too easily allied with political indoctrination, particularly by the left.[156] In the secondary and public schools, civics education was often embodied in the formal structure and conduct of school government and in the elaborate system of prefects, houses, school clubs and societies. History, however, was another matter. Imbued with the idea of evolution and progress, rich in moral exemplars of the 'right ordering of several loyalties'[157] and invigorated by the experiences of the First World War, history was supremely capable of educating for citizenship. The pupils could be led to 'realise what democracy, liberty, humanity and the feeling of nationality' were by 'watching them grow'.[158] The growth of civilisation and the progress of the community 'to culture, economic freedom and self-government' were the 'bedrock of the subject'.[159]

The various strands of the education for citizenship movement were drawn together in the 1930s by a group of political and intellectual liberals, disillusioned with the policies of the National Government and apprehensive of the growing power of Nazism, Fascism and Bolshevism. Led by Sir Ernest Simon, the group formally established an Association for Education in Citizenship to organise an educational defence of democracy.[160] The Association operated both as a private group exerting pressure on the Government and Board of Education and as a public organisation seeking to influence teachers and the leaders of educational opinion. In 1935, the Association published a book in which the role of science, and of biology in particular, in educating for citizenship was discussed by Professor D. L. Mackinnon.[161] The assertion that biology had an important contribution to make in this field was not, of course, new. J. G. Kerr, in his Presidential Address[162] to the Zoology Section of the British Association in 1926, had discussed biology in relation to the 'training of the citizen' and argued that the subject could reveal three 'great principles of communal evolution'. These were the increasing size of the community, the consequent 'increased specialisation of the individuals' and the accompanying 'increased perfection of the organisation', whereby the constituent individuals were knit together 'into the communal individuality of a higher order'. In Kerr's view, an appreciation of these principles would induce 'the biological outlook' in the mind of the citizen and encourage social stability by increasing his understanding of the complexity of social organisation.[163]

Mackinnon's case for including biology within a programme of education for citizenship rested, in part, on the same ground. What the pupil at school learnt of 'biological interdependence' could make him a 'better citizen of the world' since 'no nation lives to itself alone and what brings disaster upon one involves all that are associated with it'.[164] However, Mackinnon also claimed that biology could provide a valuable link between the 'more abstract sciences' and those that were called 'social'. Unlike pure physics or chemistry where 'dispassionate thinking' was 'not difficult', biology included problems in which human emotion and prejudices were deeply involved. As such, the subject provided an opportunity for pupils to be trained to examine their own reactions to what they were learning and 'to guard against allowing sentiment to influence a judgement on matters of fact'.[165]

The Science Masters' Association responded to the 'citizenship movement' by instituting a 'Science and Citizenship' lecture, the first of which was given by Sir Richard Gregory in January 1938 at Imperial College, London, and later published as part of the *Report of the Annual Meeting*. Arrangements for the second 'Citizenship' lecture were disrupted by the outbreak of the war but the lecture was eventually delivered by Lancelot Hogben and entitled 'Biological Instruction and Education for Citizenship'.[166] Hogben's address was a direct plea for 'biology for all' and, more particularly, for the teaching of biology in its social context. Defining education in a democratic society as 'education of the citizen to rational recognition of interests common to all', Hogben argued for the education of specialists to 'a rational appreciation of the social value of the professional work they perform'.[167] Given that biology could justify its claims to a place in universal education if, and only if, it established 'its credentials as a branch of humane scholarship', i.e. as an essential part of the intellectual equipment of the individual for the responsibilities of citizenship, the selection of curriculum content would be determined by giving prominence to those aspects of biology which were 'most relevant to human needs'. It was thus less important for a teacher of school biology to learn about 'ciliary currents in Ammocoetes or about the crystalline style of Pelecypods than to know about vitamins and nutritional diseases of babies or about iodine and calcium in relation to pig culture'.[168] Theories of the ascent of sap were of less significance in school biology than ideas about soil erosion or artificial fertilisers. Genetics should be studied in relation to the revolution brought about in crop production and animal breeding, and theories of gastrulation and the treatment of fertilisation in sea urchins should give way to the role of artificial insemination in stock breeding and to the relevance of 'recent work on sex hormones to the menopause'.

Hogben's lecture was given at the 1942 Annual Meeting of the S.M.A., the first full meeting since the outbreak of the war and one at which the science masters discussed the role of science in post-war education. Hogben's theme, the teaching of biology via its interactions with society and technology, was supported by L. J. F. Brimble in a lecture on biology as a social science. Although this lecture has been preserved only in summary form, it is clear that Brimble, like Hogben, attempted to convince the science masters of the need to abandon the conventional academic constraints upon school biology teaching. School biology courses were to be based on a firm recognition of those 'principles of social biology' which 'confront us at every turn', e.g. 'individual and public health, nutritional standards, housing, population movements, race and nation, problems of family life, relations and responsibilities of one person to another, social policy of the State'.[169] Brimble was aware that the change he advocated in the definition of school biology involved the sacrifice of at least a few sacred cows.

> Practical work well taught is of inestimable value but it runs the risk of becoming biased in favour of the potential scientists.

> Many teachers lean too much towards teaching science in the spirit of research and discovery. This may be all right in the universities but in schools it leads to (the omission) of other studies ... of equal importance.[170]

In the 1945 Science and Citizenship lecture, J. G. Crowther referred to the creation by the British Association of its Division for the Social and International Relations of Science and to the famous meeting held in 1941 to discuss 'Science and World Order'. He suggested to his audience that the S.M.A. might establish a Social Relations Committee[171] to help secure 'the necessary changes in the school curriculum' and to encourage the 'kind of science teaching and books required' by schools serving a society in which scientific activity was to be planned for the 'mutual benefit of scientists and the community'.[172]

In April 1945, when Crowther delivered his address, the world had not yet experienced the tragedy of atomic warfare and there were few shadows to cloud his vision of a post-war society in which scientific knowledge was harnessed to the service of the people. As far as biology was concerned, the educational and social benefits of biological knowledge were beyond dispute. At the same meeting at which Crowther spoke, the science masters were 'thrilled' by Alexander Fleming's account of the discovery, isolation and effectiveness of penicillin, then widely hailed as a 'miracle' drug.[173]

Cyril Bibby, then the Secretary of the Central Council for Health Education, reminded them of the importance of biology to physical and mental well-being and the science masters must have been well aware that, during the war, the Ministries of Food and Health had been trying to instil by propaganda elementary biological knowledge that ought to have been taken for granted.[174] It is thus not surprising that, in the discussion of the role of science in the future educational system, there was support for teaching science in its social context. A. W. Wellings, of Leamington College, called for a 'modification of technique and a new attitude of mind' to reorientate school science courses 'to show the relation between scientific discovery and social cause and effect'.[175] As far as biology was concerned, the desired shift was towards social biology and away from an approach based on natural history or on syllabuses which emphasised morphology and physiology and which were derived, however indirectly, from pre-medical courses of study.

The contents of Crowther's lecture and the reaction of the science masters to it,[176] indicate that the Association was responding not only to the campaign for education in citizenship but also to another development of the 1930s, the so-called 'social relations of science movement'.[177] Both Hogben and Crowther were prominent members of this movement which stemmed from the low status ascribed to science by the majority of the intellectual and political élite and from the succession of major domestic and international crises which characterised the depression years. Some of these crises involved the scientific community directly, e.g. the 'Nordic' racial theories and the growing demand for professional scientific assistance in the design of weapons and the planning of defence. As Werskey[178] has pointed out, this movement was 'neither monolithic nor cohesive' and, at no time, involved more than a few members of the scientific community. The fundamental division within the movement was between reformers, like Richard Gregory, F. G. Hopkins and Julian Huxley, who sought only to raise the prestige of, and support for, scientific research within the existing social order, and radicals, such as Bernal, Hogben, Haldane and Needham, who argued that the fullest and most humane use of science was possible only in a society reorganised along socialist lines. Despite this fundamental difference of outlook, the pressure of national survival enabled both radicals and reformers to work together throughout the Second World War. Once the war ended, the gradual improvement in the status and financing of scientific research satisfied many of the reformers who were content to be called upon to advise on government policy rather than to formulate it, as the radicals would have wished.[179]

The battle of ideas between radicals and reformers was fundamentally a conflict between alternative conceptions of the social function of science and between competing political ideologies. The radicals, many of whom were Marxists, derided the social and philosophical connotations of pure science. Crowther told his audience of science masters that the 'pursuit of purely intellectual motives' had led frequently to 'sterility' and sought to illustrate his point by reference to developments in the science of hydrodynamics. Although hydrodynamic phenomena had been studied 'for generations, mainly from a mathematical and logical point of view', the problems had proved so difficult that little progress had been made. However, when the development of aviation 'demanded solutions ... the pressure of the workshop' had proved more effective than 'pure intellectual curiosity in discovering the new science of fluid flow'.[180]

Not surprisingly, the radicals within the social relations of science movement were often pilloried as the enemies of science itself. Opposition to their views was organised by a Society for Freedom in Science which also set out to provide an alternative to the radical position. The Society required its members to adhere to five principles, the first of which is of particular significance in the present context:

> The increase of knowledge by scientific research of all kinds and the maintenance of scientific culture have an independent and primary value.[181]

In addition to the activities of the Society, several individuals took up the pen to expose the threat which they saw presented to science by 'planners' such as Bernal, Hogben, Crowther and Waddington. J. R. Baker's *The Scientific Life*, published in 1942 and written for those 'who have the welfare of science at heart' was a direct attack on the planners, the British Association which appeared to support them and on *Nature* which moved 'with what its editors (thought) to be the tide'.[182] Baker's book, an assertion of the freedom of the scientific community to investigate matters of its own choosing, inevitably placed heavy emphasis on distinguishing pure science from applied science or technology. For Baker, technology and the 'social relations of science' were identical. Crowther's definition of science as 'the system of behaviour by which man acquires mastery of the environment' was, for Baker, a definition of technology and not of science.[183] The two principal functions of science were to serve as an end in itself, 'like music' and to form a basis for technology. The eventual dominance of this view in post-war British society explains, in part, the delay in increasing the production of qualified technologists, following the reports of the Barlow and Percy Committees, and in applying scientific discoveries to the improvement of industrial practice.[184]

An international comparison with Denmark, a country with a predominantly agricultural economy, illustrates the extent of the influence of an over-rigid distinction between pure and applied science and of the failure to acknowledge the importance of the technological impulse in creating scientific knowledge. In 1948–9, Denmark produced 300 honours graduates in technology compared with twenty-two in science and mathematics, a ratio of fourteen to one. The corresponding figures for the United Kingdom in 1947–8 were 1,094 honours technology graduates and 2,344 scientists and mathematicians, a ratio of less than one technologist to every two graduates in pure science.[185]

There were several reasons why the biology curriculum and, to a lesser extent, general science, provided a focus for the battle between the reforming and radical ideologies. Many of the important and often controversial social issues of the day had a biological dimension, e.g. the menace of malnutrition,[186] the concern over the 'decline' in the 'genetic quality' of the population and the widespread threat of tuberculosis. Secondly, a significant number of the politically conscious scientists active in the social relations of science debate were themselves biologists, e.g. Baker, Huxley, Waddington, Needham and Hopkins. In addition, biology, 'the Cinderella of the sciences', was still in a state of transition from a primarily discursive, descriptive and taxonomic study to an 'unitary, experimental, quantitative science, drawing many of its basic ideas from . . . developments in physics and chemistry'.[187] As such, school biology was much less clearly defined than the established subjects, physics and chemistry. Despite the great advances made in biological knowledge since the beginning of the century, the problem of formulating an adequate statement of biological principles upon which an integrated curriculum could be constructed, remained to be solved. As Bernal pointed out in 1939, the development of a satisfactory syllabus in biology which presented the 'complex of function, form, development and genesis' as a coherent whole, still awaited 'the arrangements for greater coordination'[188] of the various biological disciplines which would come only from advances in the appropriate fields of research.

On the other hand, the relative newness of biology as a school subject allowed it some degree of immunity from criticism by those who saw a connection between the 'prostitution of science' in the war and the inadequacies of school science education. The nature of this connection was explored by Westaway in a book published in 1942, with the provocative title of *Science in the Dock: Guilty or Not Guilty?* Claiming that science was 'often credited with being the root cause of all the major evils' and was, quite properly, the 'focus of public opprobium',[189] Westaway attributed the apparent indifference of many scientists towards the use made of their work to a specialisation at school, which had forced them to drift away from non-scientific studies at an age when 'they could not have made more than a nodding acquaintance with ... the humanities'. As a result, when, later in life, scientists 'might have been expected to help towards the solution of the world's urgent problems, they were almost like children'. The personal consequences for Westaway of accepting this analysis were considerable:

> I fear that during my professional career, I advocated the claims of science teaching much too strongly and I am now quite sure that the time often devoted to laboratory practice and to the purely mathematical side of science, more especially chemistry and physics, was far too great.[190]

Although he did not ally himself explicitly with the radicals, Westaway described *Science for the Citizen* as 'noteworthy' and seems to have shared the opinion of *The Times* reviewer of Hogben's book that it was in considering science as a social activity that scientific education had most to learn from the radical position.[191]

The attempt by radicals such as Hogben, Bernal and Crowther to give a new direction to school science teaching failed principally because the reformist position triumphed in science itself.[192] The traditional features of British science, with its strong emphasis on a fundamental approach, were reasserted after the war and secondary school science, perhaps never seriously challenged, continued to subscribe to the ideology of pure science rather than to science as a social function.[193] In addition, it is doubtful whether radical influence was exercised sufficiently where it mattered most, in the construction of School Certificate and Higher School Certificate syllabuses and examinations. Despite Hogben's brilliant *Science for the Citizen* and the vision of Bernal's *The Social*

Function of Science, the radicals failed to translate their views into curriculum materials which could have provided an exemplar for the Examination Boards or a sufficient platform for teachers to construct their courses. Those who sought to realise the idea of science as a 'tool to shape ... civilisation'[194] in effective classroom practice thus faced a difficult task, which could be discharged adequately only if the full significance of 'Bernalism' were understood. This may not have been always the case. Those who urged teachers to take advantage of the 'numerous opportunities' which arose from time to time to 'point out, not perhaps at length, but with vividness and interest', 'the great sociological effects and potentialities of science'[195] were speaking the language of the reformers and not of the radicals for whom the human applications of scientific knowledge were as much part of science as its theories and science itself one of the major agents for social change rather than some mere adjunct to life.[196]

While organisations such as the British Social Hygiene Council and the Association for Education in Citizenship on the one hand, and individuals such as Lancelot Hogben and J. A. Thomson on the other, shared a common concern to encourage the teaching of biology in schools, they clearly differed in their rationale. For the organisations established to promote 'citizenship' or 'social hygiene', the widespread teaching of biology was a means of fulfilling their primary objectives. For a radical such as Hogben, school biology, together with the established sciences of physics and chemistry, offered an opportunity to illustrate the radical view of science itself and to present the subject as a liberal, humane study. It is also clear that these differences in rationale required biology curricula which differed significantly in content and emphasis both from one another and from many of the courses found in the schools which were influenced by the natural history tradition in biology or determined by the needs of intending medical students. The evolution of biology in the schools after 1930 may thus be regarded as the result of competition between somewhat different conceptions of biology as a school subject.

In the grammar and public schools, where the preparation of pupils for higher education was of fundamental importance, it was the professional influence, notably of the medical schools, which, more than any other single factor, determined the biology curriculum. Where social biology was introduced into these schools, it was granted a subordinate status and offered as an antidote to specialisation by pupils in the arts sixth or reserved as a subject of particular significance for girls.

> One form, a mixture of boys who are beginning to specialise in history, with others marking time before joining the forces, etc., does social biology once a week.
>
> All girls in the first year in the sixth form attend one lesson a week in social biology.[197]

The influence of the medical schools upon sixth-form biology courses may be traced to the late nineteenth century and, in particular, to the introduction, in 1892, of the statutory five-year course of medical training. When it became clear that the medical curriculum was seriously overcrowded,[198] the Royal College of Physicians and the Royal College of Surgeons, operating through a

Conjoint Board,[199] sought to preserve the time available for the professional elements of a medical education by recognising public schools, technical colleges and municipal schools of science as places where physics, chemistry and biology could be studied to the level of the Board's First Examination. The time spent on such study was in addition to the five years needed to qualify as a general practitioner and recognition was granted only after a satisfactory inspection of the science teaching facilities of an institution by a member of the Committee of Management of the Conjoint Board. Eton, Winchester, Charterhouse, St Paul's, Epsom, Dulwich, Cheltenham and Clifton were among the twenty-three public schools recognised in this way between 1892 and 1898, together with thirty-four municipal schools and technical colleges, and eight secondary schools. Because of the inadequate level of provision for biology teaching in the schools, recognition was often harder to obtain for biology than for physics or chemistry. Thus, Dulwich College, a public school with a well-established science side, obtained recognition by the Conjoint Board in 1895, only after additional facilities had been provided for biology teaching.[200] Although the standard of the Board's First Examination was not high,[201] particularly in biology, the activities of the Board towards the end of the century were an important incentive to a number of schools to develop their science teaching facilities.

In 1893, the General Medical Council amended its requirements for the registration of medical students to allow the first year of the five-year course to be spent at a teaching institution, other than a medical school or university, which had been recognised *after inspection by a Licensing Body*, such as the Conjoint Board, for the teaching of biology, physics and chemistry. However, the Council[202] excluded the public schools from this provision on the grounds that such schools were agents of general education and therefore unsuitable for the pre-medical teaching of physical and biological science. The Council was thus brought into conflict both with the public schools and with the Conjoint Board which was strongly opposed to the remission of time permitted by the new requirement.

In 1898, the loss of fee income from its own examinations, abandoned by students in favour of those which provided for such remission, forced the Conjoint Board to amend its own Regulations to allow one year of the curriculum, subsequent to registration with the Council, to be spent at a recognised institution for teaching science.[203] Although the intention of this amendment was similar to that of the Regulation introduced by the General Medical Council five years earlier, there were two important differences between the Registration and Licensing authorities. The Conjoint Board clearly gave a much more generous interpretation to the term 'teaching institution' than the Council was prepared to allow. In addition, the Council was unwilling to accept the procedure, adopted by the Board after inspecting Chester School of Science and Art and the Cheltenham School of Art in 1892, whereby recognition *without inspection* was granted to institutions solely[204] on the strength of the receipt of grant for science teaching from the Department of Science and Art.

Concern that recognition could be given to institutions of doubtful teaching capacity led the Council to introduce a new Regulation in January 1900, requiring it to approve those institutions recognised by the Licensing Bodies before students attending them could be registered.[205] The Royal Colleges, jealous of their independence and advised that the Council had no legal power to interfere with their choice of teaching institutions, informed the Council that they would not conform to this new Regulation and deleted any reference to student registration from their own requirements. This was possible because the General Medical Council was empowered to compel the registration of medical practitioners but not of medical students in training. An attempt to extend the powers of registration to include students was made in 1904, but it failed after representations to the Privy Council by the Royal Colleges and by the Universities of Oxford and Cambridge.[206]

However, the dispute with the Council did lead the Conjoint Board to tighten up its procedure for recognising schools and other teaching institutions.[207] It became necessary to submit plans of laboratories and lists of apparatus and specimens, together with details of the qualifications of the science staff, before an inspection could be undertaken. Separate teachers were required for physics, chemistry and biology and a laboratory and lecture room were needed for each of the three sciences. Particular importance was attached to the availability of an adequate range of biological specimens and recognition was withheld on this ground alone on more than one occasion.[208] As a result of the operation of these more stringent criteria, significant numbers of schools, particularly among those in receipt of Parliamentary grant, were removed from the list of institutions recognised by the Conjoint Board between 1900 and 1902 and applications from many others were refused.

The General Medical Council also exerted pressure on the Conjoint Board by invoking the powers available to it under the Medical Act of 1858. It called for a detailed report on all the institutions recognised by the Board and, in 1902–3, the Council's Education Committee received details of the work at fifty-nine centres which included thirty-four public and secondary schools, two Higher Grade schools and seventeen municipal technical colleges. The Education Committee's decision that not less than fifteen hours per week must be devoted to the teaching of science if any remission of time from the five-year curriculum were to be granted, imposed a condition which many of the institutions recognised by the Conjoint Board were unable to meet. Such institutions, together with a number of others which were added for more overtly political reasons, were therefore denied recognition by the General Medical Council.[209]

The Council also ordered an inspection of the Board's First Examination in physics, chemistry and biology. The subsequent severe criticism of the form of the examination and of the standard attained by many of the candidates[210] led the Conjoint Board to revise its syllabuses, introduce a written examination in biology and separate papers in physics and chemistry and to further lengthen the time of its practical examinations. After 1904, the Regulations of the Board required recognised institutions to guarantee that students had completed 180 hours of instruction and laboratory work in chemistry and 120 hours in each of physics and biology before they were admitted to the Board's First Examination.[211]

By 1909, the Board was able to illustrate the quality of the science teaching in its recognised institutions by comparing favourably the pass rates in chemistry, physics and biology of students attending these institutions with those of students who had completed their preliminary science courses at the medical schools. The figures provided ready, if somewhat suspect,[212] ammunition for those like Sir Henry Morris, President of the Royal College of Surgeons[213] from 1906 to 1909, who argued that the pre-medical teaching of physics, chemistry and biology could be transferred from the medical schools to other institutions, notably the secondary schools, without any deterioration in the standards attained. It is certain that many medical schools, especially those in London, would have welcomed some relief from the burden of teaching the preliminary courses in physics, chemistry and biology, since the provision of laboratories and equipment for these pre-clinical subjects caused severe financial difficulties.[214] These difficulties were enhanced by the declining number of students at the London medical schools,[215] a consequence of the much higher fees in comparison with medical schools in the provinces and of the severity of the Preliminary Scientific Examination which obliged many London medical students to qualify with a Conjoint Diploma rather than with a university degree.

However, opposition to the transfer of the preliminary science teaching was strong and Morris's views did not prevail, despite a vigorous campaign.[216] It is also doubtful whether such a general transfer would have been possible in the case of biology where the numbers of candidates coming forward from the institutions recognised by the Conjoint Board were much smaller than in the case of either physics or chemistry.

In such a climate of opinion, it was difficult for the General Medical Council to maintain its attitude[217] towards medical education in the public schools. The initial approaches by the A.P.S.S.M. to the Council were unsuccessful, perhaps because of some degree of ambivalence[218] on the part of the newly formed Association. Dominated as it was by the science staff from Eton and Harrow, the Committee of the Association was well aware that the group of institutions which ignored the Council's registration procedures included Oxford, London and Cambridge as well as the Conjoint Board, so that recognition of the public schools by the General Medical Council would have been of benefit only to those of their pupils intending to read for medical degrees at Scottish or provincial universities.[219] However, there was a more practical reason why such recognition was important to the public schools. Parents were withdrawing their sons at the age of sixteen to attend a 'recognised institution' where, by obtaining some remission of curriculum time, the eventual cost of a medical training would be reduced.[220] In addition, the provincial and Scottish medical schools were important to pupils attending many of the less famous public schools, the science staff of which joined the A.P.S.S.M. in increasing numbers after 1901. In 1911, the Committee of the A.P.S.S.M. addressed a Memorandum to the General Medical Council setting out the Association's case for the recognition of the public schools as institutions in which medical education could begin. On 29 May 1911, the Council adopted a Resolution which closely resembled the Regulation to which the Royal Colleges had objected so vigorously eleven years earlier and which, in effect, allowed the registration authority to approve and recognise teaching institutions chosen by the Licensing Bodies. On this occasion, however, the Colleges, alert to the problems of the London medical schools, did not oppose the Council's Resolution, the breach between the Royal Colleges and the General Medical Council was healed and the public schools gained the recognition which the A.P.S.S.M. had sought.

The introduction of the system of School Certificate examinations at the end of the First World War provided an opportunity to reduce the bewildering variety[221] of external examinations which had faced the secondary schools since 1902, since the entry requirements to the various professions could be framed in terms of the appropriate Matriculation and Certificate examinations. Unfortunately, the regulations relating to the First Medical Examination continued to vary significantly from one institution to another. Some universities allowed sixth formers to sit for this examination as external candidates. Others allowed an appropriate performance in the Higher Certificate to qualify for exemption,[222] a practice which had existed at the London medical schools since before the First World War and at Oxford since 1917. An additional complication was that some universities permitted exemption only if the Higher School Certificate were awarded by an Examination Board over which they had a degree of direct control. From 1918 until the end of the Second World War, the content of most Higher School Certificate syllabuses in biology was almost identical with that of a number of 'First M.B.' courses and, as such, reflected that particular concern with a knowledge of morphology and anatomy which was considered essential for future medical students. There were, however, sufficient differences of emphasis between the various Higher School Certificate and pre-medical syllabuses to demand some difference of approach to teaching them, e.g. Higher School Certificate syllabuses in general required that attention be given to invertebrates and to ecological issues which were inappropriate in a vocationally orientated pre-medical course. The difficulties facing a sixth-form biology teacher, required to prepare different pupils concurrently for several different examinations, are indicated[223] by the data in Table 4.9, which summarises the percentage of questions set on particular biological topics by three examining authorities between 1942 and 1947. The final column of this Table records the range of variation in the importance attached to particular topics as measured by the frequency with which they were examined. While there was undoubtedly a strong body of opinion among teachers that the various pre-medical requirements caused severe difficulty in planning sixth-form courses in biology, it must be recognised that, in the inter-war years and somewhat beyond, the needs of the intending medical students were often the principal *raison d'être* of the 'medical sixth', a group which was sometimes carefully distinguished from the 'science sixth'.

Since the work done below the sixth form was seen, in part, as a preparation for the more specialised Higher Certificate courses,[224] the influence of the

Table 4.9   Percentage of Questions on Biological Topics set by Examination Authorities between 1942 and 1947

	Biology			Botany		Zoology		
	O.C. S.E.B. Higher Cert.	Lond. First M.B.	Lond. Inter B.Sc.	O.C. S.E.B. Higher Cert.	Lond. Inter. B.Sc.	O.C. S.E.B. Higher Cert.	Lond. Inter. B.Sc.	Range %
Anatomy and Histology of Vertebrates	10.0	26.4	14.9			17.1	39.2	10–39
Invertebrates	10.0	4.2	3.2			25.7	25.7	3–26
Embryology	3.3	8.3	6.4			5.7	12.3	3–12
Animal and Plant Physiology	20.0	13.9	31.9	26.0	23.4	8.6	14.6	8–32
Morphology, Anatomy and Histology of Seed Plants	14.4	13.9	8.5	28.1	30.9			9–31
Families of Seed Plants				5.2	2.1			2–5
Spore Plants	12.2	9.7	8.5	11.5	29.8			9–30
Plant and Animal Ecology	4.4			12.5				4–13
Genetics	3.3	4.2	4.3	3.1	2.1	7.1	2.9	2–7
General Biology (e.g. Evolution)	21.1	19.5	22.4	11.5	9.6	32.9	5.3	5–33
Applied Biology	1.1			2.1	2.1			1–2

medical school entrance requirements was not confined to the sixth-form level. In so far as the more advanced courses suggested a pattern of studies to be followed by younger pupils in the school, the medical tradition in school biology raised several difficulties for those who were pressing for a more general inclusion of biology in the curriculum of the grammar school. Whilst it was widely accepted that practical work was essential in order to gain a thorough understanding of biology, the dissection, microscopic and histological studies appropriate for future medical students were often considered impossible or undesirable for classes of twenty-five or thirty pupils under the age of sixteen.[225] The attitude of these classes to dissection was occasionally a matter of concern and some authorities even expressed dislike of the possibility of pupils handling live animals.[226] In addition to the practical difficulties of obtaining an adequate number of suitable specimens[227] and of providing sufficient equipment, there were the continuing doubts whether the physiology and anatomy of sexual reproduction should be included within a main school course in biology.[228]

Moreover, the medical tradition in biology, with its emphasis on the destructive investigation of killed specimens, contrasted sharply with the approach of the naturalists who were concerned to foster a love of nature and an interest in the activities and interrelationships of *living* organisms. Although the activities of the natural history societies founded in considerable numbers in the public schools during the nineteenth century had waned with the advent of compulsory games and 'the worship of athletics', interest in natural history revived during the 1930s as field work in biology gained in importance. (See Figure 4.5.)[229] This developing interest and the need to provide appropriate facilities for field work led to the foundation in 1943 of the Council for the

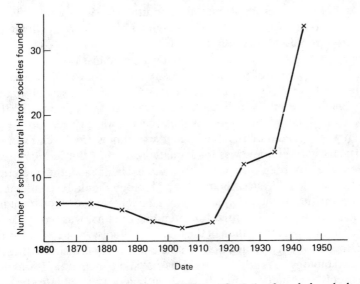

Figure 4.5 Number of School Natural History Societies founded each decade, 1860–1950

Promotion of Field Studies which, after the end of the Second World War, provided centres for field study and research at a number of locations, distinguished by the variety and profusion of their ecology or by other features of geological, geographical, archaeological or historical significance.[230] By maintaining the important tradition of making their resources available to professional biologists and amateurs alike and by enabling schools with limited opportunities for ecological studies to provide short, intensive courses for their pupils,[231] these Field Centres were to do much to encourage the natural history dimension of school biology teaching.

As biology became more widely taught in the secondary schools and the career opportunities available to qualified biologists widened, the dominant influence of medical school curricula on sixth-form biology courses became increasingly unacceptable.[232] In 1944, the Cambridge Local and the Oxford and Cambridge Examination Boards published a new Higher School Certificate syllabus designed to provide both a broader course in sixth-form biology and an adequate basis for First M.B. and Preliminary Medical

Examinations. This new syllabus included reference to animal behaviour (honey bee), parasitism (nematodes), life histories (butterfly), agricultural and economic issues (aphis) and aspects of health and hygiene (housefly and mosquito). These topics were accommodated by excluding reference to certain items such as the dogfish or the dog skull which, because of their morphological interest, formed part of almost all pre-medical syllabuses. These exclusions were sufficient to prevent the new syllabus, introduced after the war, from fulfilling an important function of its predecessor, that of permitting exemption from First M.B. examinations.[233]

Also in 1944, an Interdepartmental Committee on Medical Schools reported a 'preponderance of opinion' that all courses leading to the First Medical Examination should be taken in the universities,[234] and quoted three reasons put forward to support this view. The first was an admission that the necessary standard of knowledge of physics, chemistry and biology could be acquired at school only at the expense of a more general education. The second was that the 'definite medical trend' which should characterise the training for the First M.B. could not be ensured so long as this training was provided in the schools. Finally, it was argued that, in many secondary schools, the teaching of science, and particularly of biology, was inadequate and below the standard required. However, the Interdepartmental Committee challenged the view that the pre-medical work in physics, chemistry and biology should be conducted solely by the universities, principally because of a belief that the 'good grounding' in these sciences, deemed essential for intending doctors, was more likely to be provided in the sixth forms than in the medical schools. At many of the medical schools, the knowledge gained of 'even the elementary principles of chemistry, physics and biology' was adjudged 'superficial and ephemeral'. It was acquired 'too hurriedly' and under conditions which failed 'to stimulate the student's interest or to satisfy his mind as to the relation of these subjects to the rest of his medical studies'.[235]

The lack of consensus between the Interdepartmental Committee and the medical schools as to who should conduct the science teaching for the First Medical Examination was an indication of the difficulty of defining a satisfactory relationship between sixth-form biology on the one hand and pre-medical training on the other. Although there was widespread concern, not least among some sections of the medical profession,[236] about the effect of early specialisation on a liberal, secondary education in biology, sixth-form biology courses continued after the war to neglect those aspects of the subject which were regarded as of little or no vocational relevance to intending medical students. Field work and ecological studies in general perhaps suffered the most and moves to accommodate these aspects of biology within Higher School Certificate syllabuses were, at first, highly tentative. A scheme for testing field work was introduced by the Cambridge Local and the Oxford and Cambridge Boards in 1949 but entry to the scheme was voluntary. Candidates who wished to do so could offer themselves for an oral examination of any aspect of field work which they had carried out. A bad result was ignored but a good performance in the oral examination could be used favourably in borderline cases.

One hundred and two candidates opted for this voluntary test in 1949 and this figure increased to 273, approximately 27 per cent of the entry, in the following year,[237] the last before the introduction of the system of G.C.E. examinations.

In 1953, the British Association recommended[238] that, where any medical school exempted students from 'any part of the Statutory Pre-Medical Examination in Science before admission', passes at Advanced level in physics, chemistry and biology of any recognised Examining body 'should suffice for such exemption'. Unfortunately, the new, subject-based pattern of the G.C.E. examination did little to reduce either the multiplicity of requirements facing sixth formers intending to read for medical degrees or the accompanying problems of devising satisfactory sixth-form courses in biology. As late as 1959, the Crowther Committee reported[239] that while all medical schools, other than that at Bristol, required satisfactory passes at Advanced level in physics and chemistry in order to grant exemption from their First M.B. requirements, the regulations relating to biology varied widely. London required an A-level pass in zoology; Birmingham specified A-level biology but 'in exceptional cases' would consider pupils with passes in botany or zoology; Bristol demanded A-level biology or zoology, 'together with a good pass in botany at Ordinary level'.[240] The 'medical problem' of sixth-form biology was not to be resolved until the following decade when grammar school biology courses were redesigned as part of a wider programme of curriculum development and there were significant changes in the structure and content of medical education, following recommendations from the General Medical Council[241] and the Royal Commission which reported[242] in 1968.

In contrast to the secondary grammar schools, the biology courses in senior, and later in the secondary modern schools, were not strongly influenced by the requirements for entry into the medical profession. Whereas biology was so 'well-established' in the grammar school sector by the 1950s that there was 'little variety of organisation', modern school biology courses were so diverse as to lack any 'common denominator'. In the opinion[243] of H. J. Bonham, the Headmaster of Lutterworth Modern School, Rugby, there was no difference in the ultimate aim of teaching biology in grammar and other types of secondary school; all were concerned to develop an attitude which came from 'an understanding of biological principles and a knowledge of biological facts'. There were, however, significant differences in the contents of the biology courses and in the methods whereby such courses were taught. Whereas 'grammar school biology' was 'pure or academic' and 'imposed from without', principally via the Examination Boards, modern school biology was 'biology applied to the child and his environment[244] and, as such, compiled from 'within and subject to modification and variation' as the teacher thought desirable in the interests of his pupils. Grammar school biology was concerned with the eventual maintenance of science and secondary modern biology with science for citizenship or for 'general education', a distinction expressed in the following terms[245] at the Brighton meeting of the British Association in 1948 when the botany and zoology sections met in joint session to discuss the position of biology in the school curriculum.

There are two chief ways in which science is advanced . . . by research (and) . . . by the moving onward of . . . scientific knowledge which should form part of the equipment of the citizen in all walks of life. . . . It is in the latter field that it is necessary to include the Modern School, catering as it does for the rank and file. . . .

It was thus in the curricula of the modern rather than of the grammar schools that gardening, nutrition, food science, hygiene, health education or animal husbandry figured prominently, although these topics were more often taught in isolation or as part of a scheme of general science than incorporated in a biology course.

As far as methods were concerned, secondary modern science teachers were denied the 'incentive'[246] of external examinations and, as such, were sometimes said to need enthusiasm and skills not always assumed to be required of their grammar school colleagues. Since the interest of the secondary modern school pupil could not be taken for granted, it needed to be aroused by 'presenting figures about infant mortality from a local newspaper', by discussing a local outbreak of foot-and-mouth disease or by reporting a court case 'where an analysis of milk (had) found it to be two-thirds water'. Projects, audio-visual aids, school visits, school gardens and museums were all encouraged in these schools where the academic constraints on the curriculum were assumed not to apply but where the notion of a fixed limit to the abilities of the pupils was widely accepted. Modern school pupils 'could never be expected to master the intricacies of the microscope' and were offered experimental work which was 'qualitative largely, as opposed to the quantitative methods' of the grammar schools. The more senior pupils in the modern schools could listen to the radio in the evenings since, unlike their grammar school counterparts, they were never 'inundated with homework'.[247]

The post-war curriculum differentiation between the grammar and modern schools was not, of course, a novel feature of the educational system and it was by no means confined to biology. As with the other subjects of the curriculum, the different conceptions of a biological education realised in the modern and grammar schools were legitimised by the different social functions ascribed to the two types of school. Most pupils 'selected' for the grammar schools were assumed to 'have some profession in view'; those 'selected' for the modern schools were presumed to have 'no such immediate aims'.[248] The curriculum differentiation was also institutionalised in the allocation of funds and other resources by both central and local government after the war.[249] Surveys conducted by the British Association between 1949 and 1952 showed that whereas the 'accommodation and equipment' for biology were adequate in many grammar schools,[250] modern schools in general lacked the funds to support properly organised laboratory courses.[251] The grammar schools obtained most of the money available under the post-war school building programme[252] and suffered far less than the modern schools from the chronic shortage of specialist science teachers.[253] It is thus hardly surprising that secondary modern biology ranged from 'a total neglect' to a few very good courses 'based on gardening', with the subject, for the most part, being taught as an adjunct to hygiene.[254] It is, however, necessary to acknowledge that, during the 1950s, biology became a relatively popular subject with those pupils who had followed 'extended courses'[255] in the secondary modern schools and entered for the Ordinary level of the G.C.E. By 1960, 25,819 of the 356,617 Ordinary-level candidates were pupils attending modern schools, and biology, including human biology, accounted for 43.5 per cent of their entries in scientific subjects.[256]

Between 1952 and 1962, the number of boys and girls taking biological subjects[257] at the Ordinary level of the G.C.E. examination rose from 35,321 to over 140,000. The number of O-level entries in biology during this period increased by a factor of 2.3, a rate of growth which exceeded that of the total number of candidates. It is, of course, certain that more biology was taught in the schools than these figures indicate. Reference has already been made to the courses in social biology available in a number of grammar schools, to the largely unexamined work in the modern schools and to the entries in Ordinary-level general science of which there were 27,891 in 1962. (See Table 3.9.)

The entry in O-level zoology failed to reach 1,000 by 1957 and the botany entry rose from 814 in 1951 to only 1,057 six years later, having declined to 579 in 1954. After 1958, the numbers of entries for botany and zoology were adjudged by the Ministry of Education to be sufficiently small to be accommodated within the category of 'other subjects' in the annual published summary of statistics. Further details of the O-level entries in the biological sciences between 1952 and 1962 are given[258] in Tables 4.10 and 4.11.

Table 4.10   O-Level Entries in Botany, Zoology, Biology and Agricultural and Horticultural Science, 1951–62

	Botany			Zoology			Biology			Agriculture & Horticulture		
Year	Boys	Girls	Total*	Boys	Girls	Total*	Boys	Girls	Total*	Boys	Girls	Total*
1951	92	722	814	9	12	21	6,935	22,079	29,014	195	61	256
1952	76	337	767	0	3	47	7,718	21,203	34,252	139	59	255
1953	113	568	681	5	72	77	10,173	29,544	39,717	207	68	275
1954	101	193	579	5	8	48	9,916	25,550	42,681	185	56	352
1955	151	507	658	35	21	56	12,872	34,080	46,952	352	97	449
1956	258	542	800	31	33	64	13,518	36,620	50,138	409	69	478
1957	486	571	1,057	21	55	76	15,346	39,544	54,890	388	104	492
1958	DATA NOT PUBLISHED						17,559	45,029	62,588	491	109	600
1959							20,350	52,651	73,001	605	148	753
1960							24,035	59,954	83,989	763	171	934
1961							26,270	62,944	89,214	822	147	969
1962							25,689	73,842	99,531	878	180	1,058

* The entry in the 'Total' column sometimes exceeds the sum of the entries under 'Boys' and 'Girls' since one Examination Board failed to distinguish between boys and girls in presenting its statistics.

Table 4.11   Growth of Entries in O-Level Biology as
% of Total Entry, 1951–62

Year	No. of Girls as % of total entries by Girls	No. of Boys as % of total entries by Boys	No. of Boys and Girls as % of total entry by Boys and Girls
1951	6.49	1.74	3.93
1952	5.39	2.51	4.13
1953	6.79	1.87	4.05
1954	7.08	2.13	4.34
1955	7.40	2.21	4.49
1956	7.69	2.28	4.69
1957	7.95	2.43	4.86
1958	8.00	2.46	4.91
1959	8.23	2.51	5.03
1960	8.48	2.68	5.24
1961	8.74	2.83	5.41
1962	8.96	2.55	5.43

The relative rates of growth of botany, zoology and biology as G.C.E.
Advanced level subjects in the decade after 1952 are recorded in Tables 4.12
and 4.13. The relatively large entry in zoology may be explained, in part, by the
importance of the subject for those intending to read medicine.

Table 4.12   A-Level Entries in Botany, Zoology and Biology, 1951–62

Year	Botany			Zoology			Biology		
	Boys	Girls	Total*	Boys	Girls	Total*	Boys	Girls	Total*
1951	1,844	1,118	2,962	1,867	1,221	3,088	2,683	1,437	4,120
1952	1,600	1,051	3,013	1,649	1,131	3,144	2,697	1,329	4,413
1953	1,915	1,158	3,073	1,938	1,341	3,279	3,056	1,590	4,646
1954	2,115	1,254	3,780	2,139	1,422	3,983	2,675	1,345	4,448
1955	2,513	1,628	4,141	2,567	1,829	4,396	2,967	1,805	4,772
1956	2,875	1,827	4,702	2,883	2,064	4,947	3,052	1,865	4,917
1957	2,703	1,820	4,523	3,202	2,217	5,419	3,127	1,987	5,114
1958	2,640	1,692	4,332	3,638	2,392	6,030	3,015	1,952	4,967
1959	2,385	1,627	4,012	3,523	2,424	5,947	3,115	1,971	5,086
1960	2,679	1,813	4,492	4,175	2,845	7,020	3,474	2,359	5,833
1961	2,606	2,123	4,729	4,124	3,283	7,407	4,216	2,883	7,099
1962	2,533	2,207	4,740	4,406	3,685	8,091	4,987	3,185	8,172

* The entry in the 'Total' column sometimes exceeds the sum of the entries under 'Boys' and 'Girls'
since one Examination Board failed to distinguish between boys and girls in presenting its statistics.

As with the earlier School Certificate examinations,[259] the G.C.E. entries in
biological science at Ordinary level show a marked sex bias in favour of girls. In
1952, the ratio of the number of girls to boys entering for O-level biology was

2.75 to 1. It was virtually the same a decade later, despite the large increase in the number of candidates.

At the sixth-form level, the slight bias in favour of girls which existed[260] until 1949, disappeared as biology gained in popularity as an Advanced-level subject and a greater proportion of boys, compared with girls, remained at school after the statutory school leaving age. The ratios of the numbers of girls to boys entering for Advanced-level botany, zoology and biology were 0.66, 0.69 and 0.42 respectively in 1952, compared with the corresponding ratios of 0.81, 0.79 and 0.68 a decade later. The differentiation of the curriculum between the sexes is discussed in some detail in Chapter 5.

Table 4.13   Growth in Entries for A-Level Botany,
Zoology and Biology, 1952–62

Subject	Ratio of 1962 Entry to Entry 10 Years Earlier		
	Boys	Girls	Boys and Girls
Botany	1.58	2.09	1.57
Zoology	2.67	3.26	2.57
Biology	1.86	2.39	1.85
All Subjects	2.67	2.99	2.50

Towards the end of the 1950s, the desirability of retaining botany and zoology as distinct Advanced-level subjects was challenged by the changes which had taken place within biology itself. The enormous success of crystallographic and cytochemical studies in the field of molecular biology,[261] of which the elucidation of the structure of D.N.A. is the best-known example,[262] led to pressure to reform the teaching of the life sciences so as to incorporate both the relevant biochemistry and the reductionist/experimental approach which had brought such triumphs. While few biologists would have agreed that 'the ultimate aim' was to explain *all* biology in terms of physics and chemistry',[263] the curriculum implications of the molecularisation of biology could not be ignored, not least because the successful application of the experimental techniques and basic ideas of physics and chemistry to matters of fundamental biological significance now seemed to offer those 'arrangements for greater co-ordination' which Bernal, a generation earlier, had regarded as essential to the evolution of a rigorous, scientific biology.[264]

The move from botany and zoology to biology suggested[265] by the new paradigm in biological research also provided an opportunity to reduce the degree of specialisation of the grammar school curriculum at a time when the narrowness of the education of many sixth formers was a matter of general concern. In a situation in which the numbers of well-qualified applicants with three Advanced-level subjects exceeded the number of places in higher education, the universities' insistence[266] that two minimum passes (40 per cent) at

A-level constituted an adequate entry qualification ceased to be of practical significance.

By 1960, when the entry requirement of a science faculty at a civic university was generally 'three A-level passes in scientific subjects at 65%' and even 'one of the lesser-known London Colleges' was demanding a State Scholarship as a condition of entry to read mathematics, too many grammar school pupils were being forced into a narrow specialisation between the ages of fifteen and eighteen which did not allow adequate time for the development of other interests. A significant proportion remained in the sixth form for an additional year in an attempt to obtain A-level grades which were higher than those they had gained at the end of the conventional two-year sixth-form course and, in some schools, the Ordinary-level examinations were taken as early as possible in order to maximise the time available for Advanced-level studies.[267]

The 'narrowness and exclusivity' of the sixth form curriculum, by far its weakest feature, was unique in Western Europe or North America and was seen as contributing to the maintenance of the so-called 'two cultures', discussed by C. P. Snow in his widely publicised Rede Lecture[268] of 1959. The replacement of Advanced-level botany and zoology by a single course of biology offered schools an opportunity to counteract excessive sixth-form specialisation by providing an additional degree of flexibility in planning curricula within the existing structure[269] of the G.C.E. examinations. A particularly important advantage, given the developments which were taking place in biology itself, was the possibility of including mathematics or both physics and chemistry among the sixth-form courses followed by future undergraduates in the life sciences.

In 1959, the report of an inquiry into the suitability of Advanced-level science syllabuses as a preparation for direct entry into first degree courses in the Faculty of Science at the University of Birmingham advised intending biology undergraduates to study *either* biology, chemistry and some other Advanced-level subject, which might be scientific or non-scientific, *or* mathematics, physics and chemistry and, if possible, a non-specialist course in biology.[270] In the former case, the students were also advised that 'both mathematics and physics' were to be taken either in the sixth form or previously, 'at least to Ordinary level'. The report, based on a consideration of the Advanced-level syllabuses offered by the Joint Matriculation Board, recommended[271] that Advanced-level botany and zoology should be superseded wherever possible by a revised Advanced-level course in biology and that, 'as soon as circumstances permitted', candidates' freedom to offer Advanced-level botany and zoology at the same examination 'should be discontinued'. A specimen Advanced-level syllabus in biology was produced, intended as a basis for a thorough training in the principles of biology, yet designed to obviate the difficulties created by the variation in the entrance requirements of the different universities and medical schools. The syllabus identified several 'biological principles', e.g. the fundamental activities of living matter, the relationships of cells within organisms, and, in contrast to the more conventional syllabuses derived, however indirectly, from Huxley's type system, no particular organisms were specified for study. Indeed, the 'mention of any type (except man) was rigorously avoided'.[272] A variety of organisms could thus be used to illustrate the principles mentioned in the syllabus and schools would be free to make optimum use of the resources available to them.

The report of the committee was presented to the Joint Matriculation Board in October 1959 and no doubt encouraged the appointment of a subcommittee to review the Board's Advanced-level syllabus in biology. In 1963, a new syllabus was circulated for comment to schools and other interested organisations and individuals, emphasising that biology was an 'active experimental science', making use of the disciplines of mathematics, physics and chemistry'.[273] A new syllabus in Advanced-level biology was introduced by the Joint Matriculation Board for the examination of 1966 and, two years later, the Board's Advanced-level syllabuses in botany and zoology were withdrawn. A number of other Boards followed[274] the Joint Matriculation Board's example and introduced new Advanced-level syllabuses in biology, although most continued to offer syllabuses in botany and zoology.

The report of the inquiry conducted by the University of Birmingham was only one of a number of responses to the changing nature of biological science. Others included the Nuffield Science Teaching Project, initiated in 1962, and the publications of the American Biological Sciences Curriculum Study. The latter were of particular interest both because of the aim of the study:

> to prepare ... biology courses, suitable for wide use ... with average classes and ... to build scientific literacy to aid in the preparation of the student for later responsible citizenship[275]

and because they incorporated a choice of three conceptions of school biology. These were the so-called 'blue version' with a bias towards molecular biology, a 'yellow version' emphasising a cellular approach, and the ecologically orientated 'green version'.

Both the 'principles' and the 'type' approach to constructing biology syllabuses were to survive throughout the 1960s and beyond, producing greater differences between Advanced-level syllabuses in biological science than at any time in the past.

> Whereas A-level syllabuses in biological subjects tended to be generally similar, a situation has arisen where considerable differences exist and more are developing.[276]

Few schools seemed able to take advantage of the variety of Advanced-level syllabuses available to them. Less than 1 per cent of schools make any change of Examination Board in any one year and, in 1962, 'no real swing from or to any Board' was either 'in progress or likely'. The obstacles to changing an Examination Board for an individual subject were largely administrative and the special arrangements made later for candidates following 'Nuffield' courses in biology were, in part, a recognition of the nature of these difficulties and an attempt to overcome them.

However, the schools were not slow to favour biology at the expense of botany and zoology in the sixth form and the position of these subjects declined significantly after 1960 as Table 4.14 shows.[277] School biology 'comparable in extent and demand' with the other sciences had at last come of age. It had taken nearly a hundred years.

Table 4.14   A-Level Entrants (Summer, Boys and Girls) in Biological Science, 1961 and 1971

Subject	1961	1971	% Change
Botany	4,729	1,981	−58.1
Zoology	7,409	4,428	−40.2
Biology	7,099	21,575	+204

References

[1] For an account of Combe's educational writings, see Jolly, W., *Education: Its Principles and Practice as Developed by George Combe*, 1879.

[2] Combe, G., *On Teaching Physiology and its Applications in Common Schools*, Edinburgh, 1857.

[3] Bremner, J. P., 'George Combe (1788–1858): The Pioneer of Physiology Teaching in British Schools', *S.S.R.*, vol. XXXVIII, no. 134, 1956, p. 51.

[4] Singer, C., *A History of Biology to about the Year 1900*, 1959, p. 56.

[5] Layton, D., *Science for the People*, 1973, p. 65.

[6] Ibid., p. 60.

[7] *Clarendon Commission*, vol. IV, 1864, para. 10, Evidence of Richard Owen, F.R.S.

[8] Ibid., vol. IV, para. 75, Evidence of W. B. Carpenter, F.R.S.

[9] J. M. Wilson was senior science master at Rugby where Temple was the Headmaster.

[10] Bremner, J. P., *S.S.R.*, vol. XXXVIII, no. 136, 1957, p. 378. The book was one of Macmillan's Science Classbooks which included volumes by Roscoe (Chemistry), Lockyer (Astronomy) and Geikie (Physical Geography).

[11] Wilson, J. M., 'On Teaching Natural Science in Schools', in Farrar, F. W., (ed.), *Essays on a Liberal Education*, 1868, p. 277.

[12] Miall, L. C., Botany Teaching; London County Council Technical Education Board Conference, *Journal of Education*, February 1900, p. 119.

[13] Board of Education, *The Botany Gardens of the James Allen's Girls' School, Dulwich*, Educational Pamphlet No. 41, HMSO, 1922.

[14] *Annual Reports* of the Examiners of the Department of Science and Art, 1870 onwards and *Annual Reports* of the Cambridge Local Examinations Board, 1878–1900. The problem continued into the twentieth century; see Miall, L. C., *Journal of Education*, October 1908, p. 699.

[15] Huxley, L., *Life and Letters of Sir Joseph Dalton Hooker*, vol. I, 1918, p. 403, cited in Layton, D., op. cit., p. 62.

[16] Hooker, J. D., *Botany Science Primer*, 1876, p. 1.

[17] From 1839 to 1864, the London University Matriculation Syllabus in zoology required candidates to study 'the characteristics of the primary divisions of the Animal Kingdom and of the Classes and Orders of the Vertebrate Sub-Kingdom, according to the system of Cuvier'. Bremner, J. P., 'Some Developments in the Teaching of

Zoology in Schools in the Nineteenth Century', *S.S.R.*, vol. XXXIX, no. 137, 1957, p. 71.

[18] Brown, E. S., 'Zoology in the Schools, 1851–1951', *S.S.R.*, vol. XXXV, no. 125, 1953, p. 74.

[19] Cambridge University Local Examinations Board, *Report and Tables*, 1886, p. 28.

[20] Ibid., *Report and Tables*, 1901, p. 16.

[21] Bremner, J. P., *Some Aspects of the Teaching of the Biological Sciences in English Schools during the Second Half of the Nineteenth Century*, M.A. Thesis, University of London, 1955.

[22] Wilson, A., *Zoology*, 1877, Preface.

[23] Bremner, J. P., M.A. Thesis, op. cit., p. 161.

[24] Bremner, J. P., *S.S.R.*, vol. XXXIX, no. 137, 1957, p. 74.

[25] Department of Science and Art, *21st Report*, 1874, Appendix A., p. 2.

[26] Huxley, T. H., and Martin, H. N., *A Course of Practical Instruction in Elementary Biology*, 1875.·

[27] Cambridge University Local Examinations Board, *Report and Tables*, 1885, p. 121.

[28] Bremner, J. P., M.A. Thesis, op. cit., p. 187.

[29] Huxley, T. H., 'On the Study of Biology', in *Collected Essays on Science and Education*, 1893, p. 290.

[30] The amount expended rose from about £3,000 in 1889 to over £12,000 by the end of the century. Comber, N. M., *Agricultural Education in Great Britain*, 1948, p. 4. See also Armytage, W. H. G., *Civic Universities*, 1955, p. 230.

[31] The Yorkshire College of Science held classes in agriculture for schoolmasters in 1891–2 at five centres, with a vacation course in Leeds. Gosden, P. H. J. H., Taylor, A. J. (eds.), *Studies in the History of a University*, 1975, p. 256.

[32] Ibid., p. 270.

[33] The Chairman and the Secretary were Sir W. Hart Davies and Henry Hobhouse respectively. See Report of the Departmental Committee appointed by the Board of Agriculture and Fisheries upon Agricultural Education in England and Wales, *Minutes of Evidence*, HMSO, 1908, p. 539.

[34] The evidence of this collapse may be found in the Reports of the Royal Commission on Agricultural Depression in 1894, (Cd. 7400), in 1896 (Cd. 7981) and in 1897 (Cd. 8540), and in the twenty reports of the Assistant Commissioners which appeared between 1894 and 1896.

[35] Ware, F., *Educational Reform*, 1900, p. 62.

[36] Between 1871 and 1901, the male agricultural labourers in England and Wales 'were diminished by over one-third, while the general population increased by 43 per cent'. Ensor, R. C. K., *England, 1870–1914*, 1936, pp. 285–6.

[37] Board of Education, *The Curriculum of the Rural School*, Circular 435, April 1900.

[38] Board of Education, *Suggestions on Rural Education*, 1902, p. iii. New 'Suggestions' were issued in 1908.

[39] B.A.A.S., *Report*, 1906, p. 459.

[40] Allen, D. E., *The Naturalist in Britain*, 1976, pp. 203–4.

[41] B.A.A.S., *Report*, 1906, p. 464.

[42] For an explanation of this term, see Selleck, R. J. W., *The New Education*, 1968.

[43] Allen, D. E., op. cit., pp. 205–6, where this point is discussed in some detail. Allen also explores the effect of nature study teaching on the more scientific pursuit of 'natural history'. For other comments on 'outdoor biology', see Martin, P. G., *A History of General Studies Science and of Outdoor Biology*, M.Ed. Thesis, Bangor University, 1976.

[44] Data from *Annual Reports* of the Science and Art Department from 1863 onwards and from Cambridge University Local Examinations Board, *Reports and Tables*, 1878–1900.

[45] Modified from Shann, E. W., 'Biology in Secondary Schools', *S.S.R.*, vol. X, no. 38, 1928, p. 129.

[46] The popularity of botany, as measured by the entries for the secondary school Certificate examinations, appears to have declined.

[47] Tracey, G. W., *The Place and Role of the Biological Sciences in English School Curricula, 1902–56*. M.Sc. Thesis, University of Sheffield, 1961, p. 5.

[48] If only because botany was an inexpensive science to teach and regarded by the Taunton Commission as on a par with physics and chemistry as a subject capable of providing the necessary training in the methods of science. See Layton, D., op. cit., p. 73.

[49] Singer, C., op. cit., p. 573.

[50] Gosden, P. H. J. H., and Taylor, A. J., op. cit., p. 271–2.

[51] 'The methods of biology ... are obviously identical with those of all other sciences and therefore wholly incompetent to form the ground of any distinction between it and them.' Huxley, T. H., 'On the Natural History Sciences', *Science and Education*, 1905 edn., p. 56.

[52] B.A.A.S., Joint Discussion of Sections K and L on the Teaching of Biology in Schools, *Report*, 1907, p. 547.

[53] H. E. Armstrong was perhaps the most vocal contemporary educationist who held this view. See, Armstrong, H. E., *Training in Scientific Method as a Central Motive in Elementary Schools, 1902*, and *Science Teaching in Agricultural Districts, 1895*, reproduced in van Praagh, G., *H. E. Armstrong and Science Education*, 1973, p. 107 and p. 40.

[54] Huxley, T. H., *Science and Education*, 1905 edn., p. 64.

[55] Board of Education, *Report 1900–1*, vol. II (Report of D. H. Hoffert), HMSO, p. 271.

[56] Bryant, S., 'Natural Science', in Burstall, S. A. and Douglas, M. A. (eds.), *Public Schools for Girls*, 1911, p. 134.

[57] For a turn-of-the-century view of the ethics of vivisection, see Anderson, E. G., 'Ethics of Vivisection', *Edinburgh Review*, July 1899, pp. 147–69.

[58] B.A.A.S., *Report*, 1907, p. 549.

[59] I.C.I. set up its first pharmaceutical research department in 1936 with eight scientists in the group. Wilson, D., *Penicillin in Perspective*, 1976, p. 131. Wilson notes that in 1914, the British Pharmacopoeia listed 'just 80 synthetic drugs', mostly of the aspirin and phenacetin families, and 'all but a few were imports from Germany'. The weakness of the British pharmaceutical industry is usually attributed to the relative inadequacy of the organic chemical industry, itself usually seen as a result of the failure to develop the coal tar dye industry in the nineteenth century. See Hardie, D. W. F., and Pratt, J. D., *A History of the Modern British Chemical Industry*, 1966.

[60] *Natural Science in Education*, HMSO, 1918, para. 41.

[61] Ibid., para. 53.

[62] For an estimation of the quality of this work by a naturalist, see Allen, D. E., op. cit., pp. 203–4.

[63] Natural Science in Education, para. 89.

[64] Ibid., para. 52.

[65] Ibid., Recommendation 17.

[66] Ibid., para. 52.

[67] Ibid., para. 53. The Thomson Committee was very critical of the scientific content of courses in 'hygiene', claiming that hygiene could be considered part of a science

curriculum only if it followed a programme of systematic work in those sciences upon which the practice of hygiene depended.

[68] Ibid., para. 90.

[69] Ibid., para. 41.

[70] Ibid., para. 52.

[71] The position of botany in the curriculum, *T.E.S.*, 18 July 1918, p. 305.

[72] 'Biology in the School Science Course', *S.S.R.*, vol. I, no. 2, 1920, p. 82.

[73] Cawthorne, H. H., 'Biology and the Science Syllabus', *S.S.R.*, vol. XII, no. 45, 1930, p. 58.

[74] It should be noted that this problem was not confined to School Certificate examinations. Many Oxford and Cambridge Colleges regarded biology as an unsuitable subject for university entrance and scholarship examinations, partly because of a belief that it was possible for a candidate to do well without any 'real knowledge'. *The Times*, 21 January 1901, p. 14.

[75] Hatfield, E. J., 'School Examinations Surveyed', *Journal of Education*, vol. LXVII, February 1935, p. 70.

[76] B.A.A.S., 'Biology as an Element in the Science Curriculum of Schools', *Report*, 1925, p. 376.

[77] In 1911, the West Riding L.E.A. introduced annual summer courses for teachers on the grounds that some knowledge of biology was desirable for a teacher, even though he or she might not be required to teach the subject in a school. Crowther, J. G., *Biology in Education*, 1933, p. 148. For details of the courses organised by the Board of Education between 1919 and 1926, see Reference 79, p. 26.

[78] Armstrong, H. E., 'The Future Science of the Schools', *Journal of Education*, vol. LVII, July 1925, p. 486. In an earlier issue of the same *Journal* (January 1923, p. 11), the position of physics and chemistry was described as one of 'tyrannous predominance'.

[79] Board of Education, *Report of an Inquiry into the Conditions Affecting the Teaching of Science in Secondary Schools for Boys in England*, HMSO, 1925, p. 11.

[80] Brown, J., *Teaching Science in Schools*, 1925, pp. 122–3.

[81] *Report of the Imperial Agricultural Research Conference*, 1927, HMSO, para. 63.

[82] *S.S.R.*, vol. XI, no. 41, pp. 60 and 64.

[83] The British Association had commented upon this point in 1921. B.A.A.S., Memorandum on the Teaching of Natural History, *Report*, 1921, p. 264.

[84] Data compiled from *Annual Reports and Tables* of the Board (later Ministry) of Education.

[85] Writing in 1939, T. H. Hawkins described the growth of biology in the schools during this period as 'remarkable'. 'The Teaching of Biology in Relation to Citizenship', *Journal of Education*, September 1939, p. 595.

[86] Few schools introduced botany courses after 1928 and MacDonald (op. cit.), confirms that the teaching of biology was introduced into a large number of schools after 1930.

[87] The growing popularity of general science as an examination subject during the 1930s means that more biological science was taught to School Certificate level than is indicated by the entries for biology itself.

[88] Green, T. L., *The Teaching and Learning of Biology*, 1949, pp. 12–14. The sample was made up of forty-nine boys', forty-one girls' and forty-two coeducational schools.

[89] Board of Education, *Report of the Consultative Committee on the Education of the Adolescent*, HMSO, 1926.

[90] Board of Education, *Report of the Consultative Committee on the Primary School*, HMSO, 1931, especially pp. 182–6.

[91] B.A.A.S., *Report*, 1928, p. 397.

[92] Ibid., Appendix VI, pp. 415–28.

[93] Ibid., p. 407.

[94] Ibid., p. 399.

[95] The panel of Investigators appointed by the S.S.E.C. to inquire into the 1931 School Certificate examinations concluded that the problem of 'synthesising botany and zoology into a coherent biology course, although capable of solution' was 'not yet solved'. *The School Certificate Examination, being the Report of the Panel of Investigators Appointed by the Secondary School Examinations Council to Inquire into the Eight Approved School Certificate Examinations held in the Summer of 1931*, HMSO, 1932, pp. 132–3.

[96] *S.S.R.*, vol. XI, no. 43, 1930, p. 225.

[97] Ibid., p. 226.

[98] Armytage, W. H. G., *Sir Richard Gregory*, 1957, p. 132.

[99] Laurie, R. D., *Eugenic Education in the School*, address to the Eugenics (Education) Society, reported in *Nature*, vol. 104, January 1920, p. 513.

[100] B.A.A.S., *Report*, 1931, pp. 507–8.

[101] Huxley, J. S., *What Dare I Think*, 1931, pp. 88 and 109. See also, Huxley, J. S., *The Stream of Life*, 1926, p. 41. It should be noted that Huxley later changed his views on these issues. See Huxley, J. S., *The Uniqueness of Man*, 1941.

[102] *Nature* was also concerned with 'racial decay' and anticipated Huxley in advocating the compulsory sterilisation of the unemployed on the assumption that indigence was a symptom of 'sub-normal intelligence'. See Werskey, P. G., 'Nature and Politics Between the Wars', *Nature*, vol. 224, November 1969, pp. 462–72. Although no action of the type advocated by *Nature* was taken in Britain, many States within the U.S.A. introduced laws designed to forbid or discourage reproduction by those who were classified as feeble-minded, epileptic, habitual criminals or alcoholics. See the entry under *Eugenics* in the 1929 edition of the *Encyclopaedia Britannica*.

[103] Hogben, L., *The Nature of Living Matter*, 1930, and *Genetic Principles in Medicine and Social Science*, 1931.

[104] For example, Munro, J. W., 'Industrial Entomology', *S.S.R.*, vol. XI, no. 43, 1930, p. 196 and, in the same volume, James, W. O., 'Some Important Aspects of Plant Physiology', Part II, p. 259.

[105] School Certificate Biology Syllabus, *S.S.R.*, vol. XVII, no. 66, 1935, pp. 302–4.

[106] Farmer, J. B., 'Biology in Relation to a Career', *S.S.R.*, vol. VI, no. 22, 1924, p. 78.

[107] *Journal of Education*, February 1929, p. 131.

[108] *T.E.S.*, 19 January 1929, p. 31.

[109] See, for example, *T.E.S.*, 12 January 1929, p. 19.

[110] Economic Advisory Council, *Committee on Education and Supply of Biologists, Report*, HMSO, 1933, p. 6.

[111] Ibid., p. 42, para. 118(i).

[112] Ibid., p. 42, para. 118(ii).

[113] Ibid., p. 13, para. 27.

[114] Ibid., p. 4.

[115] Tizard, H. T., 'Science at the Universities: Some Problems of the Present and the Future'; B.A.A.S., *Report*, 1934, p. 215.

[116] Ibid., p. 216. It is perhaps worth noting that, almost a generation later, in 1962, when 1,637 students graduated with degrees in biological science, only sixteen of these were specialists in bacteriology and twelve in microbiology. See U.G.C., *First Employment of University Graduates, 1961–2*, HMSO, 1963. For comment on the U.G.C. Report, see *Institute of Biology Journal*, vol. 10, no. 4, 1963, p. 94.

[117] Economic Advisory Council, *Report*, 1933, p. 4.

[118] The numbers in individual specialisms were very small. The Natural History Museum employed ten zoologists, six botanists and five entomologists between 1918 and 1931. The Government of India 'anticipated' that the number of posts falling vacant or to be created in the decade after 1931 included six in entomology, three in mycology, three in bacteriology, six in protozoology ..., averaging five per annum. Ibid., pp. 50–1.

[119] Tizard, H. T., op. cit., p. 216.

[120] Economic Advisory Council, *Report*, 1933, p. 44.

[121] Ibid., p. 43. The Chelmsford Committee, however, was thinking only in terms of boys, e.g. 'Biology should be brought to the notice of every boy', perhaps because it saw the professional employment of biologists as a masculine preserve.

[122] Adams, J., *The New Teaching*, 1925, p. 181.

[123] Crowther, J. G. (ed.), *Biology in Education*, 1933, p. 89.

[124] For a history of the eugenic movement in Britain, see MacKenzie, D., 'Eugenics in Britain', *Social Studies of Science*, 6, 1976, pp. 499–532. For the activities of the Eugenics Society in the inter-war years, see Waterman, L., *The Eugenic Movement in Britain in the 1930s*, M.Sc. Thesis, Sussex, 1975. MacKenzie, D., op. cit., p. 518, claims that after 1918, 'eugenics seemed to lack political credibility'.

[125] Board of Education, *Handbook of Suggestions of Health Education for the Consideration of Teachers and Others Concerned with the Work of Public Elementary Schools*, HMSO, 1928.

[126] Tracey, G. W., op. cit., p. 133, describes the first ten years of its existence as 'the era of propaganda'.

[127] Sex Education and Guidance, *Nature*, vol. 151, 1943, pp. 356–7.

[128] Mander, F., 'The Teacher's Contribution', in Crowther, J. G., *Biology in Education*, 1933, pp. 145–6.

[129] Ibid., p. 150.

[130] Crowther, J. G., op. cit., p. vi. The N.U.T. issued a policy statement on sex education in schools in 1944.

[131] See, for example, Church of England Moral Welfare Council, *Sex Education and the Teacher*, 1946.

[132] The Council was set up in 1938 in response to concern at the rising divorce rate. It inevitably became involved with educational matters, including sex education and 'family planning'.

[133] *Biology and Human Affairs*, vol. 16, no. 2, 1950, pp. 57–60.

[134] Tracey, G. W., op. cit., p. 51.

[135] Chelmsford was Warden of All Souls College; Sadler was the Master of University College, Oxford; Selby-Bigge was formerly Permanent Secretary of the Board of Education and Richard Gregory was still editing *Nature*. For an account of W. M. Fletcher's work in the M.R.C., see Crowther, J. G., *Scientific Types*, 1968.

[136] Crowther, J. G. (ed.), *Biology in Education*, a handbook based on the Proceedings of the National Conference on the Place of Biology in Education, organised by the British Social Hygiene Council, 1933.

[137] Ibid., p. vi.

[138] Thomson, J. A., Geddes, P., *Life: Outlines of General Biology*, 2 vols., 1931. In their Preface, the authors describe their work as two 'large and crowded volumes'.

[139] Ibid., vol. 2, p. 1194.

[140] Crowther, J. G. (ed.), op. cit., 1933, p. 4.

[141] Ibid., pp. 4–5.

[142] Ibid., p. 5.

[143] Tracey, G. W., op. cit., p. 50.

[144] British Social Hygiene Council, *Annual Report*, 1933–4, p. 33.

[145] British Social Hygiene Council, *Annual Report*, 1935–6, p. 33.

[146] For example, with Kent L.E.A., British Social Hygiene Council, *Annual Report*, 1934–5, p. 33.

[147] For a reaction by the General Secretary of the S.M.A. to the work of the B.S.H.C., see *S.S.R.* vol. XV, no. 57, 1933, pp. 117–18.

[148] *Biology and Human Affairs*, vol. 40, no. 2, 1975, p. 54.

[149] The early issues of the *Journal* are reviewed in an editorial comment 'Forty Years On' in Ibid., pp. 53–61.

[150] Ibid., p. 60. The post-war trend was accurately predicted in the editorial of the Summer 1945 issue of *Biology and Human Affairs*: 'What is emerging is an entirely new intellectual discipline, capable, like the humanities, of embracing all aspects of human life but, unlike the humanities ... rooted in the experimental approach to all living matter.'

[151] The term 'social biology' was given a very wide interpretation by some authorities. See, for example, the proposals to establish a National Institute for Social Biology, *Nature*, vol. 149, 24 January 1942, pp. 88–102, especially p. 88. Much of this issue of *Nature* was devoted to 'social science as a basis for policy and action'. For a history of social biology, see Scoggins, J. A., *The Development of Social Biology*, M.Ed. Thesis, Chelsea College, London, 1976.

[152] Board of Education, *Code of Regulations for Public Elementary Schools*, 1906, p. vii. For an account of the Moral Instruction League, see Hilliard, F. H., 'The Moral Instruction League, 1897–1919', *The Durham Research Review*, no. 12, September 1961, pp. 53–63. For a detailed account of the citizenship movement, see Whitmarsh, G., *Society and the School Curriculum: the Association for Education in Citizenship, 1934–1957*, M.Ed. Thesis, University of Birmingham, 1972.

[153] The conference leading to the formation of the League was convened by the so-called 'New Ideal Group'. See Whitmarsh, G., op. cit., p. 13.

[154] Lloyd George told the War Cabinet in 1918 that 'Here we have a great, inflammable industrial population.' Johnson, P. B., *Land Fit for Heroes*, 1968, p. 30.

[155] J. E. C. Welldon, 1854–1937. Welldon was Headmaster of Harrow from 1885 to 1898, Bishop of Calcutta and Metropolitan of India from 1898 to 1902 and Dean of Durham from 1918 to 1933.

[156] In the year following the General Strike, the President of the Board of Education addressed the North of England Education Conference and indicated that many people were uneasy about what might be involved in teaching civics or citizenship. He could provide little reassurance since 'the president of a teacher's league' was reported 'as announcing that citizenship should come first on the list of school subjects' and that this meant 'that the child should understand the principles of socialism and should learn the fact that there is a class war in which we are all involved'. *The Times*, 7 January 1927, p. 17.

[157] Hadow, H., *Citizenship*, 1923, p. 1.

[158] Keatinge, M. W., *Studies in the Teaching of History*, 1910, p. 7.

[159] Adams, J. (ed.), *The New Teaching*, 1925, p. 263.

[160] Its President was Sir Henry Hadow and its Vice-Presidents included H. A. L. Fisher and Gilbert Murray. Its Council included Cyril Burt, Salter Davies, F. Mander, Albert Mansbridge, Cyril Norwood, W. O. Lester-Smith and Barbara Wootton amongst its members. *New Statesman and Nation*, Education Supplement, 14 July 1934, p. 63.

[161] Association for Education in Citizenship, *Education for Citizenship in Secondary*

Schools, 1935, pp. 183–93. A corresponding volume for elementary schools was published in 1939.

[162] Kerr, J. G., 'Biology and the Training of the Citizen', B.A.A.S. *Report*, 1926, pp. 102–12.

[163] Ibid., p. 109. Kerr (1869–1957) was Regius Professor of Zoology at Glasgow from 1902 to 1935.

[164] MacKinnon, D. L., op. cit., p. 186. See also Tracey, G. W., op. cit., p. 144. Dorothy Livingston MacKinnon was Professor of Zoology in the University of London from 1927 to 1949.

[165] MacKinnon, D. L., op. cit., p. 185. A Biology course devised by N. L. Houslop, Senior Biology and Senior Geography Master at Battersea Grammar School was appended to MacKinnon's essay.

[166] For Gregory's Lecture, see S.M.A., *Report for 1937 with List of Members*, pp. 16–21. The second 'Science and Citizenship' Lecture should have been arranged for 1940. For Hogben's Lecture, see *S.S.R.*, vol. XXIII, no. 91, 1942, p. 263. The S.M.A. also responded by criticising the 'literary' bias of the Spens Report, a bias which reflected the lobbying of the Spens Committee by the influential members of the Association for Education in Citizenship. These members failed in their primary objective – to get the Spens Committee to recommend the 'direct' teaching of citizenship – but they succeeded in persuading the Committee of the value of historical and literary studies in educating for citizenship. For details, see Whitmarsh, G., op. cit. Subsequent 'Science and Citizenship' Lectures were delivered by W. T. Astbury in 1948 (*S.S.R.*, vol. XXIX, no. 109, 1948, pp. 268–80) and A. H. T. Glover in 1951 (not published).

[167] *S.S.R.*, vol. XXIII, no. 91, 1942, p. 265.

[168] Ibid., p. 273.

[169] Brimble, L. J. F., 'Biology as a Social Science', *S.S.R.*, vol. XXIII, no. 91, 1942, p. 341.

[170] Ibid., p. 340.

[171] Crowther, J. G., 'The Social Relations of Science', *S.S.R.*, vol. XXVI, no. 100, 1945, p. 284. Crowther's lecture was said to be 'much to the taste of his audience', ibid., p. 372.

[172] Ibid., p. 283. Crowther may also be seen as urging the S.M.A. to respond to the 'social relations of science' as the B.A.A.S. had done at its Annual Meeting in 1936. Some of the material presented at this meeting had been reprinted in the following year. See Orr, J. B., et al, *What Science Stands For*, 1937. In addition to Orr, the contributors were A. V. Hill, J. C. Philip, Sir Richard Gregory, Sir A. Daniel Hall and Lancelot Hogben.

[173] *S.S.R.*, vol. XXVI, no. 100, 1945, p. 372. For an account of the isolation and manufacture of penicillin and of contemporary reaction it it, see Wilson, D. *Penicillin in Perspective*, 1976, *passim*.

[174] *T.E.S.*, 9 August 1941, p. 373.

[175] *S.S.R.*, vol. XXVI, no. 100, 1945, p. 376.

[176] See Note 171.

[177] Wood, N., *Communism and British Intellectuals*, 1959, p. 121.

[178] Werskey, P. G., 'British Scientists and Outsider Politics, 1931–1945', in Barnes, B. (ed.), *Sociology of Science: Selected Readings*, 1972, p. 235. Werskey's distinction between radicals and reformers is the basis of the discussion in the following paragraphs of the text.

[179] Werskey, P. G., ibid., p. 246, suggests that the radicals were left to channel their activities into organisations such as the World Federation of Scientific Workers and the Campaign for Nuclear Disarmament.

[180] Crowther, J. G., *S.S.R.*, vol. XXVI, no. 100, 1945, p. 271.

[181] Baker, J. R., *The Scientific Life*, 1942, p. 101. Baker was the author of the 'Counterblast to Bernalism', published in the *New Statesman* (29 July 1939) and, with Polyani, a founder member of the Society for Freedom in Science. Bernal's reply to Baker appeared in the subsequent issue of the same journal (5 August 1939).

[182] Baker, J. R., op. cit., 1942, Preface and p. 13.

[183] Ibid., p. 85.

[184] This was the subject of repeated warnings from the Advisory Council on Scientific Policy after the war. See, for example, the Council's *Report* for 1950–1.

[185] Sanderson, A., 'Technology: The Scientific Umbrella', *Twentieth Century*, vol. CLII, no. 910, December 1952, p. 463, quoted from Page, F. H., *Research*, vol. 4, April 1951, p. 213.

[186] See, for example, Orr, J. Boyd, *Food, Health and Income*, 1936.

[187] Bernal, J. D., *The Social Function of Science*, 1939, p. 255.

[188] Ibid., p. 256.

[189] Westaway, F. W., *Science in the Dock: Guilty or Not Guilty?*, 1942, p. 10. Westaway had written several books relating to science and education including the important *Scientific Method: Its Philosophy and its Practice*, 1912. Many scientists had shared Westaway's concern before the war, the Cambridge Scientists Anti-War group being particularly active in the thirties, picketing military bases and renting advertising space on hoardings. The Chairman of the group, W. A. Wooster, a Cambridge crystallographer, sued the Chief Constable of Cambridge for larceny of the Group's anti-war literature and was awarded damages of £1. Burhop, E. H. S., 'Scientists and Public Affairs', in Goldsmith, M., and Mackay, A., *The Science of Science*, 1964, p. 34.

[190] Westaway, F. W., op. cit., 1942, Preface. The image of childhood was carried further, e.g. 'Almost every ... distinguished man of science seems to be paddling about in his own tiny little pond.' Ibid., p. 96.

[191] Ibid., pp. 96–7.

[192] See Werskey, P. G., op. cit., p. 244ff.

[193] A continuing manifestation of this ideology is the fact that, during the 1950s, a large proportion of the more able sixth-form science specialists chose to follow courses in pure science rather than in technology which was ascribed a significantly lower status; see Oxford University Dept. of Education, *Technology and the Sixth-Form Boy*, 1963.

[194] *S.S.R.*, vol. XXIV, no. 92, 1942, p. 114.

[195] *S.S.R.*, vol. XXIV, no. 92, 1942, p. 115, taken from a reviewer's comments on *Science and Education* by S. R. Humby and E. J. F. James, published in 1942. This book was one of a series on 'Current Problems' and was the scientific counterpart to Sir Richard Livingstone's volume, *The Future in Education*. Humby and James regarded the teaching of science in relation to historical, social and economic changes as 'essentially adult in spirit' and, in large measure, impracticable with average boys and girls below sixteen years of age. The reviewer, none the less, claimed that *Science and Education* would help to promote 'the spirit and ideas of men like ... Hogben and Julian Huxley', then percolating the schools.

[196] For the educational implications of this view, see Bernal, J. D., 'Science Teaching in General Education', *S.S.R.*, vol. XXVII, no. 102, 1946, pp. 150–8.

[197] Bibby, C., 'Biology in Secondary Schools', *S.S.R.*, vol. XXVI, no. 98, 1944, p. 120.

[198] Of 400 students taking the Conjoint Diploma in 1904 and 1905, only 8.5 per cent qualified in five years, 71.5 per cent taking six years or longer. Conjoint Board, *Report of the Committee of Management*, 4 January 1906, taken from Mansell, A. L., 'The Influence of Medicine on Science Education in England, 1892–1911', *History of*

Education, vol. 5, no. 2, 1976, p. 156. The discussion in the text covering the years up to 1911 is based on Mansell's article.

[199] The Royal College of Physicians was established in 1518, that of the Surgeons in 1800. As the Examining Board in England for the Royal College of Physicians of London and the Royal College of Surgeons of England, they offered the Conjoint Diploma, L.R.C.P., M.R.C.S.

[200] Mansell, A. L., op. cit., p. 158. The statistics of institutions recognised by the Conjoint Board between 1892 and 1909 are given in ibid., p. 159.

[201] Ibid., p. 158, note 13. Biology, for example, was assessed in a fifteen-minute oral examination. The examination in physics and chemistry consisted of a single three-hour paper and a practical and oral test of not less than thirty minutes' duration

[202] Properly called the General Council of Medical Education and Registration of the United Kingdom. All the Licensing Bodies in the U.K. were represented on the Council and, as may be imagined, it was an organisation which allowed national jealousies and antagonisms to flourish. The specific influences of the Irish and Scottish interests are not considered here, although they were important since the English representatives were outnumbered. In addition, there was a well-developed relationship between secondary schools and medical education in Scotland which, in this respect, was closer to the continent of Europe. See Flexner, A., *Medical Education in Europe*, Carnegie Foundation, New York, 1912.

[203] Reduced to six months if the institutions were recognised for physics and chemistry only.

[204] There was, of course, inspection by the Department of Science and Art under the terms of its own Regulations.

[205] The Regulation is quoted in full in Mansell, A. L., op. cit., p. 160.

[206] 'Some Considerations in Medical Education', *Lancet*, IV, 20 November 1909, p. 1531.

[207] The Board, under pressure from its own examiners, had raised the standards of its examinations at the end of the nineteenth century, extending the practical examinations to two hours and revising the chemistry and biology syllabuses.

[208] Conjoint Board, *Minute Book of the Committee of Management*, 1893–1902, pp. 290 et seq., quoted in Mansell, A. L., op. cit., p. 161; e.g. at Felstead School, the Inspectors recommended that recognition be withheld until the collection of specimens 'too small to give a sufficient view of biology' was 'considerably enlarged'.

[209] Mansell, A. L., op. cit., Appendix I, pp. 167–8, lists the institutions recognised by the Conjoint Board as at 28 January 1909. He claims that the Council's decision was a 'political act aimed more at disciplining the Royal Colleges than at maintaining educational standards'. Ibid., p. 162.

[210] The Visitor and Inspector reported that it was difficult to understand why candidates, 'the depths of whose ignorance were almost unfathomable' were ever allowed to present themselves for examination. *Minutes of the G.M.C.*, vol. XXXVIII, 1901, pp. 178–80, quoted in Mansell, A. L., op. cit., p. 162.

[211] The requirement took the form of a Certificate of Study from recognised institutions.

[212] If only because the differences in pass rates were not large (e.g. chemistry 62.1 per cent and 56.7 per cent for the students from 'recognised institutions and medical schools' respectively) and the numbers of students involved were also (presumably) relatively low. For details, see Mansell, A. L., op. cit., p. 164.

[213] He was also one of the College representatives on the General Medical Council from 1904 to 1917.

[214] For some details, see Mansell, A. L., op. cit., p. 163.

[215] Between 1885 and 1889, the average entry to the London medical schools was approximately 650. Twenty years later, this had fallen to about 250. *Royal Commission on Medical Education 1965–1968*, App. 14, 298.

[216] See, for example, *Lancet*, 17 March 1906 and 1 August 1908.

[217] Archer Vassal described this as 'insulting'. *Report of the General Meeting of the A.P.S.S.M.*, 1911, p. 32, quoted in Mansell, A. L., op. cit., p. 165.

[218] According to Mansell's estimation, ibid., p. 165, the A.P.S.S.M. was 'rather an amateur affair and its initial approaches ... were firmly rebutted'.

[219] The Report of the General Meeting of the A.P.S.S.M., 1910, pp. 15–16, records that 'no advantage would be gained by urging the G.M.C. to change their present practice'.

[220] Report of the General Meeting of the A.P.S.S.M., 1909, pp. 32–4, quoted in Mansell, A. L., op. cit., p. 165.

[221] For example, at Knaresborough Grammar School in 1902, pupils were prepared for the Cambridge Local Examinations and, as required, for the 'Legal Preliminary, Medical Preliminary, Institute of Bankers, Institute of Chartered Accountants, Second Division Clerks (Civil Service), London Matriculation and Victoria Preliminary examinations. Other examinations with which the secondary schools were involved included the university and local authority scholarship examinations, the Oxford Responsions and Cambridge Previous examinations, the Preliminary Dental and the Royal College of Preceptors examinations. West Riding County Council, Education Committee, *Report on Secondary Schools*, 1904, County Hall, Wakefield.

[222] Biological Science in British Schools, *Advancement of Science*, vol. X, no. 37, 1953, p. 87. It is important to recognise that the number of candidates seeking exemption from medical examinations at school was not large, probably in the region of 500 per annum between 1920 and 1950. For details relating to the Cambridge and Oxford examinations, see Brown, E. S., op. cit., pp. 75–6.

[223] Biology in the Educational Curriculum, *Advancement of Science*, vol. VI, no. 21, 1949, p. 39.

[224] See, for example, *S.S.R.*, vol. XI, no. 43, 1930, p. 225.

[225] Ibid., vol. XI, no. 43, 1930, p. 223.

[226] B.A.A.S., *Report*, 1925, p. 377.

[227] *S.S.R.*, vol. XI, no. 43, 1930, p. 223.

[228] Some writers 'argued' that the zoology 'part' of biology was suitable only for intending medical students. See, for example, Stork, J. W., 'Biology in Schools', *Journal of Education*, vol. LXII, July 1930, p. 516.

[229] The original data, collected from H. K. Airy Shaw's *Directory of Natural History Societies*, and taken from Brown, E. S., op. cit., p. 87. Brown reports that 'probably about half the boys in a public school in 'Dr Arnold's time' were engaged in the 'compilation of floral lists and the collection of butterflies and birds' eggs'. For details of the twentieth-century development of natural history, see Allen, D. E., op. cit., Chapters 12–14.

[230] For example, Flatford Mill (1946), Juniper Hall (1948), Malham Tarn (1948), Dale Fort (1948) and Preston Montford (1957).

[231] In more recent years, the Council has worked closely with the National Trust, but its activities have always embraced organisations other than schools, e.g. youth clubs and local natural history societies.

[232] There is one 'advantage' of the medical sixth which is sometimes overlooked. First M.B. courses at the medical schools were of one year's duration. Sixth formers could complete virtually identical courses in two years.

[233] Brown, E. S., 'Zoology in the Schools, 1851–1951', *S.S.R.*, vol. XXXV, no. 125, 1953, pp. 83–4.

[234] Ministry of Health, *Report of the Interdepartmental Committee on Medical Schools*, HMSO, 1944, p. 130. This was the report of the so-called 'Goodenough Committee'.

[235] Ibid., pp. 130–1. It should be noted that in rejecting the 'preponderance of opinion', the Interdepartmental Committee presupposed both an amendment of the system of school examinations along the lines recommended by the Norwood Committee and a substantial improvement in the standard of science teaching in the schools. Neither of these conditions prevailed at the end of the war.

[236] See, for example, The Royal College of Physicians of London, *Report on Medical Education*, 1944, p. 9. 'Specialisation in scientific subjects ... in the later school years may not only interfere with the ability of self-expression, but may diminish other interests.' The influence of premedical examinations on school biology teaching was also one of the issues examined by means of questionnaires distributed by the S.M.A. to schools via the November 1942 issue of the *S.S.R.*

[237] Brown, E. S., op. cit., p. 86. The 27 per cent refers to the total entry in biology of the Boards operating the scheme.

[238] 'Biological Sciences in British Schools', *Advancement of Science*, vol. X, no. 37, 1953, p. 89.

[239] Ministry of Education, 15 to 18, a report of the Central Advisory Council for Education (England), vol. 1, *Report*, HMSO, 1959, para. 429.

[240] When the Ordinary- and Advanced-level examinations were introduced, the Ministry of Education issued Circular 227 (28 September 1950), *Professional Bodies: Requirements in Terms of the G.C.E.* These requirements were updated twelve years later by Circular 5/62, dated 24 August 1962.

[241] General Medical Council, *Recommendations as to Basic Medical Education*, 1967. In order to remove the vestiges of the concept of medical education implicit in the 1858 Medical Act, particularly those relating to registration and the statutory examinations, changes in the law were necessary.

[242] Royal Commission on Medical Education, 1965–8, *Report*, Cmnd. 3569, 1968. See especially para. 12 and Chapter 5 which recommended the abolition of the First M.B. examinations.

[243] Bonham, H. J., Modern School Biology, in 'Biology in the Educational Curriculum', *Advancement of Science*, vol. VI, no. 21, 1949, p. 42.

[244] Ibid., p. 43.

[245] Ibid., p. 41.

[246] 'In Grammar Schools, the incentive of the examination ... is felt throughout the school,' ibid., p. 44. In the opinion of L. M. J. Kramer, the Senior Biology Master at the City of London School, these same examinations had encouraged over-specialised schemes of work. Writing in 1949, Kramer claimed that 'if the fight for the recognition of biology in the grammar schools' had been won, 'the price of victory' had been the 'cultural bankruptcy of the pupils'. Kramer, L. M. J., Some Aspects of Sixth-Form Biology, *Advancement of Science*, vol. VI, no. 21, 1949, p. 35.

[247] Ibid., p. 44 and p. 43. In the modern schools, experimental work was 'best done on a large scale and with simple apparatus'.

[248] Ibid., p. 42.

[249] See pp. 239 and 275.

[250] 'Biology in Secondary Grammar Schools', *Advancement of Science*, vol. X, no. 37, 1953, p. 85. 'Reports from all sides indicate a major number ... have adequate biological equipment, although not on the scale provided for Chemistry and Physics.'

Special laboratories for biology, often 'more modern than those for physics and chemistry' were however too few in number.

251 Biology in Secondary Modern and Secondary Technical Schools, ibid., p. 84.

252 See Chapter 7.

253 In 1953, the British Association concluded that a biology teacher was 'a comparative rarity in the Modern School' and that there seemed 'little hope of improvement in the near future', *Advancement of Science*, vol. X, no. 37, 1953, p. 84.

254 'Biology in Schools', ibid., vol. VIII, no. 29, 1951, p. 66.

255 This was a development provoked by the attitude of the Ministry of Education to the entry of secondary modern pupils for external examinations in general and the G.C.E. in particular. For a summary of the issues, see Montgomery, R. J., *Examinations*, 1965, p. 188 et seq.

256 Ministry of Education, *Education in 1960*, HMSO, 1961, p. 196. The other entries, by school, were 146,496 (grammar); 20,007 (technical); 22,200 (others, including comprehensive); 20,538 (direct grant); 52,558 (independent) and 45,306 (further education).

257 Statistics from Annual Reports of the Ministry of Education, *Education in 1952* and from *Statistics of Education*, HMSO, 1962. The 'Biological Subjects' are as in Table 4.10; botany, zoology, biology and agricultural and horticultural science. Unless otherwise indicated, G.C.E. entries refer to summer examinations only.

258 The figures also illustrate trends in the relative popularity of botany, zoology and biology as main school subjects which were evident at least a decade before the system of G.C.E. examinations was introduced. See, for example, Bibby, C., Biology in Secondary Schools, *S.S.R.*, vol. XXVI, no. 98, 1944, p. 117 et seq., who shows that botany had virtually disappeared from pre-School Certificate work in all types of secondary schools.

259 For one Examination Board, the ratio of girls to boys offering biological subjects in the School Certificate examination in each of the years 1946–9, were 4.1, 4.0, 5.0 and 3.8 respectively. *Advancement of Science*, vol. X, no 37, 1953, p. 86. Not all Examination Boards distinguished boys from girls in their statistics, although the majority did so.

260 The entries for biological science(s) at Higher School Certificate level, for each of the years 1946–9, showed a girl:boy ratio of 1.02, 1.05, 1.10 and 0.91 respectively. Biological Sciences in British Schools, *Advancement of Science*, vol. X, no. 37, 1953, p. 86.

261 In some respects, these studies created the field of 'molecular biology'. Although this term was used by Astbury in 1939, *The Journal of Molecular Biology*, which made the term fashionable, was not established until 1959. A European Molecular Biology organisation was set up in 1963. See *Institute of Biology Journal*, vol. II, no. 2, 1964, p. 54.

262 For a highly personal account of this achievement, see Watson, J. D., *The Double Helix*, 1968. For a more scholarly account and wide-ranging review of the 'molecularisation' of biology, see Olby, R., *The Path to the Double Helix*, 1974.

263 Crick, F. H. C., *Of Molecules and Men*, 1966, p. 10.

264 Olby, R., op. cit., p. 426, refers to *a new kind of professionalism* in biology, 'marked by the demand that explanation must stand up to the rigorous standards of the new quantum physics'. For an account of the 'new outlook' in school biology, see *Institute of Biology Journal*, vol. 10, no. 3, 1963, pp. 71–6.

265 It was, of course, not a move welcomed universally. Much of the debate, which continued throughout the sixties, was conducted in the columns of *Nature* and con-

cerned the extent to which biologists should be trained to study organisms at a level higher than the molecular. See, for example: Stebbins, G. L., International Horizons in the Life Sciences, *Nature*, vol. 196, 16 November 1962, p. 611; Training in Biologists, ibid., vol. 195, 15 September 1962, pp. 1057–9; Yapp, W. B., ibid., vol. 198, 27 April 1963, p. 409. See also Polyani, M., Life's Irreducible Structure, *Science*, no. 160, 1968, p. 1308.

[266] Oxford University Department of Education, *Arts and Science Sides in the Sixth Form*, 1960, p. 31.

[267] Montgomery, R. J., op. cit., 1965, p. 159. As Montgomery points out, the specialisation was not a new phenomenon and competition for entry was not confined to the universities. He claims that 'pupils were driven to achieve grades in their specialist subjects at the expense of all else'.

[268] Snow, C. P., *The Two Cultures and the Scientific Revolution*, 1959.

[269] This structure was not altered throughout the sixties and is unchanged today despite the attempts by the Schools Council, set up in 1964, to broaden sixth-form curricula. Two attempts by the schools themselves at the end of the 1950s are of interest, the so-called 'ABC' schools ('agreement to broaden the curriculum') which kept one-third of the time free of specialist work in the sixth form, and the more enduring development of sixth-form general studies. See *T.E.S.*, 12 May 1961, p. 974, and Oliver, R. A. C., *General Studies (Advanced) in the G.C.E.*, 1960.

[270] University of Birmingham, *Report of an Inquiry into the Suitability ... First Degree Courses in the Faculty of Science*, 1959; the so-called Gulbenkian Report, p. A15. Some university professors even expressed a preference for undergraduates who had studied physics, chemistry and mathematics at Advanced level to the exclusion of biology. See, for example, Royal Society and the Institute of Biology, *Biological Sciences in Sixth Forms and at Universities in the United Kingdom*, 1962, p. 27.

[271] University of Birmingham, op. cit., p. A16.

[272] Ibid., p. A10. The syllabus provided generous opportunity for experimental work and it was also recommended that the applications of biology be demonstrated by 'visits to such places as farms, dairy, food factory, hospital laboratory (and) sewage treatment plant'. Ibid., p. A11.

[273] Tracey, G. W., 'The Relationship Between the Past Progress and Current Developments in the Teaching of Biological Science in English Schools, 1850–1956', *Durham Research Review*, vol. V, no. 16, 1965, p. 29.

[274] The S.M.A. and A.W.S.T. were 'out of touch' with these developments. In 1961, the two organisations reaffirmed the value of Huxley's type system and, implicitly, of syllabuses based upon such a system. S.M.A./A.W.S.T., *Science in Education, Biology for Grammar Schools*, 1961.

[275] See Kelly, P. J., 'The Biological Sciences Curriculum Study', *S.S.R.*, vol. 44, no. 153, 1963, pp. 312–23, for an account of the B.S.C.S.

[276] Royal Society and Institute of Biology, op. cit., p. 16.

[277] Data from *Statistics of Education*, HMSO, 1961, and the corresponding volume for 1971.

5
The Scientific Education of Girls

Down to 1850, and even later, it was widely assumed that the education of girls must be different from that of boys because they belonged to what was regarded as the weaker, or more euphemistically, the gentler, sex. The differences, reflecting economic, legal and social inequalities, meant that secondary education for girls, where it was provided at all, involved little more than the acquisition of the accepted feminine accomplishments. The Schools Inquiry Commissioners, in their report of 1868, presented a grave indictment of girls' education, complaining of a 'want of thoroughness', foundation and system, of inattention to rudiments and of an undue time given to accomplishments.[1] The physical sciences, read occasionally from books or presented by lectures, were 'nowhere taught systematically' to girls and were 'commonly unintelligible'.[2]

However, the fact that the Commissioners had extended voluntarily their terms of reference to include girls' schools was significant and their report marked the beginning of a new era in the secondary education of girls.[3] When the Bryce Commissioners, who included three women,[4] presented their report in 1895, they were able to survey a generation of progress in the provision of secondary schools for girls, made against opposition which was the stronger because it drew support from many different, influential groups.[5] The Girls' Public Day School Company[6] was founded in 1872 and its schools provided a model for the many others established subsequently in major cities. The Endowed Schools Commissioners and the Charity Commissioners had made steady, if unspectacular, progress in redirecting and restoring educational endowments for the benefit of girls' schools. The 1864 Commissioners mentioned only twelve endowed schools for girls in England. By 1895, there were said to be 'some eighty girls' schools' giving secondary education under the Endowed Schools Acts and other endowments under these Acts had also been made available for the secondary education of girls.[7] Even so, girls numbered less than a quarter of the pupils in endowed schools[8] in 1895, a time when secondary education was, in any case, the prerogative of the few.

The opportunities for women to receive a higher education had also been considerably extended, despite the obduracy of Oxford and Cambridge and the particular opposition to granting medical degrees to women.[9] The University of London admitted women to full degrees in 1879 and the newer, provincial institutions, such as the Victoria University and the Newcastle College of Science, made no distinction between men and women in admitting students to their courses. By the end of the century, women had access to the majority of centres offering a higher education and were able to read for first and higher degrees.

In little more than a generation therefore, the opportunities for some girls to receive a secondary and a higher education had been transformed and, in 1902, the Balfour Education Act made the provision of secondary education for girls, as for boys, the responsibility of the newly created local education authorities. The legislation, together with the grants available from the Board of Education under the successive Regulations associated with it, provided the framework for the further development of secondary education for girls during the early twentieth century. The extent of the expansion between 1904 and 1922 in the numbers of grant-aided and 'efficient' secondary schools and in the numbers of girls attending them is indicated by the data[10] in Table 5.1. In addition to those pupils receiving a secondary education in schools on the Grant List or recognised by the Board of Education as 'efficient', there were, of course, many others who attended private schools or who received an education with something 'of a secondary character' in Pupil Teacher Centres. In 1905, there were 5,380 boys and 25,294 girls receiving instruction in such Centres, but these numbers decreased rapidly as the Pupil Teacher system fell into decline.

The Secondary School Regulations introduced by the Board in 1904, which applied to boys', girls' and coeducational schools alike, attempted to ensure a 'certain measure of breadth and richness'[11] in the curriculum of grant-aided secondary schools by specifying the minimum time to be allotted to the teaching of given subjects or groups of subjects. In addition to teaching English language and literature, at least one language other than English, geography, history, mathematics, science and drawing, these schools were required to devote not less than one and a half hours each week to manual instruction.[12] In the case of girls, such instruction took the form of cookery, laundry work, dairy work or needlework or of a practical course of 'housewifery', incorporating one or more of these subjects.

The detailed nature of these 1904 Regulations was the source of particular difficulty for many headmistresses, some of whom had already expressed their concern at the 'over-crowding' of the curriculum of the girls' secondary school. As early as 1882, Elizabeth Day, the first Headmistress of the Manchester High School for Girls, confessed that she could see 'no way of giving greater prominence to Science Teaching except by lessening the time in the morning ... devoted to languages', a development which she was clearly reluctant to contemplate.[13] Sara Burstall, Miss Day's successor at Manchester, claimed that the curriculum of the girls' school had been formed historically by adding the boys' Latin and mathematics to the traditional English subjects, French and art of the girls' education and that the further incorporation of science had produced a curriculum which was 'terribly over-crowded' and which encouraged 'a scattering of interest, over-pressure, superficial knowledge and cram'.[14]

Part of the problem of providing a satisfactory curriculum for the girls' secondary school lay in the partial survival of the teaching of accomplishments and in the greater importance attached to the aesthetic subjects, such as music and art, compared with the boys' schools. However, a more significant obstacle

Table 5.1   Provision of Grant-Aided and 'Efficient' Secondary Schools for Boys and Girls, 1904–22

	1904–5	1907–8	1913–14	1921–2
1 Schools on the Grant List				
a Number of Schools for:				
i Boys	292	344	397	462
ii Girls	99	262	349	450
iii Boys and Girls	184	237	281	331
iv Total	575	843	1,027	1,243
b Number of pupils:				
i Boys	61,179	75,498	99,997	184,408
ii Girls	33,519	63,617	87,650	176,207
iii Total	94,698	139,106	187,647	360,615
2 Schools *not* on the Grant List, but recognised as efficient				
a Number of Schools for:				
i Boys	—	15	53	71
ii Girls	—	34	64	138
iii Boys and Girls	—	3	4	7
iv Total	—	52	121	216
b Number of Pupils:				
i Boys	—	3,513	13,618	21,765
ii Girls	—	5,236	8,928	22,373
iii Total	—	8,749	22,546	44,138
3 All Schools				
a Number of Schools for:				
i Boys	—	359	450	533
ii Girls	—	296	413	588
iii Boys and Girls	—	240	285	338
iv Total	—	895	1,148	1,459
b Number of Pupils:				
i Boys	—	79,002	113,615	206,173
ii Girls	—	68,853	96,578	198,580
iii Total	—	147,855	210,193	404,753

was the fact that the school day was often shorter than in boys' secondary schools, some of the older, endowed schools for girls operating morning sessions only. Even in the newer girls' schools which conducted classes during the afternoon, the morning session was usually shorter than in the corresponding schools for boys. In addition, lessons were often reduced in length, a factor which was said to be responsible for the more formal and intensive methods of teaching employed; 'more lecturing . . . and less independent though supervised work'.[15] The shorter working week found in many girls' secondary schools may be attributed to an earlier practice of escorting girls to and from school and to the 'tradition' that girls should have some freedom to contribute to the social life of the home. The Board of Education attempted to accommodate this tradition within the 1904 Regulations by permitting a reduction in the time to be devoted to science and mathematics in those girls' secondary schools in which the total instruction amounted to less than twenty-two hours each week, although a minimum of three hours' instruction in science was still required.[16]

The question whether the nature and extent of the instruction in a girls' secondary school should normally be the same as in a boys' school or, if not, what the differences should be, was the subject of vigorous debate at the beginning of the twentieth century. The evidence of national physical deterioration suggested by the programme of recruitment for the Boer War, together with the pervasive influence of Eugenic[17] and Social Darwinistic ideas[18] about the need to preserve the quality of the 'Imperial race', led to a renewed emphasis on the 'traditional' role of women as wives and mothers. This emphasis was of less immediate consequence for the work of the secondary schools than for the curriculum of the public elementary schools where it was allied with a concern to counteract the alleged reluctance of young women to breastfeed their babies, their disinclination to attend to domestic duties and their ignorance of the principles of healthy living, three factors which were widely assumed to be strongly related to, and by some to be actually responsible for, the very high level of infant mortality.[19] As George Newman, author of a classic work on infant mortality and later the first Chief Medical Officer of the Board of Education, remarked in 1906, the problem of infant mortality was 'mainly a question of motherhood'.[20]

Following the report in 1904 of an Interdepartmental Committee set up to investigate physical deterioration,[21] the Board of Education responded to these sentiments by revising the elementary school curriculum so as to provide an opportunity for imparting to the pupils who were 'destined to become the mothers and fathers of the race, the broad principles of healthy living'.[22] A *Special Report on School Training for the Home Duties of Women*, written by Alice Ravenhill, a contributor to the *Eugenics Review*,[23] reviewed the teaching of domestic science in eight European countries and in the United States and this was published[24] in three parts between 1905 and 1908. Another *Special Report on the Teaching of Cookery to Public Elementary School Children in England and Wales* was prepared in 1906 by Maude Lawrence, the Chief Woman Inspector at the Board of Education, and published[25] in the following year. Arrangements were made for the systematic and regular inspection of the teaching of domestic subjects in the elementary schools and new Regulations were introduced into the Elementary Code in 1906 in an attempt to remedy some of the worst defects highlighted by Maude Lawrence's report. The Board's attitude towards the teaching of domestic subjects in the public elementary schools is nowhere more clear than in the *Suggestions for the Consideration of Teachers*, issued in 1905. Girls were to be taught to use the simple equipment found in the kitchens of working class homes. Recipes were to be plain, rather than elaborate, and no attempt was to be made to provide 'theoretical instruction as to the methods of cooking, or as to the principles of digestion'[26] beyond that necessary for a general understanding of the subject.

The growing importance attached by the Board to the thorough teaching of domestic subjects was also reflected in the Regulations governing the curricula of the grant-aided secondary schools. Instruction in practical 'housewifery' was compulsory under the Regulations introduced in 1904 and three years later the Board sought to 'emphasise the importance of practical training for life in the case of girls'[27] by permitting those over the age of fifteen attending grant-aided secondary schools to substitute an approved course of instruction in domestic subjects for instruction in science. In 1909, this provision was extended to allow girls over the age of fifteen to substitute domestic subjects either 'partially or wholly for science and for mathematics other than arithmetic'.[28]

The Board's policy towards the inclusion of domestic subjects in the curriculum of girls' secondary schools brought it into conflict with the Council of the Girls Public Day School Trust, an organisation which, through its 'High' Schools, had sought to realise the unshakeable conviction of its founders that girls, as well as boys, could benefit from a sound, intellectual education. When the Board urged the Council to make provision for a systematic training in housewifery in its High Schools, the Council indicated that it would prefer to dispense with the Government grants and declare full independence rather than submit to the changes required by the Board which, in its view, amounted to a 'serious alteration in the aim and work'[29] of the schools for which it was responsible. However, the views of the headmistresses of several G.P.D.S.T. schools diverged considerably from those of the pioneers a generation earlier. Sara Burstall had made determined and successful attempts to improve the provision for domestic training at Manchester High School and she was particularly proud of her efforts to prepare girls for a practical life in the home.[30] Writing in 1911, the headmistress of the Haberdashers' Aske's Girls' School, London, recorded her impression that the old 'blue-stocking' type, 'who prided herself on not knowing how to sew or mend, and who thought cooking menial and beneath her',[31] no longer appealed to anyone. Rather the object was to encourage girls to develop into 'sensible, methodical, practical women' who would be competent to direct, intelligently and practically, 'the manifold duties of the home'.

Between 1909 and 1913, the teaching of domestic subjects in secondary schools was referred by the Board of Education to two separate committees. A Select Committee on Housecraft in Girls' Secondary Schools produced an interim report in 1911. The Consultative Committee was asked to consider the teaching of practical work in secondary schools and produced its report[32] two years later. These two Committees had over-lapping terms of reference, much to Morant's embarrassment,[33] and both reported on the attempts made in a number of schools to teach physics and chemistry through courses in housecraft. Arthur Smithells was a particularly strong advocate of this approach, presenting a paper on *School Training for the Home Duties of Women* to the York meeting of the British Association in 1906. Smithells argued that physics and chemistry failed to appeal to any 'feminine interest' and that scientific principles could best be taught to girls through an 'Applied Science of the Household'.[34] He was actively involved in the development of a number of suitable courses[35] and he lent his support to plans to develop the teaching of 'household science' at undergraduate level. Henry Armstrong argued the case for a scheme of instruction which would make girls 'scientific observers and thinkers in relation to all home matters' at the Leicester meeting[36] of the British Association in 1907 but his 'Suggestions for a Course of Practical Food Studies', similar in form and purpose to the schemes accepted by the Association in 1889 and 1890, were not published[37] until 1917.

Despite the obvious attractions of domestic science as a means of raising the status[38] of domestic subjects within the curriculum, there was strong opposition to the attempts to restructure the sciences to accommodate the presumed needs or interests of girls. Chemistry teachers were quick to point out that even the most simple culinary processes were based upon complex organic chemical reactions and that any scientific knowledge acquired through lessons in practical cookery could only be highly fragmented and disconnected.[39] Ida Freund, a lecturer at Newnham College and author of an influential chemical text,[40] argued forcibly[41] that the term domestic *science* was highly misleading and expressed her concern that any attempt to teach science through housecraft would be educationally disastrous since it could lead only to a lowering of the already deplorable standard of scientific education in many girls' schools.

In these circumstances, it is hardly surprising that the Consultative Committee concluded that it was too early to pronounce definitely 'as to how far the teaching of elementary Physics and Chemistry may be modified to form the basis for the scientific study of Cookery and other Domestic Arts'.[42]

In addition to the problems of accommodating domestic and other subjects within the timetable, some girls' secondary schools had also to contend with a variation in the educational standards attained by pupils on entry which was much greater than in the case of boys. Many municipal and county secondary schools admitted the majority of their pupils at approximately eleven years of age and most of these came directly from public elementary schools.[43] However, the Endowed Schools and High Schools for girls often admitted pupils who had been educated up to the age of eleven or twelve by governesses or in private day schools. While some of these schools provided a sound and systematic education, others offered curricula which were 'based on no well-considered principles' and employed teaching methods that were often 'old-fashioned and ineffective'.[44] In addition, some secondary schools operated their own junior departments for pupils between the ages of eight and twelve. Although the Board issued a Circular[45] in 1913 requiring all such Departments in grant-aided secondary schools to provide instruction in English, arithmetic, history, geography, drawing, singing and physical exercises, no very definite rules were established and 'a great variety of curricula and standards' developed.[46]

An example of a secondary school curriculum which had been 'found to work well in practice' with girls of ten to fifteen years was provided[47] by Sara Burstall in her book, *English High Schools for Girls*, published in 1907. The scheme of work for the 'A-forms' included two periods per week of general elementary science in each of three of the five years together with some nature study and biology. The 'B-forms', the 'slow trains' rather than the 'express trains' as Sadler termed them, were excluded altogether from studying physics and latin and Miss Burstall clearly envisaged that the 'B course of study', with its emphasis on English, modern languages, art and handiwork and its 'minimum of mathematics and science' could become the 'normal course of study' for the majority of girls attending a secondary school.[48]

The timetables of a number of secondary schools of different types were appended by the Board's Consultative Committee to its *Report on the Differentiation of Curricula Between the Sexes*, published in 1923. In the grant-aided coeducational day school, the youngest pupils studied science in the form of nature study for $1\frac{1}{3}$ hours each week. A course of general science (2 hours per week) was introduced into the third form, together with physics (2 hours per week) which, in conjunction with English ($1\frac{1}{3}$ hours per week), was offered as an alternative to Latin ($3\frac{1}{3}$ hours per week). The systematic study of chemistry for $2\frac{2}{3}$ hours per week was begun in the fourth form. The timetable of a grant-aided secondary school for girls, reproduced as Table 5.2, is noteworthy in that it includes no provision for the teaching of chemistry and allows considerably less time for the teaching of mathematics than the timetable of a corresponding school for boys.[49]

Where options were incorporated within the science curriculum of a girls' or coeducational secondary school, these were often arranged or exercised so as to permit girls to discontinue the study of mathematics or to study botany rather than physics or chemistry. Thus, girls in the middle and upper forms of coeducational secondary schools in Leicestershire were allowed to take botany instead of physics and to substitute needlework for trigonometry. In one of the largest of these schools, most fifth-form girls followed a course of 'general science', designed to 'meet their need in Domestic Instruction', while the boys undertook the systematic study of physics and chemistry.[50] A broadly similar pattern prevailed in the girls' secondary schools in the West Riding of Yorkshire where botany replaced the 'less elementary physics and chemistry' studied in the secondary schools for boys.[51]

The differentiation of the science curriculum between boys and girls was strongly related to the resources available for teaching physics and chemistry in the girls' schools. Of twenty-eight such schools, each with between 200 and 300 pupils, investigated by the Association of Science Teachers during the First World War, twenty had only one laboratory and ten of the thirteen larger schools in the sample were 'no better off'.[52] Specialist laboratory accommodation for the teaching of physics or chemistry was, of course, relatively expensive to provide, as the figures in Table 5.3, published[53] by the Headmistresses Association in 1907, clearly show.

Girls' schools in general lacked the funds to provide adequate accommodation and equipment for the practical teaching of the physical sciences. Many were privately and inadequately financed and few had earlier taken advantage of the grants offered by the Department of Science and Art which

Table 5.2   Time Table of a County Secondary School for Girls
(School Hours: 9.15 a.m. to 12.30 p.m., and 2.30 p.m. to 4.30 p.m.)

Form	VI	V.sp.	V	IV	Athens	Florence	Rome	Venice	III.sp.	IIA	IIB	II.sp.	I	Prep.
Average Age (Y. M.)	17 · 4	16 · 10	15 · 9	15 · 11	14 · 1	13 · 8	13 · 9	13 · 7	13 · 9	11 · 7	12 · 7	12 · 1	11 · 6	10 · 9
	hrs.	hrs.	hrs.	hrs.	hrs.	hrs.	hrs.	hrs.	hrs.	hrs.	hrs.	hrs.	hrs.	hrs.
Religious Instruction	$\frac{2}{3}$	—	$\frac{2}{3}$	$\frac{2}{3}$	1	1	1	1	1	1	1	1	1	—
English Lang. and Lit.	$2\frac{2}{3}$	$1\frac{1}{3}$	$3\frac{1}{3}$	4	4	4	4	4	$2\frac{2}{3}$	$2\frac{2}{3}$	$2\frac{2}{3}$	$2\frac{2}{3}$	$3\frac{1}{3}$	—
History	2	$1\frac{1}{3}$	2	2	2	2	2	2	2	2	2	2	2	2
Geography	—	$1\frac{1}{3}$	$\frac{2}{3}$	$\frac{2}{3}$	2	2	2	2	2	2	2	2	2	$\frac{2}{3}$
Latin	$1\frac{1}{3}$	2	4	—	2	2	2	2	—	—	—	—	—	—
French	—	$\frac{2}{3}$	—	—	—	—	—	—	—	—	—	—	—	—
German	$3\frac{1}{3}$	$2\frac{2}{3}$	4	4	$3\frac{1}{3}$	$3\frac{1}{3}$	$3\frac{1}{3}$	$3\frac{1}{3}$	4	$3\frac{1}{3}$	$3\frac{1}{3}$	$3\frac{1}{3}$	$3\frac{1}{3}$	—
Arithmetic	—	—	—	—	$\frac{2}{3}$	$\frac{2}{3}$	$\frac{2}{3}$	$\frac{2}{3}$	$1\frac{1}{3}$	$3\frac{1}{3}$	$3\frac{1}{3}$	$3\frac{1}{3}$	$2\frac{2}{3}$	—
Algebra	$1\frac{1}{3}$	$\frac{2}{3}$	$1\frac{1}{3}$	$1\frac{1}{3}$	$1\frac{1}{3}$	$1\frac{1}{3}$	$1\frac{1}{3}$	$1\frac{1}{3}$	$1\frac{1}{3}$	—	—	—	—	—
Geometry	$1\frac{1}{3}$	$\frac{2}{3}$	—	—	—	—	—	—	—	—	—	—	—	—
Trigonometry	—	—	$\frac{2}{3}$	$\frac{2}{3}$	$1\frac{1}{3}$	$1\frac{1}{3}$	$1\frac{1}{3}$	$1\frac{1}{3}$	$1\frac{1}{3}$	—	—	—	—	—
Geology	4	—	—	—	—	—	—	—	—	—	—	—	—	—
Physics	—	$1\frac{1}{3}$	$1\frac{1}{3}$	$1\frac{1}{3}$	$1\frac{1}{3}$	$1\frac{1}{3}$	$1\frac{1}{3}$	$1\frac{1}{3}$	2	$2\frac{2}{3}$	$2\frac{2}{3}$	2	$2\frac{2}{3}$	—
Botany	$2\frac{2}{3}$	$1\frac{1}{3}$	$1\frac{1}{3}$*	$1\frac{1}{3}$*	$1\frac{1}{3}$ †	$1\frac{1}{3}$ †	$1\frac{1}{3}$ †	$1\frac{1}{3}$ †	$1\frac{1}{3}$	$2\frac{2}{3}$	$1\frac{1}{3}$	$1\frac{1}{3}$	$1\frac{1}{3}$	$1\frac{1}{3}$
Drawing	1	$1\frac{1}{3}$	$1\frac{1}{3}$*	$1\frac{1}{3}$*	1	1	1	1	1	$1\frac{1}{3}$	$2\frac{2}{3}$	$2\frac{2}{3}$	$2\frac{2}{3}$	$2\frac{2}{3}$
Music and Singing	—	1	—	1	1	1	1	1	1	2	2	—	2	—
Manual Instruction	—	—	—	—	—	—	—	—	—	—	—	—	—	—
Needlework	$1\frac{1}{3}$	$1\frac{1}{3}$	$1\frac{1}{3}$	$1\frac{1}{3}$	2	2	†	2	$1\frac{1}{3}$	$1\frac{1}{3}$	$1\frac{1}{3}$	$1\frac{1}{3}$	$1\frac{1}{3}$	—
Physical Exercises	$\frac{2}{3}$	$\frac{2}{3}$	$\frac{2}{3}$	$\frac{2}{3}$	$2\frac{2}{3}$	$2\frac{2}{3}$	2	2	$2\frac{2}{3}$	2	2	2	2	—
Current Topics	—	—	—	—	—	—	—	$\frac{2}{3}$	$\frac{2}{3}$	$\frac{2}{3}$	$\frac{2}{3}$	$\frac{2}{3}$	$\frac{2}{3}$	—
Writing	—	—	—	—	‡	‡	‡	‡	$\frac{1}{3}$	—	—	—	—	—
Study	$1\frac{2}{3}$	$6\frac{2}{3}$	—	2	§	§	§	§	5	$3\frac{1}{2}$	$3\frac{1}{2}$	$3\frac{1}{2}$	$1\frac{1}{3}$	—
Homework	$7\frac{1}{2}$	$7\frac{1}{2}$	$7\frac{1}{2}$	$7\frac{1}{2}$	8	8	8	8	—	—	$3\frac{1}{2}$	$3\frac{1}{2}$	$3\frac{1}{2}$	—

* Botany or Drawing may be taken.   † Time varies and the subjects are optional.   ‡ Time varies.   § Seniors 7½ hours, juniors 5 hours.

Table 5.3   Cost of School Furniture as Estimated by the Headmistresses' Association, 1907

| | Cost per pupil | | |
	£	s	d
General School Furniture:	4	4	0
Special School Furniture:			
Science:	0	19	8
Art:	0	2	10
Domestic:	0	12	0
Total:	5	18	6

had done so much to stimulate the building and equipping of laboratories for the teaching of physics and chemistry in boys' schools.[54] In addition, it is likely that most of those in a position to influence the provision of laboratory accommodation in girls' schools shared the widely held view that girls displayed a particular aptitude for the biological sciences where they were 'helped' by their greater diligence, neatness and 'capacity for comprehending elaborate classification'.[55] In Miss Burstall's view, a girls' secondary school needed 'a biological laboratory rather than a chemical one', although she conceded that a wealthy school which intended to offer 'special facilities for science' should have laboratories of both types.[56] Not surprisingly, when the Manchester High School for Girls applied for and obtained grants for science work under the transitional arrangements which operated in 1900–1, the increased funds were used to provide a biological laboratory and a new cookery school. (See Plate 5.)

By the time the Thomson Committee reported in 1918, a number of differences in the scientific education of girls and boys were firmly established in the secondary schools. Laboratory accommodation and equipment for the practical teaching of the physical sciences were generally inferior in girls' schools compared with those of boys, and physics and chemistry were accorded a status subordinate to that of other subjects contributing to the secondary education of girls. The science subject studied by most girls was botany and few undertook any serious study of physics apart from nature study and/or an elementary course, studied in conjunction with chemistry, between the ages of twelve and fourteen.[57] The lack of systematic teaching of physics to girls was regarded by the Thomson Committee as a particularly serious problem which could not be solved until an adequate supply of suitably qualified teachers was forthcoming and means could be found of raising the low standard of attainment in mathematics.[58]

The structure of the new School Certificate examination and, in particular, the inclusion of the sciences and mathematics within the same Group, did nothing to encourage girls' secondary schools to develop the teaching of physics and chemistry. A candidate for the School Certificate awarded by the Joint Matriculation Board in 1918, for example, could satisfy the Group III requirement by presenting herself for examination in only one subject chosen from mathematics, *either* mechanics *or* physics, chemistry, geography, domestic science and *either* natural history *or* botany.[59] Girls' secondary schools were hostile[60] to the structure of the School Certificate examination from its inception, although their opposition was based not on the illogicalities inherent in the Group system, but on the status ascribed to many of the subjects traditionally important in girls' secondary education by their inclusion in the optional Group IV category. A suggestion that Group IV could be recognised as of equal value

Plate 5 Biology Laboratory, Manchester High School for Girls, formally opened in 1907.

with Groups II and III for girls, but not for boys, was firmly rejected by the Headmistresses' Association[61] and the continuing complaints from the girls' schools that the Group requirements 'bore hardly upon their candidates' were instrumental[62] in bringing about important changes in the structure of the School Certificate examination. In 1928, Group IV was reorganised, the list of subjects extended and the Secondary School Examinations Council permitted a maximum of two, rather than one, of these subjects to be offered among the five required for the award of a School Certificate. In 1938, a lower standard for satisfying the examiners of Group III subjects was accepted[63] and a pass in a simple paper in elementary mathematics became the minimum requirement in this Group. In 1938, the Group structure of the School Certificate was virtually abolished[64] and candidates were allowed to qualify for the Certificate by satisfying the minimum requirements in any two Groups, provided that one of the two was either Group II or Group III. For the remaining dozen years of the

School Certificate examination, Groups II and III were, therefore, alternatives and the aesthetic and practical subjects within Group IV were attributed a nominal parity with the more conventionally academic disciplines.

A Group structure also governed the Higher School Certificate examinations but, as Petch has pointed out, the purposes served by the Groups in the first and second examinations were 'directly contrary'.[65] When the School Certificate examination was introduced, candidates were required to present themselves for examination in subjects chosen from at least three Groups. At the Higher level, candidates were confined to one Group for Principal subjects and were permitted to choose a subject from outside that Group only for presentation at the subsidiary level. From the outset, individual Examination Boards had greater freedom to modify the arrangements for the Higher School Certificate than for the first examination where the Secondary School Examinations Council exercised more control. Some significant differences of practice thus emerged but there is no doubt that the severe constraints imposed upon the sixth-form curriculum by the requirements of the Higher School Certificate examination were a matter of widespread concern among the schools and among the girls' schools in particular. Petch's account of the work of the Joint Matriculation Board illustrates the manner in which one of the larger Examination Boards responded to pressure from the schools to reform the Group structure of the Higher Certificate Examination. In 1918, the Board required a candidate to satisfy the examiners in four subjects, three of which were to be taken at the Principal level from one of four groups.[66] In 1922, the Regulations were modified so as to require only two of the three Principal subjects to be drawn from one group but this modification proved insufficient to satisfy the girls' schools. Accordingly, the Regulations were further amended in 1928, after which date candidates were permitted to offer themselves for examination in either three subjects at Principal level or in two subjects at each of the Principal and Subsidiary levels, two Principal entries, in each case, coming from the same group. Continued pressure from the girls' schools led the Joint Matriculation Board in 1935 to recommend to the Secondary School Examinations Council that the Group structure of the Higher Examination be abolished. Although this recommendation was rejected, the Council agreed that the two subjects offered at the Principal level under either of the Board's alternative arrangements could be selected from more than one Group, thus 'granting with the left hand what was withheld by the right'.[67] In 1937, the Joint Matriculation Board 'quietly dropped' all references to Groups in the Regulations governing the Higher Certificate Examination.

Although the changes introduced by the Joint Matriculation Board into its examination schedules in the inter-war years are not always applicable in detail to other Examination Boards, there is no doubt that secondary schools in general gained a greater freedom of choice for the individual candidate during this period. The demise of the Group structure of both the first and second School Certificate Examinations was also of importance in the longer term since it paved the way for a more generous and different conception of secondary education which embraced subjects such as art and music whose status had been advanced by their wider acceptance as subjects fit for examination, particularly at the Principal level.

During the school year 1920–1, there were 1,076 secondary schools in England in receipt of Parliamentary grant via the Board of Education, providing an education for 160,779 boys and 150,979 girls, a total of 311,758 pupils. The corresponding figures for the school year 1937–8, when less than one in ten of all girls between the ages of fourteen and fifteen in England and Wales were receiving a grant-aided secondary education, are 1,244 schools, 223,975 boys, 200,643 girls and 424,618 pupils.[68] Most of this expansion in the secondary school population is explicable in terms of an increase in the average length of a secondary school education during the period.[69] About two-thirds of all the pupils who left grant-aided secondary schools in the year ending 31 July 1920 were under the age of sixteen,[70] a 'mischief' which meant not only that many pupils were failing to take full advantage of the opportunities provided, but also that such opportunities were denied to others who might have made better use of them. The 1921 Secondary School Regulations attempted to overcome this problem by making recognition of a secondary school dependent upon pupils normally remaining at school for at least four years and School Governors were empowered to give preference on admission to those pupils on whose behalf a reasonable assurance or formal undertaking to this effect could be given.[71] Inevitably, it was necessary for time to elapse before the Regulations could take effect, although there were signs,[72] even in 1921, that pupils were tending to remain somewhat longer at secondary schools. The average age of leaving rose steadily during the inter-war period and, by 1938, it was sixteen years and seven months for boys and one month earlier for girls.[73] During this period, the proportion of pupils attending grant-aided secondary schools who had come from public elementary schools also increased,[74] from almost 68 per cent in 1924 to 78 per cent in 1938. This increase was partly the result of the growth in the numbers admitted under the 'free place' system, and subsequently, after 1931, of the operation of the 'special place' arrangements which required parents to contribute to the payment of the secondary school fees. By 1938, 46.9 per cent of all pupils in grant-earning secondary schools were totally exempt, 9.7 per cent received partial exemption and the remainder (43.4 per cent) received no exemption from fees which varied considerably but usually lay between six and fifteen guineas per annum for the tuition of pupils of twelve years of age.[75]

The most significant changes in the science curriculum of girls' secondary schools in the inter-war years were undoubtedly the gradual replacement of botany by biology and the development of courses in general science.[76] As indicated in Chapters 3 and 4, each of these changes gathered momentum during the latter half of the 1930s. A Committee, appointed by the British Association to consider the provision made for instruction in botany, reported in 1932 that biology had replaced botany in 'one third of the schools reporting' and that the change had taken place within the previous five years. The Committee's conclusion was based on the responses to two questionnaires 'widely circulated among the secondary schools', but the size of the sample and the number of boys', girls' and coeducational schools within it are not given.[77] The conclusion, however, is consistent with the findings of another Committee, appointed by the Association to examine the teaching of general science in schools, which reported in the following year. These findings were based on a sample of 358 schools, approximately one-fifth of the total of 1,729 State-aided (1367) and non-aided (358) secondary schools in England and Wales in March 1931. Table 5.4 shows[78] the percentages of pupils taking various science subjects in each of three different types of school. Because of the ambiguity of the phrase 'taking chemistry' or 'taking botany', some caution is necessary in

Table 5.4   Percentage of Pupils, by Type of School, Taking Science Subjects in 1931–2

	Boys'	Girls'	Mixed
Number of Schools:	98	198	62
Average Percentage of Pupils Taking:			
Chemistry	50	26	51
Physics	55	21	50
General Science	37	40	42
Biology	21	26	28
Botany	4	31	24
Zoology	4	4	3

considering the data in the Table. Whilst many schools offered science courses which were 'taken' by pupils, by no means all of these courses were available to, or were followed to, the level of the School Certificate Examination. Of 137 girls' schools which provided courses in general science, only thirty-five entered candidates for examination in this subject at School Certificate level. In contrast, almost all of the 167 girls' secondary schools offering courses in botany and about two-thirds of those which provided teaching in chemistry, presented candidates for School Certificate examinations in these subjects.[79]

The growth of biology and general science and the decline of botany as subjects in the School Certificate Examinations between 1930 and 1938 are indicated by the data in Table 5.5. Unfortunately, the available statistics do not distinguish boys from girls among the entrants, although it is certain that the majority of candidates entering for School Certificate biology came from girls' schools.[80]

At sixth-form level, the inter-war years were a period during which the so-called 'modern studies' of English, history and French consolidated the dominant position in the secondary education of girls which had already been established by 1918. The growth in the number of advanced courses recognised for grant purposes by the Board of Education under Regulations introduced towards the end of the First World War and intended to encourage the development of sixth-form courses in secondary schools is indicated by the data in Table 5.6. Details of the distribution of the various categories of recognised

Table 5.5   School Certificate and Higher School Certificate Entries, by Subject, 1930 and 1938

	1930		1938	
i School Certificate	No. of Entries	% of total entry	No. of Entries	% of Total entry
Botany	14,785	23.4	6,828	8.9
Chemistry	25,764	40.8	25,387	33.0
Physics	16,576	26.3	19,942	25.9
General Science	1,852	2.9	8,784	11.4
Biology	1,021	1.6	15,852	20.6
Physics with Chemistry	3,431	5.4	6,913	9.0
Electricity and Magnetism	2,345	3.7	2,326	3.0
Heat, Light and Sound	3,491	5.5	2,533	3.3
Mathematics	59,272	93.9	70,048	91.0
English	64,305	99.0	77,358	99.0
ii Higher School Certificate				
Mathematics	4,048	42.2	5,501	41.7
Physics	2,860	29.8	4,040	30.6
Chemistry	2,766	28.8	3,934	29.8
Botany	543	5.7	757	5.7
Zoology	260	2.7	679	5.1
Biology	116	1.2	901	6.1
English	3,539	36.9	4,734	35.9

advanced courses among different types of grant-aided secondary school for the year 1924–5 are given in Table 5.7. Since the numbers of recognised advanced courses and of schools in which they were taught did not alter significantly[81] between 1925 and 1935, the year in which the practice of formal recognition by the Board was abolished,[82] the data in Tables 5.6 and 5.7 suggest strongly that, during this period, only about 17 per cent of the advanced courses in science and mathematics were provided in girls' schools compared with approximately 58 per cent of the courses in modern studies. There was, of course, a substantial amount of work in certain schools 'in respect of which no application was made to the Board for the formal approval of Advanced Courses',[83] but there is no reason to believe that this formally unrecognised sixth-form work was in any significant way differently biased from that conducted with the aid of grant from the Board of Education.

This bias is reflected in the subjects for which State Scholarships were awarded to boys and girls. When the State Scholarship scheme was introduced in 1920, provision was made for 200 to be awarded annually to pupils attending grant-aided secondary schools in England and Wales on the basis of their performance in the Higher School Certificate examinations.[84] The Scholarships were allotted to the Examination Boards[85] who were required to make nominations for awards in equal numbers for boys and girls. The number of State Scholarships available was increased to 300 in 1931 and to 360 in 1936, in

Table 5.6   Advanced Courses recognised by the Board of Education, by Subject, 1917–35

Year	Course A Science and Mathematics	Course B Classics	Course C Modern Studies	All Courses
1917–18	76	19	25	120
1918–19	140	26	76	242
1919–20	171	28	115	314
1920–1	193	34	144	371
1921–2	206	36	169	411
1922–3	205	36	169	410
1923–4	207	36	178	425
1924–5	212	36	177	434
1925–6	210	37	179	440
1926–7	211	36	182	445
1927–8	233	39	190	488
1928–9	229	38	185	483
1929–30	227	38	181	483
1930–1	230	37	182	494
1931–2	229	37	179	492
1932–3	232	37	175	495
1933–4	228	37	166	485
1934–5	227	36	166	481

NOTES

i In later years, the numbers in the right-hand column exceed the sum of the courses listed in the three central columns. This is because 'all courses' included Advanced, Recognised courses in Categories D, E and F. The numbers of courses in these Categories were relatively small.
ii After 1926, the *Regulations* of the Board did not specify groups of subjects but allowed schools to submit for recognition such subjects as were thought fit. The Board anticipated that the submissions would normally fall into one or other of the groups used up until 1926, so the letters A to F, associated with the groups, were retained after that date.

Table 5.7   Advanced Courses Recognised by the Board of Education, by Type of School and Subject, 1924–5

Group*	No. of Recognised Courses		
	Boys' Schools	Girls' Schools	Mixed Schools
A Science and Mathematics	141	37	34
B Classics	34	2	–
C Modern Studies	50	103	24
D Classical with Modern Studies	4	1	–
E Geography	4	0	–
F Other combinations of Subjects	0	0	0
Total:	233	143	58

* See Note (ii) to Table 5.6.

Table 5.8 Numbers of State Scholarships held by Sex, Subject and Year, 1926–37

Year*		Classics	Modern Languages	English	History	Mathematics	Science	Medicine	Engineering	Total No. awarded Annually
1926	Boys	51	27	10	26	73	86	9	17	200
	Girls	(17)	(76)	(70)	(48)	(35)	(23)	(3)	(0)	
1928	Boys	60	32	4	35	86	81	14	9	
	Girls	(30)	(80)	(59)	(47)	(24)	(26)	(5)	(–)	
1929	Boys	60	39	12	30	78	79	18	9	
	Girls	(32)	(77)	(61)	(44)	(17)	(34)	(9)	(–)	
1930	Boys	58	53	17	36	84	100	20	13	
	Girls	(34)	(74)	(70)	(40)	(22)	(42)	(8)	(–)	
1931	Boys	63	54	18	38	93	138	18	16	300
	Girls	(35)	(78)	(80)	(35)	(25)	(49)	(8)	(–)	
1932	Boys	72	77	19	47	111	156	20	18	
	Girls	(32)	(84)	(82)	(37)	(41)	(50)	(6)	(–)	
1933	Boys	80	84	19	55	108	189	21	14	
	Girls	(35)	(78)	(88)	(35)	(46)	(51)	(5)	(–)	
1934	Boys	76	89	20	53	105	110	29	27	
	Girls	(32)	(80)	(76)	(41)	(44)	(52)	(7)	(–)	
1935	Boys	75	83	31	59	122	181	23	31	
	Girls	(34)	(83)	(71)	(50)	(42)	(45)	(11)	(–)	
1936	Boys	75	76	30	60	128	191	16	35	360
	Girls	(31)	(91)	(75)	(57)	(31)	(47)	(8)	(–)	
1937	Boys	77	88	36	66	129	191	19	35	
	Girls	(26)	(82)	(67)	(64)	(35)	(49)	(10)	(–)	

* Each entry in this column refers to the academic year beginning with the date indicated. Thus 1926 refers to the academic year 1926–7.

Table 5.9   Percentages of State Scholarships held in a given Subject by Sex, Age and Year, 1926–37

Year*	Classics		Modern Languages		English		History		Mathematics		Science		Medicine		Engineering	
	B	G	B	G	B	G	B	G	B	G	B	G	B	G	B	G
1926	75	25	26	74	13	87	35	65	67	33	80	20	75	25	100	–
1928	67	33	29	71	6	94	43	57	78	22	76	24	74	26	100	–
1929	65	35	34	66	16	84	40	60	82	18	70	30	67	33	100	–
1930	64	36	42	58	20	80	47	53	80	20	70	30	71	29	100	–
1931	64	36	41	59	18	82	52	48	79	21	74	26	69	31	100	–
1932	69	31	48	52	19	81	56	44	73	27	71	29	77	23	100	–
1933	70	30	52	48	18	82	61	39	70	30	79	21	81	19	100	–
1934	71	29	53	47	21	79	56	44	70	30	77	23	81	19	100	–
1935	70	30	50	50	30	70	54	46	74	26	80	20	69	31	100	–
1936	71	29	45	55	29	71	51	49	80	20	80	20	67	33	100	–
1937	74	26	52	48	35	65	50	50	79	21	79	21	65	35	100	–

* See note to Table 5.8.   B=Boys;   G=Girls

which year candidates from non-grant-aided secondary schools also became eligible for the awards. In 1931, the allocation of Scholarships between boys and girls was made dependent upon the numbers of boys and girls entering for the examinations conducted by the Examination Board in the years immediately preceding the year of award. The numbers and percentages of State Scholarships held, by subject and sex, for each of the years 1926–7 to 1937–8 are given in Tables 5.8 and 5.9 respectively.

These figures for State Scholarships should be placed in the context of the numbers of boys and girls who left grant-aided secondary schools and proceeded to the universities. These numbers are given, for selected years,[86] in Table 5.10. It should be noted, however, that, even in 1938, by no means all

Table 5.10   Numbers of Pupils leaving Grant-Aided Secondary Schools and Proceeding to Universities and Numbers of State Scholarships Awarded

Year	No. of State Scholarships Awarded		No. Proceeding to Universities		Girls as % of boys and girls proceeding to universities
	Boys	Girls	Boys	Girls	
1909	–	–	692	316	31.3%
1920–4*	107	93 (46.5%)	1,726†	1,212	41.2%
1927	102	98 (49%)	2,057	1,312	38.9%
1931	185	115 (57.5%)	3,047	1,513	33.2%
1938	235	125 (62.5%)	2,865	1,360	32.2%

NOTES
* No new awards of State Scholarships were made for 1922–3 and 1923–4 and the system was not revived until 1924.
† The figures for university entrants are the mean for the period 1920–4. The figures for State Scholarships relate to awards made in 1924.

university entrants had taken Higher School Certificate examinations and gained a Certificate. The total number of Higher Certificates awarded in July 1938, were approximately 1,500 less than the total undergraduate entry in October of the same year and as many as a quarter of the pupils who had gained a Certificate in 1938 made another attempt in the following year. In addition, not all pupils who held a Higher Certificate proceeded to universities, either in the year in which they gained such a Certificate, or on a subsequent occasion. The explanation of these figures lies in the fact that the two older universities and the public schools associated with them assigned less importance to the Higher School Certificate examination than the more modern universities and the grant-aided secondary schools, so that a proportionally greater number of public school pupils proceeded to universities without a Higher School Certificate.

The majority of the State Scholars in the 1930s went as undergraduates to Oxford or Cambridge. Between 1927 and 1938, the percentage of State Scholars attending these two universities rose from twenty-three to thirty and from thirty-six to forty respectively. London retained about 18 per cent, whilst

Table 5.11 Numbers of Honours Degrees Awarded, by Sex and Subject, 1925–6 to 1948–9

Year	Mathematics		Natural Science*		Physics		Chemistry		Botany		Zoology		Biology	
	M	W	M	W	M	W	M	W	M	W	M	W	M	W
1925–6	139	62	142	43	113	14	277	53	15	69	8	16	–	–
1926–7	131	45	295	20	131	11	257	70	8	66	3	9	–	–
1927–8	163	51	180†		140	15	302	57	22	64	10	21	2	0
1928–9	187	62	200‡		131	4	283	63	23	61	22	18	2	0
1929–30	200	62	198	26	150	8	275	42	24	66	10	23	2	0
1930–1	191	53	208	29	166	20	280	56	28	60	19	21	4	0
1931–2	160	59	222	28	153	20	291	51	37	50	25	27	3	1
1932–3	153	79	227	26	158	18	296	54	52	57	27	27	10	0
1933–4	163	62	296	48	153	13	305	42	40	61	36	29	7	0
1934–5	189	86	311	58	154	12	343	48	43	69	48	30	8	0
1935–6	161	86	224	71	194	15	369	46	54	57	49	34	4	0
1936–7	172	58	344	68	165	10	303	50	37	50	44	23	8	0
1937–8	169	54	336	39	156	10	317	31	36	49	41	31	8	1
Total	2,718	819	3,128	511	1,964	170	3,898	663	419	779	342	309	58	2
1947–8	265	86	351	84	500	34	509	77	61	70	64	67	0	0
1948–9	328	107	367	98	463	28	612	66	61	76	78	66	0	0

NOTES:

* The term refers to B.Sc. General Degrees and Natural Science Degrees for which further details are not available.
† For the purposes of calculating a total for these columns, the 180 has been divided into 155 men and 25 women.
‡ The total has been divided into 170 men and 30 women.

the proportion attending the civic universities fell from twenty-four to twelve in the same period.[87] As indicated by the data in Table 5.8, the numbers of girls who held State Scholarships in science subjects were always relatively small. It seems likely that at least two-thirds of these girls became teachers after graduation, compared with perhaps one-third of the boys who held State Scholarships.[88]

The total numbers of women obtaining degrees in individual science subjects between the wars are not known, although figures relating to Honours degrees were published annually after 1925. These figures are summarised[89] in Table 5.11. Table 5.12 records the percentage of Honours degrees in individual science subjects awarded to women between 1925 and 1938. The data in Table 5.11 may be used to estimate the number of Ordinary degrees and, hence, the total number of science degrees awarded to women in the same thirteen-year period. The mean ratio of Honours to Ordinary degrees in all subjects granted to women between 1925 and 1938 was 2.5:1. If it is assumed that this ratio may be applied to degrees obtained solely in Faculties of Science, then the numbers of Ordinary degrees awarded in the various sciences may be estimated as in Table 5.13, which also records the estimated total numbers of Honours and Ordinary degrees obtained in these same subjects.

Table 5.12   Percentage of Honours
Graduates, by Subject, 1925–38, who were
Women

Subject	% Honours Graduates who were Women
Mathematics	27.32
Physics	7.96
Chemistry	14.53
Botany	65.46
Zoology	47.46
Biology	3.30
Natural Sciences*	14.04

* See Notes to Table 5.11.

Table 5.13   Total Numbers of Degrees, Honours and Ordinary, Awarded to
Women, by Subject, 1925–39

Subject	No. of Honours Degrees	Estimated No. of Ordinary Degrees	Estimated Total of First Degrees
Mathematics	819	328	1,147
Physics	170	68	238
Chemistry	663	265	928
Botany	779	311	1,090
Zoology	309	124	433
Biology	2	–	–
Natural Science	511	204	715

Table 5.14   Numbers of Honours Degrees, by Sex and Subject, 1951–62

Year	Subject and Numbers of Men (M) and Women (W)											
	Mathematics		Physics		Chemistry		Botany		Zoology		General Science	
	M	W	M	W	M	W	M	W	M	W	M	W
1950–51	281	87	446	24	613	84	109	81	113	69	280	45
1951–2	380	97	505	35	658	59	125	70	157	80	358	64
1952–3	329	98	495	32	712	69	111	84	125	72	348	63
1953–4	348	100	503	37	684	69	104	70	105	77	346	71
1954–5	331	100	488	43	626	75	101	78	121	75	365	79
1955–6	284	107	508	34	676	76	94	77	117	73	362	74
1956–7	314	113	531	57	703	76	102	79	105	90	365	101
1957–8	307	122	631	64	768	108	100	89	132	86	389	104
1958–9	348	125	727	77	782	101	137	88	134	121	346	116
1959–60	442	151	1,287	117	805	121	123	96	132	108	165	113
1960–1	476	155	832	89	1,016	129	126	99	175	117	387	134
1961–2	441	152	880	83	1,008	132	116	107	164	114	352	129

NOTE:

The period 1951–62 saw a marked increase in the numbers graduating in such subjects as biochemistry, metallurgy and geology. These are excluded from the Table but show a similar sex bias in favour of male graduates.

Several comments are suggested by the data in Tables 5.11 to 5.13. Over four and a half times as many women obtained first degrees in botany as obtained first degrees in physics in the same period. This dominance of botany and the very small number of women physics graduates can be attributed, at least in part, to the pattern of studies established much earlier in the century in the scientific education of girls at school. The numbers of women physics graduates produced annually[90] in England and Wales between 1925 and 1938 were clearly insufficient to support any significant expansion of the teaching of physics in girls' secondary schools, particularly at sixth-form level. This constraint on the development of physics teaching may also have been a factor which led girls' secondary schools to look more favourably upon general science than the boys' schools. General science could be taught by chemistry graduates, most of whom would have studied at least some physics and, as Table 5.11 indicates, the numbers of women chemistry graduates were not markedly less than the numbers of women graduating in botany. However, other factors were clearly operating since the near-absence of women graduates in biology proved no impediment to the rapid development of biology courses in girls' secondary schools, courses which must have been taught, at least initially, by teachers who had specialised in botany, zoology, chemistry or some other subject.

Table 5.15   Ratios of Men to Women Honours Graduates by Subject and Year (England and Wales)

Year	Mathematics	Physics	Chemistry	All Subjects
1925–6	2.24	8.07	5.22	2.20
1930–1	3.60	8.30	5.00	2.58
1937–8	3.12	15.60	10.22	3.27
1948–9	3.06	16.50	9.27	3.50
1950–1	3.23	18.58	7.29	3.45
1955–6	2.65	14.94	8.89	2.83
1960–1	3.07	9.34	7.87	3.31

In 1925–6, the ratios of Honours degrees in physics and chemistry awarded to men and women were 8.07:1 and 5.22:1 respectively, compared with 2.20:1 for all subjects.[91] The corresponding ratios for some later years, based on figures in Tables 5.11 and 5.14, are given in Table 5.15. The data in this latter Table show that the large increases in the numbers of women obtaining Honours degrees in mathematics and the physical sciences between 1925 and 1960 were insufficient to prevent a decline in the position relative to the numbers of such degrees awarded to men. In 1925–6, when 457 Honours degrees were awarded in physics and chemistry, sixty-seven (14.6 per cent) of these were gained by women. In 1960–1, women accounted for 218 (10.5 per cent) of the 2,066 Honours degrees awarded[92] in these two subjects, although it is clear that the relative position of women graduates in physical science had improved when compared with the years immediately following the end of the

Second World War. Even so, only eighty-nine women obtained an Honours degree in physics in 1960–1 compared with 374 in French, 133 in German, 289 in history, 499 in English, sixty-nine in law, 129 in chemistry, 155 in mathematics, 117 in zoology and 111 in social science.

The figures relating to the numbers of women graduating in mathematics and the physical sciences after 1951 are given an additional perspective by considering the position of these subjects in the schools. The numbers of entries by boys and girls for selected subjects at O- and A-level in each of the years between 1951 and 1962 are recorded in Tables 5.16 and 5.17 respectively. The ratio of girls to boys among these entries during the same period is given in Table 5.18.

The sex ratios among O-level entrants in 1951, A-level entrants in 1953 and Honours graduates in 1956 are compared in Table 5.19 which includes a similar comparison for the years 1956, 1958 and 1961. When compared with the sex distribution among all entrants, girls have been considerably 'under-represented' in mathematics, physics and chemistry at both O- and A-level. They may be regarded[93] as having been 'over-represented' among the entrants in biology for both examinations, although much less so at A-level than at O-level. Between 1951 and 1962, the ratio of girls to boys entering for O- or A-level physics varied little from 1 in 6, but because of the greater preponderance of boys among A-level entrants, compared with O-level, the 1:6 ratio at A-level represented a relative improvement as far as girls were concerned over the position indicated by the same ratio at O-level.[94] In addition, it should be noted that the 'under-representation' of girls among the entrants for mathematics at both O- and A-level levels is not found in the distribution among men and women of Honours degrees awarded in mathematics.

The under-representation of girls among the entrants for physics and chemistry in the G.C.E. examinations was undoubtedly a reflection of the continued imbalance in the scientific education of girls, established much earlier in the century. The Central Advisory Council for Education (England) stated the position bluntly in a Report presented in 1959:

> Physics and chemistry are the subjects most studied by boys; biology by girls.[95]

As a result, many boys' grammar schools were able to demand O-level passes in mathematics, physics and chemistry as a condition of admission to sixth-form courses in physical sciences. In the girls' schools, such a stipulation was necessarily rare. Girls were 'debarred' from a full science course in the sixth form 'because they had done virtually no physics or chemistry in the main school' or because they had 'failed in or did not take mathematics at O-level'.[96] This reference to mathematics is significant. While O-level mathematics was 'attempted by virtually every boy in a grammar school fifth form', entry by girls tended to be restricted to the more able at the subject. The others either abandoned the study of mathematics altogether or confined themselves to work in arithmetic.

The dominance of the biological sciences in the scientific education of girls has not been confined to the grammar or public schools. In sixty-nine of the 155

Table 5.16 G.C.E. O-Level Entries by Sex and Subject, 1951–62

Year	English Language		Mathematics		General Science		Physics		Chemistry		Botany		Zoology		Biology	
	Boys	Girls	Boys	Girls	Boys	Girls	Boys	Girls	Boys	Girls	Boys	Girls	Boys	Girls	Boys	Girls
1951	57,603	51,291	51,166	29,459	12,538	9,134	18,819	2,729	16,005	4,672	92	722	9	12	6,935	22,079
1952	61,326	48,642	52,418	27,306	10,420	7,799	19,916	2,837	17,722	4,979	76	337	–	3	7,718	21,203
1953	85,662	68,960	73,976	37,146	14,883	10,805	27,874	4,001	24,371	6,544	113	568	5	72	10,173	29,544
1954	70,541	56,256	62,022	30,199	11,628	8,714	25,740	3,703	22,877	5,721	101	193	5	8	9,916	25,550
1955	89,207	71,379	77,878	37,810	15,396	9,811	32,495	4,662	28,044	6,910	151	507	35	21	12,872	34,080
1956	89,621	73,002	79,213	38,393	15,741	10,006	34,583	4,872	29,159	7,231	258	542	31	33	13,518	36,620
1957	95,597	76,290	82,495	40,697	14,979	9,320	38,270	5,362	32,538	7,819	486	571	21	55	15,346	39,544
1958	108,173	87,273	93,700	46,344	15,498	9,431	44,550	6,423	37,097	9,061	–	–	–	–	17,559	45,029
1959	123,919	99,269	107,096	53,626	16,384	9,259	52,065	7,964	42,976	10,927	–	–	–	–	20,350	52,651
1960	139,964	110,107	117,664	59,612	16,886	9,545	58,539	9,541	47,290	12,353	–	–	–	–	24,035	59,954
1961	149,524	112,305	118,274	60,795	15,853	9,138	60,895	10,262	49,089	13,132	–	–	–	–	26,270	62,944
1962	151,132	142,022	130,632	69,503	15,076	9,683	67,986	11,705	52,498	14,893	–	–	–	–	25,689	73,842

Table 5.17 G.C.E. A-Level Entries by Sex and Subject, 1951–62

Year	English Literature		Mathematics		Physics		Chemistry		Botany		Zoology		Biology	
	Boys	Girls	Boys	Girls	Boys	Girls	Boys	Girls	Boys	Girls	Boys	Girls	Boys	Girls
1951	6,148	6,775	9,588	1,307	11,943	1,659	10,747	1,986	1,844	1,118	1,867	1,221	2,683	1,437
1952	5,447	5,602	9,410	1,270	11,658	1,782	10,583	2,121	1,600	1,051	1,649	1,131	2,697	1,329
1953	6,403	6,647	12,124	1,634	14,117	2,085	12,308	2,467	1,915	1,158	1,938	1,341	3,056	1,590
1954	5,613	5,980	12,196	1,590	13,909	2,197	11,831	2,498	2,115	1,254	2,139	1,422	2,675	1,345
1955	6,646	7,558	14,759	1,911	16,910	2,699	13,898	3,083	2,513	1,628	2,567	1,829	2,967	1,805
1956	7,219	8,330	16,396	2,112	18,356	2,897	14,889	3,271	2,875	1,827	2,883	2,064	3,052	1,865
1957	7,532	8,901	16,772	2,306	20,713	3,198	16,122	3,538	2,703	1,820	3,202	2,217	3,127	1,987
1958	7,745	9,241	18,069	2,474	22,876	3,457	17,860	3,753	2,640	1,692	3,638	2,392	3,015	1,952
1959	7,995	9,555	25,129	2,627	23,859	3,591	18,466	3,722	2,385	1,627	3,523	2,424	3,115	1,971
1960	9,165	11,566	28,647	4,360	26,906	4,109	20,591	4,412	2,679	1,813	4,175	2,845	3,474	2,359
1961	10,244	13,171	35,446	5,855	29,757	4,767	22,134	5,095	2,606	2,123	4,124	3,283	4,216	2,883
1962	11,333	15,081	38,083	6,243	31,575	5,090	22,850	5,378	2,533	2,207	4,406	3,685	4,987	3,185

Table 5.18   Ratio of Girls to Boys Among O- and A-Level Entrants, by Subject, 1951–62

Year	Level	English Language	Mathematics	General Science	Physics	Chemistry	Botany	Zoology	Biology	English Literature	All Subjects
1951	O	0.89	0.57	0.73	0.14	0.29	7.84	1.33	3.18	–	0.85
	A	–	0.14	–	0.14	0.18	0.61	0.65	0.53	1.10	0.45
1952	O	0.79	0.52	0.75	0.14	0.28	4.43	–	2.74	–	0.78
	A	–	0.13	–	0.15	0.20	0.66	0.68	0.49	1.03	0.42
1953	O	0.80	0.50	0.73	0.14	0.27	5.02	14.40	2.90	–	0.79
	A	–	0.13	–	0.15	0.20	0.60	0.69	0.52	1.04	0.41
1954	O	0.79	0.49	0.75	0.14	0.25	1.91	1.60	2.57	–	0.77
	A	–	0.13	–	0.16	0.21	0.59	0.66	0.50	1.06	0.39
1955	O	0.80	0.48	0.64	0.14	0.25	3.35	0.60	2.64	–	0.79
	A	–	0.13	–	0.16	0.22	0.65	0.71	0.61	1.14	0.43
1956	O	0.81	0.48	0.64	0.14	0.25	2.10	1.06	2.71	–	0.80
	A	–	0.13	–	0.16	0.22	0.63	0.72	0.61	1.15	0.44
1957	O	0.79	0.49	0.62	0.14	0.24	1.17	2.61	2.58	–	0.79
	A	–	0.14	–	0.14	0.22	0.67	0.69	0.63	1.18	0.43
1958	O	0.81	0.49	0.61	0.14	0.24	–	–	2.56	–	0.79
	A	–	0.14	–	0.15	0.21	0.64	0.66	0.65	1.19	0.42
1959	O	0.80	0.50	0.56	0.15	0.25	–	–	2.59	–	0.79
	A	–	0.10	–	0.15	0.20	0.68	0.69	0.63	1.19	0.42
1960	O	0.79	0.51	0.56	0.16	0.26	–	–	2.49	–	0.79
	A	–	0.15	–	0.15	0.21	0.67	0.68	0.68	1.26	0.44
1961	O	0.75	0.51	0.58	0.17	0.27	–	–	2.39	–	0.77
	A	–	0.16	–	0.16	0.23	0.81	0.79	0.68	1.28	0.45
1962	O	0.94	0.53	0.64	0.17	0.28	–	–	2.87	–	0.81
	A	–	0.16	–	0.16	0.23	0.87	0.84	0.64	1.33	0.47

Table 5.19   Sex Ratio (Girls/Boys) Among O- and A-Level Entrants and Honours Graduates

O-Level in 1951	Mathematics	0.57	O-Level in 1956	0.48
	Physics	0.14		0.14
	Chemistry	0.29		0.25
	Biology	3.18		2.71
Total Entries:		0.85		0.80
A-Level in 1953	Mathematics	0.13	A-Level in 1958	0.14
	Physics	0.15		0.15
	Chemistry	0.20		0.21
	Biology	0.52		0.65
Total Entries:		0.41		0.42
Honours Degrees Awarded in 1956	Mathematics	0.38	Honours Degrees Awarded in 1961	0.32
	Physics	0.07		0.11
	Chemistry	0.11		0.13
All Honours Degrees:		0.35		0.28

coeducational senior schools investigated by H.M. Inspectorate in 1930, the boys followed courses of 'purely physical science' while the girls were confined to work in biology or 'more accurately', in botany.[97] In some senior schools for girls, there were continued attempts to accommodate the teaching of basic physical and chemical principles within courses of housecraft or domestic science, but, for reasons already mentioned, these were rarely successful. Domestic science often involved little more science than 'a series of unrelated chemical tests',[98] so that pupils failed to acquire a coherent body of scientific knowledge or to realise that there was 'order in the natural world' of which they formed a part.[99]

In the post-war secondary modern schools, the dominant position of the biological sciences in the scientific education of girls was consolidated[100] by the chronic shortage of teachers of physics, chemistry and mathematics. By 1961, when a number of secondary modern schools had well-established G.C.E. courses in a variety of subjects, this dominance was evident in the pattern of entries in the sciences at O-level. (See Table 5.20.) The numbers of secondary modern school pupils taking A-level subjects were very small so that the ratio of girls to boys among the entrants fluctuated considerably during the later 1950s and early 1960s. However, the data in Table 5.20 indicate a pattern similar to that found among the entries from boys and girls attending grammar schools.[101]

The pressures on the curriculum of girls' secondary schools in the early years of this century and the continuing debate over the extent to which secondary education of girls should differ from that of boys, eventually led the Board of Education to refer the question of curriculum differentiation between the sexes to its Consultative Committee. The Report of this Committee, published in

Table 5.20   G.C.E. O- and A-Level Entries, 1961, by Boys and Girls Attending Modern Schools*

Subject	O-Level			A-Level	
	Boys	Girls	Girl:Boy Ratio	Boys	Girls
Physics	2,345	53	0.02	9	0
Chemistry	277	46	0.16	2	0
Mathematics	7,479	1,806	0.24	22	3
Biology	418	2,716	6.50	3	5
General Science	2,508	420	0.17	–	–
All Subjects	48,385	34,409	0.71	212	252

* The data include candidates from the very small number of 'all-age' schools in 1961.

1923, discussed at some length the relative position of the physical and biological sciences in the scientific education of girls and the alleged lower attainment of girls in subjects such as physics, chemistry and mathematics. Interest in these issues was revived after the Second World War when successive Governments assumed an almost direct relationship between a growth in the supply of qualified scientists and technologists and an increase in national economic prosperity. Girls became part of 'a pool of untapped scientific ability'. In addition, the relative neglect of the physical sciences in their education was regarded as incompatible with the need to produce a more scientifically literate population in which those who were not science specialists had 'enough understanding of the scientific side of human knowledge' to hold their own in 'an increasingly scientific and technological world'.[102] It is appropriate, therefore, to conclude this chapter with a review of some of the factors which have been held responsible for the relative contribution made by the physical and biological sciences to the education of girls and for the apparent reluctance of girls to embark upon careers as professional physicists, chemists or technologists. As Figure 5.1 shows, using data drawn from the 1966 Sample Census,[103] the proportion of women with scientific qualifications in the various age groups altered little between 1925 and 1965, except in the case of medicine where the proportion of women increased from approximately 10 per cent of those qualifying in 1930 to about 30 per cent in 1965.

There is little doubt that, throughout the period under discussion, the conditions for teaching physical science in girls' schools have, in general, been less favourable than those in corresponding schools for boys. A British Association Committee, reporting[104] in 1917, noted that 'as a rule', the number of hours per week devoted to science teaching was 'much less than in boys' schools'. Over forty years later, a headmistress told[105] a conference organised by the same Association that girls could be given 'a full and equal choice' of science specialisms only if the 'quantity of science teaching in the main school' were substantially increased.

Perhaps of greater significance than the time made available for teaching physics or chemistry in girls' schools is the manner in which the timetables have been organised so as to present individual subjects or groups of subjects as options. Generalisation about the patterns of curriculum organisation within girls' schools is clearly impossible, one study, reported in 1963, recording 'more than a hundred ... ways of designing the main lines of a science course for

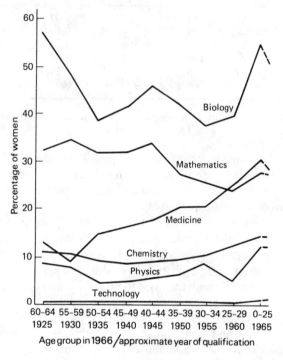

Figure 5.1 Percentages of those qualified in science who are women, by age groups.

the 11–15 age group in a girls' grammar school'.[106] None the less, there can be little doubt that the options available within the timetables of many girls' schools have been such as to discourage, or even prevent, a more advanced study of physics, chemistry or mathematics. In 1962, only 40 per cent of the girls' grammar schools in England taught *any* physical science in the fifth year, a figure which fell to nearer 20 per cent when general science was excluded. In other words, 60 per cent of the pupils attending girls' grammar schools in England in 1962 were studying no physics or chemistry after the age of fourteen.[107] These figures, which have important consequences[108] for the career opportunities available to girls, are given an added significance by Bremner's evidence[109] of an 'unexpected, if low, percentage of sixth formers in girls' schools' who were 'ready to take up physics and chemistry as special studies when the opportunity arose later in their careers'.

The provision of laboratory accommodation and equipment available for teaching the physical sciences has also been less satisfactory in girls' schools than in those for boys, a point noted[110] by the Consultative Committee in 1923 and by the Science Masters' Association and other organisations a generation later when the laboratory accommodation in all types of girls' grammar schools was described[111] as 'inferior to that of boys' and 'often markedly so'. This assessment was reported in 1957 when, despite the post-war building programme, the provision of laboratory accommodation in many grammar schools for boys failed to meet the standards established by the Ministry of Education. Significantly, the Ministry advised different standards of laboratory provision for boys' and girls' schools. Four laboratories were recommended for a two-form entry boys' or coeducational school compared with three for a girls' grammar school of the same size.[112] Each of these recommendations specified a degree of provision lower than that incorporated in the standards established by the Industrial Fund for the Advancement of Scientific Education in Schools which was set up in 1955 to finance the building, expansion, modernisation and equipping of science accommodation in direct-grant and independent schools.[113]

In addition, girls' schools of all types have been affected more severely than boys' schools by the problem of recruiting adequate numbers of specialist teachers of physics, mathematics and, to a lesser extent, of chemistry. The magnitude of the potential supply of women graduate teachers of physics has already been indicated and, in the inter-war period, girls' grammar schools were able to recruit a sufficient number of such teachers only because of the limited scale on which the subject was taught. After the war, the rapid growth in the demand for qualified scientists and technologists, the accompanying expansion of the education service and broader social changes such as the trend towards earlier marriage, generated an acute shortage of qualified teachers of physics and chemistry. This shortage had particularly severe consequences not only for girls' schools but also for the modern schools, many of which were able to devote no more than 1½ hours each week to the teaching of science[114] during the mid-1950s.

While the allocation of funds for laboratory accommodation and equipment and the distribution of limited teaching resources have, in general, been to the disadvantage of the education of girls in physics and chemistry, such factors are inadequate to account for the enduring under-representation of girls among those studying the subjects at different levels within the educational system. Several studies[115] have established that the tendency of girls to specialise in foreign languages or English rather than in the physical sciences is often less marked in single sex schools than in coeducational schools where the resources available for science teaching have been closer to those found in boys' rather than in girls', schools.

The possibility that differences in the pattern of subject choices between boys and girls could be attributed to sex differences in ability was discussed at length by the Consultative Committee in its Report on the Differentiation of the Curriculum in 1923. However, most of the expert evidence available at the time was based on studies which did not involve pupils of secondary school age and the Committee was left to conclude that there were no 'very trustworthy data to warrant explicit differentiation in the education of the sexes on psychological grounds'.[116]

Since 1923, the field of sex differences in ability has been studied extensively and a number of significant differences in the levels of performance of boys and girls in tests designed to measure such 'specific abilities' as verbal reasoning, spatial thinking and manual dexterity, seem to have been well-established.[117] Despite these findings, there are several reasons for doubting whether differences in performance on tests on this kind have any relevance to the relative levels of attainment or interest in subjects such as physics, chemistry and mathematics by boys and girls at school. Many of the test results relate to average male and female scores and the extent of any overlap is frequently ignored, despite its obvious importance even when the difference between the scores of the two populations is statistically significant. Secondly, specific ability, although more satisfactory than general intelligence as a working concept, is a difficult notion and caution is necessary in inferring the degree of possession of a particular ability from the performance by boys and girls at particular tasks. It has been shown, for example, that some tests described as measuring spatial ability could be completed by verbal processes and vice versa.[118] In addition, the distinction between 'ability' and other personal characteristics is one of convenience which may be misleading, if only because abilities are estimated by the performance of particular tasks and, as in any test procedure, the degree of success at such performance will be influenced by levels of motivation, expectation and anxiety as well as by the more specifically physiological differences between boys and girls. Finally, and perhaps of greatest importance, it is by no means certain which 'specific abilities', allied with given personality characteristics, can be regarded as necessary for interest in the physical sciences at school or for eventual success in the practice of physics or chemistry.

Differences between the several scientific disciplines suggest that science cannot be regarded as a uniform intellectual activity and studies of the relationship between achievement in the sciences and competence at tests designed to measure given abilities have produced inconsistent results. The evidence that numerical ability correlates closely with achievement in the sciences is, for example, inconclusive.

To admit that relative levels of performance on tests of specific abilities fail to provide sufficient grounds to justify a differentiation of the curriculum between the sexes is not, of course, to deny that many of those in a position to influence the scientific education of boys and girls at school have acted as though such grounds were established. Not all were as cautious as Sara Burstall who wrote[119] in 1907 that it appears that boys do better, *caeteris paribus*, in mathematics, chemistry and physics; girls in literature, history and biology'. The teachers and examiners who gave evidence to the Consultative Committee in 1923, while accepting that 'variations in educable capacity between individual members of the same sex were probably greater than any differences between boys and girls', were in 'almost general agreement' that girls, as a rule, 'showed equal or superior originality and capacity in English literature, history, modern languages, and possibly the biological sciences, but were definitely inferior to boys in . . . those branches of natural science which specially require a knowledge of mathematics'.[120] Although the Consultative Committee was careful to point out that the differences in the achievements of the two sexes in certain subjects should be accepted 'with considerable reserve', it was apparently prepared to admit a 'comparative lack in girls of an attitude of scepticism and curiosity' which gave the best approach to natural science and that girls had 'an aptitude for the biological sciences' in which they were 'helped by their greater diligence and neatness'.[121] Boys, on the other hand, were said to excel in experimental work, 'in initiative, in the capacity for judging phenomena and in reasoning'. It is not difficult to move from opinions such as these to a position in which girls are expected to be less interested in, or to do less well at, physics and chemistry than boys and such expectation becomes institutionalised in the timetable and in the allocation of resources within schools or incorporated within official thinking. It was the Newsom Committee which, in 1963, advised[122] that 'the girl may come to the science lesson with a less eager curiosity than the boy'.

The different expectations of boys and girls by parents and teachers and the consequent different demands which may be made upon the two sexes play an important part in determining the eventual social functions of men and women, although many other powerful and subtle influences are clearly operating, often before children enter school.[123] There is little doubt that in British society, as in most of Western Europe, the practice of physical science has been a male-dominated activity. In 1955, only 373 of the 13,635 members of the Royal Institute of Chemistry were women.[124] In 1961, women accounted for a mere 500 of the 151,090 engineers and technologists recorded in the Census of that year.[125] As late as 1965, Wynne-Jones could lament[126] that it was 'taken for granted' that girls should not study physical science professionally or otherwise. Whereas social science was 'respectable' and biological science 'just permissible', physical science was 'beyond the pale' and engineering 'absolutely prohibited'. Such an attitude was reflected in Hudson's finding in 1966 that it was the 'divergent' rather than the 'convergent' girl who chose to specialise in physics and it helps to explain his assumption that it required a 'divergent mentality' for a girl to act contrary to the expectations of her society.[127] society.[127]

The importance of social rather than intellectual factors in determining the representation of women in the scientific and technological professions is emphasised by comparative studies of scientific employment. According to the 1971 Census, there were fifteen men employed as chemists and 130 as engineers for every woman practising each of these professions within the United Kingdom. In science teaching, including university teaching, and in the medical profession, there were about four men for every woman. These figures, which reflect a pattern of employment broadly similar to that prevailing in most of the countries of Western Europe and in North America, are in marked contrast to those found in countries of the Eastern Block. In Poland, for example, women accounted for 11 per cent of the engineers and 44 per cent of the doctors and dentists in 1965, compared with approximately 30 per cent and 77 per cent respectively in the Soviet Union.[128]

Girls have also been under-represented among the students following apprenticeship schemes or other courses of training leading to science-based qualifications, many of which have been provided since 1945 in colleges within the further education sector. The majority of girls entering this sector on leaving school have enrolled for courses related to employment in the secretarial and commercial fields. As Kathleen Ollerenshaw remarked[129] in 1958, the 'mere sight' of a woman student in those technical colleges specialising in engineering or building caused 'quite a stir'. During the 1950s, as at any time since 1902, most girls simply left school[130] as soon as they were legally permitted to do so. Once in employment they were often denied the opportunities more generally available to boys to obtain qualifications or further training on the basis of the day-release system. As Figures 5.2a and b illustrate,[131] such a system had barely developed for girls in many sectors of employment, even by 1962.

In addition to presenting science and technology as activities undertaken principally by men, society has also fostered a number of assumptions about the nature of these activities and of the intellectual and emotional characteristics of those engaged in them. These assumptions have underpinned the images of science and scientists presented through plays, novels, poems, science fiction, cinema, radio and, since the Second World War, television. The images are complex and, as might be expected, show some sensitivity towards broader social and historical changes.[132] Nevertheless, it is possible to discern several recurrent elements which have served to characterise scientific research as a remarkably pure, logical, ethically neutral and unemotional activity. It is as if the imaginative, aesthetic, social and craft elements of scientific creation have been suppressed and excluded from the popular account of scientific practice, much as they are ignored in the conventional and, in Medawar's term[133] 'fraudulent' scientific paper. The personal characteristics ascribed to scientists are entirely consistent with the intellectually mechanical and insulated activity in which they are assumed to be engaged. The positive virtues of superior intelligence, total dedication and commitment to objectivity have often been coupled with a total egocentricity, emotional sterility and a relative lack of interest in people and their relationships within society.[134] It is this latter trait which has proved too convenient for those who, at different times and for different reasons, have chosen to attack science through its manifestations in technology.[135]

Quarrying literature or other material in search of profiles and attitudes is a hazardous undertaking since it involves a highly personal assessment. However, it is not difficult to find examples of those stereotypes of science and its practitioners which have already been described. Some features of these stereotypes have a long ancestry[136] and appear to be recognised by at least some of those who are, or have been, intimately concerned with scientific activity.

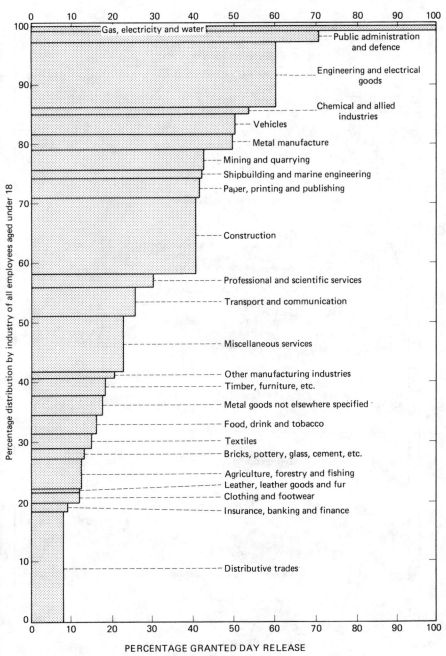

Figure 5.2a Percentage of employees aged under 18 granted day release in 1962 (Boys).

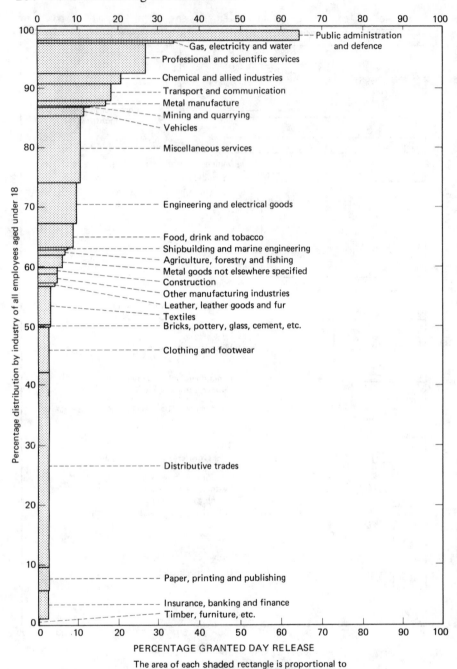

Figure 5.2b *Percentage of employees aged under 18 granted day release in 1962 (Girls).*

Thus, A. N. Whitehead in 1929 warned[137] of the danger of 'a celibacy of the intellect which is divorced from the concrete contemplation of the complete facts' and, in more recent times, Dainton has acknowledged[138] the view that a scientist is 'a man (*sic*) voluntarily withdrawn from human contact; disassociating himself from personal and societal problems ... a man who is "objective" to an objectional degree'. Some support for the existence of this stereotype is found in the work of Hudson in England and of Mead and Metraux in the United States.[139]

School science education must perhaps take some responsibility for failing to encourage a more accurate and comprehensive picture of science and its practitioners. Such a picture will evidently need to accommodate the differences between individual sciences as well as incorporate the imaginative, craft, aesthetic and social elements of scientific activity within a framework which distinguishes between 'revolutionary' and 'normal' science.[140] For the present, it is perhaps not too much to postulate that the relative neglect of the human and social dimensions of physical science has been of particular disadvantage to girls. It is appropriate to note Ormerod's conclusion that few girls have opted to study physics and chemistry because these subjects, while occasionally intellectually engaging, are perceived by most girls as devoid of any personal or social implications.[141] Such a conclusion is consistent with Hutchings's view that girls have been deflected from physical science, not because of a lack of ability or willingness to work but because they found most science lessons 'hardly relevant to their main interests'.[142] School biology is presumably exempted from this criticism on the grounds of the personal, domestic and social dimensions of biological knowledge and the more direct relationship of such knowledge to employment in those occupations where girls have had secure career expectations, e.g. nursing, midwifery.

Finally, it is necessary to emphasise that the scientific education of girls has been affected by many of the difficulties which have beset their education in other disciplines. These difficulties include not only the problems of early leaving and the lack of parental support for study beyond the statutory school leaving age, but also the more fundamental question of the extent to which the education of girls should prepare them explicitly for their future roles as wives and mothers. The Consultative Committee on the Differentiation of the Curriculum in 1923 had no doubt that it was the girls and not the boys who were to be the makers of homes but it warned of the dangers of differentiating the curriculum for boys and girls on the basis of differences in the work done by men and women:

> Experience suggests that the division of work between the sexes has changed frequently in the past and that the range of employment followed by women is likely on the whole to increase.[143]

This was to prove to be an accurate prophecy, although the Committee could not have foreseen the extent of those changes which have taken place in society during this century, many of which have been of particular significance for the education of girls. Between 1906 and 1956, the expectation of life for girls at birth rose[144] from 52.4 to 73.3 years. The proportion of women aged between fifteen and nineteen who were married rose from 15 per cent in 1901 to 44 per cent fifty years later. The corresponding figures for women aged between twenty and twenty-four are 24 and 27 per cent. The trend, although not uniform throughout the century, has been for a greater proportion of women to get married and to do so much earlier.[145] (See Table 5.21.) The size of the 'average family' has decreased steadily and the proportion of married women engaged in paid employment has increased. In 1901, 22 per cent of all the women 'gainfully occupied' were married. By 1951, this figure had risen[146] to 40 per cent and, by 1961, to 50 per cent. Over one-third of all married women

Table 5.21   Proportions of Women (per thousand) of Different Age-Groups who were or had been married on given Census Dates, 1901–61

	Year of Census					
	1901	1911	1921	1931	1951	1961
All ages	340	356	383	413	488	498
15–19 years	15	12	18	18	44	66
20–24 years	272	242	270	257	480	577
25–29 years	579	558	568	587	770	835

There was no census in 1941.

in 1963 were earning a wage or salary,[147] compared with a quarter in 1951 and a tenth in 1921. The range of occupations in which women have been employed has also widened considerably from 1901 when no less than 80 per cent of all women in employment were either engaged in the textile, food and tobacco trades or working as domestic servants.[148] The most significant areas of growth have been in the secretarial, nursing, welfare and teaching sectors of employment.[149]

The conditions of employment of women and the secondary education of girls have been slow to respond to these changing social patterns, thus intensifying the conflict between motherhood and full-time employment. Awareness of this conflict has doubtless increased as the opportunities for women in employment and in further and higher education have expanded. Gallagher showed[150] in 1957 that many girls rejected further education because their parents expected them to marry, and Pheasant, in 1961, reported[151] that girls were reluctant to undertake a long course of training for the same reasons. Seear, Roberts and Brock, in 1964, claimed[152] that women rejected engineering as a career partly because of the difficulties of returning to such a profession after fulfilling family obligations. This claim is given added significance by the findings of Hall and Veness[153] that many girls in the science sixth forms in the early 1960s were consciously seeking a career which would allow them to reconcile their domestic and occupational responsibilities, a problem which Karl Pearson, writing in 1894, described as *par excellence*, the woman's problem of the future'.[154]

It is clear that many questions relating to the education of girls have been determined by reference to the contemporary views about the status and function of women within a particular society. Such views, which have changed with time and shown a marked dependence upon social class, have inevitably been reflected in the attitudes of teachers and pupils and in the policies pursued by those responsible for the allocation of resources within the educational system. Only with the advent of the so-called 'women's movement' in the 1970s did the subtle processes of the social construction of sex differences begin to receive the detailed scrutiny they had long deserved.[155]

References

[1] Schools Inquiry Commission, *Report of the Commissioners*, vol. 1, 1868, chap. VI, pp. 548–9. It should be noted that the Commissioners applied many of their strictures to the secondary education of boys.

[2] Ibid., p. 550.

[3] Kamm, J., *Hope Deferred: Girls' Education in English History*, 1965, chap. XV.

[4] They were Lady Frederick Cavendish, Dr Sophie Bryant (*née* Jex-Blake) and Mrs E. M. Sidgewick. Kamm, op. cit., p. 225, is incorrect in stating that Miss Beale was a member. Miss Buss, who was appointed originally, died on Christmas Eve in 1894 and she was replaced by Mrs Bryant.

[5] For an account of this opposition, see Burstyn, J. N., *Higher Education for Women: The Opposition in England During the Nineteenth Century*, London University, Ph.D. Thesis, 1968.

[6] It became a 'Trust' in 1906.

[7] Royal Commission on Secondary Education, *Report*, vol. 1, 1895, pp. 15 and 76.

[8] Kamm, J., op. cit., p. 214.

[9] Ibid., chap. XVIII. Emily Davies' Women's College, founded in 1869 at Hitchin, soon moved to the outskirts of Cambridge to become Girton College. Other women's colleges founded during the period were Bedford (London) in 1869, Newnham (Cambridge) in 1871, Somerville and Lady Margaret Hall (Oxford) in 1879 and Holloway in 1886. Cambridge admitted women to degrees on equal terms with men only in 1948. For an account of the opposition to women becoming doctors see Mead, K. C. H., *Women in Medicine*, 1938, and Manton, J., *Elizabeth Garrett Anderson*, 1965.

[10] Data taken from *Report of the Consultative Committee on the Differentiation of the Curriculum for Boys and Girls Respectively in Secondary Schools*, HMSO, 1923, p. 42. This Report is hereafter referred to simply as *Report on Differentiation*, HMSO, 1923.

[11] Ibid., p. 39. The Regulations were 'to provide against Schools recognised under that name (i.e. Secondary) offering only an education which is stunted, illiberal, unpractical or over-specialised'.

[12] Board of Education, *Regulations for Secondary Schools*, 1904, Cd. 2128, para. 4 and para. 12(d).

[13] Burstall, S. A., *The Story of the Manchester High School for Girls*, 1911, p. 107. Miss Burstall quotes from Miss Day's Report of 1882.

[14] Burstall, S. A., *English High Schools for Girls*, 1907, p. 107.

[15] *Report on Differentiation*, HMSO, 1923, p. 133.

[16] Board of Education, *Regulations for Secondary Schools*, 1904, para. 5.

[17] For an account of the Eugenics Movement in Britain at the beginning of the century, see MacKenzie, D., Eugenics in Britain, *Social Studies of Science*, vol. 6, 1976, pp. 499–532.

[18] See Dyhouse, C., 'Social Darwinistic Ideas and the Development of Women's Education in England, 1880–1920', *History of Education*, vol. 5, no. 1, 1976, pp. 41–58.

[19] For a review of this issue, see Dyhouse, C., 'Good Wives and Little Mothers: Social Anxieties and the Schoolgirl's Curriculum, 1890–1920', *Oxford Review of Education*, vol. 3, no. 1, 1977, pp. 21–35.

[20] Newman, G., *Infant Mortality: A Social Problem*, 1906, p. 257.

[21] *Report of Inter-Departmental Committee on Physical Deterioration*, 1904.

[22] Board of Education, *Report for the Year 1903–04*, Cd. 2271, HMSO, 1905, p. 16.

[23] Ravenhill, A., 'Eugenic Ideals for Womanhood', *Eugenics Review*, vol. 1, 1909–10, p. 267: 'Woman must be an Eugenicist', to answer 'the trumpet-call which sounded out her weighty obligations, as much imperial as domestic or social'.

[24] Board of Education, *Special Reports on Educational Subjects, School Training for the Home Duties of Women;* Part I, *The Teaching of Domestic Science in the United States of America*, 1905; Part II, *Belgium, Sweden, Norway, Denmark, Switzerland and France*, 1906; Part III, *The Domestic Training of Girls in Germany and Austria*, 1908.

[25] Board of Education, *Special Report on the Teaching of Cookery to Public Elementary School Children in England and Wales*, HMSO, 1907. Another 'General Report' on the teaching of Domestic Subjects was issued in 1912.

[26] Board of Education, *Suggestions for the Consideration of Teachers and Others Concerned in the Work of the Public Elementary Schools*, 1905, pp. 78–9.

[27] Board of Education, *Regulations for Secondary Schools, 1907*, Cd. 3592, HMSO, para. 8 of Prefatory Memorandum.

[28] Board of Education, *Regulations for Secondary Schools, 1909*, Cd. 4691, HMSO, para. 9.

[29] Kamm, J., *Indicative Past: One Hundred Years of the Girls' Public Day School Trust*, 1971, pp. 144–6.

[30] See, for example, Burstall, S. A., op. cit., 1907, chap. 13.

[31] Burstall, S. A., and Douglas, M. A., (eds.), *Public Schools for Girls*, 1911, p. 153.

[32] Board of Education, *Report of Consultative Committee on Practical Work in Secondary Schools*, HMSO, 1913.

[33] According to Dyhouse, op. cit., 1977, p. 33, the Board had been 'literally bombarded' with inquiries about housecraft teaching in secondary schools. The correspondence relating to this matter is in *P.R.O., Ed.*, 24/386.

[34] B.A.A.S., *Report*, 1906, pp. 781–4.

[35] See Flintham, A., M.Ed. Thesis, Leeds, op. cit., 1974, Appendix 1, p. 251 and pp. 197–8. For an account of the background to Smithells's involvement with courses of this kind, see Jenkins, I., *Some Aspects of the Work of the Yorkshire Ladies Council of Education, 1871–1891*, M.A. Thesis, University of Leeds, 1976, p. 73.

[36] Armstrong, H. E., 'The Need of a Scientific Basis to Girls' Education from a Domestic Point of View', B.A.A.S., *Report*, 1907, p. 721. (The paper is not reprinted.)

[37] Suggestions for a Course of Practical Food Studies, B.A.A.S., *Report*, 1917, pp. 188–202.

[38] Many teachers in girls' secondary schools appear to have regarded the domestic subjects, whether described as housecraft or as domestic science, as fit only for the less

intelligent of their pupils. See, for example, Burstall, S. A. and Douglas, M. A. (eds.), op. cit., p. 154.

[39] Board of Education, *Report of Consultative Committee on Practical Work in Secondary Schools*, 1913, pp. 46–7, 50–51.

[40] Freund, I., *The Experimental Basis of Chemistry*, 1920. The book was published posthumously, Miss Freund having died in 1914.

[41] Board of Education, *Report of Consultative Committee on Practical Work in Secondary Schools*, 1913, pp. 312–16. See also, Freund, I., 'Domestic Science – A Protest', *Englishwoman*, vol. X, 1911, pp. 147–63 and pp. 279–96.

[42] Board of Education, ibid., pp. 42–52.

[43] *Report on Differentiation*, HMSO, 1923, p. 50. Only a small proportion of public elementary school pupils succeeded in gaining entry to a secondary school. The percentage of such pupils aged ten to eleven 'on March 31st of the previous year' who were admitted to secondary schools was 9.50 in 1920, 12.90 in 1930 and 14.34 in 1938.

[44] Ibid., p. 57. The difference in the standard of attainment of junior pupils at entrance was described in 1923 as 'one of the greatest practical difficulties with which many Girls' High Schools had to contend'.

[45] Circular 826, *The Curricula of Secondary Schools*, 1913.

[46] *Report on Differentiation*, HMSO, 1923, p. 58. Junior Departments were, however, inspected and reported upon on the occasion of a Full Inspection of a secondary school.

[47] Burstall, S. A., op. cit., 1907, p. 115.

[48] Ibid., pp. 45, 46 and 115. This was a distinction which clearly makes nonsense of Miss Burstall's claim that the 'B girl can get to the same terminus, and does, only she takes longer over it' (p. 45).

[49] *Report on Differentiation*, HMSO, 1923, Appendix VI, pp. 187–93.

[50] Ibid., p. 56.

[51] Ibid., pp. 55–6.

[52] *Natural Science in Education*, HMSO, 1918, para. 79. The Association of Science Teachers was an association of women science teachers, mainly in secondary schools.

[53] Quoted in Burstall, S. A., op. cit., 1907, Appendix B, p. 223.

[54] See Chapter 7.

[55] This was the opinion of the teachers and examiners as assessed by the Consultative Committee in its *Report on Differentiation*, HMSO, 1923, p. 104.

[56] Burstall, S. A., op. cit., 1907, p. 81.

[57] *Natural Science in Education*, HMSO, 1918, para. 27 and para. 79.

[58] Kamm, J., op. cit., 1965, p. 237, asserts that many girls attending secondary schools studied no mathematics at this time but the Thomson Committee (*Natural Science in Education*, HMSO, 1918, para. 25), suggested that in many girls' schools, a greater amount of time was devoted to the study of mathematics than was really needed 'to attain the standard aimed at'.

[59] The four groups were (i) English subjects, (ii) languages, (iii) science and mathematics, (iv) music, drawing, manual work, housecraft. For details of the J.M.B. programme, see Petch, J. A., *Fifty Years of Examining*, 1953, pp. 80–9.

[60] Petch, J. A., op. cit., pp. 91 and 92.

[61] Burstall, S. A., *Retrospect and Prospect, Sixty Years of Women's Education*, 1933, p. 238. Miss Burstall also indicates the frustration she experienced in attempting to accommodate the curriculum of her school to the needs of the School Certificate Examination and the Board of Education Regulations in the early 1920s. She acknowledges that 'a local inspector was very helpful in suggesting possibilities'. (Ibid., p. 240.)

[62] Petch, J. A., op. cit., p. 91.

[63] The standard was also reduced in Group II by abolishing the *requirement* that candidates wrote a composition in a foreign language. However no candidate was allowed to offer both of the 'lower alternatives' for Groups II and III.

[64] But for the Second World War, the Group system would probably have been abolished much earlier than 1950.

[65] Petch, J. A., op. cit., p. 101, from which the details relating to the J.M.B. in the paragraph are taken.

[66] The groups were (i) Greek, Latin, ancient history; (ii) English, history, languages (excluding Greek), pure mathematics; (iii) history, languages (excluding Latin), economics, geography; (iv) mathematics and the sciences. Petch, J. A., op. cit., p. 101. In 1925, pure mathematics was removed from the second group and another group (higher mathematics) introduced to meet the needs of mathematical specialists.

[67] Ibid., p. 103.

[68] Figures from *Board of Education, Report for the Year 1920–1*, Cmd. 1718, p. 26 and *Education in 1938, Being the Report of the Board of Education and the Statistics of Public Education for England and Wales*, Cmd. 6013, p. 129. 9.7 per cent of girls and 11.2 per cent of boys between fourteen and fifteen years of age attended grant-aided schools in 1938.

[69] As a result, the average size of a secondary school also increased, to about 350 by 1938.

[70] Board of Education, *Report for the Year 1919–20*, Cmd. 1451, p. 26.

[71] Board of Education, *Report for the Year 1920–1*, Cmd. 1718, p. 25.

[72] For example, the entries for the Higher Certificate Examinations increased by 56 per cent between 1919–20 and 1920–1 (from 2,032 to 3,026), ibid., p. 31.

[73] Board of Education, *Education in 1938*, p. 15.

[74] Lawson, J., Silver, H., *A Social History of Education in England*, 1973, p. 388.

[75] Board of Education, *Education in 1938*, pp. 15 and 132.

[76] Petch, J. A., op. cit., p. 83, regards the introduction of general science as 'perhaps the greatest change in secondary school science teaching in this period'.

[77] B.A.A.S., Report of Committee appointed to consider and report on the provision made for Instruction in Botany in courses of Biology and matters related thereto, *Report*, 1932, p. 293.

[78] B.A.A.S., Final Report of Committee on the Teaching of General Science in Schools, with Special Reference to the Teaching of Biology, *Report*, 1933, p. 319.

[79] An additional need for caution arises from the fact that the figures are *averages* and almost certainly disguise a wide spread.

[80] Data from Board of Education, *Report for the Year 1930–1*, pp. 24–5 and *Education in 1938*, pp. 149–50. In 1949, when the School Certificate entries for the J.M.B. examination in Biology numbered 10,929, the ratio of girls to boys among the entrants was 5:1. Petch, J. A., op. cit., p. 84.

[81] In 1924–5, there were 311 schools and 434 recognised advanced courses; in 1934–5, there were 329 schools and 481 courses. The data for Tables 5.6 and 5.7 are taken from the appropriate *Annual Reports* of the Board of Education.

[82] Grant support, however, continued.

[83] The Board used this phrase in several of its Reports, but gave no indication of the extent of the 'unrecognised' work.

[84] Special examinations were held in Wales until 1927 when the system became the same as in England.

[85] In 1921, 178 were distributed to the Examination Boards in England. (Oxford 12,

Cambridge 20, Oxford and Cambridge 36, Bristol 5, Durham 4, J.M.B. 75.) The remaining 22 went to Welsh Scholars.

[86] The data are taken from appropriate *Annual Reports* of the Board of Education.

[87] Board of Education, *Education in 1938*, p. 57.

[88] Ibid., p. 58.

[89] The data are taken from University Grants Committee, *Returns from Universities and University Colleges in Receipt of Treasury Grant*, HMSO, published annually except during the Second World War.

[90] The numbers of women graduating in physics in some years were *very* small, e.g. four in 1928–9, eight in the following year, so that many university physics departments had no female undergraduates reading for Honours degrees in the inter-war years.

[91] In French, the ratio was 1 to 1.24 and in English 0.91 to 1.

[92] The figures exclude 'joint' degrees in, for example, physics and chemistry or chemistry and geology. In general, the numbers following such courses were small and most of the undergraduates were men. The data in Table 5.14 are taken from U.G.C., *Returns from Universities ...* , HMSO.

[93] Equally, boys may be regarded as having been 'under-represented' in this respect.

[94] It should be noted that because the numbers of girls/women studying physics were low throughout this period, small changes in these numbers could have produced marked alterations in some ratios.

[95] Central Advisory Council for Education (England), *15–18*, vol. 1, HMSO, 1959, para. 318.

[96] Ibid., paras. 317 and 318.

[97] Board of Education, Educational Pamphlet no. 89, *Science in Senior Schools*, HMSO, 1932, p. 8.

[98] Ibid., p. 7.

[99] West Riding County Council, *The Senior School Curriculum*, 1931, chap. iv, 'The Teaching of Elementary Science Including Gardening', p. 54. In 1917, the British Association (*Report*, 1917, p. 141) was told that 'if domesticity' were dominant, work in domestic science could not be regarded 'as a proper substitute for a science course'.

[100] The Crowther Committee recognised this point in 1959, noting that the pattern of G.C.E. courses in modern schools was 'a reflection of the strength and weaknesses of their staffing', *15 to 18*, ibid., para. 116.

[101] The data in Table 5.20 are taken from Ministry of Education, *Education in 1961*, HMSO, 1962.

[102] The Crowther Committee invented the term 'numeracy' to describe the characteristics of such understanding. *15 to 18*, vol. 1, HMSO, 1959, para. 401. In more recent times, the relative neglect of physics and chemistry in the education of girls has received attention from the so-called 'women's movement'.

[103] General Register Office, *Sample Census, 1966, Scientific and Technological Qualifications*, Table 7. *Economic Activity Tables*, Table 3. The percentages are corrected to allow for varying male/female ratios in the different age groups.

[104] B.A.A.S., *Report*, 1917, p. 133.

[105] Huxstep, E. M., 'Scientific Education for Girls', in Perkins, W. H. (ed.), *Science in Schools*, 1958, p. 26.

[106] Joan of Arc, Sister St, 'An Inquiry into the Teaching of Physical Science in Girls' Grammar Schools', *Contemporary Physics*, IV, 1963, p. 376.

[107] Ibid., p. 377.

[108] For an examination of some of these consequences, see Brown, N. M., 'Some Educational Influences on the Choice of a Science Career by Grammar School Girls',

B.J.Ed.Psychol, vol. 23, 1953, p. 188, and Pheasant, J. H., *The Influence of School Organisation and Curriculum on the Choice of Examination Subjects and Careers made by G.C.E. Candidates*, University of London, Ph.D. Thesis, 1960.

[109] Bremner, J. P., 'Science for Girls', *S.S.R.,* vol. XL, no. 142, 1959, p. 590.

[110] 'With some notable exceptions, girls' schools possess less adequate equipment for science teaching' (than boys' schools), *Report on Differentiation*, HMSO, 1923, p. 124.

[111] 'The Provision and Maintenance of Laboratories in Grammar Schools', *S.S.R.*, vol. XXXIX, no. 139, 1958, p. 438 and ibid., vol. XLI, no. 145, 1960, p. 461.

[112] Similar 'reasoning' governed the provision recommended for three- and four-form entry schools.

[113] Of a sample of 373 maintained grammar schools in 1957, only 44 per cent reached the Ministry's own standards and only one school reached the standard established by the Industrial Fund. Perkins, W. H., (ed.), op. cit., p. 66. It should be noted that the grammar schools gained a large proportion of the post-war school building programme, accommodating more than a third of the 4,000 or so school laboratories built between 1945 and 1957. Lawrence, B. E., 'Science Facilities: the Role of Local Education Authorities', in Perkins, W. H. (ed.), op. cit., p. 124. See also Boulind, H. F., 'Accommodation and Equipment', in ibid., p. 72.

[114] This figure was based on a 'review of timetables of over 1,500 modern schools' by Lawrence, B. E., op. cit., p. 122.

[115] The Crowther Report (15 to 18, vol. 1, para. 371) touched upon this point. Other studies include, Sutherland, M. B., 'Coeducation and School Attainment', *B.J.Ed. Psychol.,* 31, 1961, p. 158 ff; Dale, R. R., 'Mixed or Single-Sex Schools?' (3 vols.), 1969–74; Schools Council, *The Examination Courses of First Year Sixth Formers*, 1973; D.E.S., *Curricular Differences for Boys and Girls*, 1975. M. B. Ormerod expressed the matter succinctly: 'It is pretty certain that if all girls were in single sex schools more of them would study the physical sciences.' *Single Sex and Coeducation: An Analysis of Pupils' Science Preferences and Choices and their Attitudes to other Aspects of Science Under these Two Systems* in *Girls and Science Education – Cause for Concern?*, 1975, p. 71. Ormerod's conclusion should be set in the context of the finding that at all levels the number of science students tends to reflect the general standard of teaching. See Seear, N., Roberts, V., Brock, J., *A Career for Women in Industry*, 1964, and Hall, S. M., *An Investigation of Factors Involved in Girls' Choices of Science Courses in the Sixth Form and of Scientific Careers*, B.Litt. Thesis, Oxford, 1965.

[116] *Report on Differentiation*, HMSO, 1923, p. 121. The Committee referred to the evidence of Thorndike, Burt, Stanley Hall, among others, in its Report.

[117] For a review, see Maccoby, E. E., and Jacklin, C. N., *The Psychology of Sex Differences*, 1975, and Fairweather, H., 'Sex Differences in Cognition', *Cognition*, 4, 1976, pp. 231–80.

[118] Coltheart, M., Hull, E., and Slater, D., 'Sex Differences in Imagery and Reading', *Nature*, vol. 253, 1965, pp. 438–40.

[119] Burstall, S., op. cit., 1907, p. 13.

[120] *Report on Differentiation*, HMSO, 1923, pp. 93 and 101.

[121] Ibid., p. 104.

[122] Central Advisory Council for Education (England), *Half Our Future*, vol. 1, HMSO, 1963, para. 421.

[123] For an account of some of these influences, see Sharpe, S., *Just Like a Girl: How Girls Learn to be Women*, 1976.

[124] Oliver, M., 'Women in Chemistry', *J.R.I.C.*, August 1955, p. 413.

125 General Register Office, Census 1961, *Summary Tables* and *Scientific and Technological Qualifications*, HMSO, 1962, Table 6.

126 A.S.E., *Bulletin*, September 1965, no. 14, p. 15.

127 Hudson, L., *Contrary Imaginations*, 1966, and *Frames of Mind*, 1968.

128 Hall, S. M., *An Investigation of Factors Involved in Girls' Choices of Science Courses in the Sixth Form and of Scientific Careers*, Oxford B.Litt. Thesis, 1965, p. 2. See also Couture-Cherki, M., 'Women in Physics', in Rose, H., and Rose, S. (eds.), *The Radicalisation of Science*, 1976, pp. 65–76 for a radical view of the employment of women in academic science.

129 Ollerenshaw, K., *Education for Girls*, Conservative Political Centre, 1958, p. 32.

130 Ollerenshaw, (ibid., p. 33) records that, in 1958, more than three-quarters of all girls left school before they were sixteen and 'not more than half' of these girls attended 'any further education course whatsoever, day or evening'.

131 Ministry of Education, *Statistics of Education*, 1962, p. 35.

132 See, for example, an analysis by Hirsch of the image of the scientist in science fiction in the United States between 1926 and 1950, in Barber, B., and Hirsch, W., *The Sociology of Science*, 1962, ch. 17.

133 Medawar, P. B., 'Is the Scientific Paper a Fraud?' *Listener*, 12 September 1963, pp. 377–8.

134 For a survey of the attitudes of American students, see Mead, M., and Metraux, R., 'The Image of the Scientist among High School Students: A Pilot Study', and Beardslee, D. C., and O'Dowd, D., 'The College Student Image of the Scientist', in Barber, B., and Hirsch, W., op. cit., chaps. 15 and 16. For the British context, see A.S.E., 'Attitudes to Science and Scientists', *S.S.R.*, vol. 51, no. 174, 1969, p. 11.

135 For a review of the 'attack' through literature, see Davenport, W. H., 'Anti-technology Attitudes in Modern Literature', *Technology and Society*, vol 8, no. 1, April 1973, pp. 7–14.

136 For example, the attitude of the seventeenth-century wit towards scientists as men who could admire nothing 'except fleas, lice and themselves', a reference to Hooke's *Micrographia*. Syfret, R. H., 'Some Early Critics of the Royal Society', *Notes and Records of the Royal Society of London*, vol. 8, October 1950, pp. 20–64.

137 Whitehead, A. N., *Science and the Modern World*, 1929, p. 245.

138 Dainton, F. S., *Science; Salvation or Damnation?* University of Southampton, 1971, p. 18.

139 Hudson, L., op. cit., 1966 and 1968, and Mead, M., and Metraux, R., op. cit., 1962.

140 The distinction is due to Kuhn, T. S., *The Structure of Scientific Revolutions*, 1962.

141 Ormerod, M. B., *S.S.R.*, vol. 54, no. 189, pp. 645–60.

142 Hutchings, D., 'The Science Scene', *New Education*, April 1966, p. 17. Hutchings's article is based on the findings of Hall, S. M., op. cit.

143 *Report on Differentiation*, HMSO, 1923, p. 130.

144 *15 to 18*, vol. 1, HMSO, p. 28.

145 *Census, 1961*. Marital Condition, Proportion at Successive Censuses per 1,000 in each Group (Table 13), *Age, Marital Condition and General Tables*, HMSO, 1966.

146 *15 to 18*, vol. 1, p. 30, and Census, 1961, *Summary Tables*, Table 32, HMSO, 1966.

147 Anderson, K., Dame, *Women and the Universities: A Changing Pattern*. Fawcett Lecture, Bedford College, 1963, p. 16.

148 *15 to 18*, vol. 1, HMSO, p. 30.

149 In 1951, 89.2 per cent of the nursing profession were women as were 57.5 per cent of all welfare workers. The corresponding figures for 1961 are 90.1 per cent and 47.3 per cent.

[150] Gallagher, M., 'The Prospect of Marriage: a Study of the Attitudes towards Further Education of a Sample Group of Secondary Technical and Secondary Grammar School Leavers', *B.J.Ed.Psychol.*, vol. 27, 1957, p. 24.

[151] Pheasant, J. M., 'The Influence of the School on the Choice of Science Careers', *B.J.Ed. Psych.*, vol. 32, 1961, p. 38.

[152] Seear, N., Roberts, V., and Brock, J., *A Career for Women in Industry*, 1964.

[153] Hall, S. M., op. cit.; Veness, T., *School Leavers, Their Aspirations and Expectations*, 1962, pp. 57–60.

[154] Pearson, K., 'Women and Labour', *Fortnightly Review*, May 1894, p. 576.

[155] For an introduction, see Sharpe, S., op. cit., especially chap. 2 and Marks, P., 'Femininity in the Classroom: An Account of Changing Attitudes', in Mitchell, J., and Oakley, A., *The Rights and Wrongs of Women*, 1976, pp. 176–98. For a Marxist perspective on women and science, see Stehelin, L., 'Sciences, Women and Ideology', in Rose, H., and Rose, S. (eds.), op. cit., chap. 4.

6
The Supply of Teachers

As with other subjects of the curriculum, the widespread teaching of science demands a large number of suitably qualified teachers. The adequacy of the supply of such teachers depends upon the balance of several factors which include the numbers produced via the several teacher-training mechanisms, the so-called 'wastage-rate' arising from resignation, retirement or death, the extent and nature of alternative careers and opportunities available to qualified teachers and the numbers of pupils to be taught in the schools. In the years leading up to the First World War, this last factor was of particular significance.

Between 1904 and 1914, the number of grant-aided secondary schools almost doubled and the number[1] of pupils receiving a secondary school education rose from 64,000 to nearly 188,000. This growth in the numbers of pupils attending secondary schools was, in part, a consequence of the revised teacher-training Regulations introduced by the Board of Education after 1903 which required all future elementary school teachers to receive 'a sound, general education in a Secondary School for three or four years'. Local education authorities were urged to provide secondary-school scholarships for intending teachers and, by 1906, these accounted for almost half (48.5 per cent) of the total of 23,500 scholarships available to secondary schools in England and Wales.[2]

The expansion of secondary education in the early years of this century was also encouraged by the system of 'free places' introduced by the Board in 1907. Under the 1907 Regulations, 25 per cent of the places in grant-aided secondary schools were to be given, free of tuition and entrance fees, to pupils who had spent the previous two years at a public elementary school. By 1916–17, almost a third of the 200,000 pupils attending grant-aided secondary schools paid no fees, although many of these were technically scholarship holders.[3]

The expansion of secondary education was not the only development which increased the demand for qualified teachers. The reorganisation of some elementary schools led to the employment of more[4] assistant teachers and reference has already been made to the emergence of central schools which offered an education to pupils between the ages of eleven and fifteen. The staffing of these central schools was often on a liberal scale and, by 1913–14, schools of this type in London were providing[5] an education for 16,163 pupils.

The new teachers required by the expanding educational system came from two principal sources, the teacher-training colleges and the universities. In 1900, there were sixty-one colleges, training 5,608 students. By 1913–14, the number of colleges had increased by twenty-six and the number of teachers in training had more than doubled[6] to 11,728. Some of these colleges were day colleges operating in conjunction with universities or university colleges; others were residential and controlled by the local education authorities or the voluntary bodies. Despite the growth in the number of training college places after 1900, the elementary schools were faced with a shortage of teachers, largely as a result of a too-rapid decline in the pupil-teacher system. In 1906–7, over 11,000 pupil-teachers were admitted to the register. By 1912–13, this number had fallen[7] to below 1,500 and the pupil-teacher system was virtually obsolete, although it lingered in some areas until the Second World War. (See Table 6.1.) Although the Board of Education, on several occasions, expressed[8] concern at the shortage of teachers, the system did not survive to any significant extent beyond the end of the First World War.

Table 6.1   No. of Pupil-Teachers Recognised for the First
Time (England Only)

Year	No. of pupil teachers
1906–7	11,018
1907–8	10,297
1908–9	5,209
1909–10	3,850
1910–11	2,612
1911–12	1,955
1912–13	1,469
1913–14	1,454
1914–15	1,886
1915–16	2,168
1916–17	1,951
1917–18	1,815
1918–19	1,737
1919–20	1,588

Almost all of the students attending the training colleges followed a two-year course leading to the Teacher's Certificate, but provision was also made for other types of student. Teachers who were already qualified could be admitted in order to gain a 'wider range and firmer basis for their work' and some students 'who had passed certain public examinations' were eligible to follow a one-year course leading to certification as a teacher.[9]

The extent and nature of the science studied by the teachers trained in the colleges are difficult to determine. In 1900, 4,323 candidates at fifty-nine colleges were examined, under a 'payment by results' system, in a variety of 'science' subjects which included mathematics, mechanics, magnetism and electricity, heat, light and sound, botany, human physiology, elementary biology, hygiene and physiography. However, the distribution of the entries among the individual subjects, recorded[10] in Table 6.2, confirms that very few student-teachers attending the training colleges at this time made any serious study of the physical sciences or of mathematics.

After 1900, the Board abolished the payment by results system and regulated the Exchequer grant by means of a capitation formula dependent upon the courses taken in science subjects. Some colleges offered 'special, optional courses' and, in 1903–4, out of a total of only 681 men taking such courses, 218 studied 'advanced' science, 189 'advanced' mathematics and 187 modern languages, excluding English.[11]

Table 6.2   Statistics of Examinations in Science in the Training Colleges in 1900

No. of Colleges Examined	59
No. of Classes Examined	291
No. of Individuals Examined	4,323
No. of Papers Worked In	
Practical Plane and Solid Geometry	1,701
Mathematics	23
Theoretical Mechanics (Solids)	331
Theoretical Mechanics (Fluids)	55
Sound, Light and Heat (Elementary)	550
Sound (Advanced and Honours)	117
Light (Advanced and Honours)	4
Heat (Advanced and Honours)	22
Magnetism and Electricity	372
Inorganic Chemistry	403
Inorganic Chemistry (Practical)	286
Human Physiology	294
Botany	665
Physiography	3,119
Principles of Agriculture	25
Hygiene	1,146
Total	9,113

The new teacher-training Regulations introduced by the Board in 1904 marked an important development in teacher education. The Board assumed a greater degree of control over the appointment of staff to the colleges[12] and remodelled the curriculum to provide a much more liberal course of study than had been permitted previously. Elementary science was a compulsory subject in the revised curriculum, together with English, history, geography and elementary mathematics and every college was obliged to have at least one well-equipped laboratory. There was, however, considerable freedom to construct alternative schemes of study within the prescribed framework. In the case of 'elementary science', 'even more latitude' was given than to other subjects and each training college was free to devise its own course after careful consideration of the needs of its students and the facilities available for science teaching.[13] The inevitable result was a diversity in the science courses offered by the colleges although this was perhaps less than might have been anticipated. In 1913, the Board commented[14] that while 'some students' took a course in physics and chemistry, the kind of work which had found 'most favour and ... made most advance in recent years' was best described by the 'necessarily vague title of Nature Study'. Whatever the content of the various courses in elementary science, there seems little doubt that much of the work was of such a low standard that it ought to have been done in the secondary schools or pupil-teacher centres rather than in the training colleges.[15]

In 1913, in response to pressure from the colleges, the teacher-training Regulations were amended to allow students to take fewer subjects and to study those selected to a more advanced level. Science henceforth ceased to be a compulsory component of the two-year Certificate course and an opportunity to remedy the neglect of physical science in the training of elementary school teachers was lost. Of the 3,392 student-teachers who sat the Board's Final Examination in 1915, only 1,731 (51 per cent) were examined in Elementary Science and most of these, 1,549, were women. The numbers of student-teachers who were examined in more advanced courses in physics or chemistry were very small. (See Table 6.3.)

Table 6.3   No. of Training College Students Taking the Final Examinations in Science in 1915

	Men	Women	Total	Passed with Credit	Passed with Distinction
Elementary Science	182	1,549	1,731	401	–
Advanced Courses					
Physics	52	4	56	23	4
Chemistry	39	14	53	13	1
Botany	12	267	279	180	40
Rural Science	36	41	77	37	4
Total Number of Students			3,392		

The universities and university colleges were also involved in the training of elementary school teachers. Much of the work in the new institutions of higher education founded towards the end of the nineteenth century[16] involved evening and occasional students and the development of full-time courses in the Faculties of Arts and Sciences was dependent upon the recruitment of adequate numbers of students with appropriate financial support. A memorial to the Royal Commission on Elementary Education in 1887 proposed that the courses of study and examinations of the Yorkshire College and similar institutions be accepted for teacher-training purposes and that appropriate grants be provided to meet the costs of teaching and supporting the students.[17] When the Committee of Council eventually accepted the recommendation of the Royal Commission that day training courses be established in the university institutions, teacher-training departments were quickly set up and the university colleges began to recruit intending elementary school teachers as full-time students. There were forty of these vocationally orientated, subsidised students at the Yorkshire College in 1896, in which year six of the twenty-six men gained degrees of the Victoria University.[18] Apart from their professional training, these students had followed regular university courses and studied alongside other undergraduates in the Faculties of Arts and Science.

These grant-earning students were important to the university colleges and continued to be so long after most of them had gained full university status early in the twentieth century. Just how important is indicated by the data in Table 6.4. Of 3,318 science graduates of universities other than Oxford or Cambridge[19] between 1907 and 1914 (inclusive), 1,077 (32 per cent) had signed a 'declaration', binding them to teach in a grant-aided school for a period of seven years. Until 1907, this pledge related to service in a public elementary school but, in response to an anticipated shortage of secondary school teachers, the declaration was subsequently amended to require the bonded graduate to teach either in an elementary school or a grant-aided secondary school if a suitable vacancy existed.[20] Inevitably, a considerable number of these graduates gained appointments in the expanding secondary system so that they were, as the Thomson Committee lamented,[21] 'not available for elementary teaching'.

Those students who were bound by their declaration to teach were not, of course, the only undergraduates to embark upon a career in school teaching once they were qualified to do so. Some, a minority, followed a one-year course of professional teacher-training, and the relevant figures for the period 1908–14 are recorded in Table 6.5. If it is assumed that 40 per cent of those following such courses were science graduates who had all graduated in the academic year immediately prior to that in which they were trained, the data in Tables 6.5 and 6.6. suggest that these students accounted for an additional 9 per cent of all those graduating in science between 1907 and 1912.

Table 6.4   Distribution of Student Teachers Among University Graduates*, 1907–14

Year	B.A. All Students	B.A. Student Teachers	B.Sc. All Students	B.Sc. Student Teachers	B.A.+B.Sc. All Students	B.A.+B.Sc. Student Teachers
1907	271	115	293	103	564	218
1908	299	112	338	119	637	231
1909	312	138	312	108	624	246
1910	381	135	462	118	843	253
1911	386	204	461	186	847	390
1912	438	197	464	162	902	359
1913	503	190	512	145	1,015	335
1914	490	192	476	136	966	328
Totals	3,080	1,283	3,318	1,077	6,398	2,360

* Other than Oxford and Cambridge graduates. See Reference 19.

The compound figure of 41 per cent for the proportion of would-be teachers among science undergraduates in these years before the First World War must be further increased to accommodate those students who, upon graduation, entered school-teaching directly, i.e. without undertaking a one-year course of professional training. The numbers of such students were significant since many

Table 6.5   No. of Graduates Following One-Year
Teacher-Training Courses, 1908–14

Year	No. of Graduates Following One-Year Teacher Training Courses
1908	64
1909	79
1910	77
1911	71
1912	109
1913	114
1914	107

Table 6.6   No. of Persons Recognised as Intending Teachers for
Elementary Schools in England and Wales 1908–20

Year Beginning 1 August	Boys	Girls	Total
1908	2,722	6,892	9,614
1909	2,308	5,759	8,067
1910	1,558	4,627	6,185
1911	1,388	4,291	5,679
1912	1,167	4,065	5,232
1913	1,155	4,642	5,797
1914	1,251	5,117	6,368
1915	1,304	5,743	7,047
1916	1,097	5,447	6,544
1917	928	5,332	6,260
1918	809	5,279	6,088
1919	1,094	5,510	6,604
1920	1,350	6,507	9,857

headteachers were unconvinced of the value of, or of the need for, professional training for secondary school teaching and most of the teachers already employed in the secondary schools were not[22] themselves professionally trained for this work. Between 1909–10 and 1912–13, the number of untrained graduates employed in the schools rose[23] by 489. If the proportion of these untrained graduates who held degrees in science subjects is assessed[24] at 245 (i.e. 50 per cent), this figure represents approximately 20 per cent of those who had graduated in science in the period under consideration. It is thus a reasonable estimate that, between 1907 and 1914, over 60 per cent[25] of the undergraduates reading for science degrees at grant-aided universities and university colleges were destined to become schoolteachers.

The reasons for this state of affairs are not hard to seek. The declaration to teach offered financial support to relatively large numbers of undergraduates who would otherwise have been unable to afford an university education and the rapid pre-war development of the system of secondary education ensured an adequate supply of teaching appointments for graduates in general. In addition, the career opportunities available within other sectors of employment, including postgraduate research, were severely limited. In 1913–14, there were only 189 postgraduate students in grant-aided colleges in England and Wales pursuing scientific research or reading for higher degrees by examination. Even the Cavendish Laboratory, with its distinguished record of achievement in fundamental physics, could claim 'only about 25 research students' at this time. If allowance is made for the number of science research students at London and the two older universities, it is doubtful whether, in 1913, there were more than 300 students engaged in systematic scientific research for higher degrees.[26]

There was little demand from industry for qualified scientists, whether graduate or not, and what demand existed was principally for chemists to work in such industries as dyeing, explosives, oils, fats, paper, confectionery, brewing and heavy and pharmaceutical chemicals. In 1902, Dewar estimated[27] that the various industries employed a total of 1,500 chemists, although most of these had little or no formal training. Not more than 220 of these 'industrial chemists' were graduates, a figure which may be compared with the 550 or so graduate teachers of chemistry employed, at the same time, in the elementary and secondary schools and in the institutions of higher education.[28] In addition to these 770 graduate chemists engaged in education and industry, a number of chemists were self-employed as private consultants. The Institute of Chemistry had 250 consulting chemists among its members in 1902 and these probably constituted the majority of chemists employed in this way, although it is unlikely that more than 40 per cent of them were graduates.[29]

Graduates probably formed a similar proportion of the 250 scientists employed in the scientific service of the government in 1902. For the most part, these scientists were engaged in the Geological Survey (forty-two), the South Kensington Museums (thirty-six), the Patent Office (eighty) and the Observatories (twelve). The Civil Service provided almost no opportunity for science graduates or indeed for any graduates other than those of the universities of Oxford and Cambridge.[30]

There is some evidence to suggest that the opportunities offered by industry to graduate scientists increased in the early years of the century,[31] e.g. forty firms accepted graduate scientists into employment between 1911 and 1914 compared with twenty-one in the four years after 1906. Yet this expansion was clearly limited, although it may have been on a much greater scale than most historians have allowed.[32] In 1918, Sir James Dobbie, the retiring President of the Institute of Chemistry, recalled[33] that, at the outbreak of the war, one-seventh of the members of the Institute had been working abroad because of the lack of opportunities available to them at home.

Although most of the 6,000 or so science graduates produced by British universities between 1902 and 1914 embarked upon a career in school teaching, the number proved insufficient to meet the demand which the schools made for graduate teachers of physics and chemistry. In the three years up to 1914, the numbers of full-time students in the arts and science faculties of the grant-aided universities and university colleges actually fell and the number of science graduates produced dropped from 512 in 1913 to 476 in the following year, a mere dozen more than in 1910. In the same period there was also some decline in the numbers of teachers being trained[34] for elementary and secondary school work by the training colleges. (See Tables 6.6 and 6.7.) Re-

Table 6.7   No. of Students Completing a Course of Training for Secondary Schools Under the Regulations of the Board of Education, 1909–25

Year	Men	Women	Total
1909–10	35	139	174
1910–11	30	133	163
1911–12	43	156	199
1912–13	38	178	216
1913–14	38	167	205
1914–15	19	218	237
1915–16	11	203	214
1916–17	2	124	126
1917–18	6	109	115
1918–19	19	125	144
1919–20	43	182	225
1920–1	78	180	258
1921–2	213	265	478
1922–3	341	335	676
1923–4	255	381	636
1924–5	259	509	808

presentatives of the Association of Science Teachers, giving evidence to the Thomson Committee, claimed that there had been a 'great shortage of science teachers for some years before the war' and supported their claim by reference to seventy-two schools, containing '200–400 girls of all ages', only thirty-nine of which had the 'services of two full-time science mistresses'.[35] The representatives of the Association of Public School Science Masters, on the other hand, can hardly be said to have presented the Thomson Committee with an account of an acute shortage affecting the schools with which they were concerned. They merely 'drew the attention' of the Committee to the fact that many members of their Association no longer found it possible 'to devote time to boys who come voluntarily to do work in the laboratory'.[36] If the other organisations which submitted oral or written evidence to the Thomson Committee made explicit reference to the problems of science teacher supply, the

Committee did not quote this evidence to support its assertion that the supply was 'inadequate for existing needs, quite apart from the abnormal conditions created by the war',[37] the latter being a reference to the depletion[38] of the schools caused by the belated recruitment of qualified scientists, especially chemists, to serve the national war effort.

The supply of science teachers was discussed by the British Association Committee on Science in secondary schools which reported in 1917. The Committee found that the supply of masters was 'being maintained at its present level' only by the 'large influx of clever pupils' who passed from the public elementary schools to the secondary schools and hence to the training colleges and universities. The anxieties of this Committee appear to have been for the future rather than for the present and much of its comment is related to the conditions under which science teachers were employed. Tenure was insecure, a superannuation scheme had not yet been devised and salaries were inadequate.[39] The salaries of male assistant teachers in elementary and secondary schools were consistently well below the average annual earnings of salaried employees and there was marked discrimination against women who earned perhaps a third less than their male colleagues occupying similar posts. In 1914, the *average* salaries of graduate and non-graduate teachers were as shown in Table 6.8. By 1917, a newly qualified graduate might command a

Table 6.8 Average Salaries of Teachers at 31 January 1914 and in the First Year of the Burnham Scales (March 1922)

	31 Jan. 1914		31 March 1922	
	Graduates	Non-Graduates	Graduates	Non-Graduates
Men	£225 p.a.	£165 p.a.	£451 p.a.	£357 p.a.
Women	151	123	343	272
Men and Women	194	139	400	301

salary within the range £120 to £150 per annum, a figure which had improved considerably during the first two years of the war,[40] but which, in the opinion[41] of the British Association Committee, was unlikely to be enough to compensate for job insecurity or the absence of adequate pension arrangements.

Within a few years of the end of the war, at least two of the conditions likely to improve the supply of science teachers had been fulfilled. National 'Burnham' salary scales for elementary and secondary school teachers had been negotiated successfully and the School Teachers (Superannuation) Act had passed into law. However, the attitude of the State and of industry towards science and technology had changed, largely as a result of the war, and the expectation that science-based industries 'born of war conditions, would not be allowed to perish'[42] with the advent of peace was seen as a threat to the future supply of well-qualified science teachers for the schools. The Thomson Committee remarked[43] in 1918 that industry had 'already begun to compete for the services of those who, in former times, would have looked forward to science teaching as a profession' and warned that the competition was likely to grow more severe. The British Association Committee made the same point, referring[44] to the 'fast-growing demand for scientific experts from the various branches of manufacture and industry', to the attractions 'offered by medicine as a profession for women' and commenting that these developments would accentuate the 'scarcity of well-qualified science masters and mistresses'.

Although the 'great eagerness' of men who had previously gone into banking, insurance and clerical posts to 'take up engineering as a profession'[45] and the post-war 'rush of the younger generation'[46] to train as chemists owed much to the harnessing of science to the prosecution of the war, the pre-war involvement of the State in scientific research should not be underestimated since it provided the basis of much that was to follow. Government expenditure on civil science and grants to scientific societies had risen[47] from approximately £62,000 in 1900 to £238,828 ten years later. Financial support for the National Physical Laboratory, formed in 1898 under the auspices of the Royal Society and a 'vocational oasis' for physicists, was likewise transformed. Its income increased five-fold between 1900 and 1914, although much of the capital for development came from private sources, and an Aeronautics Research Committee was established at Teddington to build up the air service on 'a foundation of science'.[48] The Development Act of 1909, designed to promote 'the economic development of the United Kingdom', led to the establishment of Agricultural Research Institutes,[49] twelve of which were created by 1914, and a similar pattern of organisation was envisaged for the Medical Research Committee set up in 1913. The Research Institutes provided a small number of scholarships for the training of students in the appropriate fields of agricultural research and, equally important, offered some prospect of a research appointment to the trained graduate.

British manufacturing industry, on the other hand, was often untouched by science.[50] The desperate need for materials and equipment denied to manufacturers by the outbreak of the war produced desperate measures which eventually gave way to a variety of uncoordinated activities.[51] The Royal Society established a War Committee to organise the scientific work of importance to the war effort, using the laboratories of schools, colleges and universities. The Institute of Chemistry surveyed the general shortage of laboratory glassware, most of which had been produced hitherto in Germany. More planning and coordination were needed but, in the absence of a government policy for science, there could be no machinery to harness the talents available within the scientific community. Many scientists had joined the Armed Forces and some had been killed in action. The best known example is perhaps the death of H. G. J. Moseley at Gallipoli in 1915 which left Rutherford to complain[52] bitterly of the 'national tragedy' caused by the 'inelastic organisation' which directed scientific men to the firing line. By 1915, when 300 Fellows of the Institute of Chemistry had enlisted, the munitions factories were complaining of the lack of trained chemists and were employing young, inexperienced workers who received their training on the job. Not until June 1915 were systematic attempts made by Lloyd George's Ministry of Munitions to direct scientific expertise towards specific technical objectives. One hundred and fifty chemists were withdrawn from military service to work in the munitions industry and, in 1916, chemistry became a reserved occupation.[53]

In July 1915, the Government issued a White Paper, outlining its *Scheme for the Organisation and Development of Scientific and Industrial Research*. Five days later, on 28 July 1915, the Privy Council established a Committee for Scientific and Industrial Research, advised by a Council whose terms of reference allowed it to initiate research into specific problems, to establish specific institutions for research in applied science and to provide finance to support research students and Fellows. The first report[54] of the Committee, issued in 1916, clearly recognised and stated the need to build and organise scientific laboratories, staffed with adequate numbers of qualified scientists trained in research. The Committee for Scientific and Industrial Research, which became the Department of Scientific and Industrial Research in 1916, assumed responsibility for the National Physical Laboratory and a number of Research Boards and Associations were set up in conjunction with it. By the end of the war, when the country was almost self-sufficient in the supply of many of those articles which had been a German monopoly in 1914, the importance of scientific knowledge and of scientists to military and industrial capability was more clearly understood than at any time in the past and, as Cardwell has pointed out,[55] the apparatus of the modern scientific world had been assembled.

The immediate post-war prospects for science were, therefore, rosy, although some concern was expressed that the application of science to the service of industry or the State weakened the position of science as a mode of pure, self-justifying, intellectual inquiry. This concern was to be voiced on many occasions[56] between the wars, becoming, as has been noted in Chapter 4, something of a *cause célèbre* in the years shortly before and during the Second World War. In 1919, the scientific community, infused with a new confidence, could note the sharp increase in the numbers of students reading for scientific and technological qualifications in the universities, partly as a result of a scheme for the higher education of 'ex-service students' which began its effective operation in January 1919. Grants were made by the Board of Education to help suitable students, who had returned from the war, to follow full-time courses of higher education in subjects other than pharmacy, agriculture, forestry and veterinary science. The courses of study approved for awards by the Board in 1919 are given[57] in Table 6.9.

The threat to the supply of science teachers for the schools posed by the promised, post-war expansion of investment in scientific research and manufacturing industry, and so clearly anticipated by the Thomson Committee and the British Association, was not to be realised for a generation. By the end of 1920, the post-war euphoria had evaporated and, in G. D. H. Cole's words, 'the world passed swiftly into a fit of morbid depression'. The policy of successive governments between the wars may be seen as one of 'feeding' this depression by reducing financial and other support for scientific research in precisely those areas which might have led to some amelioration of the economic difficulties. As Lord Balfour remarked[58] in 1927, the Government had brought many scientific research activities to an ineffectual conclusion not because they were bad, but 'because the depressed condition of Industry (showed) they (were) especially necessary'. The activities of the Department of Scientific and Industrial Research were affected severely as Governments sought to imitate the weakest aspects of private enterprise by reducing the funds available for scientific research and development. The first post-war depression led to a reduction in the Departmental expenditure to 17 per cent below the estimates of 1920–1 and a further, similar cut, was introduced a year later.[59] Another attempt by the Treasury to cut the Departmental estimates by 10 per cent in 1927 was resisted, but the net result of the successive economies and delays in

Table 6.9   Higher Education of Ex-Service Students. Numbers of Awards made and Courses of Study Followed by 1919

Course of Study	No. of Awards
Classics, Philosophy, etc.	2,009
Art, Architecture, etc.	2,229
Pure Science and Mathematics	2,407
Engineering and Technology	6,491
Medicine and Dentistry	2,732
Commerce	2,975
Miscellaneous	2,241
Total	21,084

financing the work of the D.S.I.R. was that its expenditure rose from £497,000 in 1922–3 to only £536,000 by 1929–30. The State subsidy of the various research associations fell from £103,000 in 1922–3 to £54,000 in 1928 and, in the absence of a Government example, little money was forthcoming from a depressed industrial economy. Not surprisingly, six research associations ceased[60] to function between 1923 and 1928.

Research in agricultural science escaped, for the most part, the economic blizzard which swept over medical and industrial scientific research in the decade or so after 1920. Financial aid to agricultural research increased from £334,692 in 1920 to £892,691 in 1930, largely because of the more readily recognised relevance of such research to the improvement of agricultural productivity.[61] As has been noted, there was even some short-lived concern at the shortage of qualified biologists to meet the needs of the agricultural industry at home and in the colonies.

Following the great 'slump' of 1931, there was a marked change in the attitude of Government to the Department of Scientific and Industrial Research, partly because the gradual revival in trade brought a renewed confidence in the economic potential of applied science. The grant for medical research rose[62] from £139,000 in 1933–4 to £195,000 in 1937–8 and industry followed the example of Government in increasing its financial support for the research associations. The D.S.I.R., noting[63] that, by 1936, several large industrial undertakings had set 'well-balanced teams of research workers, including chemists, engineers and biologists, to solve a particular problem or develop a new product', commented that the previous five years had marked 'an important development in the industrial outlook of the country'. Clearly, therefore, some of the more enlightened sections of industry were prepared to invest in scientific research in the hope of boosting their profitablity. However, it is unlikely that this attitude was widespread in manufacturing industry in the mid-1930s and evidence collected by the Association of Scientific Workers in 1936 suggests that much of the scientific activity was on a small scale.[64] Of thirty-three firms which provided details of their costs to the Association, twenty-five were spending less than £5,000 per annum on research and the maximum expenditure, by the United Steel Company, was £20,000.

The increased investment in scientific research by both industry and government brought new opportunities of employment for those with appropriate scientific qualifications. By 1939, the D.S.I.R. was spending almost £1m on its research programme and supporting research associations for twenty-two industries.[65] Data collected by the Federation of British Industries suggest[66] that, between 1930 and 1938, the number of scientific and technically qualified personnel in industrial employment increased by approximately 217 per cent while the number of firms employing them rose by almost half. (See Table 6.10.) The proportion of unemployed members of the Institute of Chemistry, which had stood at 3.3 per cent in 1932, fell steadily after this date and, in 1938, the Government recruited ninety-three chemists, over five times the number it had appointed at the beginning of the decade.[67]

The virtual stagnation of the demand for qualified scientists and technologists for much of the inter-war years did nothing to stimulate the teaching of science and technology at the universities. The industrial depression after 1926 produced something of a 'swing' to arts subjects among undergraduates (see Tables 6.11 and 6.12) and, of the seventy-one new professorships created in the quinquennium after 1925, only twenty-two were in science and technology.[68] The proportion of students reading for first degrees in science and technology, which stood at approximately 19 per cent and 12 per cent respectively in 1922–3, fell to about 16 per cent and 10 per cent by 1938–9 (see Figures 6.1 and 6.2),[69] and for some university departments of applied science, notably mining and textiles, faced with a shortage of students and of funds for research, the inter-war years were especially bleak.[70]

As in the years before the First World War, the civic universities continued to rely heavily on students with teacher-training grants in order to maintain their undergraduate numbers. They were able to recruit few State Scholars, almost all of whom[71] attended the universities of Oxford, Cambridge or London. Not surprisingly, a suggestion by Eustace Percy when he became President of the Board of Education, that the system of binding impecunious students to teaching be ended, brought vigorous and prompt reactions from a number of Vice-Chancellors.[72] In the event, the system survived the Government of which Percy was a member and the arrangements were not formally reconsidered until the Board undertook the planning of the programme of post-war educational reconstruction in 1941. The combined degree and training grant was eventually abolished, together with the 'Declaration' and post-war graduate students became eligible for a grant to meet the cost of the one-year postgraduate, teacher-training course.

Table 6.10   Industrial Employment of Scientific and Technically Qualified Personnel, 1930–8

Year	No. of Firms Employing Scientific and Technically Qualified Personnel	% increase on Previous Figure	No. of personnel employed	% increase
1930	384	–	1,381	–
1935	432	12.5	2,566	85.8
1938	520	20.4	4,382	70.7

Table 6.11   Degrees Awarded, by Faculty, 1919–20 to 1937–8 (England & Wales)

Year	Arts	Pure Science	Medicine and Dentistry	Technology	Total
1919–20	828	766	422	224	2,244
1920–1	1,240	1,217	496	540	3,500
1921–2	1,831	1,654	477	1,105	5,101
1922–3	1,760	1,512	544	833	8,257
1923–4	2,315	1,885	686	716	9,118
1924–5	1,864	1,473	731	606	9,157
1925–6	2,590	1,890	657	668	7,257
1926–7	3,643	1,914	659	693	7,324
1927–8	3,915	1,996	520	670	7,517
1928–9	4,021	1,989	500	715	7,555
1929–30	4,309	2,087	495	738	7,727
1930–1	4,430	2,117	596	788	8,048
1931–2	4,372	2,242	563	889	8,191
1932–3	4,523	2,242	597	905	8,394
1933–4	4,728	2,279	586	806	8,489
1934–5	4,588	2,442	641	862	8,627
1935–6	4,811	2,484	639	857	8,926
1936–7	4,564	2,402	838	921	8,853
1937–8	4,603	2,377	965	877	8,951

NOTES

i The totals for 1922–3 to 1928–9 inclusive include the number of diplomas awarded annually. These were large in some fields, e.g. dentistry. The totals in all cases also include the relatively small numbers of degrees awarded in agriculture, forestry, horticulture and dairy-work.
ii The totals refer to both higher and first degrees. The importance of the University of London in producing science graduates is not revealed by this Table but should be noted. The University awarded 23.2, 28.5, 31.3, 21.6 and 20.9 per cent of all first degrees in natural science granted by English universities in 1920–1, 1930–1, 1937–8, 1950–1 and 1960–1 respectively. The corresponding percentages for technology degrees are 36.4, 26.8, 27.0, 18.7 and 18.0.

The failure of both Government and industry to provide adequate financial support for scientific research for most of the inter-war period, allied with the continued provision of grants for intending graduate teachers, ensured that, as in earlier years of the century, schoolteaching was the most important field of employment for science graduates. Jobs, however, were hard to obtain and, as if this were not enough, teachers' salaries were cut by 15 per cent in 1931. The

Table 6.12   Degrees Awarded, by Faculty, 1947–8 to 1963–4 (England and Wales)

Year	Arts	Pure Science	Medicine and Dentistry	Technology	Totals
1947–8	6,845	3,662	1,336	1,853	14,083
1948–9	7,968	3,918	1,301	1.948	15,684
1949–50	7,999	4,429	1,419	1,989	16,433
1950–1	7,515	4,460	1,594	1,982	16,153
1951–2	7,645	4,823	1,676	2,039	16,743
1952–3	7,454	4,832	1,906	1,994	16,727
1953–4	7,385	4,657	1,840	1,906	16,263
1954–5	7,424	4,792	1,925	1,921	16,575
1955–6	7,664	4,661	1,950	2,035	16,766
1956–7	7,813	4,999	1,896	2,298	17,465
1957–8	8,410	5,330	1,764	2,413	18,415
1958–9	8,944	5,840	1,869	2,686	19,877
1959–60	9,534	6,436	1,905	3,206	21,672
1960–1	9,796	6,699	1,914	3,375	22,350
1961–2	9,982	6,982	1,984	3,462	23,006
1962–3	10,547	7,743	2,124	3,338	24,328
1963–4	11,284	8,794	1,946	3,821	26,466

NOTES

i The totals exclude degrees awarded in agriculture, forestry and veterinary science.

ii From 1959–60 onwards, the degrees awarded in 'social studies' were recorded separately in the U.G.C. statistics. These have been included under 'Arts' to allow comparison with earlier years.

iii From 1961–2 onwards, technology degrees are categorised as 'Applied Science'.

iv Totals refer to both higher and first degrees. The numbers of higher degrees awarded by Faculty are not available for earlier years. In 1950–1, the ratio of higher to first degrees in science was 0.24. In 1954–5, it was 0.27 and in 1960–1, 0.23. Most British universities did not institute the degree of Ph.D. until after the First World War.

number of posts available annually in secondary schools in the 1930s was approximately 300, compared with perhaps 1,000 newly qualified teachers seeking appointments. Headmasters commonly received a hundred applications for a post in a grammar school[73] and the difficulties facing trained graduate teachers, even towards the end of the inter-war period, are illustrated by the data[74] in Table 6.13. College-trained elementary and secondary school teachers faced even greater difficulties in gaining appointments. It is estimated that 1,100 newly qualified teachers were unemployed[75] at the end of 1932, a year in which admissions to the training colleges were cut by 2½ per cent. Further cuts of 10 per cent and 8 per cent were introduced in 1933 and 1934 respectively.

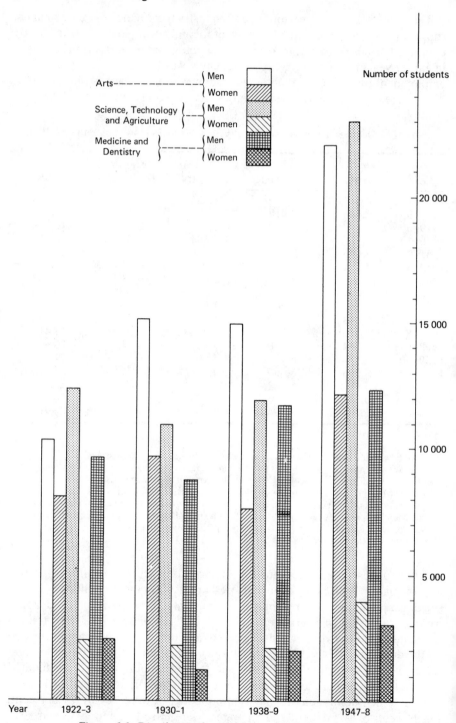

*Figure 6.1 Distribution by Faculties of Full-Time Students,
Men and Women, 1922–47.*

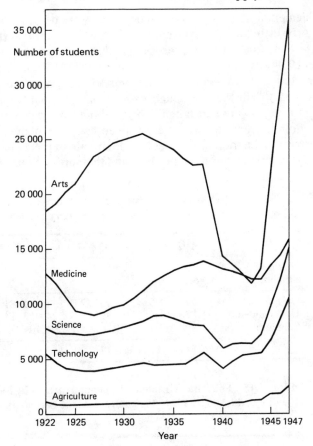

Figure 6.2. Distribution by Faculties of Full-Time Students, 1922–47.

Table 6.13   Employment in Grant-Aided Secondary Schools of Graduates Completing Training in University Departments of Education in July 1936, 1937 and 1938

Year	Qualified Leavers		Appointments Obtained	
	Men	Women	Men	Women
1936	933	688	269	245
1937	888	662	236	232
1938	860	682	152	172

To describe the problem of the inter-war years as a chronic over-supply of teachers is to tell only half the story. The other half, recounting the failure of successive Governments to develop the education service, even to raise the school leaving age, is not the concern of this book but one response to the continuing unemployment of teachers was of seminal importance. The National Union of Teachers made a particularly determined attempt to exclude from the elementary schools those teachers who were not Certificated and its success may be estimated from the data[76] in Table 6.14. As far as the secondary schools are concerned, the proportion of male, trained graduate assistant teachers in 1938 was almost the same as it had been in 1927, the corresponding figures for women showing a rise of just over 15 per cent in the same period. (See Table 6.15.)[77] The fact that a high level of unemployment among graduate teachers in the inter-war years failed to bring about a more general increase in the proportion of graduates who were trained can be explained by the continuing mistrust of the training courses and doubts about their value on the part of secondary school headmasters, teachers and their professional organisations which represented them.

Table 6.14   Numbers and Percentages of Different Grades of Recognised Teachers in Public Elementary Schools

	1921		1931		1938	
Grade of Teacher	No.	%	No.	%	No.	%
Certificated	118,071	71.5	126,245	77.0	131,941	81.9
Uncertificated	35,178	21.2	30,632	18.6	24,058	14.9
Supplementary	12,898	7.3	7,270	4.4	4,905	3.2
Totals	166,147		164,147		160,904	

Table 6.15   Full-Time Graduate Assistant Teachers by Sex and Qualifications, 1927–38, in Grant-Aided Secondary Schools

	1927	1930	1933	1936	1938
Men					
Trained	5,314	5,226	5,014	5,785	6,271
Untrained	3,433	3,720	3,929	4,036	4,071
% Trained	60.75	58.41	56.06	58.90	60.63
Women					
Trained	3,022	3,836	4,534	5,120	5,487
Untrained	2,508	2,594	2,552	2,409	2,370
% Trained	54.64	59.65	63.99	68.00	69.83

Section L of the British Association was told[78] in 1925 that most members of those schools represented at the Headmasters' Conference did not require training since 'the personality of the teacher was more valuable than his scholarship, his method or his equipment'. The Incorporated Association of Headmasters supported[79] postgraduate, professional training for secondary school teachers in a Resolution passed in 1934, but many of its members were clearly unconvinced of the value of such training. The Incorporated Association of Assistant Mistresses instructed its Executive in 1938 to examine and report upon the training of secondary school teachers but the education subcommittee of the Association, to whom the instruction was referred, regarded the problems as too complex and more appropriate for investigation by the Board of Education. Such an inquiry was due to be undertaken in 1939 when the Second World War began.[80]

As far as science was concerned, the circumstances under which the country entered the Second World War were different in at least two important respects from those which had prevailed in 1914. The numbers of qualified scientists and technologists were much greater and there was a mechanism whereby the Government could initiate and finance research of importance to the prosecution of the war and, if necessary, deploy or coordinate scientific manpower accordingly. The extent of the coordination is impressive. Scientific work related to munitions involved the Ministry of Supply with sixty teams of workers in sixteen different universities and 114 different firms,[81] in addition to the relevant research pursued by the Department of Scientific and Industrial Research and the Research Associations.[82] The development of radar alone involved nearly 5,000 staff drawn from the universities, electrical engineering industries and armed forces and many thousands more were employed in production.[83]

There were, inevitably, problems in harnessing science to the service of the war, some of them stemming from a failure to anticipate the kind of scientific endeavour needed. The supply of physicists soon proved inadequate to meet the demands in such fields as telecommunication and radar but not until 1941 was a bursary scheme introduced to allow suitable personnel to attend 'crash' courses at the universities or elsewhere in such subjects as radio and engineering.[84] Yet the war revealed and confirmed what could be achieved by planning the application of science to industrial development and it transformed Government and public thinking about the role of science in society.

That society was also looking for a transformation of its educational system. The McNair Committee,[85] reporting in 1944 on the training of teachers, noted how the 'nation as a whole' had 'woken up to the deficiencies of its public educational system' and was determined upon its reform. The Education Act which became law in August 1944 was the instrument of that reform. Despite the unprecedented debt and physical damage caused by the war, educational principles were suddenly seen as more important than the immediate economic concerns. Secondary education was to be provided for all, within a tripartite system and in accordance with the age, ability and aptitude of each pupil. A shortage of teachers was to prove an unacceptable excuse for maintaining the school leaving age at fourteen. An emergency training scheme was introduced at the end of the war and the leaving age was raised to fifteen in April 1947. Most of the increase in the supply of teachers between the end of the war and 1950 was due to the emergency training scheme which eventually contributed 22,000 men and 11,000 women to the schools.[86] Many of these teachers were older and maturer than their colleagues produced in the normal way via the training colleges and universities and they helped, not only to restore the general staffing level in the schools in 1950 to its January 1947 figure, but also to improve the staff–pupil ratio in the secondary schools.

The 1944 Act was also a landmark in the development of further education in that it required, rather than permitted, local education authorities to make adequate provision for such post-school education in the administrative areas for which they were responsible. The legislation provided the framework for what has been called[87] the 'explosion' of further education, based upon sandwich, part-time, day-release and evening courses, and eventually embracing institutions as diverse as evening institutes and polytechnics. The extent and nature of the expansion of further education between 1946 and 1963 is indicated by the data[88] in Table 6.16. A discussion of the post-war expansion of further education is beyond the scope of this book but two aspects are of particular significance in the present context. Many further education colleges came to prepare students for a variety of G.C.E. examinations, both at Ordinary and Advanced levels, a provision which was especially important at a time when the majority of secondary modern schools did not offer G.C.E. courses to their pupils. In addition, a considerable number of the college courses, taken by students as the preparatory steps towards higher qualifications such as Ordinary and Higher National Certificates and Diplomas, were in science subjects and, as such, made demands upon the supply of science teachers at a time when the schools were often hard-pressed to appoint suitable staff.

Table 6.16   Expansion of Further Education, 1946–63

No. of Students (in thousands)	Year		
	1946	1956	1963
Full Time (inc. Sandwich)	45	76	184
Part-time Day	196	469	613
Part-time Evening	527	724	779
Evening Institute	827	980	1,075
Totals	1,595	2,249	2,651
No. of Teachers – Full time			
Major Establishments	4,383	12,116	28,204*
Evening Institute	184	153	⎫
Service divided between			⎬ 402
2 or more establishments	163	208	⎭
Totals	4,630	12,477	28,606

* Includes Colleges of Advanced Technology.

The blueprint for the expansion of further education was the Percy Report,[89] although its message could hardly claim to be new. The Report clearly elaborated the role of science, particularly applied science, in the planned post-war economy, and emphasised that the economic prosperity of the country depended, first and foremost, on the fullest possible application of science to industry. The Percy Committee recommended that some technical colleges should develop their work to university level, acquire university status and operate within a national system of higher technological education coordinated by a Committee for Technology in conjunction with Regional Advisory Councils. The recommendations within the Percy Report were supported by the Barlow Committee which, in May 1946, reported[90] on the future needs of the country for qualified scientific manpower.

However, when considered together, the Reports of the Percy and Barlow Committees hint at some difference of opinion as to how scientific expertise should be harnessed to the service of the State. During peacetime, priorities are less easily established and the appropriate balance of effort beween pure and applied science less easily recognised than in a nation engaged in war. For the Barlow Committee, 'teaching and fundamental research' constituted the first priority[91] and, as such, these activities should have first claim on the scientific manpower available during the period of post-war reconstruction. For the Percy Committee, the priority lay with the development of technology – what the Barlow Committee described as 'civil science, both Government and Industrial' – at the highest level. This difference of opinion was to some extent institutionalised in the post-war development of higher and further education. The Percy recommendations led the National Advisory Council on Education for Industry and Commerce (N.A.C.E.I.C.) to support[92] an expansion of higher technological education based on the technical colleges. The Barlow recommendations, endorsed by the Advisory Council on Scientific Policy, proved more immediately acceptable to post-war Governments which preferred to allocate scarce financial resources to the development of technological education within the university sector. Cotgrove, who has examined this issue in some detail, sees in it the 'dead hand of tradition', hindering 'the adjustment of the educational system to the changing needs of society'.[93] Only after the publication of the White Paper[94] on Technical Education in 1956, did the Government initiate developments along the lines recommended by the Percy Committee and the N.A.C.E.I.C. In 1957, a number of technical colleges were designated Colleges of Advanced Technology. By 1961, these had become 'direct-grant' establishments and, following the Robbins Report on Higher Education in 1963, they became independent, technological universities.[95]

The post-war expansion of scientific and technological education at all levels was, of course, stimulated and sustained by the increasing demands of industry and Government for qualified scientists and technologists. The £4m spent by Government on civil research in 1939 had increased almost ten-fold by 1960, excluding research supported by the State but contracted to industry.[96] In 1954, defence research and development cost twice as much as only three years earlier and, by 1956, defence work accounted for two-fifths of all scientists and engineers in employment.[97] This commitment to defence during the period of cold-war politics severely hampered the post-war development plans of the D.S.I.R., but, even so, expenditure by the Department rose from[98] £4m in 1948 to nearly £13m by 1960. Medical and agricultural research shared in this expansion and the universities became increasingly dependent upon 'contract' income. In 1938–9, payment for research under contract accounted for 7.4 per cent of the total income (approximately £6m) of British universities, compared with a 35.8 per cent Exchequer grant and 29.8 per cent from fees. By 1958–9, when Government grants represented 69.7 per cent of the greatly increased total income of £52m, the proportion received from 'contract research' had risen to 12.1 per cent.[99]

In 1928, expenditure on scientific research by British industry represented approximately 0.001 per cent of the National Income.[100] This percentage reached 0.0025 by 1938 and 0.01 by 1958 when the National Income stood at a much higher level. The major part of this increased investment in scientific research was accommodated within the larger industrial concerns such as Imperial Chemical Industries and Unilever, the latter company employing 290 graduates in their research laboratories in 1960 compared with 180 a decade earlier.[101] This increased industrial investment in scientific research may be illustrated in another way. While total employment in manufacturing industry rose by 14 per cent between 1948 and 1959, employment in the chemical and related industries grew by 24 per cent and in electrical engineering[102] by 40 per cent. Only a fraction of these increases can be attributed to an increase in the employment of graduate scientists and technologists in a research capacity; some were employed in personnel and managerial work and many more were engaged in production at plant level. It seems likely that the increase in the numbers employed in this latter capacity was important among the factors which contributed to the chronic post-war shortage of qualified scientific man-power in other fields, notably, but not exclusively, in the teaching of physics and chemistry within the schools.

Between 1947 and 1950, the numbers of graduates employed in maintained and aided grammar schools increased by 12.4 per cent and there was a slight improvement in the overall teacher:pupil ratio.[103] The number of graduates admitted to professional training for teaching also increased in this period, from 2,359 in 1947 to 2,886 in 1950, a rise of 22.3 per cent.[104] In the immediate post-war years, therefore, the overall supply of trained graduate teachers and the numbers employed in the grammar schools both increased substantially. However, the increases were inadequate in two important respects. The expansion in teacher supply was insufficient to allow the staffing ratio which prevailed in 1950 to be maintained when the greatly increased number of children born after the war were accommodated within the secondary schools. In addition, the increase in the supply of graduate teachers was not distributed equally among the various subjects of the grammar school curriculum, there being a marked preponderance of arts graduates among these new entrants to the profession.

The National Advisory Council for the Training and Supply of Teachers drew attention to both of these points in its first report, covering the period from July 1949 to February 1951. The Council also raised the more con-tentious issue of quality, commenting that it appeared 'at least doubtful' whether the quality of the new entrants to the profession, as measured by the class of their degrees, was 'good enough' to maintain the existing 'level of quality of the whole body of teachers in grammar schools'.[105] Not everyone who commented on the quality of the new recruits to the science teaching profession at this time was as cautious as the National Advisory Council. A British Association Committee was so convinced of a deterioration in the quality of school biology teaching that it found it 'difficult to resist the conclusion'[106] that an 'arbitrary statistical judgement' had been made to the marks obtained in the School Certificate examinations in biology between 1946 and 1950.

In the years immediately following the publication of the first report of the National Advisory Council, the total number of graduates seeking to enter the teaching profession was well maintained. However, the imbalance between arts and science graduates increased, so much so that, by 1953, some unemployment of arts graduates was reported.[107] Whilst the number of male mathematics and science graduates entering the profession was 'sufficient to make good ordinary wastage', it was inadequate to meet the demands of the expanding secondary schools or to remedy the deficiency in staffing which already existed. The supply of women graduates in science and mathematics presented even more serious problems since the numbers entering the schools in 1952–3 were insufficient to compensate for those leaving the profession.[108]

The inadequacy of the supply of mathematics and science graduates to meet the demand current in 1953 was serious enough. Since this demand was estimated to rise very substantially during the remainder of the decade, the National Advisory Council concluded that 'extraordinary measures' would be needed if the staffing ratios in the schools were to be maintained. A number of measures were introduced, including a programme of extensive advertisement designed to recruit science and mathematics graduates for the schools, although none could be described as 'extraordinary'. In 1955, teachers were allowed to continue teaching for a maximum of five years after the normal retirement age[109] of sixty or sixty-five and, in March 1956, approval was given to the Burnham Committee's proposals[110] for special allowances to be paid to those teachers undertaking advanced work in the schools. These proposals applied to all teachers, irrespective of subject, but it was believed that they would 'help to make teaching more attractive for scientists' by improving salaries and thus serve to stimulate recruitment.

Later in 1956, the Ministry of Labour and National Service agreed that the indefinite postponement of national service, already granted to first- and second-class Honours graduates in science and mathematics who entered a number of occupations in the Government service and industry, would be extended to similarly qualified graduates who wished to take up posts in schools which were grant-aided or recognised as 'efficient' and which provided sixth-form courses. As the Ministry of Education admitted, the effect of this change would not be noted immediately and it was 'not likely' to be great numerically. It was, in fact, of considerable assistance to the schools. In the first year of operation, 201 graduates obtained deferment and 169 of these were appointed to posts in maintained schools. Of these 201 graduates, twenty-one were mathematicians, eighteen were physicists, seventy-four chemists, and forty biologists, and thirty-three of the 201 (16.4 per cent) had graduated with first-class Honours degrees.[111] The arrangements for deferment were quickly

extended to cover graduates in chemistry, biology or general science irrespective of the class of their degrees, to arts graduates with first- or second-class
Honours degrees who had successfully completed an approved course of
teacher training, and, finally, to all graduates in mathematics and science.
These extensions of the arrangements for deferment of national service contributed significantly to the improvement in the recruitment of graduate
teachers of science and mathematics which took place[112] after 1956. (See Table
6.17.)

Table 6.17   Numbers of Mathematics and Science Graduates Teaching Senior
Children in Maintained Primary and Secondary Schools, 1952–60

Year (as at 31 March)	Men	Women	Total	Net Increase
1952	7,161	3,316	10,477	–
1953	7,193	3,457	10,650	173
1954	7,516	3,460	10,976	326
1955	7,591	3,548	11,139	163
1956	7,687	3,670	11,357	218
1957	8,078	3,738	11,816	459
1958	8,339	3,780	12,119	303
1959	8,829	3,902	12,731	612
1960	9,419	4,095	13,514	783

Throughout the 1950s and for some years beyond, concern at the shortage of
graduate science teachers was sustained not so much by reference to the value
of science as a vehicle of a liberal education, as by an emphasis on the
importance of scientific expertise in generating national economic prosperity.
For the National Advisory Council for the Training and Supply of Teachers,
'nothing' was 'so important to the future of the nation' as 'the science that was
taught in the grammar schools and in the public schools and in those secondary
modern schools which (were) providing G.C.E. courses'.[113] Similar, if less
exaggerated, claims were made by the Federation of British Industry, the
Advisory Council for Scientific Policy,[114] the British Association[115] and the
teachers' organisations. Anthony Eden, introducing the White Paper on
Technical Education in 1956, expressed the point in somewhat more com-
petitive terms, warning that 'the prizes' would 'not go to the countries with the
largest population' and that 'those with the best systems of education' would
'win'.[116]

Notwithstanding these sentiments, many schools continued to experience
difficulty in recruiting science staff. In 1953, there were over 100 science posts
unfilled in maintained grammar schools for boys, a situation which contrasted
sharply with the 'golden age' of recruitment before the war when some science
graduates, in order to gain a job, had taught subjects such as woodwork or
physical education. By 1957, when grammar schools of all types were accommodating greatly increased numbers of pupils in their sixth forms, at least 250
science posts remained unfilled, 222 were said to be filled unsatisfactorily and

614 posts in grammar schools were held by non-graduates.[117] In round figures, therefore, at least one-seventh of all science posts in maintained grammar schools were either unfilled or filled unsatisfactorily at this time. Some public schools fared little better, appointing science staff 'with third-class or pass degrees ... (who) ... would not have (been) considered before the war', or recruiting scientists with good Honours degrees only by taking them away from other schools.[118]

Secondary modern and girls' schools of all types suffered worst from the effects of the shortage of science teachers. In 1957, the 877 secondary modern schools providing O-level courses had eighty-nine unfilled posts, 152 new posts to be filled, 177 filled unsatisfactorily and a total of 1,375 non-graduates, many of them emergency-trained, teaching science.[119] A headmistress of a girls' grammar school admitted in 1958 that her school had been 'without a chemistry and physics mistress for some years'. Another recorded that her pupils were taught chemistry by 'four part-time people of whom only one (was) satisfactory'; two were men and one of these had taught for only one year, 'from 1914 to 1915'.[120] The Incorporated Association of Headmistresses collected details of the difficulties experienced by its members in filling teaching posts at various times during the 1950s and the data relating to mathematics, physics and chemistry for the period 1954–8 are summarised[121] in Table 6.18.

Table 6.18   Percentage of Vacancies Filled
Satisfactorily as Reported by Members of the Inc.
Association of Headmistresses

Year	Mathematics	Physics	Chemistry
1954	77	66	66
1955	66	57	77
1956	55	45	65
1957	52	45	55
1958	48	50	52

The shortage of graduate teachers of science and mathematics during the 1950s was a consequence of the failure of the expanding school system to attract an adequate number of such graduates in the face of severe competition from other fields of employment, despite the fact that the annual output of qualified scientists and technologists had almost doubled from about 5,000 in 1945 to approximately 10,000 a decade later. In addition, the number of men graduating in science or arts from U.K. universities in 1950 who entered school teaching was greater than at any time previously, although the figure of 925 represented a lower proportion (24.5 per cent) of those graduating in that year than had been the case in 1930 (32.7 per cent) or in 1937 (26.1 per cent). Table 6.19 summarises[122] the first employment of men graduates in 1950 and the class of degree they were awarded, and it seems likely that the pattern of male, graduate employment indicated by the data in this Table did not change significantly during the rest of the decade.[123] As far as science and mathematics

Table 6.19   First Employment by Class of Degree (Male Graduates of U.K. Universities in 1950)

First Employment	No.= 100%	Class of First Degree		
		First %	Second %	Other %
Teaching (Mathematics and Science)	265	5	32	62
Other Teaching	660	5	58	37
Civil Service and Local Government	265	11	51	38
Civil Service (Scientific)	218	25	47	28
Universities	166	53	41	6
Commerce	296	4	53	43
Industry	1,218	13	41	46
Law, the Churches, 'Cultural Occupations'	397	6	52	42
Other	243	10	49	41
Total	3,728	12	47	41

were concerned, the numbers of graduates entering the schools were insufficient to meet the needs of the secondary schools which, by the later 1950s, were accommodating the so-called 'bulge' in the post-war birth-rate and the 'trend' for pupils to remain at school beyond the statutory leaving age. The 'bulge' and the raising of the school-leaving age in 1947 increased the number of pupils in grant-aided schools in England and Wales from just over 5 million in 1946 to approximately 7 million in the early 1960s and, between 1953 and 1960, the proportion of grammar school pupils remaining at school to the age of seventeen increased by more than half.[124] Not surprisingly, therefore, the 1950s were a period when the schools 'lived on capital' and both the quantity and the quality of science teaching were seriously threatened. (See Figures 6.3 and 6.4.)[125]

Finally, it is appropriate to emphasise that, after 1945, the competition between various types of employer to recruit staff from a limited stock of qualified scientists and technologists was, as far as the schools were concerned, on terms which were much less favourable than those which had prevailed before the war. Caution is necessary in interpreting simple salary comparisons which ignore career and promotion prospects or other conditions of service and there is little doubt that teachers were much better paid after 1956 than in the earlier half of the decade. Yet, to some extent, the facts can speak for themselves. In 1938, the maximum of the university lecturer scale was £500 per annum, compared with £480 per annum for a graduate teaching in a grammar school and the difference between the salary maximum of a university senior lecturer and a senior science master was not more than £24 per annum. By 1958, the university lecturer could expect to earn a maximum of £1,650 per annum in that grade, compared with £1,075 per annum as a graduate school-

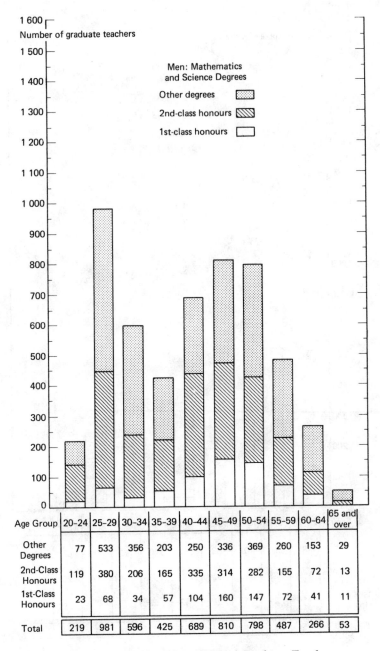

Age Group	20–24	25–29	30–34	35–39	40–44	45–49	50–54	55–59	60–64	65 and over
Other Degrees	77	533	356	203	250	336	369	260	153	29
2nd-Class Honours	119	380	206	165	335	314	282	155	72	13
1st-Class Honours	23	68	34	57	104	160	147	72	41	11
Total	219	981	596	425	689	810	798	487	266	53

Figure 6.3 Age Distribution in 1958 of Graduate Teachers Maintained secondary grammar schools (England and Wales).

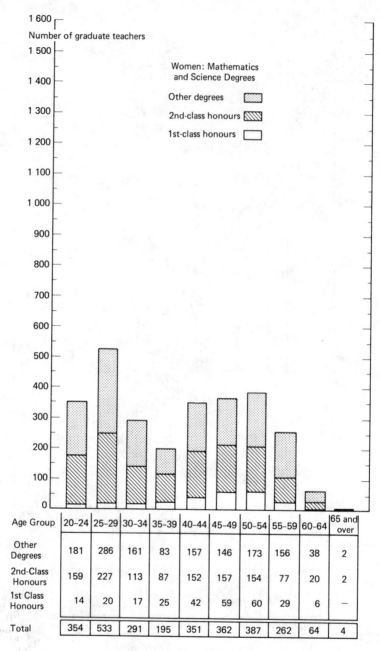

Figure 6.4 *Age Distribution in 1958 of Graduate Teachers Maintained secondary grammar schools (England and Wales).*

master and the difference between the salary maxima of the university senior lecturer (£2,100 per annum) and the senior science master (£1,400 per annum) had widened[126] to £700 per annum.

Comparisons of teachers' salaries with those of similarly qualified graduates in industry are less easily made because of the wide range of salaries offered by very different sectors of industry. However, there seems little doubt that graduate teachers' salaries have, in general, been lower, and sometimes very much lower, than those offered by industry. In 1930, most (62 per cent) Associate Members of the Institute of Chemistry earned[127] a salary within the range £250–499 per annum and just under a quarter (24.6 per cent) were paid between £500 and £999 per annum. The average salary[128] of a male graduate teacher on 31 March 1930 was £436 per annum and that of a woman £366 per annum and, as has been noted, these were cut by 15 per cent in the following year. Although this cut was eventually restored (in two parts) by 1935, graduate teachers' salaries, like those of qualified chemists generally, deteriorated during the 1930s.

In 1945, a common salary scale for all qualified teachers was introduced, but post-war comparisons of graduate salaries in industry and schoolteaching are complicated by the various additional differential payments introduced by the Burnham Reports of 1948, 1951, 1954 and 1956. The new scheme of graded posts and head of department allowances incorporated in the 1956 Burnham settlement was particularly significant since it involved a clear recognition of the need to pay graduate teachers more than their non-graduate colleagues if the former were to be attracted in adequate numbers by the schools and, as such, it undermined the philosophy underlying the notion of a common scale for all qualified teachers.[129] The point was made explicit by the Crowther Committee in 1959:

> ... the great difference between the University graduate and the student leaving a training college is that there is severe competition ... to secure the services of the former and ... it is therefore necessary to offer much more pay to get him into teaching.[130]

By the end of 1959, the average salary[131] of teachers (£947 per annum) was slightly less than double the 1945 figure of £513 per annum, but the salaries earned by graduate teachers had increased more than these figures suggest, principally because grammar school teachers had more generous allowances than their colleagues in secondary modern or primary schools. Even so, the 1959 average, if applied to a chemistry or physics graduate with an Honours degree, compares unfavourably with the median annual income (£1,180) of a member of the Institute of Chemistry[132] aged between thirty-one and thirty-five in 1956 or in 1959 (£1,370). It compares even more unfavourably with the median annual salary of scientific personnel within the same age range and employed in industry which, in 1959, stood[133] at £1,420.

Notwithstanding these comparisons, the overall improvement in the salaries of graduates teaching in the schools between 1945 and 1959 was both substantial and real, although much of the increase came in the latter half of the

1950s. Attributing arbitrary values of 100 to both the retail price index in 1945 and to the average salary of a male graduate teaching in the same year, the salary had reached 264 by 1959 while the index had risen[134] to only 182.

For women teachers, salaries have been lower at every age and at every point in time until April 1961, when the principle of equal pay, agreed in 1955, eventually came fully into operation. The effects of these lower rates of pay on the recruitment of women science graduates to school teaching must remain a matter for conjecture, although it is clear that the supply of women teachers for the schools has been influenced by a number of other factors which are social in origin, rather than narrowly economic.

In 1961, the Minister of Education urged the Burnham Committee to retain salary differentials between graduates and non-graduates and, if possible, to increase such differentials 'still further', on the grounds that the schools were facing a continuing shortage of teachers of science and mathematics.[135] The 1961 salary settlement introduced a basic scale of £570 to £1,170 per annum with graduate and Honours degree additions of £100 per annum each, Heads of Department allowances ranging from £165 to £545 per annum and a series of 'graded posts', worth between £100 and £230 per annum. Such a pay policy, which favoured graduates at the expense of non-graduates, and grammar school teachers at the expense of their secondary modern and primary colleagues, dominated official thinking in the early 1960s. Despite protests from, and sanctions[136] by, the National Union of Teachers, it was a policy unlikely to be changed so long as the shortage of specialist graduate teachers was regarded as severe and concern at such shortage was sustained by reference to the economic rather than to the educational function of scientific education. The possibility of 'subject differentials', i.e. additional payments to teachers of shortage subjects, was never a practical proposition[137] and, as a result, a change in pay policy had to await a more general improvement in the supply of graduate teachers.[138] Such a condition prevailed in the later 1960s and the 1971 Burnham settlement significantly turned its attention to emphasising the long-serving and more senior teachers in the schools.[139]

References

[1] Board of Education, *Annual Report* and *Statistics of Public Education* for the relevant years. The development of secondary education up to 1923 is reviewed in the Board's *Report for the Year 1923–4*, pp. 9–40.

[2] In 1900, about 5,500 children from public elementary schools received 'assistance from public funds', principally in the form of scholarships available under the Technical Instruction Acts, to finance their secondary education. Whilst this figure cannot be compared directly with that for 1906 quoted in the text, the figures undoubtedly indicate a substantial increase in the numbers of scholarships available. For a review of the passage from the elementary to the secondary school, see Board of Education, *Report for the Year 1911–12*, HMSO, Cd. 6707, pp. 24–8.

[3] Not all free (i.e. non fee-paying) places were 'free places' in the special sense of the 1907 Regulations which provided that, where private or L.E.A. Scholarships and

awards for intending teachers did not make up the required 25 per cent of places, the gap was to be bridged by an appropriate number of 'free places'.

4 In 1901, the number of teachers employed in public elementary schools was 149,804. Ten years later, it was 164,271.

5 Board of Education, *Report for the Year 1913–14*, HMSO, p. 60.

6 Board of Education, *Report 1900–1*, vol. 1, p. 49 and *Report for the Year 1913–14*, p. 159.

7 Data from Board of Education, *Annual Report* for each of the relevant years.

8 In its *Report for the Year 1915–16*, the Board commented (p. 47) that for some years it had called attention 'to the serious deficiency in the supply of elementary school teachers' and that 'since last year' the position had become 'still more critical'.

9 In 1903–4, 2,244 men and 4,071 women were following training college courses leading to recognition as a teacher; twenty-six men and eighty-three women were certificated teachers following a one-year course; *Statistics of Public Education, 1903/4/5*, Cd. 2782, pp. xvi-xviii.

10 Board of Education, *Report 1900–1*, vol. 1, p. 51 and vol. 2, p. 556.

11 Board of Education, *Statistics of Public Education, 1903/4/5*, Cd. 2782, pp. xvi-xviii.

12 Board of Education, *Report for the Year 1912–13*, HMSO, pp. 35–6.

13 Ibid., p. 37.

14 Ibid., p. 38.

15 *Natural Science in Education*, HMSO, 1918, para. 88. The data in Table 6.3 are also taken from this source.

16 E.g. Yorkshire College, Owens College and similar colleges at Liverpool, Sheffield, Birmingham and Newcastle. See Armytage, W. H. G., *Civic Universities*, 1955.

17 Gosden, P. H. J. H. and Taylor, A. J. (eds.), *Studies in the History of a University*, 1975, p. 45. Cardwell comments that the university colleges perceived in the training of elementary school teachers, 'a vast field waiting to be cultivated'. Cardwell, D. S. L., *The Organisation of Science in England*, 1957, p 162.

18 Gosden, P. H. J. H. and Taylor, A. J. (eds.), op. cit., p. 46.

19 The data in Table 6.4 are taken from *Statistics of Public Education in England and Wales* for the years 1907 to 1914 and *Returns from Universities and University Colleges in Receipt of Government Grant* 1907–8, annually to 1913–14. As such, Oxford and Cambridge graduates are excluded from the numbers in Table 6.4.

20 It follows that, until 1907, many of the new universities and university colleges contained two groups of intending teachers; those would-be elementary school teachers supported from public funds and intending secondary school teachers who were self-supporting.

21 *Natural Science in Education*, HMSO, 1918, para. 88.

22 Of a total of 5,246 men employed in grant-earning secondary schools in 1913, 1,970 had been trained for elementary work, 180 for secondary school work and the rest were untrained. Gosden, P. H. J. H., *The Evolution of A Profession*, 1972, p. 214.

23 The actual numbers are given in Cardwell, D. S. L., op. cit., p. 166.

24 It should perhaps be pointed out that this figure of 50 per cent for those entering teaching without training and the earlier estimate of 40 per cent for those science graduates who opted for professional training are, to some extent, mutually compensating. No attempt has been made to differentiate between the sexes but the proportion of trained women teachers in secondary schools at this time was 47.4 per cent, significantly higher than the figure for men of 37.5 per cent. Gosden, P. H. J. H., op. cit., p. 215.

[25] Cardwell, D. S. L., op. cit., p. 166, using some common data but a number of different assumptions, concludes that the figure was 66 per cent 'at the very lowest'. Oxford and Cambridge graduates are excluded from Cardwell's analysis, as from that in the text. The Thomson Committee claimed that the number of first- and second-class Honours degrees awarded annually between 1910 and 1914 by those two universities averaged 146. *Natural Science in Education*, HMSO, 1918, para. 171.

[26] Cardwell, D. S. L., op. cit., p. 165. Apart from the '1851 Exhibition' Scholarships introduced in 1895 and some funds available for agricultural research (see Reference 49), there were few grants available to support full-time postgraduate research students, the Treasury having rejected the recommendation of the Haldane Committee in 1905 that a 'moderate sum . . . be set aside for distribution by way of payment to postgraduate students'. University Colleges (Great Britain), Grant in Aid, *Third Report of the University Colleges Committee*, HMSO, 1905, Cd. 2422, p. ix, para. 10. The D.S.I.R. scheme of funding postgraduate research was not introduced until 1915–16.

[27] B.A.A.S., *Report*, 1902, p. 15. 1,500 was a 'liberal' estimate, while, 'at the very outside', the figure could not be put higher than 'somewhere between 1,500 and 2,000'.

[28] Of these, perhaps 400 were employed in secondary schools. Cardwell, D. S. L., op. cit., p. 159, calculates the figure on the assumptions that about 1,000 of the 8,000 graduate schoolmasters in secondary school teaching in 1902 held degrees in science and that 40 per cent of the science graduates were chemists. Pike, R. M., estimated that 'there were about 2,000 scientists of graduate standing in Britain in 1902, excluding teachers in Scottish schools and in a few universities'. *The Growth of Scientific Institutions and Employment of Natural Science Graduates in Britain, 1900–60*, M.Sc. Thesis, University of London, 1961, p. 35.

[29] Pilcher, R. B., *A History of the Institute of Chemistry, 1877–1914*, 1914, p. 165. In 1914, 40 per cent of the members of the Institute were graduates.

[30] *Civil Estimates* and *Forces Estimates, 1902–3*. The figures must be regarded as approximate since it is likely that some departments, e.g. the Patent Office, employed non-scientists, while others, e.g. the meteorological department, employed scientists in a scientific capacity but were excluded from the estimates.

[31] *Natural Science in Education*, HMSO, 1918, para. 169. Of 110 men who read chemistry in Part II of the Tripos between 1900 and 1916, eighty went into the chemical industry. Sixty of the 100 chemistry students of Sir William Ramsay entered manufacturing industry or public service between 1891 and 1910.

[32] It has, for example, been suggested that research was being undertaken by an increasing number of firms before the war and that its extent might have been deliberately obscured by trade secrecy. Sanderson, M., 'Research and the Firm in British Industry, 1919–39', *Science Studies*, vol. 2, 1972, p. 107 et seq.

[33] Dobbie, J. J., Presidential Address, *Proc.Inst.Chem.*, (Pt. II), 1918, p. 33.

[34] The data are taken from the appropriate annual *Reports of the Board of Education*, HMSO.

[35] *Natural Science in Education*, HMSO, 1918, para. 71. The four representatives of the Association of Science Teachers were Miss Saunders (Newnham), Miss Drummond (Camden School), Miss Monk (Roedean) and Miss Stern (North London Collegiate).

[36] The A.P.S.S.M. representatives before the Thomson Committee were A. Vassal (Harrow), D. Berridge (Malvern), C. L. Bryant (Harrow), M. D. Hill (Eton) and D. R. Pye (Winchester).

[37] In 1912 and 1913, the Board asked L.E.A.s to supply details of the number of posts for Certificated and un-Certificated teachers existing in their schools and of the number of vacancies. In London, in these two years, 0.75 per cent and 0.79 per cent of such posts

were unfilled compared with 2.57 and 2.69 per cent for the County L.E.A.s and 0.64 and 0.77 per cent for the County Boroughs. *Report of the Board of Education, 1912–13*, HMSO, Cd. 7341, 1914, p. 86.

[38] Dobbie, J. J., op. cit., Pt. II, p. 33, referred to men flocking back from abroad, schools being depleted of their teachers and 'many who were on the point of abandoning chemistry' finding 'at last the opportunity which had been denied them'.

[39] B.A.A.S., *Report*, 1917, p. 142. It should perhaps be noted that some industrial salaries were even worse. As late as 1915, firms offered 'first-rate chemists', 30s a week and a graduate chemist at Woolwich Arsenal was offered £2 0s 6d. Haber, L. F., *Chemical Industry in the Nineteenth Century*, 1958, p. 195. For a wrathful comment on the latter see *Proc.Inst.Chem.*, 1915 (Pt. II), p. 30. Not surprisingly, there were moves to organise collective protection among scientists by forming professional associations cum trades unions, e.g. the British Association of Chemists (1917), the Institute of Physics (1919), the Association of University Teachers (1919), the National Union of Scientific Workers (1918). For a study of one aspect of this phenomenon see McLeod, E. K., *Politics, Professionalisation and the Organisation of Scientists: The Association of Scientific Workers, 1917–42*, Ph.D. Thesis, University of Sussex, 1975.

[40] For details, see Gosden, P. H. J. H., op. cit., especially Chapter 2 which discusses teachers' salaries in the years before the introduction of 'Burnham' scales. The data in Table 6.8 are taken from *Report of the Committee on National Expenditure*, HMSO, Cmnd. 3920, 1931, p. 50.

[41] B.A.A.S., *Report*, 1917, p. 142.

[42] Dobbie, J. J., *Proc.Inst.Chem.*, 1917 (Part II), p. 19. Dobbie anticipated a 'greatly increased demand' for chemists 'competent to set going and control industrial concerns'.

[43] *Natural Science in Education*, HMSO, 1918, para. 71.

[44] B.A.A.S., *Report*, 1917, p. 143.

[45] Quoted from the *Liverpool Daily Post* in Sanderson, M., *The Universities and British Industry*, 1972, p. 237.

[46] Pilcher, R. B., *The Profession of Chemistry*, 1927, p.v.

[47] *Government Scientific Organisation in the Civilian Field*, HMSO, 1951, Appendix, p. 41.

[48] Minutes of the Executive Committee of the National Physical Laboratory, vols. 1–4, 1900–17, quoted in Pike, R. M., op. cit., p. 52. For the importance of the N.P.L. as a source of employment for physicists, see Moseley, R., *The Growth of Physics and its Emergence as a Profession in Britain*, M.Sc. Thesis, University of Sussex, 1973, ch. 2.

[49] The Act provided £2.9m for aiding and developing agricultural and rural industries, improvement of land and waterways, construction of harbours, etc. The Institutes were to be under the control of the Ministry of Agriculture and Fisheries.

[50] Pike, R. M., op. cit., p. 56, concludes that 'apart from some sections of the chemical and engineering groups', British industry 'remained in a state of happy ignorance'.

[51] For contemporary accounts of the interaction of science and the Great War, see, e.g., Lord Moulton, *Science and War*, Rede Lecture, Cambridge, 1919; Poulton, E. B., *Science and the Great War*, Romanes Lecture, Oxford, 1915. On the shortage of optical glass and instruments, see Winter, J. (ed.), *War and Economic Development*, 1975, pp. 165–203. For dyes, see Haber, L. F., *The Chemical Industry*, 1971, pp. 184–217.

[52] See Marwick, A., *The Deluge*, 1965, p. 228, and Reid, R. W., *Tongues of Conscience: War and the Scientists' Dilemma*, 1969, p. 39.

[53] *History of the Ministry of Munitions*, HMSO, 1918–22, vol. VI, part I, p. 49.

[54] *Report of the Committee of the Privy Council for Scientific and Industrial Research for the Year 1915–16*, 1916. The members of the Committee were Sir W. S. McCormick, Sir

G. T. Beilby, W. Duddell, Professor J. A. McClelland, R. Meldola, R. Threlfall, Sir C. A. Parsons and Lord Rayleigh.

[55] Cardwell, D. S. L., op. cit., p. 173.

[56] Two critics of particular importance were Abraham Flexner, an American, and Sir Ernest Barker. Essentially these critics challenged the right of vocational subjects to a place in the university curriculum. Flexner, A., *Universities: American, English and German*, 1930, and Barker, E., *Universities in Great Britain: Their Position and Their Problems*, 1931. The criticism served to generate a healthy reaction. See Armytage, W. H. G., op. cit., p. 266 et seq.

[57] Board of Education, *Report for the Year 1918–19*, HMSO, Cmd. 722, p. 84. It should, however, be noted that the increase of 56.9 per cent in full-time students at universities and university colleges between 1919 and 1924 coincided with a cut of £300,000 in 1922–3 in the quinquennial budget and with a marked reduction in the levels of local support in many cases. The result was a period of 'acute anxiety' for the universities who were already, as Soddy pointed out, 'packed with men, crammed, three to a bench, into laboratories which even before the present influx, were ... a disgrace to the nation'. U.G.C., *Returns from Universities and University Colleges, 1919–20 to 1923–4*, HMSO, 1924, p. 6; ibid., 1923–4 to 1928–9, p. 3, and *Scientific Worker*, Supplement to May 1920, p. 17.

[58] Tizard, Sir Henry, *A Scientist in and out of the Civil Service*, 1955, p. 15. The government expenditure on civil research, approximately £1.2m in 1920, reached only £3.1m in 1930 and just under £4m by 1939 compared with perhaps £2m and £2.8m on defence research in 1934 and 1937 respectively (all figures are approximate). *Government Scientific Organisation in the Civilian Field*, HMSO, 1951, and Bernal, J. D., *The Social Function of Science*, 1939, pp. 62–3.

[59] D.S.I.R., *Annual Report*, 1920–1, p. 6.

[60] Pike, R. M., op. cit., p. 66, points out that the government had assumed that the various research associations would rapidly become financially independent once established with State aid.

[61] *Government Scientific Organisation in the Civilian Field*, HMSO, 1951, Appendix on Research Expenditure, p. 38.

[62] Quoted in Pike, R. M., op. cit., p. 70.

[63] D.S.I.R., *Annual Report*, Cmd. 5350, 1935–6, p. 15.

[64] Association of Scientific Workers, *Industrial Research Laboratories*, 1936.

[65] Argles, M., *South Kensington to Robbins*, 1964, p. 80.

[66] Federation of British Industries, *Industry and Research*, 1943, p. 7. The F.B.I. survey is almost certainly incomplete since it did not cover all firms engaged in scientific work. Much of the Government aid to scientific research was, of course, for defence purposes.

[67] It had stood at 1.2 per cent in September 1929. Chapman, D., 'The Profession of Chemistry During the Depression', *Progress and the Scientific Worker*, Autumn 1939. Chapman regarded the figures as 'small'.

[68] Argles, M., op. cit., p. 75. The data in Tables 6.11 and 6.12 are taken from the *Annual Returns of Universities and University Colleges in Receipt of Government Grant*. 'Arts' included theology, fine art, law, music, commerce, economics and education.

[69] The figures are taken from U.G.C., *University Development from 1935 to 1947*, HMSO, 1948, pp. 30–1.

[70] At Leeds, for example, consideration was given to the abolition of the chair in mining and to the combination of teaching in the Leeds and Sheffield departments, although neither took place. Gosden, P. H. J. H., and Taylor, A. J. (eds.), op. cit., p. 288.

[71] About one-sixth of State Scholars attended the University of London and two-thirds

the Universities of Oxford and Cambridge; the remaining one-sixth were distributed among all the other universities.

[72] The Vice-Chancellor of Leeds wrote to Percy 'strongly opposing' the suggestion and a meeting with Percy and the Head of the Education Department at the University took place on 21 December 1928. Gosden, P. H. J. H., and Taylor, A. J. (eds.), op. cit., pp. 50–1.

[73] Gosden, P. H. J. H., op. cit., p. 174.

[74] Hansard, 23 November 1938, vol. 341, cols. 1765–8.

[75] Simon, B., The Politics of Educational Reform, 1920–1940, 1974, p. 215.

[76] Data from Annual Reports of the Board of Education for the relevant years.

[77] Gosden, P. H. J. H., op. cit., p. 280.

[78] B.A.A.S. Report, 1925, p. 372.

[79] Journal of Education, February 1934, p. 112.

[80] Gosden, P. H. J. H., op. cit., p. 281.

[81] Scott, J. D., Hughes, R., The Administration of War Production, 1955, p. 284.

[82] The staff of the D.S.I.R. increased from 2,153 in 1939 to 2,772 in 1945. D.S.I.R. Annual Report, 1947–8, Cmd. 7761. This surveys the period 1938–48.

[83] Crowther, J. G., Whiddington, R., Science at War (D.S.I.R.) 1947, pp. 30–1 and p. 84.

[84] In 1941, Britain had perhaps 1,100–1,200 trained physicists. The shortage was world-wide, e.g. in the U.S.A. in 1941, there were 4,500 physicists, of whom 1,400 were engaged in war work. The shortage in Britain may be attributed in part to the failure of the physics-based industries to develop on a significant scale in the inter-war period.

[85] The Report of a Committee appointed by the President of the Board of Education to Consider the Supply, Recruitment and Training of Teachers and Youth Leaders, 1944.

[86] Ministry of Education, Training and Supply of Teachers. First Report of the National Advisory Council, HMSO, 1951, p. 5.

[87] Cantor, L. M., Roberts, I. F., Further Education in England and Wales, 1972, p. 1.

[88] Taken from ibid., p. 1 and p. 2.

[89] Ministry of Education, Higher Technological Education, HMSO, 1945.

[90] Scientific Manpower: Report of a Committee appointed by the Lord President of the Council, Cd. 6824, HMSO, 1946.

[91] Ibid., p. 18.

[92] Ministry of Education, The Future Development of Higher Technological Education. Report of the National Advisory Council on Education for Industry and Commerce, HMSO, 1950.

[93] Cotgrove, S. F., Technical Education and Social Change, 1958, chapter 13.

[94] Technical Education, HMSO, 1956.

[95] The C.A.T.s were often as large as some universities, e.g. Birmingham C.A.T. had 5,172 students in 1961–2.

[96] Pike, R. M., op. cit., p. 79.

[97] Ibid., p. 80.

[98] Ibid., p. 81. Pike points out that most of this increase came after 1954 when a five-year plan was established to fulfil at least 95 per cent of the 1946 proposals by 1959.

[99] Advisory Council on Scientific Policy, 13th Annual Report, Cmnd. 1167, 1959–60, p. 6.

[100] Carter, C. F. and Williams, B. R., Science in Industry, 1959, p. 9.

[101] Pike, R. M., op. cit., p. 122.

[102] Ibid., p. 119.

[103] Ministry of Education, *Training and Supply of Teachers*, 1951, p. 14. The ratio improved from 39.7 to 40.5 teachers per thousand children.

[104] Ibid., p. 11.

[105] Ibid., p. 14.

[106] Biological Sciences in British Schools, *The Advancement of Science*, vol. X, no. 37, 1953, p. 87. 'There seems little doubt that both the quality and the quantity of biology teachers has rapidly deteriorated.' The Committee also expressed concern at the 'dilution' of the grammar schools: a reference to the great number of pupils in them after the war.

[107] *Graduate Teachers of Mathematics and Science*, Report of the National Advisory Council on the Training and Supply of Teachers, HMSO, 1953, p. 1.

[108] Ibid., pp. 1–2. There was also a general concern over the quality of science graduates entering the grammar schools, the Council regarding as 'possibly significant', the decline from 14.7 per cent to 4 per cent in the proportion of men with 'Firsts' in science or mathematics who left training in 1938 and 1953 respectively.

[109] Barton, A. W., 'The Supply of Science Teachers', in Perkins, W. H., *Science in Schools*, 1958, p. 56.

[110] Ministry of Education, *Education in 1955*, p. 12.

[111] Ibid., p. 12, and *Education in 1956*, p. 14. This is one of the few published statistics which refer to individual science subjects. The problem was generally discussed in terms of 'science and mathematics' but there is little doubt that the shortage was much more severe with physics and mathematics than with chemistry or biology.

[112] Ministry of Education, *Education in 1959*, p. 17. The deferment arrangements were also extended to all men, whether or not graduates, who had successfully completed an approved course of teacher training. See also *Education in 1960*, pp. 19–20.

[113] Quoted in Barton, A. W., op. cit., p. 52.

[114] 'It is an essential condition of our survival that the number of trained scientists and technologists in industry be greatly increased.' Advisory Council for Scientific Policy *Sixth Annual Report, 1952–3*, Cmd. 8874, HMSO.

[115] Perkins, W. H., op. cit., *passim*.

[116] Quoted in Argles, M., op. cit., p. 92.

[117] Barton, A. W., op. cit., p. 53. Pike, R. M., op. cit., claims that in 1957, over 1,000 science teaching posts were 'either unfilled' or 'inadequately filled'.

[118] Barton, A. W., op. cit., p. 54.

[119] Ibid., p. 55.

[120] Huxstep, E. M., 'Scientific Education for Girls', in Perkins, W. H., op. cit., pp. 28, 29 and discussion on p. 39.

[121] Ministry of Education, *15 to 18*, HMSO, 1959, vol. 1, p. 242.

[122] P.E.P., *Graduate Employment*, 1956, chapter 3.

[123] This was the view of the Crowther Report in 1959; *15 to 18*, HMSO, 1959, vol. 1, p. 237.

[124] Lawson, J., Silver, H., *A Social History of Education in England*, 1973, pp. 427 and 428.

[125] Taken from Ministry of Education, *15 to 18*, HMSO, 1959, vol. 1, pp. 234–5.

[126] The figures in this paragraph are taken from Barton, A. W., op. cit., p. 58, who hints that grammar school masters might have been 'overpaid in 1938'.

[127] *Proc.Inst.Chem.*, Part III, 1931, p. 197. The Institute of Chemistry introduced surveys of the salaries of its members in 1920. For details of this period, see *Proc. Inst.Chem.*, 1921, p. 44. Unfortunately, the early survey was based on category of

employment and the later surveys on age and grade of Institute membership so that direct comparison is not always possible.

[128] *Report of the Committee on National Expenditure*, Cmnd. 3920, 1931, p. 50.

[129] It was, of course, a reversal of the 'egalitarian' policy pursued by the Ministry of Education in the immediate post-war years. A Graduate Teachers' Association was established to oppose this policy whose 'decline set in with the increase of differential payments'. Gosden, P. H. J. H., op. cit., p. 76.

[130] Ministry of Education, *15 to 18*, HMSO, 1959, vol. 1, p. 440.

[131] Conway, F., *School Teachers' Salaries, 1945–59*, Manchester School of Economic and Social Studies, 1962, Part III.

[132] *J.R.I.C.*, September 1956, p. 518 and ibid., September 1959, p. 485. Pike, R. M. (op. cit., p. 138) describes the increase in salaries of chemists in general between 1942 and 1959 as 'spectacular', adding that such salaries may not have improved in real terms until 1953 because of increases in the cost of living and in taxation.

[133] Pike, R. M., op. cit., p. 139 (note).

[134] Based on figures in Greenhalgh, V. C., 'The Movement of Teachers' Salaries', *J.Ed., Admin. and History*, December 1968, pp. 23–6.

[135] *Schoolmaster*, 28 July 1961, p. 162.

[136] In 1963, the N.U.T. Annual Conference resolved to reject any settlement which increased the so-called primary-secondary differential and urged its negotiators to seek an improvement of the basic scale. Sanctions were introduced in 1967, taking the form of refusing to supervise school meals, to work with unqualified teachers, etc. For details, see Gosden, P. H. J. H., op. cit., p. 80ff.

[137] Ibid., p. 74.

[138] A survey carried out by the Headmasters' Association of posts vacant in 1969 suggested that schools were having less difficulty in appointing teachers of biology, chemistry and physics than teachers of English or music. See also, 'Scientists to Spare?', *Times Educational Supplement*, 29 August 1969, p. 11.

[139] This had long been the policy of the National Association of Schoolmasters which had gained representation on the Burnham Committee in 1962.

7
Laboratory Provision and Design

Despite the general neglect of physical science by the public and endowed grammar schools for much of the nineteenth century, it is to some of these schools that credit must be given for the early provision of facilities for the practical teaching of physics and chemistry. Stonyhurst College, which was teaching physical science by 1808, spent over £2,000 on a lecture room, chemical room and mathematical room in that year and made an appeal for funds to purchase apparatus.[1] Classes in experimental physics were conducted at University College School in 1835 and the City of London School set aside a room 'specially adapted for practical science'[2] in 1847. At the Bristol Trade School, opened in 1856, boys of twelve years and upwards conducted chemical analyses in a laboratory attached to the school and the pupils were encouraged to make some of the apparatus needed for laboratory work in physics.[3] Wilson began teaching science at Rugby 'in the cloakroom on the ground floor in the Town Hall', although a small chemical laboratory was completed at the school by 1860 and more generous accommodation was provided shortly afterwards.[4] Yet, as the Public School Commissioners reported in 1864, Rugby was the exception among the nine public schools they had investigated, most of which 'altogether omitted' physical science from their curricula.

The Taunton Commissioners, reporting in 1868, discovered a similar lack of laboratory accommodation in the endowed schools. Few of these schools took immediate advantage of the permission given to them in 1868 to use part of the endowment of the school to provide funds with which to finance the building of laboratories. Of the 128 endowed grammar schools sufficiently interested to reply to an inquiry from the Devonshire Commissioners in the early 1870s, science was taught in sixty-three, of which only thirteen had a laboratory and eighteen, 'scientific apparatus of any kind'.[5] The Devonshire Commissioners were, however, able to record some progress in the major public schools, partly because, by 1872, Harrow, Eton and Charterhouse were either building or planning new science laboratories. This example was followed by other schools such as Rossall, Wellington, Cheltenham, Dulwich, Christ's Hospital and the grammar schools at Bradford and Manchester. Almost all of these laboratories were equipped for the teaching of chemistry, rather than physics, although the pioneering work of Worthington at Clifton is a distinguished exception.[6]

Science was also taught in the organised science schools and classes supported by funds from the Department of Science and Art. From 1868 onwards, the Department offered building grants to such schools and classes at a rate rising to a maximum of 2s 6d per square foot of internal area, although in no instance could the grant exceed £500 for the buildings in any one school or be greater than the funds provided by the school itself. On receipt of a certificate showing that the building and conveyance were completed, an Inspector was sent to examine the accommodation. Assuming that the school could provide its share of the cost and the Inspector's report was satisfactory, the grant was then used to finalise the account.[7] Strict conditions were also attached to the use of the facilities provided in this way. For example, the grant to be given towards the cost of building a chemistry laboratory was allowed only if the laboratory constituted 'a room or part of a room set apart for the study of Practical Chemistry'. Such accommodation could thus not be used to teach other subjects although it could be made available for 'practical work in other experimental sciences' when not required for practical chemistry.

Grants were also given towards the purchase of apparatus, up to a maximum of 50 per cent of the cost, and towards the purchase of laboratory fittings, 'not exceeding $33\frac{1}{3}$ per cent of their cost', provided that the laboratory had a mean height of not less than fifteen feet and the fittings, apparatus and chemicals were those required to teach the appropriate syllabuses prescribed by the Department of Science and Art.[8] The total grant paid for science instruction rose from £20,118 in 1870 to £240,822 by the end of the century as the Department made a 'vigorous onslaught against teaching that was unillustrated by experiment'.[9]

The design of laboratories and fittings to meet the specifications of the Department of Science and Art owed much to William de W. Abney who, after eight years of teaching 'some branches of physical science at the School of Military Engineering' was appointed a Departmental Inspector for Science in 1876 and eventually became Director for Science in 1893. Addressing the British Association in 1903 as President of Section L, Abney referred to some of the earlier laboratories financed by the Department as having a 'sealed pattern efficiency' which, whatever its shortcomings, had the virtue of telling 'people what is the least that is expected of them'. As the number of such laboratories increased and their limitations became more obvious, marked improvements in design were introduced, the 'sealed-pattern' fell into abeyance and 'any properly equipped laboratory' was recognised by the Department so long as it met 'the absolute necessities of instruction'.[10]

Some of the School Boards, particularly those in the larger industrial towns, were quick to take advantage of the funds available under the Regulations of the Department of Science and Art. After the passage of the 1870 Act, it was not long before new laboratories were established in Board Schools for the benefit of 'Sixth Standard children' and those attending organised science classes, often provided in the Higher Grade Elementary Schools. Some of these schools achieved a nationally recognised standard in science teaching[11] and, until the 'Cockerton' decision in December 1900, were able to use both rate aid and government grant to support their work in this area of the curriculum. After the administrative reorganisation at the turn of the century, the laboratories built in these 'elementary' schools remained to provide the basis for the work in chemistry and physics in those secondary and central schools created from them.

The endowed grammar schools were more reluctant than the School Boards to take full advantage of the grants available from the Department of Science and Art to build and equip laboratories. Of the ninety-eight schools recognised as 'organised science schools' in 1894, only sixteen were endowed schools,[12] a proportion which it is not difficult to explain. The principal purpose of a grammar school, as confirmed by the Grammar School Act of 1840, was to teach Latin and Greek, other subjects being allowed only if their inclusion in the curriculum did not undermine the terms of the foundation. From 1872, the Department of Science and Art required that an organised 'day' science school provide systematic instruction in science for not less than three years in accordance with the schemes of work elaborated in the Directory, and that not less than fifteen hours per week be devoted to those subjects taught under the aegis of the Department. Few endowed grammar schools were prepared to seek recognition as organised science schools under these terms, particularly since there was likely to be the additional financial burden of building and equipping a laboratory and of employing staff to teach the science subjects. Towards the end of the nineteenth century, the requirements for recognition were relaxed[13] and the changed circumstances encouraged more endowed schools to apply for the status of an organised science school, 169 being so recognised[14] by 1897. Some endowed schools also took advantage of the interim arrangements, operated by the Board of Education after 1899, whereby special grants were available for science work conducted in day secondary schools. The Governors of the Manchester High School for Girls used funds obtained under these arrangements in 1900–1 to build a cookery school and a biology laboratory.[15] school and a biology laboratory.[15]

Inspection was, inevitably, a condition of grant, under the Regulations of both the Department of Science and Art and, subsequently, of the Board of Education. An organised science school had to be 'open at all times to the visit and inspection' of the appropriate officers, another condition likely to have been unacceptable to a number of endowed grammar schools, particularly those where the teaching left something to be desired. The Manchester High School for Girls had no anxieties on this account and the visit of Her Majesty's Inspectors at the beginning of the century was adjudged to have had little practical effect on the general work of the school, except perhaps on the 'feelings of the mistress'.[16]

After 1890, other means were available to encourage the endowed grammar schools to build specialist accommodation for the teaching of science. In that year, surplus government funds, the so-called 'whisky money', arising from the abandonment of some provisions of a Local Taxation (Customs and Excise) Act, were made available to the newly created local authorities to be spent on technical education and/or the relief of rates. Some authorities, e.g. the West Riding, allocated all of the income to technical education, administering the money via the Technical Instruction Committees which they had been empowered to establish under the Technical Instruction Act[17] of 1889. Some of the 'whisky money' went to continuation schools but funds were also made available to local grammar schools, sometimes in the form of an annual grant and, at other times, as a lump sum to build and equip science laboratories.[18]

Between 1890 and 1902, the Technical Instruction Committee of the West Riding County Council aided the provision of thirty-one physical laboratories, thirteen chemical laboratories and three 'combined laboratories' in those grammar schools to which it awarded scholarships.[19] The Manchester Grammar School similarly received a grant from the Corporation to extend its facilities for the practical teaching of physics and chemistry.[20] Both the grants and the scholarships administered by the Technical Instruction Committees were regarded as legitimate activities, undertaken by the authorities to encourage the development of technical education and substantial sums of money were often involved. In 1893–4, the West Riding Committee spent almost £10,000 on scholarships and perhaps a third as much on grants to secondary schools.[21] The capital allowance for building gained in importance after 1897 when the Department of Science and Art discontinued its building grants but still required an organised science school to meet its specified standards of laboratory accommodation and fittings.

The timing of these activities of the Technical Instruction Committees was particularly fortunate in that the availability of 'whisky money' coincided with the growing momentum of Armstrong's campaign to base school science teaching on practical, heuristic investigation. In addition, the programme of school laboratory building should be seen in the context of parallel developments in the field of higher education. By the end of the nineteenth century, practical instruction in chemistry and physics was an established component of undergraduate science education in every institution of university rank. This was particularly the case in the London colleges and in those institutions which were shortly to become independent civic universities. The public schools, a frequent target of Armstrong's invective and often free from many of the financial problems facing the endowed grammar schools, were provided with rather less of a lead by the two ancient universities. Practical experimental work was not made a compulsory part of the education of physics undergraduates at the Cavendish Laboratory until Rayleigh[22] succeeded Maxwell in 1879. Chemistry under Odling at Oxford suffered from the general failure of that University to show any sympathy with the contemporary educational and social changes, a failure which led Abney to conclude in 1903 that it was necessary to look to the modern universities 'to lead the movement in favour of that kind of education which is best fitted for the after-life of the large majority of people of this country'.[23]

By 1902, the view that school science should be based on laboratory work, not necessarily of a heuristic kind, was widely held and it has not been seriously challenged to this day. Abney estimated[24] that there were 1,165 school laboratories 'recognised' for the teaching of chemistry (758), physics (320), metallurgy, biology and mechanics (eighty-seven) at this time and Sutcliffe asserts[25] that over 1,100 of these had been built since 1877. The considerable experience of laboratory design and furniture that had accumulated during the

Plate 6 Class in a chemistry laboratory, Liverpool, 1902.

Plate 7 School physics laboratory, 1911.

last quarter of the nineteenth century was incorporated in several important and influential treatises. Robins's *Technical School and College Building*,[26] published in 1887, is notable for its highly detailed comparison of laboratory design in England with other countries, especially Germany. Felix Clay's *Modern School Buildings*, which appeared in 1902, contains a lengthy chapter[27] on 'rooms for the teaching of science and art', but T. H. Russell's *The Planning and Fitting of Chemical and Physical Laboratories*, published[28] in 1903, is undoubtedly the most thorough survey of the state of development of laboratory design and fitting at the beginning of the century. Plates 6 and 7 and Figures 7.1 and 7.2 illustrate the kinds of laboratories in which physics and chemistry were taught at this time.[29]

After 1904, the Regulations of the Board of Education governing the curricula of grant-aided secondary schools required that the instruction in science include 'practical work done by the pupils' but no indication was given of the

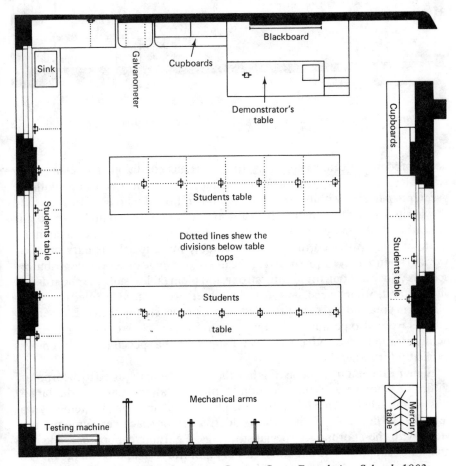

Figure 7.1 The Physical Laboratory, Cowper Street Foundation School, 1903.

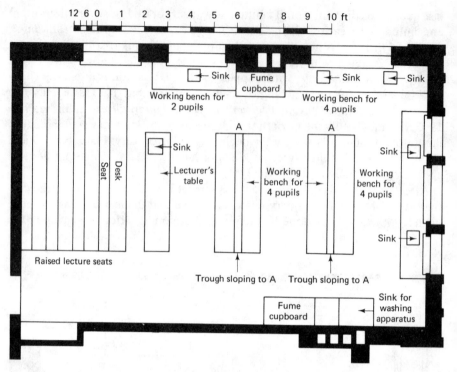

Figure 7.2 The Chemical Laboratory, New School for Girls, Clapham, 1903.

accommodation deemed necessary to satisfy this condition. The elementary school Regulations were much more detailed in this respect, reflecting both the greater experience within the central administration of schools of this type and the limited contribution that it was estimated science would make to the education of the majority of the population. Article 85(a) of the Elementary Code of 1902 provided that 'a room suitably fitted for elementary practical work in science may be provided for the use of one large or several contributory schools'. Such a room, fitted with 'strong and plain tables, sinks, cupboards and shelves and, where necessary, a fume closet' was not, as a rule, to exceed 600 ft.² in area and had to be provided with a 'proper supply of gas'. Elementary schools were also permitted to equip a conventional classroom 'with a simple demonstration table and gas and water supply' but a special lecture room was explicitly forbidden.[30]

Higher Elementary Schools, on the other hand, were required to incorporate sufficient laboratory accommodation to provide 'at one time for the largest class in the school'. One laboratory for physics and another for chemistry was regarded as desirable, each allowing 30 ft.² of floor space per pupil and provided with the appropriate specialist fittings, e.g. fume cupboards, sinks, gas and water supplies. The minimum size of laboratory, computed on the basis of twenty pupils per class, was 600 ft.², but a somewhat larger size was advocated in anticipation of an increase in the number of pupils working in the laboratory at any one time. Higher Elementary Schools could also be provided with a small balance room, a preparation room and a lecture room, the latter 'having an area of about 750 sq. ft.'[31]

The Board of Education issued Building Regulations for both elementary and secondary schools in 1907. These were updated and re-issued[32] in 1914, partly as 'a statement of principles of school planning' upon which the Board proceeded in 'criticising the plans submitted to them' and partly as a statement of what the Board believed to be 'the best current practice in the application of these principles'. The laboratory accommodation suggested for elementary schools was evidently meant to be simple and inexpensive. Where the Board approved the provision of a room for teaching science in such schools, 'between 20 and 25 sq. ft. of floor space' was to be allowed for each pupil working in the laboratory and this was to be fitted with 'benches of a simple character with water and gas laid on in suitable positions'. In contrast, grammar schools were to be provided with laboratories built to standards higher than those set by the Department of Science and Art at the end of the nineteenth century. In no case was there to be less than 30 ft.[2] of floor space per pupil and each laboratory was to be sufficiently large to make it unnecessary to divide a class into small groups for the teaching of practical science. It was recommended that each pupil be allowed a working surface of $3\frac{1}{2}$ ft. by $2\frac{1}{4}$ ft. to be provided on either single or double laboratory benches. The Board discouraged the placing of central reagent shelves on double benches, preferring side-bench accommodation for such 'special purposes'. A demonstration table was regarded as essential in any laboratory to be used for main school teaching of science. For more advanced work, the Board favoured smaller rooms, although a separate balance room was deemed unnecessary unless delicate balance work was to be undertaken.

The Building Regulations also contained recommendations about the number of laboratories appropriate for secondary schools of a given size. The Board considered that a school with 150 pupils over the age of twelve would require at least one laboratory, and probably two if the school were coeducational. Larger schools, with more than 300 pupils on the roll, required a correspondingly more generous provision and three laboratories were recommended. The importance of adequate and convenient storage and preparation facilities was also recognised and schools of more than 250 pupils were regarded as sufficiently large to justify the additional provision of separate lecture room accommodation.

The suggestions and recommendations incorporated within the Building Regulations allowed architects ample scope for initiative in laboratory design, but few new laboratories were built during the First World War. The position in 1918 was summarised in the Report of the Thomson Committee which recorded[33] that in the newer, grant-aided secondary schools and in those which dated 'back to the days of the Department of Science and Art', the provision of laboratories and lecture rooms was, in general, adequate. The position in the public schools appears to have been somewhat less satisfactory, despite the improvements which had been made in the earlier years of the century. Of the fifty-five public schools represented at the Headmasters' Conference, thirty had 'three and more laboratories', twenty-one had two laboratories and only four schools, each with fewer than 200 pupils, were limited to one. However, in 'certain schools', the scale of laboratory provision was either 'insufficient for the needs of those taking science', or sufficient only because so many boys did not study physics or chemistry. As has been noted already, the provision of laboratory accommodation in girls' secondary schools, whether or not state-aided, was generally less satisfactory than in the corresponding schools for boys. Of twenty-eight girls' secondary schools, each with between 200 and 300 pupils, twenty had only one laboratory and ten out of thirteen larger schools were 'no better off'.[34] In the public elementary schools, particularly those outside the larger towns, a specially equipped laboratory was the exception rather than the rule, and the Thomson Committee advocated that every elementary school should have 'a large room with flat tables and a supply of water (and, where possible, gas and electric light)'.[35] Such a room was to be available for the general use of the school and 'not restricted to the daily instruction of one class'.

For most of the inter-war period, laboratory building, along with other forms of school accommodation, was severely restricted by the economy measures introduced by successive Governments. The elementary schools were badly affected as local authorities delayed their building programmes and implemented 'absurd economies on buildings and staff',[36] in order to curtail their educational expenditure. Some secondary schools were able to take advantage of the grants provided by the Board of Education to finance 'recognised advanced courses'[37] at sixth-form level. These grants were usually sufficiently generous to allow some of the money to be spent on equipping a laboratory or on adapting existing accommodation for the practical teaching of science. The need to modify existing classrooms under conditions of severe economic constraint when the secondary school population was expanding, does much to explain the size of many school science laboratories which became 'standardised' at 960 ft.[2] by the 1930s. Figure 7.3 illustrates[38] how the demolition of appropriate partition walls enabled standard classroom units, 20 ft. by 24 ft., arranged along a 6 ft. wide corridor, to be converted to provide two laboratories, each of 960 ft.[2] area and a preparation room with dimensions of 20 ft. by 18 ft. Some public schools were able to increase their laboratory accommodation by using funds collected to build a memorial to their former pupils killed during the First World War. A number of public school 'science schools or blocks' thus date from the decade or so after 1918, e.g. at the City of London School[39] in 1927 and at Cheltenham College in 1921, where two old museum rooms were converted into laboratories at a cost of £3,500 of which £1,200 was spent on fittings.[40]

When the Hadow Committee, reporting in 1926, advised the establishment of modern schools, it was clearly aware of the importance of ensuring that the work of these schools was not hampered by a provision of equipment and accommodation which was markedly inferior to that prevailing in the grant-aided secondary grammar schools. The Committee thus recommended that the 'construction and equipment of Modern Schools should approximate to the standard required from time to time by the Board in schools working under the Regulations for Secondary Schools'.[41] The prospect of a greater number and variety of 'secondary' schools, created as a result of Hadow reorganisation, made it necessary for the Board of Education to review its Secondary School Building Regulations. The 1914 Regulations, supplemented in 1925 by a Circular dealing with science accommodation and school libraries,[42] were

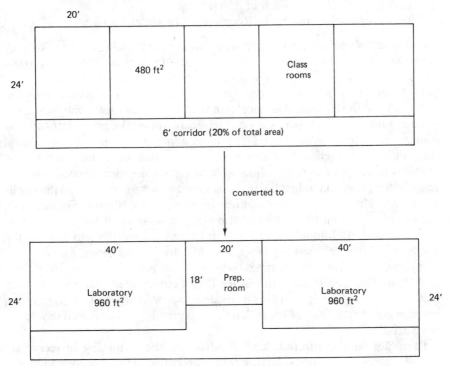

Figure 7.3 Conversion of five classrooms to two 960 ft² laboratories and one 360 ft² preparation room.

replaced by new *Suggestions for the Planning of New Buildings for Secondary Schools*, issued, as Educational Pamphlet no. 86, by the Board[43] in 1931. The change from 'Regulations' to 'Suggestions' is less significant than may appear to be the case since the earlier Regulations, although cast in an appropriate form, were not 'strictly speaking . . . regulations at all'.[44] Both the Regulations and the Suggestions stated, with adequate precision, the expectations of the Board in the matter of school building and the Suggestions were distinguished only by the inclusion of a more extensive commentary upon the Board's views.

Pamphlet no. 86 contained specimen schedules of accommodation and details of the 'science rooms' regarded as appropriate in grant-aided schools of various sizes and types.[45] For a single form entry boys' school, the Board recommended one general laboratory (960 ft.²) and a preparation/store room of about 230 ft.^{2} in area. For a four-form entry boys' school with about 620–660 pupils on the roll, the Board advised the following schedule of science accommodation:

> One Elementary Laboratory for Physics and Biology of 960 ft.^{2}
> One Elementary Laboratory for Chemistry of 900 ft.^{2}
> One Advanced Laboratory for Physics of 450 ft.^{2}
> One Advanced Laboratory for Chemistry of 450 ft.^{2}
> Two Lecture Rooms, each of 550 ft.^{2}
> Two Preparation and Store Rooms each of about 230 ft.^{2}

The absence of specialist accommodation for the advanced teaching of biology is noteworthy, as is the suggestion that the needs of teaching elementary physics and biology could be met by a single, dual-purpose, laboratory.

The laboratory provision suggested for girls' schools reflected both the dominance of the biological science(s) in the curricula of these schools and the smaller numbers of girls who stayed at school to undertake post-Matriculation courses in science. Where the latter condition did not prevail, the Board suggested that the schedule of laboratory accommodation should be the same as that which applied in boys' schools of a corresponding size. In coeducational schools, the provision 'might be on the same scale as it would be if all the pupils were boys', although a number of alternatives were also offered. For example, the Board suggested that a specialist biology laboratory of 900 ft.^{2} might be included, with additional space for storage and preparation, to replace the combined 960 ft.^{2} elementary laboratory for physics and biology.

In smaller schools, of all types, where it was not possible to justify the provision of advanced laboratories, the Board commented that it would 'help matters . . . if . . . the original plans (provided) two ordinary classrooms in such a position near to the Science room that they may readily be converted should the need arise'.

Pamphlet 86 also offered detailed advice on the furnishing of secondary school science laboratories, lecture rooms and other related accommodation. Preparation rooms were to 'be 10 feet wide', 'run the full width of the labora-tory' and be so designed as to provide adequate storage space. A greenhouse, preferably with access directly from a laboratory, was regarded as 'desirable' in those schools in which biology was taught. A separate balance room was regarded as unnecessary since it led to 'overcrowding' and made it difficult for the teacher to supervise the pupils. Laboratory walls were not to be plastered because they provided 'useful working surfaces' and windows were to be 'disposed so as to leave as large an amount of wall space as possible'. Special 'dark rooms' were not recommended but it was thought necessary to make arrangements to partially darken advanced physical laboratories and lecture rooms.

The most detailed recommendations in Pamphlet 86 relate to the design and fitting of laboratories for the teaching of chemistry. The Board advised that benches should never be placed with one end 'abutting on a wall' and that sufficient 'island' benches be provided to 'accommodate a normal class'. Single benches, 2 ft. wide, and double benches, $3\frac{1}{2}$ ft. wide, were to be separated by gangways of 3 ft. and 4 ft. respectively. The advantages of double benches in 'saving' floor space and in making 'traffic and supervision easier' were emphasised and specifications were offered for a 10 ft. demonstration bench and a 30 ft. length of side bench to accommodate balances and other items of equipment.[46] Figure 7.4 illustrates an arrangement of single benches, wall bench and demonstration bench in a 960 ft.² laboratory which Savage, writing in 1964, described[47] as the commonest 'a generation or more ago', i.e. during the 1930s.

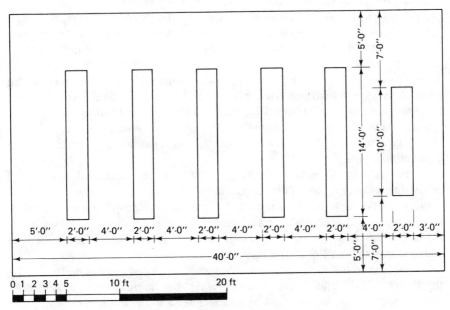

Figure 7.4 Elementary Laboratory with five single benches.

When the Hadow Report was published in 1926, the Board of Education withdrew the 1914 Building Regulations for Public Elementary Schools. No new Building Regulations for this type of school were issued until 1939, when the Board responded to representations about the 'inconvenience caused to Local Authorities, Managers and Architects by the absence of any reasonably accessible indication ... of the principles which should govern the planning of new schools, especially those for the education of senior children'.[48] There are significant differences in the provision suggested in 1931 for the secondary schools and that recommended in 1939 for the new 'senior schools', to be planned with a school leaving age of fifteen in view. The enduring nature of these differences, based as they were on the advice given by the Board[49] to local authorities after 1926, was to be a particular handicap to those secondary modern schools created from senior schools in the reorganisation of secondary education following the 1944 Act. In the 1939 Suggestions for the planning of buildings for public elementary schools, the term 'science room' is preferred to 'laboratory' and the schedules of accommodation suggested[50] for two and three form entry senior schools include only one such room of 960 ft.[2] which could, in appropriate circumstances, be replaced by two rooms, each of 600 ft.[2] . The schedule of accommodation for smaller senior schools, i.e. those with an annual intake of approximately 40 pupils and a maximum of 160 pupils following a four-year course, was thought to raise particular problems. The Board's solution was to recommend[51] the building of 'at least two' multi-purpose rooms in schools of this kind, one of which, not less than 900 ft.[2] in area, could be devoted to 'Manual Instruction and Science'.[52]

In furnishing the science room(s) of a senior school, the 'principal aim' was 'simplicity', the only special feature regarded by the Board as necessary being a demonstration bench 'at least eight feet long by about two feet' or, at most, 'two feet six inches wide', and 'two feet nine inches high'. It was not necessary for pupils' benches to be 'of an elaborate type' and ordinary solid tables with drawers were preferred to other types of furniture. These tables were to be without sinks and without fixed points for gas supply. The science room, although equipped primarily for general science, also needed to meet the requirements of biology teaching and a 'small glass-house', very close to the science room and 'accessible from it', was regarded as valuable in this connection.

As far as storage and preparation facilities were concerned, the Board advised that the equipment and apparatus of the science room was 'part of the furnishing'. As such, much of it could be kept in the Room where it would be readily available for use. Where a separate store or preparation room was to be provided, the Board argued[53] that the science room itself could[54] then be reduced in size to a floor area of 900 ft.[2] .

In addition to the Regulations and Suggestions issued from time to time by the Board of Education, there were several other publications which offered advice and information to teachers and architects in the matters of laboratory design, furniture and fitting. Munby's *School Laboratory Fittings*, published in 1929, is one of the more readable, yet wide-ranging, surveys of the problems of equipping science laboratories and lecture rooms to be published in the inter-war period. Intended primarily 'to help the Science Master . . . to crystallise his ideas and put them into a form capable of transmission to those who have to carry them into practice',[55] the book includes an account of the problems of providing current electricity, other than for lighting, in a school laboratory and is now of additional interest because of the estimated costs quoted for various laboratory fittings. A double chemical bench was 'usually worth £7 10s to £8 per foot of its length', inclusive of the cost of gas, water and drainage services. The corresponding figures for a lecture bench and 'plain physics table' were £3 10s per linear foot and 7s per square foot respectively. Fume cupboards 'with tiled bases, sink drainage, gas supply and a gas flue' cost approximately £9 per foot of length for short ones of about 4 feet' or '£8 or less for long ones'.[56]

Architects were able to turn to more technical sources and, in particular, to professional journals which occasionally carried accounts and illustrations of the construction of individual science laboratories or 'blocks'. The suite of laboratories and classrooms completed in the mid-1930s at St John's School, Leatherhead, to 'take the place of those out of date', was described in some detail[57] in the *Architects' Journal* of 2 July 1936. The two-storey building, comprising fourteen classrooms, mathematics room, lecture room and laboratory accommodation for physics and chemistry, together with appropriate storage and preparation facilities, was completed at a total cost[58] of £18,312 or 1s 6d 'per foot cube', inclusive of all laboratory fittings.

It is difficult to assess with any precision the extent to which the provision of laboratories and equipment during the inter-war years matched the recommendations of the Board of Education. However, it seems likely that very few schools exceeded the Board's specification and that the science accommodation in many elementary, senior and secondary schools fell below the standards scheduled in the Board's 'Suggestions'. Of a sample of thirty-nine urban secondary schools for boys, each with over 400 pupils and offering a recognised advanced course in science in 1925, nineteen possessed laboratory and ancillary accommodation which H.M. Inspectorate adjudged unsatisfactory, either because the number and size of rooms were insufficient to provide for the work required or because the rooms were badly planned.[59] In some cases, a 'good deal' of the science teaching in these schools was provided in classrooms not adapted in any way for experimental work. In other instances, the accommodation available severely curtailed the scope and amount of science work which could be undertaken. In ten of the thirty-nine schools, one or more advanced laboratories were needed and seven of the schools had no science lecture room or a similar facility for demonstration. The Inspectors concluded that custom had reconciled the science teachers to bad conditions and that many of them thus lacked adequate standards with which to compare their own accommodation and facilities.[60]

It is difficult to relate these impressions of the Inspectorate to the data obtained two years later by the Science Masters' Association from questionnaires returned from a large sample of 649 secondary schools.[61] However, both sources emphasise the wide variation in the nature and extent of laboratory provision in the secondary schools at this time. Table 7.1 shows[62] the

Table 7.1 Laboratory Accommodation Classified by the Examining Authority to which Schools submitted their Pupils 1927

Group of Schools	Average ft.²/boy	ft.²/boy period
Oxford Local	9.07	1.66
Central Welsh Board	10.67	1.48
N.U.J.M.B.	8.39	1.46
Cambridge Local	8.61	1.46
Oxford and Cambridge	9.82	1.42
Bristol University	7.66	1.37
Durham University	7.52	1.22
London University	7.78	0.99

range of working laboratory space in secondary schools in 1927, categorised by reference to the Examination Boards for whose School Certificate examinations the responding school normally submitted candidates. In the words of the Science Masters' Association, why schools associated with the Oxford Local and London Boards diverged 'so much and in the opposite direction' from what seemed to be a mean was 'not easily accounted for'.[63] The Association noted that lecture room accommodation also varied 'a great deal', adding that since 'the average of accessory rooms' (balance rooms, preparation rooms, store rooms, etc.) was less than one per school in its sample, 'a very great number of schools' were also without facilities of this kind.

There seems little doubt, therefore, that the science teaching accommodation in a significant number of boys' secondary schools during the 1920s, and probably somewhat beyond, fell below the standards being urged by the Board of Education. Such a situation may be attributed to three factors; the effect of economy measures on the building programme, an increase in the numbers of boys attending secondary schools, and an extension of the scope of the work undertaken in science, notably at sixth-form level.[64] In general, the position in girls' schools continued to be much less satisfactory than in the secondary schools for boys, although the smaller numbers of girls studying physical science may have eased the pressure on such accommodation as was available and obviated the serious overcrowding of laboratory classes which was commonplace in many boys' schools in the inter-war years. As far as the senior schools were concerned, the Board noted in 1931 that some of these schools were working under restrictions imposed by their accommodation and that those which were housed in 'older buildings' were hampered by the unsuitability of the rooms available for practical work.[65]

The variation in laboratory provision from one school to another was matched by a corresponding variation in the money available for the purchase of science teaching apparatus and materials. The sample data, published by the Board of Education in 1925 and summarised in Table 7.2, revealed a range from 33s to 2s 2d in the amount of money spent annually per pupil on purchasing equipment and chemicals.[66] Some caution is necessary in making any inference from these figures since a low annual per capita expenditure may indicate that a school was well equipped and adequately supplied with chemicals and other consumable materials. It is thus important to note that H.M. Inspectors reported 'a sufficiency of apparatus and chemicals' up to the level of the School Certificate examination in the sample of schools to which the data in Table 7.2 refer.[67] As far as chemistry is concerned, it is likely that the principal deficiency in equipment related to the teaching of sixth-form physical chemistry, a branch of the subject which developed rapidly at this level in the secondary schools in the inter-war period. It is also important to record the Board's more general view that, although the conditions affecting science teaching in many boys' schools were 'far from ideal' in 1925, they represented 'a real and substantial advance' when compared with those which had prevailed fifteen years earlier.[68]

Table 7.2 Variation of Expenditure on School Science per (boy) pupil, 1925

No. of Boys in a School Doing Science	Total Cost per Head per Year	
	s	d
720	10	4
380	7	6
800	4	0
515	18	8
530	6	10
329	12	1
510	18	2
420	21	2
509	13	3
643	11	1
418	10	8
598	14	2
290	6	10
420	33	0
608	2	2
390	12	4
380	9	0
330	13	9
500	6	2
330	11	6
540	4	6
275	5	11
301	21	10
200	14	4
350	16	6
320	17	6
411	19	6
423	18	0
560	10	0
313	10	0

Since the expansion of school science teaching which took place after 1918, especially at sixth-form level, was not matched by a general increase in laboratory provision, it was inevitable that attention would be focused on the optimum use of those laboratories which were available. Adequate technical support and efficient laboratory management were both regarded as important in this respect. The Thomson Committee had advocated 'the employment of a mechanic sufficiently skilled to be able to repair instruments, and to make simple pieces of apparatus for teaching', but, of the thirty-nine boys' secondary schools investigated by the Inspectorate in 1925, eleven possessed no laboratory assistance of any kind. As a result, the laboratories in these schools were ill-kept, valuable apparatus was left unused or deteriorating and science teachers were 'wasting their time' doing work which could have been done more economically by men 'of more modest qualifications'.[69] The Science Masters' Association felt strongly on this latter point, arguing that just as it paid 'a firm of doctors to keep a dispenser and errand boys', so it paid 'a school to keep skilled and unskilled assistants in addition to the masters'. The matter was simply one of sound business economics.[70] Fifteen of the thirty-nine schools employed laboratory 'attendants', but, for the most part, these were youths who were badly paid and who left to get a better job 'just when they were beginning to be useful'.[71] Occasionally, schools endeavoured to deal with the shortage of laboratory assistance by providing the science teaching staff with an unusually generous allowance of non-teaching periods but a more economically sound and long-term solution was clearly needed. The London County Council allowed its schools to employ laboratory assistants in accordance with the schedule summarised[72] in Table 7.3. Under this scheme, boys were paid 5s a

Table 7.3   L.C.C. Schedule for Employment of
Laboratory Assistants, 1926

Type of School	Laboratory Assistants Permitted
400+ pupils, approved advanced course in science and mathematics	1 adult and 1 boy
400+ pupils, no advanced course	1 adult
Less than 400 pupils with an advanced course	1 adult
Other Schools	1 boy

week, rising to 7s 6d after three months, and to 10s after a further twelve months. Men received 20s a week, rising to 35s a week by annual increments of 2s 6d, with a minimum of 25s on attaining the age of twenty-one. Even when these basic rates were supplemented, as they were[73] in 1926, they remained well below the level of pay of many other occupations and, in particular, of the best-paid and trained technicians employed by some of the more distinguished public schools.[74] None the less, the L.C.C. scheme, which seems to have been without parallel in other authorities at this time, was 'something definite towards which, as a minimum, an effort should be made'.

An alternative arrangement for securing laboratory assistance was to employ pupils who had completed their School Certificate course and who wished to continue their education but were unable to do so without some financial aid. Such pupils were often expected to give half of their time to the service of the school and to attend classes during the other half, preparing themselves for the London Matriculation or other examination. Such arrangements were widely adopted and they were particularly important and formalised in some areas, e.g. at the Swindon and North Wiltshire Secondary School and Technical Institution.[75]

The Science Masters' Association gave attention on a number of occasions between the wars to remedying the 'unbusiness-like and uneconomical' administration of secondary school science laboratories. The most thorough survey of the problem was undertaken by a subcommittee on laboratory assistants which reported to the General Committee of the Association in November 1938. The investigation involved 175 schools, although, in the words of the subcommittee, had the facts been 'available from every secondary school which teaches science', the whole position would have been found to be 'even less satisfactory' than that revealed by those schools in the sample.[76] In 35 per cent of the schools, there was 'no laboratory assistance whatsoever' and in another 40 per cent, the assistance was 'inadequate', often because pupils of the school operated as part-time assistants, a practice condemned by the Science Masters' Association. As a result of its findings, the Association decided to accept the responsibility of framing a suitable course upon which prospective laboratory assistants could be tested by examination, successful candidates receiving the Association's 'Certificate of Competence'. In addition, a scheme of classification and remuneration of school laboratory technicians was proposed.[77] This work of the Association was an important attempt to break the vicious circle which appeared to govern the employment of laboratory assistants in the secondary schools. The few posts available to trained laboratory stewards had branded the job as a 'blind alley' occupation, so that the supply of candidates willing to prepare for such work was inadequate, both in quality and in quantity, and the appropriate training facilities remained undeveloped.

However, the image of a 'blind-alley' occupation was not to be shed easily and the work of the Science Masters' Association subcommittee acquired a more enduring value only in 1950 when the City and Guilds of London Institute adopted a modified form of the syllabus, suggested by the Association, as the scheme of work leading to its Intermediate Certificate Examination for laboratory technicians. Although the intentions of the Association were inevitably frustrated by the outbreak of the war, there is no doubt of its commitment to increasing the quantity and the quality of assistance available to science teachers working in the grammar and public schools. Asked by the Norwood Committee, during the war, whether there were any circumstances or conditions of a general nature which it would specially indicate as hampering the full development of science in the secondary schools, the Association referred to the 'inadequate laboratories and equipment in some schools' and the 'inadequate (sometimes complete lack of) laboratory assistance'.[78] Both these points were re-emphasised in the evidence of the Association of Women Science Teachers but, significantly, the women's organisation gave priority to the shortage of competent science teachers in the girls' grammar schools.

Throughout the inter-war period, and for well beyond, the majority of science teachers were forced 'to struggle with the sole help of some students who, naturally, (had) received little or no instruction in the care of the laboratory and its apparatus, nor even in the preparation of the necessary reagents'. It was to meet the needs of these teachers that Sutcliffe's *School Laboratory Management*[79] was published in 1929. The book was a pioneering work in its field and served to supplement the more narrowly technical publications dealing with glass manipulation and other laboratory arts. It was reprinted in 1937 and reissued in 1950 as a second edition which incorporated the changes made necessary by the Education Act of 1944 and the new Building Regulations issued by the Ministry of Education in 1945. It remained a useful book in the field of school laboratory management throughout the 1950s, passing out of print only as the new school science curricula initiated at the end of the decade made different and increased demands on laboratory design, techniques, reagents and apparatus.

Sutcliffe's book contained only a passing reference to the contribution which pupil-based practical work should play in school science teaching.[80] This issue, a matter of lively controversy at the time of the Thomson Committee's criticism of Armstrong's heurism, gained added significance with the development of schemes of work in general science. Although the debates within the Science Masters' Association and the British Association failed to identify[81] the relative advantages of demonstration and pupil-based laboratory work, the view that practical science should be based firmly on exercises conducted by the pupils rather than on demonstrations performed by the teacher came to be strongly reinforced in the inter-war years. In the 1927 *Handbook of Suggestions for Teachers*, it is possible to discern the reaction of the Board of Education to the earlier excesses of heurism. The Board warned that 'the experienced teacher will never dispense entirely with the demonstration lesson', the value of which had been 'too often forgotten'. Ten years later, the Board chose to press a somewhat different point, claiming that 'the ideas which a child gets from doing things for himself' became 'part of his mental equipment more completely than those he (gained) from seeing things done or hearing or reading about them'.[82] The response of the Science Masters' Association to this change in the climate of opinion and, more particularly, to the charge that its general science course encouraged demonstration exercises at the expense of pupils' practical work, was to include an appropriate chapter and schedule of experiments in the post-war edition of *The Teaching of General Science*.

Under the provisions of the 1944 Education Act, the Minister of Education assumed responsibility for prescribing the standards of accommodation to which new schools built and maintained by local education authorities were required to conform. The relevant Regulations, issued in March 1945, were accompanied by a Memorandum[83] consisting of 'short explanatory notes on the various matters dealt with in the Regulations, together with three appendices'. No attempt was made to prescribe in detail 'the precise number and type of the individual practical rooms' needed in schools of various types so that local authorities were allowed considerable discretion, provided only that the specified 'total aggregate area' was not exceeded. The Ministry's suggestions for the 'distribution of practical accommodation' were included in Appendix 2 of the Memorandum, in the form of a Table indicating how the 'aggregate area' could be distributed within secondary schools of different sizes and types. The schedule of science teaching accommodation recommended for a three-form entry, eleven to eighteen secondary school is summarised[84] in Table 7.4. For smaller eleven to eighteen schools, the recommended provision was reduced appropriately, but eleven to sixteen schools were expected to make do with a single, multi-purpose laboratory of 960 ft.² whatever the size of their annual intake.[85]

Table 7.4   Recommended Schedule of Science Accommodation for a Three-form entry, 11–18 Secondary School (Ministry of Education, 1945)

Type of Accommodation	Area /ft.²	Number Recommended
General Laboratory	960	3
Advanced Laboratory	450	1
Lecture Room	540	1
Preparation Room	230	3

Under the Regulations issued in 1945, local authorities and other interested parties submitted details of their school building projects, together with estimated costs, to the Ministry of Education for approval. It soon became clear that the costs of apparently comparable projects varied widely, in some instances by almost a factor of two.[86] With hindsight, it is not difficult to explain this variation. The cessation of school building during the war, coupled with changes in building costs, constructional techniques and standards of educational provision, meant that no post-war consensus existed about the realistic cost of a school place. Accordingly, in 1949, the Ministry of Education introduced a system of cost limits per pupil place which, in conjunction with the annual building programme[87] and the Building Regulations, controlled the massive expansion in school building which took place during the 1950s and 1960s.

New Building Regulations were issued[88] in 1949, 1951, 1954 and 1959 and, whenever new wage settlements or regulations were introduced in the building industry, the cost limits per pupil place were adjusted and local authorities informed via Circulars issued by the Ministry. In 1962, the Ministry introduced the so-called 'Building Code'[89] which consolidated, in a loose-leaf form, 'all the information on limits of costs, standards and procedures' required by local education authorities and which had previously been 'dispersed over a number of circulars and administrative memoranda'. The Building Code was subsequently updated by the incorporation of amendment lists issued under cover of a circular, administrative memorandum or letter as appropriate.

The legislative framework outlined in the various Building Regulations issued after 1945 was supplemented by more detailed examples of school construction described in a series of Building Bulletins. However, local authorities were under no obligation to accept the advice implicit in the Building Bulletins except in so far as the guidance given was specifically stated to be an explanation or amplification of a requirement[90] in the Building Regulations. Building Bulletin no. 2, issued[91] in February 1950, was concerned with the provision of accommodation in secondary modern schools containing between ten and twenty classes, i.e. two- to four-form entry schools. Only one science laboratory of 930–990 ft.^{2} in area was recommended for schools of this kind, although it was recognised that a single laboratory could not accommodate all the work in science which would normally be required in the larger schools with which Building Bulletin no. 2 was concerned. Accordingly, it was recommended that the science laboratory be planned with 'one of the general classrooms adjacent' so as to provide additional space for demonstration and group work. A preparation room, 'not less than 10 ft. in width and 250 sq.ft. in area', was regarded as an essential adjunct to the laboratory which was to be 'fully equipped for specialist use'.[92]

Table 7.5   Science Laboratories and Other Practical Rooms, Each of 960 ft.^{2}, suggested for Coeducational Secondary Modern Schools, 1954

Size of School (Form Entry)	No. of Science Laboratories	No. of general practical rooms
1	1 Handicraft & Science Room	
2	1	1
3	2	1
4	2	2
5 or 6	3	2

Building Bulletin no. 2 was supplemented in 1951 by no. 2A, which sought to examine how the principles underlying the planning of secondary modern schools could be applied to 'other types and sizes of secondary schools'. However, in 1954, the Ministry prescribed reduced minimum areas of teaching accommodation for one- and two-form entry schools and, as a result of the consequential changes in the formula for calculating cost limits, a new edition[93] of Building Bulletin no. 2A became necessary. The emphasis in designing secondary modern schools was still placed on flexibility and, in particular, on the use of adjacent accommodation if more laboratory space were needed, although two or three science laboratories were suggested[94] for modern schools with 450 or more pupils on the roll. (See Table 7.5.) In the grammar schools, where laboratories were usually 'very different, both in number and in character' from those needed in the modern schools, it was recommended that the science accommodation be planned so as to enable 'from 40 to 70 per cent of sixth-form pupils to undertake advanced work in at least two sciences'.[95] Since the advanced laboratories of about 450 ft.^{2} in area, once considered adequate to accommodate sixth-form practical classes, were clearly too small for contemporary needs, it was also suggested that the advanced work could be undertaken by groups of sixteen to twenty-four pupils working in a 960 ft.^{2} elementary laboratory, designed for the larger group of thirty pupils. Official recognition of the problems of using a 960 ft.^{2} laboratory for both elementary and advanced work did nothing to temper the criticism of this suggestion by the Science Masters' Association.[96]

The numbers of laboratories and demonstration rooms for grammar schools of various types and sizes, suggested in Building Bulletin no. 2A, are summarised[97] in Table 7.6. The figures in this Table represent a higher standard of laboratory provision than that regarded officially as adequate in 1945, but it should be noted that Building Bulletin no. 2A endorsed the view that it was not necessary to incorporate the same standard of laboratory accommodation when designing boys', girls' and coeducational grammar schools of a given size. This, too, was criticised by the Science Masters' Association.[98]

Table 7.6   Numbers of Laboratories (L) and Demonstration Rooms (D) Suggested for Grammar Schools, 1954

| Type of School | Size of School | | | | | |
| | 2 form Entry | | 3 form Entry | | 4 form Entry | |
	L	D	L	D	L	D
Boys	4	0	5	1	–	–
Girls	3	0	4	0	–	–
Coeducational	4	0	5*	0*	5‡	1‡
Coeducational	–	–	5†	1†	6§	1§

*   90 Sixth-form pupils
† 180 Sixth-form pupils
‡ 120 Sixth-form pupils
§ 240 Sixth-form pupils
Each laboratory=960 ft.^{2}. Demonstration Room between 650 and 750 ft.^{2}.

In addition to providing examples of the science teaching accommodation likely to be needed in secondary modern and grammar schools, Building Bulletin no. 2A discussed the problems of providing such accommodation in secondary technical, bilateral and multilateral schools. Comprehensive schools, which clearly involved a rejection of the assumption that pupils could be classified according to their fitness for a grammar, modern or technical curriculum, were discussed only briefly. The official view was that it was 'impracticable and probably undesirable' to make recommendations about the planning of comprehensive schools with expertise still so 'rudimentary'.[99] It was considered, however, that a comprehensive school was likely to need much the same kind and amount of teaching accommodation as a multilateral school with the same annual intake.

Throughout the 1950s and beyond, the Development Group of the Architects and Building Branch of the Ministry of Education collaborated with local education authorities in research into the educational and technical requirements of the developing secondary schools. The results of the joint investigations, often embodying unusual features of design, planning or construction, were made available to others by means of the Building Bulletins and were an important contribution to the transformation of British school design which began in the early 1950s. Expertise of another, if related, kind was to be found in those authorities associated with CLASP, a consortium founded in 1957 to share and develop the system of school building pioneered[100] by the Nottinghamshire L.E.A. The success in 1960 at the twelfth Milan Triennale of a primary school, designed by the County Architect of Nottinghamshire using the CLASP method of construction, was an international recognition of the quality of the best of the post-war British school building programme.

This was a programme which involved a race against time and which could not get under way until the emergency needs arising from the destruction or damage of about 5,000 schools during the war had been met. It was necessary to accommodate greater numbers of pupils than at any time in history, many of whom stayed at school longer than ever before and architects were required to be receptive to new ideas both in education and in construction techniques. Some elements of the achievement may be quantified. In 1949, it was estimated that at least $2\frac{1}{4}$ million new school places would be needed by 1961. This soon proved to be a serious under-estimate and, by 1959, the stock of school places had been increased by 3 million.[101] Between 1945 and 1959, £19 million were spent on school science teaching accommodation and £4 million on equipment and materials for teaching the science subjects.[102] Plate 8 illustrates[103] a school science laboratory which is typical of the many built during this period.

Plate 8   Chemistry laboratory built for Hertfordshire C.C. in 1958.

Despite the overall magnitude and quality of the achievement of the school building programme, teachers in less than 10 per cent of maintained grammar schools in 1957 considered their science accommodation to be adequate and less than half of these schools could meet the Ministry's own standards for laboratory and ancillary accommodation in new buildings.[104] Provision remained uneven across the country and many older grammar schools faced a serious shortage of laboratory accommodation at a time when the proportion of pupils specialising in science subjects in the expanding sixth forms was increasing steadily.[105] Girls' grammar schools, in which the level of laboratory provision was generally below that found in grammar schools for boys, were particularly affected by the expansion in the sixth-form population.[106] The science teaching facilities in many modern schools also remained seriously deficient, partly because the grammar schools gained a disproportionate share of the money available for laboratories within the post-war building programme.[107]

Table 7.7   Standards of Laboratory and Ancillary
Accommodation, 1954–7

| | | Total Teaching Spaces Based on | |
Size of School	Type of School	Building Bulletin 2A	Industrial Fund Standards
2-form Entry	Boys	4	6
	Girls	3	6
	Mixed	4	6
3-form Entry	Boys	6	10
	Girls	4	10
	Mixed	5	10
4-form Entry	Boys	7	11
	Girls	5	11
	Mixed	6	11

The Ministry's recommended standards of laboratory provision were, at all levels, below those set by the panel of Assessors to the Industrial Fund for the Advancement of Scientific Education in Schools, established in 1955 to provide capital grants to improve science teaching facilities in those independent, public and direct-grant schools which could not 'receive assistance from public funds for capital works'.[108] The Assessors accepted that separate accommodation should be provided for elementary (960 ft.^{2}) and advanced work (600 ft.^{2}) in physics and chemistry and assumed that a laboratory or lecture/demonstration room could be regarded as 'fully used' if it were used for teaching purposes for two-thirds of the total time available for teaching during a school week. Using these guidelines, the Assessors recommended[109] that a three-form entry 'grammar' school should incorporate three elementary laboratories (960 ft.^{2}), two advanced laboratories for physics and chemistry, each of 600 ft.^{2} and two Demonstration Rooms, one for physics and one for chemistry, each of approximately 540 ft.^{2} . If one advanced and one elementary biology laboratory, together with a lecture/demonstration room, are added to this schedule of accommodation, a three-form entry selective school would have a total of ten 'teaching spaces' available for science. Comparable figures, computed for schools of other sizes, are presented[110] in Table 7.7 which also compares these standards of provision with those suggested in Building Bulletin no. 2A.

In 1957, the provision of laboratory accommodation in schools of the 'grammar school type' was investigated by means of a questionnaire distributed on behalf of a joint committee of the Science Masters' Association, Association of Women Science Teachers, National Union of Teachers and the 'Joint Four' Secondary Associations. Two thousand questionnaires were issued but, of the 566 schools which responded, only 472, involving some 250,000 pupils, provided statistically useful data. The analysis of the responses highlighted the problem of defining a standard of adequacy of laboratory provision and the results were therefore presented with reference to both the Ministry's standards and those established by the panel of Assessors to the Industrial Fund. The data in Table 7.8 may represent a somewhat optimistic picture of the position in maintained grammar schools in 1957 since there were grounds for believing that the sample of schools responding to the questionnaire were probably above average in staffing, equipment and accommodation. In addi-

Table 7.8   Laboratory Provision in Schools Compared with Theoretical Standards, 1957 and (1959)

| Size of School | Type | No. in Sample | | Percentage Adequate with Respect to | | | |
				Ministry Standards		Industrial Fund Standards	
2 form entry	G	110	(140)	27.3	(34)	0	(2)
	D.G.	21	(23)	66.7	(87)	9.5	(39)
	I	25	(23)	84.0	(78)	20.0	(61)
3 form entry	G	206	(258)	49.3	(48)	0.5	(0)
	D.G.	14	(25)	85.5	(76)	7.2	(4)
	I	2	(15)	50.0	(87)	0	(60)
4 form entry	G	57	(149)	61.4	(50)	0	(0.7)
	D.G.	2	(8)	100.0	(100)	0	(13)
	I	3	(5)	100.0	(100)	33.3	(60)
All Schools	G	373	(547)	44	(45)	0.3	(0.7)
	D.G.	37	(56)	78	(84)	8	(20)
	I	30	(43)	83	(84)	20	(60)

G   = Grant Aided
D.G. = Direct Grant
I   = Independent
Figures given thus ( ) refer to the later 1959 survey (see text).

tion, it should be noted that, if the same standards of laboratory provision were applied to girls' schools as applied to boys' schools, then the percentages quoted for 1957 in column four of Table 7.8 would decrease by a factor of approximately two.[111]

Unlike the Ministry of Education, the Committee administering the Industrial Fund made specific recommendations about the provision of ancillary rooms for science, arguing that each science subject required its own preparation room and advising the provision of a balance room when sixth-form work in chemistry was undertaken. In addition, a chemical store and a workshop were regarded as essential to the efficient operation of a science department of whatever size. Table 7.9 indicates the percentages of grammar, direct-grant and independent schools which were adequately provided with ancillary rooms in 1957 when judged by these standards.[112] In the view of the Chairman of the joint investigating committee, there were 'marked shortages of preparation rooms, store rooms, demonstration rooms and balance rooms'.[113]

Table 7.9   Adequacy of Provision of Ancillary Rooms in Schools by Industrial Fund Standards, 1957 and (1959)

Type of School	No. of Schools in sample		Preparation Room		Balance Room Chemical Store		Workshop	
			\% of Schools in which Accommodation is adequate with respect to					
L.E.A. Grammar	362	(570)	21	(34)	52	(54)	10	(16)
Direct Grant	36	(58)	31	(45)	47	(67)	22	(40)
Independent	23	(44)	36	(64)	57	(80)	26	(66)

Figures given thus ( ) refer to 1959: see text.

The joint committee also examined the extent of the laboratory assistance available to the science teachers in public, direct-grant and maintained grammar schools in 1957. The findings of the Committee, summarised in Table 7.10, show that 25 per cent (ninety-two) of the sample of maintained grammar schools in England and Wales had no laboratory assistance of any kind at this time. For reasons already indicated, the proportion for maintained grammar schools as a whole was almost certainly higher, perhaps closer to the 46 per cent reported in a study only three years earlier.[114] The supply of laboratory technicians indicated[115] in Table 7.10 may be compared with the staffing establishment recommended for grammar and technical schools by the Science Masters' Association in 1955. The Association's standards are quoted[116] in Table 7.11 and, if these were applied to the sample of schools investigated in 1957, none of the boys' schools, four girls' schools and only two coeducational schools would be regarded as adequately staffed with laboratory assistants. In

Table 7.10   Provision of Laboratory Technicians in Schools 1957 and (1959)

Type of School	Number in Sample	Numbers of Technicians						% with at least one Senior and one Junior
		None	Part Time	One Junior	Two Juniors or more	One Senior	One Senior and one Junior	
L.E.A. Grammar	362 (568)	92 (126)	31 (48)	78 (127)	14 (18)	93 (163)	54 (86)	15 (15)
Direct Grant	36 (58)	20 (17)	1 (8)	6 (2)	0 (1)	4 (15)	5 (15)	14 (26)
Independent	23 (44)	7 (7)	3 (1)	3 (2)	1 (0)	2 (9)	7 (25)	30 (57)
Comprehensive	10 (13)	3 (3)	0 (0)	1 (2)	1 (1)	0 (2)	5 (4)	50 (31)

Figures given thus ( ) refer to 1959: see text.

addition, if the standard of laboratory provision accepted for boys' grammar schools were applied to girls' and coeducational schools of the same size, then not one[117] of the maintained grammar schools in the sample of 472 schools was staffed to the standards recommended by the Science Masters' Association in 1955.

Table 7.11   Minimum Number of Technicians
Related to Number of Teaching Spaces, as
Recommended by the Science Masters'
Association in 1955

Number of Teaching Spaces in Full-Time Use for Science	Minimum number of Technicians
8	2 Senior+2 Junior
7	1 Senior+3 Junior
6 or 5	1 Senior+2 Junior
4 or 3	1 Senior+1 Junior

'Senior' refers to Grades III and IV and Junior to Grades I and II as defined in the 1955 S.M.A. Report on Laboratory Technicians.

In the circumstances, any other finding would have been surprising. The Association quite properly emphasised the need to employ technicians who had been suitably trained and recommended the City and Guilds Laboratory Technicians Intermediate Certificate as an appropriate qualification for a school laboratory technician. However, the facilities for studying for such a qualification, although expanding, were severely limited. In 1954, only twenty-four centres, mainly technical colleges, offered appropriate and recognised courses of instruction and the numbers of candidates, eighteen in 1951, ninety-six in 1954, were small.[118] In addition, many other opportunities, usually better paid and with more favourable career prospects, were available outside the schools which were thus unable to attract more than a few of the small number of laboratory technicians who were formally qualified.

In its earlier advocacy of the need to provide laboratory assistance on an adequate scale in the schools, the Science Masters' Association had emphasised the importance of making optimum use of the time and skill of the more highly qualified school science teachers.[119] In the 1950s, a new dimension was added to the argument, namely that the inadequate supply of trained laboratory technicians, like the shortage of science teachers, was adversely affecting the production of qualified scientific manpower, with 'grave consequences to the nation'.[120] Despite this claim, it is clear that a solution to the problem could emerge only gradually, as training facilities were expanded, qualifications were rationalised and recognised by employers and a career structure, with appropriate salary scales, for laboratory technicians became established on a national basis. Such conditions began to exert a beneficial influence on the schools only in the 1960s although, as subsequent studies by the Association for Science Education showed,[121] many obstacles remained to be overcome. Even in 1968, school laboratory assistants accounted for only 0.4 per cent of the country's technical manpower, compared with 1.4 per cent then needed to provide a level of support regarded as adequate when judged by the Association's own criteria.[122]

The 1957 inquiry by the Science Masters' Association and other organisations revealed that a significant number of science laboratories were planned or actually being built in both the maintained and the private sector of secondary education. For this reason, and because the response rate was low, the questionnaire was reissued in 1959 to about 2,000 L.E.A. grammar, direct-grant and independent schools, of which 734 provided data which was statistically useful in at least some respects. The relevant figures from this subsequent investigation are given[123] in parenthesis in Tables 7.8–7.10. Despite the building or completion of 486 laboratories in the sample of 547 maintained grammar schools in 1958–9, the proportion of those schools in which the science teaching accommodation was adequate by the Ministry's own standards was almost the same in May 1959 as it had been in the smaller sample two years earlier. Another 482 new laboratories were 'approved, but not yet started' within the 547 maintained schools, suggesting that, between 1958 and 1960, the science teaching accommodation in these schools increased at a mean rate slightly in excess of one new laboratory per school. Even allowing for this projected laboratory building programme, the provision of science accommodation in the sample of maintained schools in 1959 was much inferior to that found in the direct-grant and independent schools which had, by this date, taken advantage of the resources available to them from the Industrial Fund for the Advancement of Scientific Education in Schools.

Unlike the maintained grammar schools, where the proportion of schools with at least one senior and one junior laboratory assistant remained constant at 15 per cent, the direct-grant and independent schools also considerably increased[124] their level of technical assistance between 1957 and 1959.

All types of secondary school seem to have shared, although not equally, in the improvement in ancillary accommodation for science teaching which took place between 1957 and 1959 (see Table 7.9). As with laboratories and technical assistance, the provision of ancillary rooms was much more nearly adequate in direct-grant and independent schools than in schools in the maintained sector. Girls' schools, of whatever type, were significantly worse off in all three respects than the corresponding schools for boys.

The disparity between maintained grammar schools on the one hand and direct grant and independent schools on the other, extended to the money available for science teaching and to the ways in which it could be spent. Both of these issues were investigated in 1957 and again in 1959 when the financial position was said not to have 'noticeably improved'. The variation in the amount spent per year per pupil taking science in 1957 was described as 'colossal'. At one extreme,[125] an independent boys' school had '£3 8s 10d per year', while, at the other, one boys' grammar school had 'only 1s 1d'. This condition had not altered by the time of the later survey, with the result that the majority of the grammar schools and of girls' direct grant and independent schools were still subjected to financial constraints which were 'frustrating and inimical' to the work they were called upon to do.[126] Table 7.12 indicates the

Table 7.12   Average Amounts Spent per annum per pupil Taking Science by Type of School, 1959

Type of School	No. in Sample	Boys s d	Girls s d	Coeducational s d
L.E.A. Grammar	578	12 3	8 8	10 10
Direct Grant	54	20 11	8 3	–
Independent	43	27 1	9 8	–
Comprehensive	12	–	–	4 9

average amounts spent per annum per pupil studying science in schools of different types in 1959. The amounts refer to all three principal sciences and were used by the joint investigating committee to suggest that an average amount of 12s 6d was the minimum adequate expenditure per year per pupil studying science. The numbers and types of schools failing to meet this minimum standard, already exceeded by many schools in the independent sector, are given[127] in Table 7.13. It should be added that thirty-six of the 578

Table 7.13   Numbers of Schools Spending Less Than 12s 6d per Annum per Pupil Taking Science, 1959

Type of School	Number in Sample	Number and percentage spending less than 12s 6d per annum per pupil	
L.E.A.			
Boys' Grammar	224	132	59%
Girls' Grammar	166	140	84%
Coeducational Grammar	188	120	64%
Direct Grant			
Boys	34	10	29%
Girls	20	16	80%
Independent			
Boys	34	4	12%
Girls	9	7	78%

L.E.A. grammar schools responding to this element of the questionnaire spent less than 4s 6d per pupil per annum on science and one of these 'acknowledged less than 1s 6d per pupil'.[128] Clearly, the range and variation in expenditure revealed by the Board of Education in 1925 had not disappeared with the passage of over a generation.

Finally, what of school laboratory design in the years since the end of the Second World War? By 1945, some of the disadvantages of the arrangement of benches illustrated in Figure 7.4 had become clear. The restriction in the length of working space imposed by the use of single benches was probably less important than the fact that such an arrangement was particularly expensive to service with gas, electricity, water and drainage. Double-sided laboratory benches helped to overcome both of these difficulties and Figure 7.5 illustrates[129] an arrangement of such benches adopted by the London County

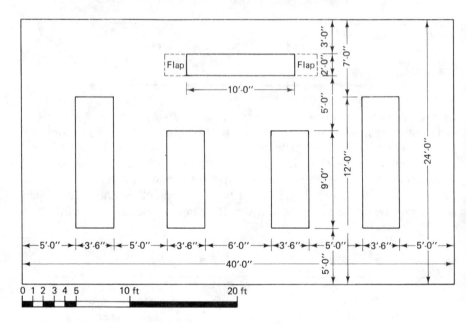

Figure 7.5 Laboratory in which the long wall is used as a teacher's base. (c. 1945).

Council in 1945 and, subsequently, by other education authorities. The 'long wall' of the elementary laboratory is used as the teacher's base and the arrangement provides 84 linear ft. of working space compared with the 70 linear ft. of the arrangement represented in Figure 7.4. However, the angle of viewing of the teacher's bench is increased for some pupils and the arrangement in Figure 7.5 is thus not entirely satisfactory for either class teaching or for demonstration purposes. In an attempt to remedy these deficiencies, many post-war elementary laboratories were built to a shape which was more nearly square (30 ft. by 32 ft.) than rectangular (24 ft. by 40 ft.) while retaining the overall floor area of 960 ft.[2] This pattern was 'widely adopted'[130] despite the fact that the square shape required a larger roof span and thus increased building costs, unless the laboratory was sited at the end of a building.[131]

The design of specialist advanced laboratories continued to be much influenced by the requirements of the practical examinations conducted by the Examination Boards at sixth-form level. In the case of chemistry, the emphasis was on systematic, inorganic qualitative analysis and on volumetric exercises and these required the incorporation of suitable ventilation and weighing facilities in the design of advanced chemistry laboratories. With the introduction into schools of semi-micro techniques of qualitative analysis, the centrally mounted racks of analytical reagents became obsolescent during the 1950s, their function being assumed by smaller, portable units which could be stored in a drawer or cupboard or on a side-bench. With the need for central racks of reagents thus obviated, it became easier to use an advanced chemistry laboratory for general class teaching or demonstration. The smaller, 450 ft.² advanced laboratories were clearly too small to accommodate a class of thirty or more pupils, but developments of this kind undoubtedly made it easier for schools to implement the suggestion, made officially in 1954, that new schools should incorporate 960 ft.² laboratories which could be used for either advanced or elementary work. This larger size also allowed part of the laboratory area to be reserved for a particular activity, e.g. a lecture demonstration, by incorporating an appropriate design feature such as tiered seating.

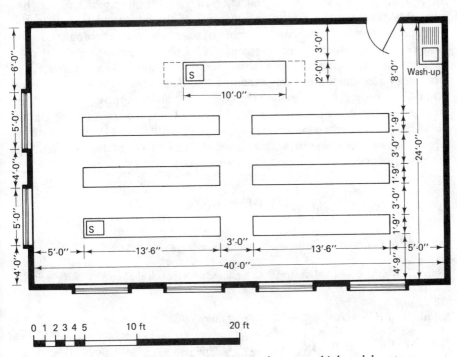

Figure 7.6 Arrangement of benches in an elementary biology laboratory.

The requirements of advanced physics laboratories have been simpler than in the case of chemistry. A reduced level of gas and water services to the pupils' benches has been the norm, emphasis being placed on the provision of flat and uninterrupted working surfaces. Sinks and gas taps have often been confined to side benches although, in some instances, the latter were mounted on the side of the pupil's bench with access via a small hole in the working surface. The benches or tables have, in general, been fixed in position to facilitate the supply of low-voltage d.c. and mains electricity. This restriction was effectively removed with the advent of portable power supplies during the later 1950s, making it unnecessary to incorporate a low voltage facility in the design of advanced physics laboratories.[132]

The needs of elementary biology teaching have, for the most part, been met by laboratories similar in design to that illustrated in Figure 7.6. Until very recently, biology has been much less exacting in its demands for laboratory furniture and equipment than either chemistry or physics and, because of its later arrival in the secondary school curriculum, architects and teachers have had less experience upon which to draw. A recently built advanced biology laboratory, described by Savage in 1964, was only 483 ft.[2] (23 ft. by 21 ft.) in area, although supplemented by a natural history room (180 ft.[2]) and a greenhouse.[133]

The post-war design of school science laboratories, especially those intended for advanced work in physics and chemistry in the grammar schools, has inevitably reflected the major commitment of the education system to the production of a greatly increased number of scientists and technologists. In the modern schools, which were relatively free from the pre-professional constraints upon the grammar school science curriculum, a lower standard of laboratory accommodation was accepted and design seems to have involved often little more than optimising the use of the multi-purpose laboratory or laboratories available for science teaching. Not surprisingly, neither design philosophy was to prove satisfactory as, during the 1960s and 1970s, secondary education was reorganised and science teachers explored the problems of teaching science in unstreamed or 'mixed-ability' classes.

References

[1] Ministry of Education, *Science in Secondary Schools*, Pamphlet no. 38, HMSO, 1960, pp. 7–8.
[2] Sutcliffe, A., 'Student Laboratories in England: A Historical Sketch', *S.S.R.*, vol. XI, no. 42, 1929, p. 86.
[3] Ibid., p. 87.
[4] Ministry of Education, op. cit., 1960, p. 9, and Sutcliffe, A., op. cit., p. 87.
[5] Devonshire Commission, 1872–5, *Report*, vol. VI, p. 1. The 'permission' to use endowment funds to finance laboratory accommodation was a consequence of the Taunton Commissioners' recommendation.
[6] Sutcliffe, A., op. cit., pp. 87–8.
[7] Department of Science and Art, *Directory for Science and Art Schools and Classes*, 1891, Appendix A, pp. 108–10.
[8] Ibid., p. 26 and Department of Science and Art, *Report*, 1870, C. 174, Appendix A and pp. 19–20.
[9] Abney, W. de W., Presidential Address to Section L, B.A.A.S., *Report*, 1903, p. 868. For expenditure 1860–1902, see ibid., p. 875.

[10] Ibid., pp. 868–9. Abney pointed out that the 'sealed-pattern' could 'be trotted out as a bogey'. Sutcliffe, A., op. cit., p. 89, ascribed the 'monotonous similarity' of the early laboratories financed by Departmental funds to Abney's approach to laboratory design.

[11] Thus, A. P. Laurie, visiting the Leeds Higher Grade School in 1894, found it 'impossible to convey ... the impression which this school makes upon one of efficiency, energy and vitality' and he thought that no one could fail to realise 'the presence of a new educational force'. For alternative views of these schools, see Simon, B., *Education and the Labour Movement, 1870–1920*, 1965, the Bryce Commission *Report* and *Minutes of Evidence*, and Cruickshank, M., *Church and State in English Education*, 1963.

[12] Gosden, P. H. J. H., *The Development of Educational Administration in England and Wales*, 1966, p. 48.

[13] In 1894, the minimum of fifteen hours was reduced to thirteen, and, in the following year, literary, commercial and manual subjects were made a compulsory part of the curriculum and the basis of calculating the attendance grant was changed.

[14] Gosden, P. H. J. H., op. cit., pp. 48–9.

[15] Burstall, S. A., *The Story of the Manchester High School for Girls*, 1911, p. 186.

[16] Ibid., p. 185.

[17] This Act also empowered the authorities to levy a rate up to one penny in the pound for the provision of technical and manual instruction.

[18] Graves, J., *Policy and Progress in Secondary Education, 1902–1942*, 1943, p. 17.

[19] National Association for the Promotion of Technical and Secondary Education, *Record*, July 1902, p. 366.

[20] Mumford, A. A., *The Manchester Grammar School 1515–1915*, 1919, p. 411, quoted in Lawson, J., Silver, H., *A Social History of Education in England*, 1973, p. 340.

[21] Bryce Commission, *Report*, vol. 1, 1895, p. 34.

[22] Rayleigh's first aim was to make the organisation of the laboratory, and especially the teaching, more systematic. Two demonstrators appointed by Rayleigh, R. T. Glazebrook and W. N. Shaw, developed the laboratory course and their practical notebooks provided the basis of the famous textbook 'Practical Physics'. Crowther, J. G., *The Cavendish Laboratory, 1874–1974*, 1974, Chapter 6.

[23] Abney, W. de W., op. cit., p. 872.

[24] Ibid., p. 875.

[25] Sutcliffe, A., op. cit., p. 90. Sutcliffe's figure is derived from Abney's data.

[26] Robins, E. C., *Technical School and College Building*, 1887.

[27] Clay, F., *Modern School Buildings: Elementary and Secondary*, 1902. Despite the title, the book concentrates on secondary schools.

[28] Russell, T. H., *The Planning and Fitting of Chemical and Physical Laboratories*, 1902. In addition to these specialised 'architectural' texts, it was common for practical science texts to include details of laboratory design, e.g. Worthington, A. M., *A First Course of Physical Laboratory Practice*, Sixth Edition 1903, and Stewart, B. and Gee, W. W. H., *Practical Physics for Schools and the Junior Students of Colleges*, 1902.

[29] Figures from Clay, F., op. cit., pp. 135 and 146. Plates from *Record*, vol. XI, no. 47, July 1902, p. 332 and Laurie. A. P. (ed.), *The Teacher's Encyclopaedia*, 1911–12, vol. III, p. 82.

Elementary School Code and its schedule. Clay, F., op. cit., Appendix, p. 442.

[31] Ibid., p. 443.

[32] Board of Education, *Building Regulations for Public Elementary Schools*, 1914, Cd. 7516, and *Building Regulations for Secondary Schools*, Cd. 7535, 1914.

[33] *Natural Science in Education*, HMSO, 1918, para. 79.

[34] Ibid., and B.A.A.S., *Report*, 1917, p. 206.

[35] *Natural Science in Education*, HMSO, 1918, para. 90.

[36] Birchenough, C., *History of Elementary Education in England and Wales from 1800 to the Present Day*, Third Edition, 1938, p. 206.

[37] I.e., 'Physics, chemistry and mathematics, along with other complementary studies to be taken more lightly', Board of Education, *Curriculum of Secondary Schools*, 1913, Circular 826.

[38] Lloyd, W. H., 'Designing a Laboratory – 1', *Educ. in Chem.*, vol. 9, no. 4, July 1972, pp. 142–3.

[39] Douglas-Smith, A. E., *City of London School*, 1965, p. 395. The accommodation included advanced and elementary chemical laboratories, a chemistry lecture room, a science masters' common room, a balance room and a laboratory and lecture room for physics.

[40] Morgan, M. C., *Cheltenham College: The First Hundred Years*, 1968, Cheltonian Society, p. 167.

[41] Board of Education, *Report of the Consultative Committee on the Education of the Adolescent*, HMSO, 1926, p. 178.

[42] Board of Education, Circular 1364, *Science Accommodation and School Libraries*, 1925.

[43] Board of Education, *Suggestions for the Planning of New Buildings for Secondary Schools*, Pamphlet no. 86, HMSO, 1931.

[44] Ibid., p. 4.

[45] The information in this and the ensuing paragraphs is extracted from ibid., pp. 29–36.

[46] In a chemistry laboratory, there would also be need for space to accommodate a fume cupboard. 'Two or three fume cupboards', each 3 ft. by 2 ft., were regarded as necessary in most such laboratories, although a larger size (4 ft. by 2¼ ft.) was recommended for an advanced laboratory.

[47] Savage, Sir G., *The Planning and Equipment of School Science Blocks*, 1964, p. 21, from which source Fig. 7.4 is taken.

[48] Board of Education, *Suggestions for the Planning of Buildings for Public Elementary Schools*, Pamphlet 107, 1939.

[49] The 1939 Suggestions were, of course, published too late to provide the advice authorities had sought since 1926.

[50] Board of Education, *Pamphlet 107*, 1939, p. 108.

[51] Ibid., p. 30.

[52] Almost a generation later, the Newsom Report was critical of the continued existence of this kind of accommodation. The Report contains a photograph (Plate 8b) of an improvised workshop in an under-sized room. *Half Our Future*, HMSO, 1963.

[53] The information in this and in the preceding paragraph is taken from Board of Education, *Pamphlet 107*, pp. 40–5.

[54] The store room was to extend the whole width of the science room and have a 'depth of about eight feet', ibid., p. 41.

[55] Munby, A. E., *School Laboratory Fittings*, 1929, Preface.

[56] Ibid., p. 85.

[57] Milne, O. P., 'Science Block, St John's School, Leatherhead', *Architects' Journal*, 2 July 1936, p. 15.

[58] Ibid., p. 17.

[59] Board of Education, *Report of an Inquiry into the Conditions Affecting the Teaching of Science in Secondary Schools for Boys in England*, HMSO, 1925, p. 14.

[60] Ibid., p. 15.

[61] *S.S.R.*, vol. XI, no. 41, 1929, pp. 59–64.

[62] Taken from ibid., p. 62.

[63] Ibid., p. 59.

[64] Board of Education, *Report of an Inquiry ...*, HMSO, 1925, p. 14.

[65] Board of Education, *Educational Pamphlet No. 89*, 1932, pp. 10–11.

[66] Board of Education, *Report of an Inquiry ...*, HMSO, 1925. The list does not contain all thirty-nine schools investigated. At least two of the schools excluded had an annual per capita expenditure of less than 2s 2d which is the lowest quoted in the Table. The figures of 1s 8d and 2s 0d are given in ibid., p. 12.

[67] Ibid., p. 18.

[68] Ibid., p. 4.

[69] *Natural Science in Education*, HMSO, 1918, para. 73 and para. 80, and Board of Education, *Report of an Inquiry ...*, HMSO, 1925, p. 10.

[70] 'Laboratory Assistants in Schools', *S.S.R.*, vol. VIII, no. 30, 1926, p. 102.

[71] Board of Education, *Report of an Inquiry ...*, HMSO, 1925, p. 10.

[72] *S.S.R.*, vol. VIII, no. 30, 1926, p. 104.

[73] In 1926, the rates were subject to a temporary cost of living addition of £4. The boys' figure thus became 9s, rising to 18s, and the men's scale 36s, rising to 63s. The S.M.A. quoted average (weekly) contemporary wages of £3 16s for a coal hewer, £2 16s for a shipwright and £2 10s for a roadsweeper in a London borough.

[74] £5 10s was quoted as the maximum wage in a big public school where conditions were 'exceptionally favourable'. *S.S.R.*, vol. VIII, no. 30, 1926, pp. 103 and 106.

[75] For an outline of this scheme and the subsequent careers of boys appointed under it between 1904 and 1918, see ibid., pp. 108–10.

[76] 'Report of the Subcommittee on Laboratory Assistants', *S.S.R.*, vol. XXI, no. 83, 1940, p. 978.

[77] Class A, Boys; Class B, Stewards; Class C, Senior Stewards. The salary scale suggested for a Senior Steward, qualified with an H.N.C. in Chemistry, was £215×£15 to £260 p.a. Ibid., pp. 985–6.

[78] 'Science in Schools', *S.S.R.*, vol. XXIV, no. 92, November 1942, p. 99.

[79] Sutcliffe, A., *School Laboratory Management*, 1929, Preface.

[80] Thus, on p. 2 (1929 edition), Sutcliffe rejects Armstrong's 'advice' to dispense with a demonstration bench.

[81] The B.A.A.S. discussed the relative efficiency of teaching science by demonstration methods and via individual laboratory work at its Annual Meeting in 1934. In the development of those characteristics termed generally 'scientific ability', neither method was found to establish superiority. Demonstration methods were said to produce better results with those who were 'mentally bright' and who had received previous systematic training. B.A.A.S., *Report*, 1934, p. 393. The 'results' presented in 1934, while not startling, should be viewed with some scepticism.

[82] Board of Education, *Handbook of Suggestions ...*, 1929, p. 227 and ibid., 1937, p. 488.

[83] Ministry of Education, *Memorandum on the Building Regulations*, Being the Regulations dated 24 March 1945, Prescribing Standards for School Premises made under Section 10 of the Education Act, 1944, HMSO, 1945. This replaced the Draft Building Regulations and an associated Memorandum issued on 3 November 1944. See also Ministry of Works, *Standard Construction for Schools*, Post-War Building Studies, HMSO, 1945.

[84] Ibid., Appendix 2, p. 21.

[85] The Appendix to the Memorandum also included suggested schedules of accommodation for schools with pupils of eleven to sixteen (or over) and which had a commercial or a technical bias.

[86] Morrell, D. H. and Pott, A., *Britain's New Schools*, 1960, p. 13.

[87] From 1949, L.E.A.s and the Church authorities were invited each year to submit their building programmes which outlined projects to be started during a twelve-month period beginning perhaps two years ahead. In this way the Ministry could produce a national school building programme.

[88] Ministry of Education, *Premises Amending Regulations* 1949 (S.I. 2279), 1949; *Standards for School Premises Regulations* (S.I. 1753), 1951; ibid., 1954 (S.I. 1473), and 1959 (S.I. 890).

[89] Ministry of Education, *The Building Code; Limits of Cost, Standards and Procedures for Building Projects carried out by L.E.A.s*, 1962.

[90] Ibid., para. 1.1, p. 9.

[91] Ministry of Education, *New Secondary Schools*, Building Bulletin no. 2, February 1950, HMSO.

[92] Ibid., p. 43.

[93] Ministry of Education, *New Secondary Schools: Supplement*, Building Bulletin 2A, August 1954, 2nd edition, HMSO.

[94] The data in Table 7.5 are taken from ibid., pp. 13–26.

[95] Ibid., paras. 65 and 66, p. 30.

[96] *S.S.R.*, vol. XXXIX, no. 139, 1958, pp. 440–1.

[97] The data are taken from Ministry of Education, *Building Bulletin 2A*, 1954, pp. 31–41.

[98] S.M.A. *Provision and Maintenance of Laboratories in Grammar Schools*, John Murray, 1958. See also, Kerr, J. F., *Practical Work in School Science*, 1963, p. 70.

[99] Ministry of Education, *Building Bulletin 2A*, 1954, para. 148, p. 75.

[100] For an account of the Consortium of Local Authorities Special Programme see, Ministry of Education, *The Story of Clasp*, Building Bulletin 19, June 1961, HMSO.

[101] Morrell, D. H. and Pott, A., op. cit., pp. 5–6. Although the expenditure on education increased massively between 1938 and 1958, the Crowther Report (1959) estimated that it had done 'little more than keep up with the general expansion of the national income'.

[102] Hill, J. W. F., 'Science Facilities – The Role of Local Education Authorities', in Perkins, W. H. (ed.), *Science in Schools*, 1958, p. 109.

[103] Plate taken from Hertfordshire County Council, *Building for Education 1948–61*, 1961.

[104] *S.S.R.*, vol. XXXIX, no. 139, 1958, pp. 443 and 444.

[105] For details, see Edwards, A. D., *The Changing Sixth Form in the Twentieth Century*, 1970, p. 52.

[106] In 1951, the number of girls aged eighteen or over in the grammar schools represented 6.1 per cent of the fourteen-year-olds four years earlier. By 1963, the corresponding percentage was 11.4. Ibid., p. 52.

[107] Lawrence, B. E., in Perkins, W. H., op. cit., p. 118; 'There is a very big and indeed much larger deficiency of laboratories in Modern Schools.'

[108] Boulind, H. F., 'Accommodation and Equipment', in Perkins, W. H., op. cit., p. 63.

[109] *S.S.R.*, vol. XXXIX, no. 139, 1958, p. 441.

[110] The data are taken from ibid., p. 442.

[111] Ibid., p. 442 and p. 443.

[112] Ibid., p. 443.

[113] Ibid., p. 444.

[114] Chapman, K. M. H. and Coulson, E. H., 'An Inquiry into the Conditions Affecting Science Teaching in Grammar Schools', *S.S.R.*, vol. XXXV, no. 126, 1958, p. 176.

[115] *S.S.R.*, vol. XXXIX, no. 139, 1954, p. 444.

[116] Modified from *S.S.R.*, vol. XXXVI, no. 130, 1955, p. 402. See also vol. XLI, no. 145, 1960, p. 473.

[117] *S.S.R.*, vol. XXXIX, no. 139, 1958, p. 444.

[118] 'Report of the Subcommittee on Laboratory Technicians', *S.S.R.*, vol. XXXVI, no. 130, 1955, p. 396.

[119] Report of the Subcommittee on Laboratory Assistants, *S.S.R..*, vol. XXI, no. 83, 1940, p. 979.

[120] *S.S.R.*, vol. XXVI, no. 130, 1955, p. 402.

[121] For example, 'Supply of Laboratory Technicians', *Educ. in Science*, no. 28, June 1968; 'Education and Training of Science Laboratory Technicians', ibid., no. 48, June 1972; 'Duties and Responsibilities of Laboratory Technicians', ibid., no. 53, June 1973.

[122] *Education in Science*, no. 28, June 1968, p. 34.

[123] The data are taken from 'Provision and Maintenance of Laboratories in Grammar Schools (1959)', *S.S.R.*, vol. XLI, no. 145, 1960, p. 465 ff.

[124] However, the 1959 figure of 15 per cent may represent something of a regression because of the increased proportion of boys' grammar schools in the later and larger sample. See ibid., p. 469.

[125] *S.S.R.*, vol. XXXIX, no. 139, 1958, p. 445.

[126] *S.S.R.*, vol. XLI, no. 145, 1960, p. 470.

[127] Ibid., pp. 469–70.

[128] Ibid., p. 470.

[129] Savage, Sir G., op. cit., 1964, p. 23. For an illustration of a laboratory built to this design, except that all of the benches are of the same length, see ibid., p. 16.

[130] Lloyd, W. H., op. cit., 1972, p. 143.

[131] Savage, Sir G., op. cit., 1964, p. 29.

[132] Developments in electrical instrumentation also made it unnecessary to incorporate such features as wall-mounted galvanometer brackets in the design of school physics laboratories.

[133] Savage, Sir G., op. cit., 1964, p. 43 and Plate 5. Figure 7.6 is taken from ibid., p. 25.

8
Methods and Examinations

Any discussion of the methods by which science has been taught in schools since 1900 raises a number of formidable problems. It is, for example, difficult to describe teaching methods in terms which are sufficiently precise to allow the extent to which these methods have been used at different times to be estimated. This difficulty is illustrated by Fowles's claim[1] in 1937 that a few definite ways of teaching chemistry were 'more or less known and practised'. These were identified as the informative, heuristic, normal experimental, historical and modern methods, the latter seeking to present inorganic and organic chemistry as a series of related phenomena explicable in terms of fundamental physical principles. It is clear, even from a superficial analysis, that Fowles's categories (which may be extended as appropriate to other sciences) share a number of common methodological elements. Classroom discussion, the dictation of notes or laboratory and field-based practical studies are not associated exclusively with any one method. Moreover, the overlap between the methods extends to some of the objectives they were intended to fulfil. It is difficult to imagine a method of teaching school science which is not designed to help pupils acquire some scientific knowledge or gain at least some insight into the procedures whereby such knowledge has been established. To some extent, therefore, the differences between science teaching methods lie in the role ascribed to, and the emphasis placed upon, a number of common methodological components such as laboratory exercises or class demonstration.

There is the additional problem of sources. Books on science teaching methodology are statements of intent rather than accounts of actual practice and, for much the same reason, official publications are of limited direct help. The Thomson Committee went to some lengths to condemn the worst excesses[2] of heurism in the schools and favoured no one teaching method. The Hadow Report[3] devoted more attention to the content than to the methods of school science teaching and the Spens Report pressed the case for general science without reference to how the subject was actually being taught. Even specialised reports, dealing with the position of science in schools, have excluded detailed comment on methods.[4]

To be entirely convincing, an account of the methods by which science has been taught in schools since 1900 must be based on the results of a large scale and complex investigation of classroom and laboratory practice. While such an investigation cannot be conducted in retrospect, science lessons have been observed and commented upon by a number of observers, notably by members of L.E.A. and H.M. Inspectorate. The comments of local authority advisers and inspectors seem to have been informal and, as such, are not recorded. The reports of general inspections of schools, conducted by H.M. Inspectorate, are available for consultation, although subject to the normal rules governing access to public documents. Such reports can, at best, provide only a discontinuous record of school science teaching under the abnormal conditions of inspection and, for the most part, they are confined to schools supported by public funds. Scrutiny of a sample of thirty general inspection reports, covering a variety of schools over the period 1904–45, indicates that such reports are a scant source of information about science teaching methods. This, to some degree, is to be anticipated since the reports relate to a general inspection in which comments upon the teaching of science would be given prominence only if the visiting inspector(s) regarded such teaching as, in some way, 'distinguished'. Where favourable comment is recorded, it is usually general in nature, e.g. the science work at the Johnston School in Durham in 1932 was described[5] as 'capably conducted' and achieving 'a satisfactory standard'. In only one of the thirty reports examined is there favourable *and* specific comment on the methods by which science was taught and the implication is that such methods were exceptional. At Redditch Secondary School in 1923, the Inspectors commented[6] upon the inclusion of a lively class discussion of the 'historical and economic aspects of scientific discovery' within the main school, adding that the 'proper emphasis on accuracy' was a characteristic of the pupils' 'independent practical work'.

As might be expected, adverse comment by the inspectorate was more specific in nature and therefore of greater interest in the present context. At Blyth Secondary School in 1927, the inspectors deprecated[7] 'the practice of dictating notes in the lower forms', on the grounds that it stifled initiative and 'failed to develop the descriptive powers of the boys'. At the Lady Margaret School, Fulham, in 1930, the Inspectors commented[8] upon the low standard of botanical drawing and at Tamworth Girls' High School in the same year, a series of 'thoughtfully planned' demonstrations were said not to leave 'a deep impression on the girls'.[9]

Some schools were inspected on more than one occasion between 1904 and 1945, e.g. King Edward VII School, King's Lynn, in 1914 and 1933. Unfortunately, no useful comparisons can be drawn from the relevant reports since different aspects of the work were the subject of comment on the two occasions.

Research theses, which might have been expected to constitute an important secondary source of information about science teaching methods, are, in general, disappointing. Atherton's study[10] of the *Modern Approach in Science Teaching*, presented in 1939, is more concerned with matters of content (biology and general science) than with methods of teaching. He does, however, claim that, in the years up to the outbreak of the Second World War, the majority of graduate science teachers 'followed the method and taught what they themselves had learned at the Universities'.[11]

The methods of science teaching at the Universities and, in particular, the development of laboratory classes is too large a topic to be considered in detail here. In the case of chemistry, Liebig's laboratory at Giessen was a seminal influence. As far as physics is concerned, the introduction and mode of organisation of practical physics courses owe much to such individuals as Clifton (at Oxford), Carey Foster (London), Glazebrook and Shaw (Cambridge) and ultimately to E. C. Pickering in the United States. Books such as Worthington's *A First Course of Physical Laboratory Practice* provided the pattern for much that was to follow for the schools and included a prototype set of 'rules' for pupils working in laboratories. The 'third rule' is of particular interest:

> The form in which the experiment is to be recorded should be got ready beforehand so that as soon as an observation is made it can be recorded in the right place in the form.[12]

The influence of university teaching methods upon grammar school science education was confirmed by Ramsay in an investigation reported[13] in 1950. He claimed that, apart from heurism, 'the main method of teaching science' had been with 'the aid of organised courses of laboratory work, supported by practical demonstration, after the style of the laboratory courses of the University.[14] Ramsay issued questionnaires to teachers, seeking information about the size of practical classes, methods of organising practical work and of learning scientific definitions and nomenclature. The teachers were invited to suggest changes in the teaching of science which they thought desirable and to indicate any methods of teaching science which they had actually tried out in the classroom, laboratory or field. The response to Ramsay's questionnaire was disappointing (168 from 1,401) and an elaborate statistical technique does not make his findings easy to summarise briefly. He concluded[15] that over 40 per cent of the science teachers in his responding sample required definitions and principles to be precisely worded and 'learnt by heart' and that practical work was employed more for 'learning the content' of the science syllabuses than for inculcating a scientific attitude towards problems. Little use was made of projects or 'elementary research exercises' and a 'good deal of time' was spent on note taking, the writing up of practical work or answering questions on the work done. In Ramsay's view, most of the activities described by the science teachers in his sample were 'useful, no doubt, but not peculiar to science as an educational subject'.

The impression gained from Ramsay's survey is supported by an analysis of the contents of pupils' class and laboratory notebooks. The exercise books of different members of the same class often contain identical and formal statements of laws and principles, suggesting that these statements were dictated by the teacher or copied from the blackboard or a textbook. Laboratory notebooks used by pupils in grammar schools in different parts of the country and at different times often reveal a marked similarity in the work done and in the manner in which such work was recorded and presented. Many of the experiments in physics and chemistry conducted by grammar school pupils between the wars were being repeated by their successors a generation later and, for the most part, the accounts of such experiments have been clearly derived from a standard format: Test, Observation Inference, or Title, Apparatus, Method, Observation, Results and Conclusions.[16]

When a clear and coherent account can be got fairly readily, it may be written up on the blackboard and entered up in books, the descriptive matter being simplified as far as possible by the use of diagrams.

The work is to be headed clearly and, when done, to be summarised in a brief conclusion.[17]

The available evidence, limited though it is, suggests that the methods by which science has been taught in the grammar schools have not shown the diversity which might have been expected to follow from the freedom given to teachers to organise their own work. It is conventional to attribute this lack of variety to the restricting influence of the Examination Boards. While it is undoubtedly true that School Certificate syllabuses in chemistry and, to a lesser extent, in physics, were remarkably 'well-standardised'[18] as early as 1925, this conventional explanation is inadequate in several respects, not least because many of the skills assessed in public examinations in science can be taught in a variety of ways. What cannot be disputed, however, is that these examinations have been remarkably consistent, both in the skills they have tested and in the manner of testing them. When questions have been set on particular topics within the science syllabus (e.g. hydrogen sulphide, latent heats, reproduction) the form and precise content of such questions have, in large measure, been predictable. It also seems that examination questions in chemistry have been much more susceptible to this influence of 'tradition', at least at the level of the First Examination, than have questions in physics or biology.[19]

In physics, it is possible to set an infinite variety of problems and calculations related to a given scientific principle and this possibility itself provides for some variation in physics questions. The following two questions are therefore of some significance. The first was set in an N.U.J.M.B. School Certificate paper in 1927, the second in an Ordinary-level paper of the same Board over a quarter of a century later.

1 A ball weighing 6 oz. rests in a right-angled groove of which the two sides are equally inclined to the vertical. With what force does the ball press on one side of the groove?
2 A ball weighing 2 lb. rests in a right-angled groove of which the two sides are equally inclined to the vertical. With what force does the ball press on each side of the groove?

There have, of course, been significant changes in the contents of School Certificate and G.C.E. science syllabuses, e.g. the introduction of atomic theory and bonding in chemistry, of current electricity in physics, of biochemical and physiological topics in biology. To determine whether the new content has required science teachers to encourage the development in their pupils of new cognitive skills, it is necessary to classify the skills tested in the various examination papers set in physics, chemistry and biology.

In a comparison of J.M.B. Advanced-level biology papers set between 1962 and 1966, Tracey classified individual questions on the basis of 'cheap recall, simple recall, expensive recall, intelligent guessing, teaching recall and open-ended' or 'loose' questions. He concluded that the introduction of a new syllabus during this period had not led to any significant change in the cognitive skills measured by the Board's examination in biology at Advanced level. The emphasis on factual recall was largely undiminished and Tracey described[20] the new examinations on the new syllabus as a 'lost opportunity'.

Any analysis based on a complete examination paper fails to take account of the choice of questions available to candidates and this may be significant unless each question is equally difficult and tests comparable intellectual skills. An alternative approach is that of Spurgin[21] who analysed Advanced-level physics papers in terms of the marks awarded for bookwork and description, calculations and 'understanding'. The results of applying[22] Spurgin's technique to Higher School Certificate and Advanced-level papers in physics and chemistry, set by the J.M.B. at ten year intervals since 1922, are summarised in Table 8.1. These data also illustrate the enduring importance of factual recall and suggest that sixth-form pupils have been required to learn a body of knowledge for reproduction in a relatively standard form if they were to gain high marks in their H.S.C. or A-level examinations in chemistry and, to a lesser extent, in physics.

Table 8.1   Analysis of N.U.J.M.B., H.S.C./A-Level Papers at Ten Year Intervals since 1922

	1922		1932		1942		1952		1962	
	P	C	P	C	P	C	P	C	P	C
Bookwork and description	55	72	47	65	48	75	52	67	49	56
Calculations	33	15.5	37	10	37	5.5	31	14.5	30	17
Understanding	12	12.5	16	25	15	19.5	17	18.5	21	27
Number of questions in two papers	24	16	20	16	20	18	24	24	24	24
Number to be answered in two papers	14	12	14	12	10	10	12	10	12	10

Numbers refer to % marks awarded for the category indicated in physics (P) and chemistry (C).

An emphasis on factual recall has not been confined to science papers at the sixth-form level. Table 8.2 summarises the results of an analysis of School Certificate and Ordinary level papers in physics, chemistry and biology, using a modified form of Bloom's *Taxonomy of Educational Objectives*.[23] In this analysis, the sub-classes of the Taxonomy (knowledge of facts, of principles, of terminology, etc.) have been ignored and the six broad classes reduced to four: knowledge, comprehension, application, and analysis and synthesis. 'Evaluation' was excluded since none of the papers investigated were found to test this skill, a finding which is not altogether surprising.[24] Analysis and synthesis have also been amalgamated since it was found impractical to isolate the latter.

The use of these four categories permits comparison of the data with the results obtained[25] by Crossland and Amos from an analysis of School Certificate and Ordinary level papers in the period 1948–64. In their study, Crossland and Amos allocated ten marks to each question on an examination paper and then distributed these marks among four categories; acquisition of facts, interpretation of facts, application of scientific principles to new situations and the designing/planning of experiments. The inadequacy of this procedure is recognised but it does permit a comparative study and there seems little reason to assume that the limitations of the technique invalidate the conclusions. In addition, it is possible to defend the use of an 'unofficial mark scheme' on the grounds that it represents the 'consumer's viewpoint'.[26] The data in Table 8.2 are consistent with the findings of Crossland and Amos and suggest that, at the level of the First School Examination, the papers in biology have consistently placed a greater emphasis on factual recall as an examination objective than have the corresponding papers in physics and chemistry.

To what extent can the J.M.B., to which the data in Table 8.2 refer, be regarded as representative of the Examination Boards as a whole? Scrutiny of the science papers of the various Boards throughout the years after 1918 reveals that the examinations set by each Board have a recognisable and distinctive style and format. Yet, as in the case of the J.M.B., questions on given topics have tended to reappear in a standardised form, demanding similar skills of the candidates. Spurgin's analysis[27] suggested that, in the Advanced level physics papers set in 1962 by the J.M.B., London and Oxford and Cambridge Joint Boards, candidates were asked to display approximately the same skills, although some of the 'larger differences' may have been significant.[28] Crossland and Amos's study revealed no serious discrepancies[29] between the science papers of the J.M.B., and the Welsh, Cambridge and Oxford Boards at School Certificate and Ordinary levels so that the J.M.B. may reasonably be regarded as typical so far as the skills assessed in its written papers in science are concerned.

The practical examinations in science conducted by the various Boards raise a number of other issues. The J.M.B. has conducted optional and little used practical examinations in physics, chemistry and biology at Ordinary level whereas the corresponding examinations of some other Boards, e.g. the Oxford and Cambridge Joint Board have been compulsory. Kerr, who has explored the problems associated with practical examinations in school science, has suggested that, by 1963, such examinations had become a 'major obstacle to the full achievement of the most important educational values of experimental work'.[30] The skills tested in practical examinations are not discussed here in detail since the contribution of the practical marks to an overall assessment has varied from one Board to another and there have also been important differences between one science subject and another in the proportion of marks allocated to a practical assessment.[31] However, it seems clear that changes in the regulations governing practical examinations have had a direct effect on the work of some teachers, e.g. the introduction of a dissection exercise into practical examinations in biology meant that teachers were required to give

Table 8.2   Analysis of S.C./O-level science papers in terms of Bloom's Taxonomy (modified)

	Biology*				Physics				Chemistry		
Year	K.†	C.	A.	A/S	K	C	A	A/S	K	C	A	A/S
1922	–	–	–	–	48%	9%	32%	11%	50	11	12	27
1923	–	–	–	–	43	11	34	12	59	9	9	23
1924	–	–	–	–	50	6	27	17	57	8	17	18
1925	–	–	–	–	41	11	40	8	57	11	11	21
1926	–	–	–	–	53	4	40	3	61	13	8	18
1927	–	–	–	–	43	7	41	9	50	9	22	19
1928	–	–	–	–	46	8	32	14	59	10	7	24
1929	–	–	–	–	51	9	31	9	54	11	7	28
1930	–	–	–	–	49	13	28	10	53	4	28	15
1931	69%	16%	2%	13%	46	10	25	19	54	11	19	16
1932	81	5	0	14	49	4	32	15	58	13	9	20
1933	74	11	0	15	47	9	32	12	54	17	7	22
1934	75	6	0	19	54	8	32	6	57	10	15	18
1935	80	5	0	15	47	5	41	7	55	13	10	22
1936	69	14	2	15	58	6	25	11	58	7	11	24
1937	63	16	0	21	60	4	25	11	53	8	16	23
1938	71	13	1	15	51	12	24	13	61	11	7	21
1939	75	12	0	13	59	9	22	10	50	10	15	25
1940	81	9	0	10	43	4	49	4	54	10	17	19
1941	84	9	3	4	50	3	41	6	49	8	20	23
1942	71	11	0	18	53	8	31	8	50	12	19	19
1943	75	5	1	19	41	7	41	11	56	6	17	21
1944	78	8	0	14	48	3	39	10	60	4	9	27
1945	84	6	2	8	42	6	45	7	60	11	9	20
1946	71	6	1	22	49	5	34	12	65	11	10	14
1947	79	6	0	15	40	11	45	4	55	9	14	22
1948	75	4	1	20	43	10	39	8	50	9	16	25
1949	79	2	0	19	39	5	49	7	60	6	6	28
1950	78	3	4	15	57	4	30	9	58	7	15	20
1951	79	6	0	15	58	2	27	13	61	5	13	21
1952	79	2	0	19	55	7	28	10	54	7	11	28
1953	83	2	2	13	60	10	20	10	63	9	11	17
1954	75	2	1	22	49	2	42	7	56	4	21	19
1955	71	2	1	26	57	6	32	5	57	8	13	22
1956	78	2	0	20	42	14	39	5	61	3	14	22
1957	79	4	0	17	58	6	32	4	54	7	16	23
1958	77	10	3	10	49	8	32	11	58	8	11	23
1959	79	5	2	14	58	7	26	9	61	4	19	16
1960	80	3	2	15	55	4	28	13	63	3	15	19
1961	81	2	3	15	61	9	27	3	64	2	12	22
1962	84	4	2	10	50	4	34	12	59	6	12	23
1963	85	4	2	9	54	4	33	9	57	5	10	28
1964	85	6	2	7	58	8	28	6	61	8	12	19

* No paper until 1931.
† K=knowledge; C=comprehension; A=application; A/S=analysis/synthesis.

their pupils an opportunity to acquire the necessary skills. Scrutiny of a number of practical science papers reveals how the innovatory, e.g. dissection, quickly became the orthodox and routine. The questions set in these papers also lend support to Kerr's claim that the format of practical examinations came to be determined by organisational as well as educational considerations.[32]

In so far as the Examination Boards have exerted little or no pressure on science teachers to reconsider either their objectives or their methods, they may be regarded as having exerted a conservative influence upon the practice of grammar school science teaching. The emphasis placed in public examinations in science on the ability to recall scientific knowledge and to reproduce it in a relatively standard form has, until recently, survived all criticism, including that levelled by the Thomson Committee[33] in 1918, the British Association[34] in 1928, the Spens Committee[35] in 1938, the so-called 'Gulbenkian' Committee[36] in 1959 and by the Association for Science Education[37] during the 1960s. As a consequence, the dictation of notes, the rote learning of formal definitions and other techniques likely to lead directly to the acquisition of the appropriate information have flourished.

> ... for many of us, the burden is fashioned by the demands made by public examinations. If these require learning by heart masses of information, this must be our own approach.[38]

More significantly, teaching activities likely to foster the acquisition of skills or attitudes not rewarded in the public examinations have, to some degree, been discouraged. Armstrong in 1928, referred[39] to the 'stranglehold' of examinations, mastering the schools, making rational teaching and the development of the spirit of inquiry all but impossible. The British Association, more temperately, admitted that what the examination system did not encourage, it 'tended to frustrate'[40] and the Science Masters' Association, advocating its general science course a decade later, was forced to recognise that the acquisition of such skills as 'the ability to plan experiments and test statements' required a different approach to science teaching from that then prevailing in the grammar schools.[41] However, it was not until more recent times, when the Nuffield Science Teaching Project sought to extricate grammar school science education from the 'straitjacket of chronic success'[42] that assessment became an integral part of curriculum reform.

> Even the most wonderful teaching programme would be largely spoiled ... if it had to be tied to examinations that did not fit its methods or its spirit.[43]

This 'chronic success' also owes much to school science textbooks which, perhaps inevitably, have emphasised the skills assessed in public examinations rather than reflected the broader aims of school science education urged by organisations such as the Science Masters' Association and the British Association or by individuals such as Armstrong, Bernal, Gregory, Hogben and Nunn. Texts which attempted to alter the approach to elementary science teaching 'disappeared from the bookseller's shelves' if they failed to meet the precise requirements of the examination syllabuses in science, however inadequate these requirements may have been.[44] The books which have survived have shown a remarkable and occasionally depressing uniformity, especially in the case of chemistry.

Writing of Ordinary-level chemistry texts used in schools in 1960, Bassey commented[45] that it was as though the '400 pages of a common ancestor' had been shuffled and reprinted, 'with the addition of a handful of pages to mark the individuality of the "new" book'. The 'approach, the style and the choice of photographs' were the author's own but each 'new' chemistry text intended for pupils following an Ordinary-level course brought no appreciable change.

Successful school science texts, once established, have been assured of a long life. Holderness and Lambert's *School Certificate Chemistry*,[46] first published in 1936, was reprinted twice in 1937 and three times in 1939, 1940, 1941, 1943, 1944, 1946 and 1947. The second edition of 1948, reprinted in 1949 and 1950, led to a third edition in 1951 which was reprinted in the same year and again in 1952 and 1953. The fourth edition was produced and reprinted in 1954 with two reprints in each of the following five years, the 1960 reprint being reset in 1961. In contrast, *Elementary Chemistry* by E. J. Holmyard, first published in 1925, remained unchanged from 1934 to 1960 when it was still being regularly reprinted.[47]

Similar publishing successes may be recorded in other areas of school science, e.g. Sherwood Taylor's *General Science for Schools*[48] and Harrison's *Elementary General Science*.[49] In biology, *Elementary Biology for Matriculation and Allied Examinations* by Phillips and Cox, first published in 1930, had reached its tenth edition by 1952 and a new impression was issued in 1957. F. J. Wyeth's *Elementary General Biology* (1933) was reprinted thirteen times by 1947 in the same edition, the revised edition of 1949 being reprinted in 1952, 1953, 1954 (twice), 1955 and 1956. Brimble's *Everyday Botany*[50] which was issued in 1934, was reissued in 1945, 1949, 1952 and 1953.

It is perhaps unnecessary to labour the point by a detailed reference to school physics texts. To choose but one example, Mackenzie's *Light* (1936), was reprinted[51] in 1939, 1943, 1945, 1946, 1948, 1950, 1954 and 1957. The 'principal change' incorporated in the second edition of 1954 was described as the rearrangement of the plates to appear at the end of the book.

Bassey has commented[52] that Ordinary-level chemistry texts have followed 'one familiar and well-worn' path which, by 1960, had become a 'rut rather than a highway'. There is little doubt that this judgement may be applied, although to a lesser extent, to school texts in biology and physics. One aspect of the rut is illustrated by the data in Table 8.3 which compares the contents of three established chemistry texts, first published in 1936, 1950 and 1961, with those of twenty-three school chemistry books published[53] between 1924 and 1931. It seems that many school chemistry texts, like the relevant examinations, have largely ignored the social dimensions of chemistry, despite detailed accounts of the processes underlying the chemical industry, and have excluded virtually all reference to the imaginative, personal and craft elements of scientific creativity. The emphasis has been upon chemistry as a body of knowledge,[54] established by pure, self-justifying inquiry, although not all

Table 8.3 Comparison of content of selected school chemistry texts* 1924–61 (after Pullan)

	Pullan's data	Book 1	Book 2	Book 3
Date of publication	1924–31	1936	1950	1961
Content	%	%	%	%
1 Chemical information	49.5	60	55	71
2 Chemical theory	20.3	19	19	13
3 Chemistry of industrial processes	5.2	14	15	13
4 Practical instructions	16.4	15	18	16
5 Aids to learning (revision questions, diagrams, etc.)	14.3	18	17	12

* The three books are respectively: Holderness, A., Lambert, J., *School Certificate Chemistry*, 1936. Goddard, F. W., Hutton, K., *A School Chemistry for Today*, 1950 and Kingdon, J. E. H., *Chemistry*, 1961. It should be noted that Pullan's data is presented in greater detail than in the above table.

authors would have subscribed to the views expressed by Kemp[55] and Littler[56] in the introduction to their respective texts:

... of the two sides of science, *Pure* science is infinitely the more important.

... it cannot be too often insisted upon that the true scientist studies chemistry for its own sake and not simply for the material benefits that the study brings in its turn.

A similar disappointing lack of variety and a corresponding failure to reflect some of the broader aims of school science education have characterised science texts intended for use at sixth-form level. Without elaborating on long-established sixth-form texts in chemistry, physics and biology such as those by Holmyard, Nightingale and Grove and Newell respectively,[57] it will be sufficient to assert, on the basis of Bassey's evidence,[58] that the contents of the texts have strongly reflected the collective contents of the syllabuses of the Examination Boards to the near exclusion of all else. As with School Certificate and Ordinary-level texts, the sixth-form books have been rich in questions taken from previous examination papers and have presented their information in the form required to answer them. The premise upon which a majority of school science textbooks appear to have been constructed was perhaps stated most explicitly by Holmyard in the preface to his highly successful sixth-form text *A Higher School Certificate Inorganic Chemistry*:

... the allotment of space to individual topics is roughly in proportion to the frequency with which these topics appear in the examination papers.[59]

The constraints imposed upon school science education by the external examinations have been confined almost entirely to the grammar and public schools. Teachers in other types of institutions, such as the senior, elementary, trade, junior technical and secondary modern schools which have provided an education for the majority of the population for most of this century, thus appear to have had more opportunity than their grammar school colleagues to experiment with methods of organising and teaching science. To what extent, if at all, has this opportunity been realised?

There is evidence of the introduction of innovative practice into individual senior or modern schools at various times since 1902. Dent has reported[60] an unnamed school which in 1928, 'scrapped the timetable and its list of subjects' and formed staff and pupils into small groups 'each under a leader' to undertake a project entitled 'Our Future Home'. Greenhough has provided an account[61] of an 'experiment' in the boys' senior school of which he was Headmaster in the 1930s and he records how pupils in their last year (fourteen to fifteen years of age) were encouraged to construct 'individual timetables' by making a selection from a wide range of activities. According to Dent,[62] experiments of this kind and others 'ran into the hundreds' during the inter-war years and paved the way for much that was to follow in the curricula of the secondary modern schools after 1944. A few of these experiments were even translated into publishing ventures as authors sought to reflect the emphasis placed upon individual work in a number of elementary and senior schools by producing complete courses of 'individual assignments' in natural science, intended for use by the pupils and sometimes accompanied by a suitable 'cabinet' of elementary science apparatus and materials.[63]

Tweddle, reviewing[64] a scheme of science work used in post-primary schools between 1940 and 1950, noted that it was not the function of secondary modern schools 'to attempt to train scientists', adding that in some secondary modern schools, 'too much time' had been spent on the verification of principles 'discovered by scientists long ago'. He describes a curriculum organised on a topic basis, the topics being related to the theme of 'Science and Our Daily Lives'. The scheme of work, summarised diagrammatically in Figure 8.1 is probably representative of similar schemes followed by many secondary modern schools in the years shortly after the end of the Second World War.[65] The topics were taught by a variety of methods, many of which would clearly have not been out of place in a grammar school.

> After a preliminary discussion during which the key question is posed, the experiment undertaken, the facts are observed and noted and the pupil is asked to draw his conclusions. . . . . Notebooks are . . . used for recording the results of experiments. . . . The sequence of events is summarised under the four headings of the object of the experiment, the diagram, the method and the result.[66].

> . . . after studying expansion we note how it is made use of in thermometers, thermostats and other appliances or in technical processes. At other times, we proceed in the reverse way. We start with an appliance – an electric bell say – and try to find out how it works.[67]

In the immediate post-war period, many secondary modern schools 'launched out in a large way upon projects', sometimes to the near exclusion of other forms of teaching. Dent has commented[68] that 'in all but the best schools' which

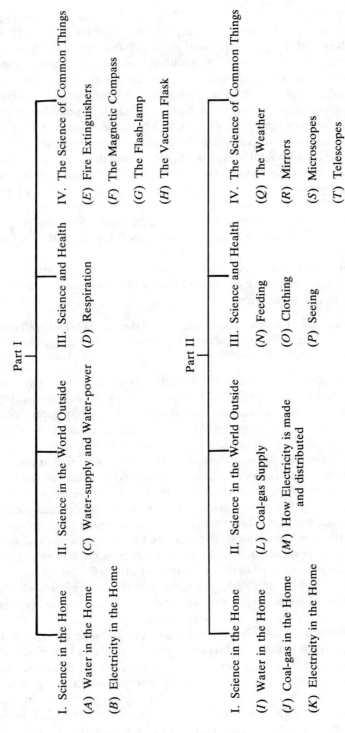

Figure 8.1 *Scheme of work for a secondary modern school, c. 1950.*

relied largely upon project or 'centre of interest methods', 'not very much solid or systematic learning' was achieved, and the Ministry of Education, in its Annual Report for 1949, expressed concern[69] that relatively few secondary modern schools had 'come to grips with the problems of how to meet intellectual needs and how to stimulate fullest effort'. During the 1950s, the public and official pressure 'to raise standards' led to something of 'a retreat from extreme unconventionality'[70] in a number of modern schools, although the freer and less formal methods were rarely abandoned completely. A few local education authorities responded by developing more systematic courses for use in their modern schools. These courses, more often than not, had 'a bearing on future employment' although care was taken to emphasise that they were not 'trade courses in any narrow sense', intended to train a boy or girl for a particular job.[71] As an example, science teachers in Cheshire cooperated with representatives of local industries to produce 'alternative courses', intended for use in both the modern and the grammar schools for which the authority was responsible.[72]

In 1956, Loukes concluded[73] that there was 'no secondary modern curriculum', only a multitude of curricula 'framed in response to the needs and opportunities of each school'.

> ... in one place, a broad academic bias, because there are able children needing it; in another a strong bias to local industry; in another attention to basic manual skills to serve many industries; in another, attention to the arts of leisure.

Two years later, Dent claimed[74] to detect something of a pattern in this diversity. Some modern schools, few and declining in number by 1958, had risen little, if at all, beyond the level they had reached as public elementary schools. Others were doing 'highly effective senior elementary work' and a third, 'very large' group consisted of schools which 'consciously or unconsciously', attempted to realise the aim of the modern school, that of providing a 'good, all-round secondary education, not focused primarily on the traditional subjects of the school curriculum, but developing out of the interests of the children'.[75] This third group included schools which taught the academic subjects 'in much the same way, though to a less advanced level, as they (were) taught in the grammar schools' but omitting foreign languages and specialised branches of physical science, and a smaller sub-group which constructed their curricula largely upon projects or 'centres of interest'.

By 1963, Taylor felt able to comment that the modern schools were displaying signs of an 'academic attitude' towards subject matter. He remarked upon the extent to which the modern school curriculum had 'withstood the onslaught of educational ideas' which at one time had seemed likely to alter the subject-centred timetable, 'in favour of projects, centres of interest, individual assignments and subject groups', adding that schools in which the work was 'based on such approaches' were clearly 'exceptional in the general run of modern schools'.[76] In some instances, this development of an 'academic attitude towards subject matter' may be attributed to the need to establish parity of prestige with the grammar schools, a need reflected in the pressure from some modern schools to be allowed to develop G.C.E. courses.[77] In other cases, the move to re-establish subject teaching along relatively conventional lines probably owed more to the growing realisation of the weaknesses of some of the alternative methods.[78]

It thus seems clear that, by the end of the 1950s, the 'opportunity to develop science teaching along fresh lines' in conditions 'free from the cramping traditions'[79] of examinations had been realised in a variety of ways and to different degrees in different modern schools. A large minority, perhaps even a majority, of these schools were 'attacking the problems of the "new" secondary education with imagination and energy'.[80] Some demonstrated the academic influence to which Taylor has referred and others, probably a declining minority, continued to reflect that 'remarkable efflorescence of new model courses and curricula'[81] which characterised the work of so many modern schools in the immediate post-war period.

Finally, it is necessary to acknowledge that the teaching of science, in schools of all types, has been influenced, directly and indirectly, by such technological innovations as radio, the cinematograph and television which were not developed principally for educational use but which have done much to inform and determine twentieth-century society. The British Broadcasting Corporation began radio transmissions in 1922 and, by 1925, almost a million people owned radio receivers. By the outbreak of the Second World War, this figure had risen to nearly 9 million and radio broadcasting was an established means of mass communication.[82] The educational possibilities of radio were realised early and, following experimental broadcasts[83] in 1924, the BBC initiated a regular, daily series of educational programmes. There was extensive use of radio programmes by the schools during the 1930s and, by the end of the decade, educational radio was a well-developed resource available to most schools.[84]

The potential usefulness of film to the teacher was also recognised by the end of the First World War and the film enthusiasts were quick to cite[85] evidence from the United States which purported to establish the educational advantages of the medium. However, there was little immediate response from schools or local authorities[86] although a number of scientific films, notably on biological topics, were made and used. As early as 1924, E. N. Lovell of Charterhouse commended[87] to his fellow members of the Science Masters' Association, the 'excellent Secrets of Nature series, produced by the New Era Film Company'. The general slowness of the response may be attributed to the high cost of a cine-projector,[88] the lack of a convenient power source in many schools[89] and the inadequate number of worthwhile films available for use, a point emphasised by a committee on the 'Kinematograph in education' which reported in 1924:

> ... the supply is almost necessarily waiting upon the demand, and the demand does not arise until the supply is assured.[90]

This committee, composed of representatives of the Board of Education, the Educational Associations and the cinematograph industry, had no doubt that films had a distinctive and important contribution to make to the work of the teacher. It was left to Oswald Latter to indicate some of the advantages of the cine-film for the teaching of biology. Processes such as the 'germination of seeds, movement of tendrils, and changes involved in the life history of ... the lower forms of life' could all be speeded up by the use of film. Similarly, those changes which were so rapid that the 'eye could not appreciate them at their normal rate' could be 'slowed down'. Such changes included the movements of bird wings in flight and of fish in water.[91]

Members of the Science Masters' Association discussed the contribution of the cinematograph to their work at their Annual Meeting in 1924 when 'much interest' was evinced in the possibilities.[92] During the later 1920s, attempts were made to discover how films could best be used in teaching[93] and some local authorities arranged or encouraged the showing of educational films to pupils.[94] By 1930, the merits of sound and silent films had been compared but the lack of suitable films of either type remained a serious problem which discouraged the more widespread use of film for educational purposes.

As more films specially for schools were produced, often with help from teachers,[95] exhibitions were held and a large number of educational films were shown[96] at the Annual Meeting of the British Association held in 1935. School science teachers could learn about new science teaching films from the educational press and, in particular, from the reviews in the journal of the Science Masters' Association. An opportunity for members to view new films became an established feature of the Association's Annual Meeting.

By 1935, over 700 schools possessed equipment suitable for projecting sound films[97] and the Board of Education recognised the growing importance of such films in a pamphlet on optical aids, published in 1938. Perhaps because of the near universality and popularity of the sound film in the cinemas, the Board also drew the attention of teachers to other, longer-established devices such as the episcope, diascope and epidiascope.[98] By the outbreak of the war, schools in general were well provided with apparatus for audio-visual aids although the supply of film projectors remained inadequate.[99]

After the war, stimulated by the activities of the National Council for Visual Aids in Education and the Educational Foundation for Visual Aids, schools made a greatly increased use of a wide variety of audio-visual materials and techniques. During the prosperous later 1950s, these techniques came to include television, television sets entering the schools in much the same way as radio receivers had done a generation earlier. The particular needs of science teachers were catered for by the contributions of organisations such as the BBC Natural History Unit and by the films sponsored by the large international science-based companies such as I.C.I., B.P. and Shell.

By the 1960s, with the widespread use of tape recorders, the introduction of film loops and the extensive programme of school broadcasts offered by the BBC and by the ITA, school science teachers were faced with a greater range of audio-visual resources than at any time in the century and many organisations, such as museums, traditionally concerned with the supply of audio-visual materials to the schools, were forced to reconsider their educational functions.[100] For the teachers, the problem was no longer a shortage of adequate visual material on film. Rather it was that of familiarisation with the films, tapes, slides, charts, photographs, tape-slide sequences, film loops and strips being produced, of distinguishing the worthwhile from the mediocre, and of organising and deploying the audio-visual resources of a school science department to help to meet the formidable challenge of science education for all.

References

[1] Fowles, G., *Lecture Experiments in Chemistry*, 1937, p. 497. In some instances, it is possible to associate these teaching methods with particular individuals who may be said to have pioneered their use in school or university science teaching, e.g. heurism with H. E. Armstrong, the normal experimental method with Ida Freund, the historical method with E. J. Holmyard.

[2] *Natural Science in Education*, HMSO, 1918, para. 42.

[3] Board of Education, *The Education of the Adolescent*, HMSO, 1926, pp. 220–26.

[4] E.g. Board of Education, *Report of an inquiry into the conditions affecting the teaching of science in secondary schools for boys in England*, HMSO, 1925.

[5] *P.R.O., Ed. 109/1191*, p. 6. There is no shortage of comment in the reports on such matters as laboratory accommodation, the time allowed for teaching science, the provision of science books for a library. Occasionally, a comment reminds the reader of how much times have changed, e.g. at Blyth in 1927, the inspectors observed that 'the installation of power current in the laboratories, if it could be achieved, would be a very valuable asset to the science work'. *P.R.O., Ed. 109/4563*, p. 11.

[6] *P.R.O., Ed. 109/6748*, p. 1, p. 2.

[7] *P.R.O., Ed. 109/4653*, p. 11.

[8] *P.R.O., Ed. 109/3704*, p. 1.

[9] *P.R.O., Ed. 109/5331*, p. 11.

[10] Atherton, W., *The Modern Approach in Science Teaching, having particular reference to courses for secondary school pupils of eleven to sixteen years of age*, M.Ed. Thesis, University of Manchester, 1939.

[11] Ibid., p. 88.

[12] Worthington, A. M., *A First Course of Physical Laboratory Practice*, 1903 edition, p. 11.

[13] Ramsay, M. P., *A Psychological Analysis of the aims and methods of science teaching in secondary grammar schools*, M.Sc. thesis, University of London, 1950.

[14] Ibid., p. 4.

[15] Ibid., p. 111.

[16] See, for example, the contents of exercise books in the *Bicknell Collection*, University of Leeds Museum of the History of Education.

[17] Preface to Hutton Grammar School, Lancashire, *General Science syllabus*, 1935 and *Physics Course*, 1935; these syllabuses (typescript) are in the University of Leeds Museum of the History of Education.

[18] Holmyard, E. J., *An Elementary Chemistry*, 1925, Preface.

[19] Jenkins, E. W., 'Public Examinations and Science Teaching Methods in Grammar Schools since 1918', *Durham Res. Review*, vol. VI, no. 26, 1971, pp. 548–56.

[20] Tracey, G. W., 'Some difficulties involved in relating examinations to the ideals of a new Advanced-level Biology syllabus', *J.Biol.Ed.*, vol. 1, 1967, pp. 243–9. See also Holway, P. H., 'A-level Papers in Biology as Tests of Scientific Thinking', *J.Biol.Ed.*, vol. 2, 1968, pp. 207–18, who claims that since 1962, there has been a 'slight tendency' for A-level biology papers to move closer to testing 'scientific thinking skills' and therefore somewhat away from assessing the ability to recall facts.

[21] Spurgin, C. B., 'What Earns the Marks?' *Physics Education*, vol. 2, 1967, pp. 306–10.

[22] As a check that the use of Spurgin's method did not lead to any inconsistency with Spurgin's own data, an analysis of the 1962 J.M.B. A-level physics paper 1 was carried out and sufficient agreement obtained to warrant further use of Spurgin's (modified) categories.

[23] Bloom, B. S., *Taxonomy of Educational Objectives*, vol. 1, Cognitive Domain, 1956.

[24] See, for example, Lindquist, E. F. (ed.), *Educational Measurement*, 1951, pp. 509–10.

[25] Crossland, R. W. and Amos, R., 'What do O-level Examinations in Biology Test?', *Biology and Human Affairs*, vol. 26, no. 2. 1961, pp. 38–41, and 'Towards New O-level Examinations in Biology', *Biology and Human Affairs*, vol. 30, no. 3, 1965, pp. 35–9.

[26] Spurgin, C. B., op. cit., p. 309.

[27] Ibid., p. 307.

[28] This is hardly surprising since one of the functions of the Secondary School Examinations Council was to 'oversee' the School Certificate examinations, a task taken somewhat more seriously by the Schools Council after 1964.

[29] Crossland, R. W. and Amos, R., op. cit., 1961, p. 40.

[30] Kerr, J. F., *Practical Work in School Science*, 1963, pp. 59–60.

[31] Ibid., p. 67.

[32] Ibid., p. 97.

[33] *Natural Science in Education*, HMSO, 1938, para. 43.

[34] B.A.A.S., *Report*, 1928, p. 469.

[35] Board of Education, *Secondary Education*, HMSO, 1938, p. 243.

[36] *Report of an enquiry into the suitability of the G.C.E. Advanced syllabuses ...*, University of Birmingham, 1959.

[37] A.S.E. (S.M.A./A.W.S.T.) *Science and Education, A Policy Statement*, 1961, p. 9.

[38] Nuffield Foundation, *Chemistry: Introduction and Guide*, 1966, p. 3.

[39] B.A.A.S., *Report*, 1928, p. 523.

[40] Ibid., p. 446.

[41] Lewis, D. G., 'Objectives in the Teaching of Science', *Edu. Research*, 1965, vol. VII, no 3, p. 187.

[42] Nuffield Foundation, *Chemistry: Introduction and Guide*, 1966, p. 4.

[43] Nuffield Foundation, *Physics: Teacher's Guide I*, 1966, p. 6.

[44] Bassey, M., 'A Field Review of O-level Chemistry Textbooks', *Technical Education and Industrial Training*, vol. 2, no. 12, 1960, p. 14, refers to Dootson and Berry's *First Principles of Chemistry*, published in 1929. The book omitted the 'obsolete laws of multiple and reciprocal proportions' but, as Bassey points out, such laws were 'present in the examination syllabus' and so had to 'be used in the schoolroom'.

[45] Bassey, M., op. cit., p. 13.

[46] Holderness, A. and Lambert, J., *School Certificate Chemistry*, 1936.

[47] Bassey, M., op. cit., p. 13. 'Over half a million copies' of this book were sold by 1960 and Bassey used it as 'the standard treatment' with which to compare other chemistry books.

[48] Taylor, F. Sherwood, *General Science for Schools*, 1939. Reprinted in the same year and in 1944, 1945 and 1946.

[49] Harrison, J. M., *Elementary General Science*, 1941. Reprinted five times by 1948, new edition in 1952.

[50] Brimble, L. J. F., *Everyday Botany*, 1934.

[51] Mackenzie, A. E. E., *Light*, 1936.

[52] Bassey, M., op. cit., p. 14.

[53] The technique of analysis is drawn from Pullan, J. M., *School Textbooks in Chemistry*, M.A. thesis, University of London, 1932, which also provides the data for the books published between 1924 and 1931.

[54] Bassey, M., 'Some Conclusions', *Technical Education and Industrial Training*, vol. 3, no. 2, 1961, p. 15.

[55] Kemp, B. C. L., *Chemistry for Schools*, 1931 (new editions until 1956).

[56] Littler, W., *Elementary Chemistry*, 1931 (new editions until 1959).

[57] Holmyard, E. J., *A Higher School Certificate Inorganic Chemistry*, 1939; Nightingale, E., *Higher Physics*, 1948; Grove, A. J., Newell, G. E., *Animal Biology*, 1942. The latter book clearly reveals the 'medical influence' on sixth-form biology sources.

[58] Bassey, M., 'Field Review of "A/S" level chemistry textbooks', *Technical Education*, November 1964, pp. 538–9.

[59] Holmyard, E. J., op. cit., preface, p.v. In addition, those sections which dealt with stock examination questions were 'kept for the most part within such limits' as would 'enable a candidate to reproduce them or their substance within half an hour'. To be fair to Holmyard, he recognised that the 'cultural aspect' of chemistry was 'seldom reflected in examinations' but it must receive due attention in a book which aspired to do something other than cram.

[60] Dent, H. C., *Secondary Modern Schools, An Interim Report*, 1958, p. 7. Dent is quoting from an article in *The Times Ed. Supp.* of 28 January 1928.

[61] Greenhough, A., *Educational Needs of the 14–15 Group: a record of an experiment in a senior school*, 1938.

[62] Dent, H. C., op. cit., p. 8.

[63] See, for example, Sharp, F. E., *The Individual Natural Science: A four years course of assignments*. N.D. There were also 'individual books' in geography, history, literature, arithmetic, drawing, English composition and literature.

[64] Tweddle, T. A., *The Science Teacher's Handbook*, 1950, p. 9.

[65] Ibid., p. 11 and Chapman, J. V., *Your Secondary Modern Schools: an account of their work in the late 1950s*, 1959, p. 181.

[66] Chapman, J. V., op. cit., pp. 179–80.

[67] Kneebone, R. M. T., *I work in a secondary modern school*, 1957, p. 130. The author was headmaster of a modern school in York.

[68] Dent, H. C., op. cit., pp. 37–8.

[69] Ministry of Education, *Education in 1949*, HMSO, 1950, p. 23.

[70] Dent, H. C., op. cit., p. 39.

[71] Cheshire Education Committee, *The Secondary Modern School*, 1958, p. 10.

[72] Cheshire Education Committee, Alternative Courses in Secondary Modern Schools. The representatives included staff from British Rail(ways), the Alkali Division of I.C.I., Lever Brothers, the Cheshire Branch of the National Farmers' Union. Other examples of specialised courses encouraged by L.E.As. (pre-nursing, technical, engineering, business) may be found in (e.g.) Southampton Education Committee, *Special Courses in Secondary Modern Schools, Report after Five Years*, 1954 and Nottinghamshire Education Committee, *The Secondary Modern School and its Curriculum*, 1949.

[73] Loukes, H., *Secondary Modern*, 1956, p. 69.

[74] Dent, H. C., op. cit., pp. 29–30.

[75] Ibid., p. 34.

[76] Taylor, W., *The Secondary Modern School*, 1963, p. 84.

[77] Successive post-war Ministers of Education refused to sanction a national examination of a lower level than the G.C.E. between 1944 and 1960. The 'gap' was partly filled by the examinations of the College of Preceptors, the Royal Society of Arts, the Union of Educational Institutions and by examinations organised by local authorities in conjunction with groups of modern schools.

[78] Dent, H. C., op. cit., p. 39.

[79] The phrase is that of the Board of Education and was originally applied to Senior Schools. 'We are free from cramping traditions and the necessity of preparing for examinations and this offers us an opportunity to develop science teaching along fresh lines; to take what is good from old ideas and experiment freely with new ones.'

[80] Dent, H. C., op. cit., p. 17.

[81] Ibid., p. 9.

[82] Pimlott, J. A. R., *Recreations*, 1968, chap. 5.

[83] 'Educational Broadcasting', *Times Ed. Supp.*, 2 May 1925, p. 182.

[84] Parker, L. W., *School Broadcasting in Great Britain*, 1937.

[85] Powell, F., 'The Cinema in Education', *Journal of Education*, March 1922, p. 146.

[86] Note on new educational films, *Times Ed. Supp.*, 3 February 1923, p. 55.

[87] *S.S.R.*, vol. V, no. 19, 1924, p. 153.

[88] About £30 in 1924.

[89] Not all schools possessed current electricity at this time, in which case 'recourse may be had to limelight which is quite sufficiently powerful and . . . not difficult to manipulate now that oxygen is readily obtainable compressed in cylinders'; *S.S.R.*, vol. V, no. 19, 1924, p. 155.

[90] 'Technical Description of Projector and Films', ibid., p. 156.

[91] 'The Kinematograph and Science Teaching', ibid., pp. 152–3. The particular contribution of 'moving film' to biology teaching was recognised before the First World War. See 'Cinematograph', *Journal of Education*, June 1912, p. 372.

[92] *S.S.R.*, vol. V, no. 19, 1924, p. 154.

[93] *Report of an experiment on the use of sound films in schools, 1930*; the experiment was undertaken in 1929 by six authorities in Middlesex, jointly with the N.U.T. See also, 'Talking Films in Schools', *Times Ed. Supp.*, 4 April 1931, p. 124.

[94] 'Cinematography', *Journal of Education*, June 1927, p. 432.

[95] Films for use in schools, *Times Ed. Supp.*, 7 January 1933, p. 4.

[96] For a comment, see 'Films of Insect Life', *Times Ed. Supp.*, 14 September 1935, p. 334.

[97] 'Teaching by Films', *Times Ed. Supp.*, 23 March 1935, p. 96.

[98] Board of Education, *Pamphlet No. 115*, HMSO, 1938, p. 5.

[99] Review of Cine Biology, *Times Ed. Supp.*, 11 October 1941, p. 482. See also Paterson, R. N., 'The Future of Visual Aids in the Schools', *Journal of Education*, 1947, p. 186.

[100] Museums played an important part in the work of the elementary schools early in the twentieth century especially in the hands of such pioneers as H. Crowther, E. E. Lowe and J. Hutchinson. As always, the nature, extent and effectiveness of the contribution made by a particular museum to the work of the schools depended upon the needs of the

schools, the interests and commitments of the professional staff of the museum and the resources available within it. For reviews, see Smythe, J. E., *The Educational Role of the Museums and Field Centres in England from 1884*, M.A. thesis, University of Sheffield, 1966 and McCabe, G. I., *Museums in Education: the educational role of museums in the United Kingdom*, M.A. thesis, University of Sheffield, 1975.

Index

345